Juvenile Delinquency
Causes and Control

Robert Agnew
Department of Sociology
and
Violence Studies Program
Emory University

Roxbury Publishing Company
Los Angeles, California

Library of Congress Cataloging-in-Publication Data

Juvenile delinquency: causes and control
Robert Agnew, 1953–
p. cm.
Includes bibliographical references and index
ISBN 1-891487-47-7
1. Juvenile delinquency. I. Title.
  Juvenile Delinquency
HV9069.A55 2000
364.36–dc21

00-020278
CIP

Publisher: Claude Teweles
Managing Editor: Dawn VanDercreek
Production Editor: Renée M. Burkhammer
Assistant Editor: Michael Sametz
Typography: Synergistic Data Systems
Cover Design: Marnie Kenney

Printed on acid-free paper in the United States of America. This paper meets the standards for recycling of the Environmental Protection Agency.

ISBN 1-891487-47-7

Photos (listed by page number) courtesy of: Royaltyfreephotos.com—cover photo; Robert Agnew—257; Corbis—243, 244, 252; Scott Decker—155, 172, 178, 185, 325; Digital Stock—33, 49, 71, 87, 95, 123, 139, 209, 212, 233, 285; Mark Ide—3, 11, 17, 19, 103, 105, 115, 201, 277, 294, 299.

A **website** for this text is available at http://www.roxbury.net. A comprehensive **instructor's resource guide/testing program** is also available in book form or on disk.

Roxbury Publishing Company
P.O. Box 491044
Los Angeles, California 90049-9044
Tel: (310) 473-3312 • Fax: (310) 473-4490
Email: roxbury@roxbury.net
Website: www.roxbury.net

The Roxbury Series in Crime, Justice, and Law

Series Coeditors:

Ronald L. Akers, University of Florida

Gary F. Jensen, Vanderbilt University

This new series features concisely and cogently written books on an array of important topics, including specific types of crime and central or emerging issues in criminology, justice, and law.

The books in this series are designed and written specifically for classroom use in criminology, sociology, deviance, delinquency, criminal justice, and related classes. The intent of the series is to provide both an introduction to the issues and the latest knowledge available—at a level accessible to undergraduate students.

Brief Contents

Part III: The Control and Prevention of Delinquency

Detailed Contents

Part I

The Nature and Extent of Delinquency

Part II

The Causes of Delinquency

Part III

The Control and Prevention of Delinquency

Acknowledgments

I would like to thank several people for their help in preparing this book. They include Ron Akers and Gary Jensen, who encouraged me to write the book and provided much useful feedback. Claude Teweles, who gave me the time and freedom to write the type of book I wanted. Frank Cullen, a valued friend and colleague, who has taught me much about crime and its control. Everett K. Wilson, whose ideas about teaching have had a tremendous influence on this book. The students in my juvenile delinquency classes. Several additional individuals who provided valuable comments on all or portions of the book are: Thomas J. Bernard, Patricia Brennan, Scott Decker, Finn-Aage Esbensen, Stephanie Funk, Michele Hussong, Marvin Krohn, David Mackey, Judge Robin Nash, Dean Rojek, Joseph Sanborn, Frank Scarpitti, Randall Shelden, Sherod Thaxton, and Richard A. Wright. And my wife Mary and children Willie and Jenny. Mary provided the support and encouragement necessary to write this book, while Willie and Jenny provided the inspiration.

An Important Message for Instructors

Criminologists often complain about the limited impact of criminology on public perceptions and crime control policy. I believe that a major reason for this limited impact lies with our introductory textbooks. Our texts are perhaps the major way in which we communicate with the larger community. Yet, with a few notable exceptions, they do not provide students with a clear sense of what causes delinquency and what can be done to control delinquency. Rather, our texts tend to overwhelm and confuse students. Students get lost in all the theories of delinquency that are presented; they have trouble drawing conclusions from the discussions of empirical research, since contradictory studies are often described, with little effort to sort between them; and they are not provided with a good overview of the most promising approaches to delinquency control and prevention. If we were to ask the readers of such texts why juveniles engage in delinquency or what should be done to control delinquency, I venture to say that most would respond with blank stares or jumbled answers.

This book is very different from most delinquency texts now on the market. This book is:

Shorter and More Focused

First, it is shorter and more focused than current texts. The dominant texts attempt to cover all the major research on delinquency, and they are often 500 pages or more in length. This text does not attempt to cover all major areas in the field. Rather, it devotes serious attention to what I consider to be the three major questions in the field: What is the nature and extent of delinquency? What are the causes of delinquency? What strategies should we employ to control delinquency? Students reading this text should be able to give reasonable answers to these questions. I am not sure that this is the case with many current texts.

At the same time, you may feel that this text does not devote adequate attention to certain topics. But the shortness and relatively low cost of this text make it easy for you to cover whatever additional topics you like with supplemental readings. In fact, I encourage this approach. I believe that it is important for students to read articles and paperbacks that describe original research and discuss particular issues in detail. There are many wonderful articles and books on delinquency, like *Code of the Street* by Anderson (1999) and *The Saints and the Roughnecks* by Chambliss (1973). I think it would be unfortunate for students to take a delinquency course without being exposed to these materials. And I believe that this view is becoming more common, as reflected in the increased number of delinquency readers and "companion" texts being offered by publishers.

A More Synthetic Approach to Delinquency Theory and Research

Second, this text differs from most current texts in that it employs a more "synthetic" approach to delinquency theory and research. Most texts spend a great deal of time *describing* delinquency theories and research but make little effort to synthesize such theory and research. For example, they describe (often superficially) the four or five different versions of strain theory that now dominate the literature. They also describe the research on each of these versions of strain theory, noting both supportive and nonsupportive studies. They do not, however, attempt to draw on this theory and research in order to develop an up-to-date, comprehensive version of strain theory. Students reading such texts get caught up in trying to memorize all the different versions of strain theory (and other theories) and the mixed evidence on these versions. They come away confused and overwhelmed. Unlike virtually all other texts, my text does *not* describe the different versions of all the major delinquency theories. Rather, I attempt to synthesize the best of the current delinquency theories into a set of three "generic" theories: a strain-based theory, a social learning theory, and a control-based theory. Since these generic theories represent a synthesis of the best of current theory and research, my empirical assessments of them are somewhat more optimistic than those found in other textbooks. This synthetic approach also saves much space, since current texts devote much coverage to the different versions of the major delinquency theories, as well as to the history of delinquency theories.

After describing these three generic theories, I devote several chapters to the major *research* on the causes of delinquency, moving from the biopsychological research to the macro-social research. I make a special effort to state, in a clear, concise manner, the major conclusions that can be drawn from these different areas of research. At the same time, I do make note of problems in the research and I attempt to sort through contradictory studies where necessary. The final section of the book provides a brief overview of the police, courts, and corrections but focuses on general strategies that appear to hold some promise for the control and prevention of delinquency. These strategies fall in four areas: deterrence, incapacitation, prevention, and rehabilitation. While I give examples of successful programs and policies in these areas, my major focus is on describing the *general features* of those programs/policies that appear most successful.

Many instructors may object to this synthetic approach, especially as it applies to delinquency theories. I do not explicitly discuss certain popular theories. The three theories I present, however, dominate the delinquency literature, and I believe that broadly interpreted, they capture the essential ideas of most other theories. My discussion of these three theories, and the research on them in particular, presents the major arguments associated with labeling, rational choice, routine activities, self-control, social disorganization, and certain aspects of conflict and feminist theories. For example, I state that social learning theory predicts that crime is more likely when motivated offenders encounter suitable targets in the absence of capable guardians (the essential ideas of the routine activities perspective). Like Bernard and Snipes (1996) and others, I believe that there are too many theories in criminology. I think that the essential ideas of most theories can be presented in terms of the three generic theories, making life much simpler for students and researchers and making criminology more useful for policy makers.

More Student (and Instructor) Friendly

Third, I have done several things to make this text *more student (and instructor) friendly.* Unlike most other texts, this book is organized around questions rather than topics. For example, instead of a section on "the sociodemographic correlates of delinquency," there is a section on "who is most likely to engage in delinquency?" Students find questions more interesting than topics; questions invite students to become more actively involved in the learning process, and they better convey what the research process is about; answering questions that teachers and researchers feel are interesting and important (see Goldsmid and Wilson, 1980). The subheadings under each question essentially form a sentence outline of the book. Students, then, can gain a quick overview of each chapter and section before reading it, and they can easily review the major points of each chapter/section after reading it.

The book also has a common theme: using the three delinquency theories to understand the basic facts about delinquency, to interpret the research on the causes of delinquency, and to evaluate and develop policies for the control of delinquency. For example, I stress that much of the research on delinquency was inspired by the three theories discussed and that all of the research is interpretable in terms of these theories. To illustrate, the biopsychological research describes several traits that are conducive to crime, such as impulsivity, sensation seeking, and irritability. I stress that the effect of these traits on crime can be explained in terms of the three theories: such traits increase strain, reduce concern for the costs of crime, and make crime seem more rewarding. This common theme helps students master the material, since the book comes across as an integrated whole rather than a series of discrete facts. Chapters build on one another (although they can also stand on their own), and certain points are reemphasized throughout the text.

The book is also written in a more informal, conversational style than that found in most texts. I believe this style makes the book more interesting and accessible to students. Further, the book is divided into twenty-three relatively short chapters, each focusing on a discrete topic, which makes it easier for instructors to assign readings. With other texts, instructors frequently end up assigning portions of a chapter (e.g., they assign the four and a half pages of a chapter that deal with strain theory). Students should also appreciate the fact that the chapters are shorter and generally more coherent than those found in many other texts.

Having said all this, I should note that this book does not contain a lot of pictures or tables and figures. These features are nice, but I avoid them for two reasons. First, I want to keep the cost of the book as low as possible. In my experience, students prefer a cheaper textbook to one with a lot of pictures. Second, many students ignore tables and figures, and many others are overwhelmed by them. Rather than presenting students with a lot of numbers, I prefer to stress the essential points that these numbers are designed to convey.

Promotes Active Learning

Fourth, my text attempts to *promote active learning*, especially the application of text materials. Most notably, students are provided with numerous examples of how one might use the major theories of delinquency to explain the basic facts about delinquency, to understand the research on the causes of delinquency, and to develop and evaluate programs and policies for controlling delinquency. Also, students are frequently asked to engage in such applications themselves. Students are also asked to apply the text materials to their own lives. Unlike authors of many texts, I do not include a list of discussion questions at the end of each chapter. Rather, I regularly pose questions for students throughout the text. This emphasis on the application of text materials is crucial in my view: It dramatically increases the students' understanding of the materials, and the materials are of little use unless students develop the ability to apply them.

Further, the text not only describes what criminologists know about delinquency, it also gives students a sense of *how* criminologists know what they know, that is, how criminologists collect and analyze data. In particular, I spend much time discussing how criminologists measure delinquency, how they test theories—especially how they determine whether one variable causes another, and how they determine whether a program or policy is effective in controlling delinquency. Students, then, are not asked to accept the findings of criminology on faith. They are given a sense of what the research process is like. I frequently apply these materials, pointing to problems in research studies and discussing the need for further research in certain areas. Further, I ask the students to apply these materials.

I Appreciate Your Feedback

I am most interested in receiving your impressions of the text, including things that you like and do not like (e.g., topics I should devote more coverage to, sections that are unclear or too "dry," statements that you disagree with, literature that I should have cited, etc.). I will consider your comments carefully when revising the text. Please e-mail me at *bagnew@emory.edu* or write to me at The Department of Sociology, 1555 Pierce Drive, Emory University, Atlanta, GA 30322.

An Overview of the Book

The media have lately been filled with reports of juvenile crime. In the midst of my writing this book, two students shot thirteen others to death at Columbine High School in Colorado. Other reports of juvenile crime—including more school violence—followed. For example, a 15-year-old student in Conyers, Georgia—a short distance from my home town of Atlanta—fired a 22-caliber rifle into a group of between 150 and 200 students gathered in the commons area of his high school. Six students were injured, but none died. These incidents have led people throughout the country to ask a number of fundamental questions about juvenile delinquency: How common is juvenile delinquency? Is it increasing? Who is most likely to commit delinquent acts? What are the causes of juvenile delinquency? What can be done to control or prevent delinquency? These are the questions addressed in this book.

The book is in three sections. The four chapters in the first section focus on the *Nature and Extent of Delinquency*. These chapters deal with the "basic facts" about delinquency, such as: What is delinquency? How much delinquency is there? Is delinquency increasing? and who is most likely to commit delinquent acts?

The twelve chapters in the second section focus on the *Causes of Delinquency*. These chapters first describe the three leading theories, or explanations, of delinquency. They then describe the research on delinquency inspired, in large part, by these theories. This research examines the extent to which delinquency is caused by individual traits (e.g., intelligence, impulsivity), family factors (e.g., broken homes, poor supervision), school factors, delinquent peers and gang members, and a range of other factors, such as the mass media, religion, the nature of one's community, drugs, and guns. The material in this section helps explain many of the basic facts about delinquency presented in the first section, such as the fact that some juveniles are more delinquent than others and that males are more delinquent than females.

The seven chapters in the final section focus on the *Control and Prevention of Delinquency*. These chapters describe what the police, juvenile courts, and juvenile correctional agencies do to control delinquency. In particular, they describe how these agencies operate, how effective they are, what they might do to be more effective, and the extent to which they discriminate against certain groups in their efforts to control delinquency. These chapters then describe four general strategies for controlling delinquency that involve all of these agencies as well as other groups: the "get tough" strategies of deterrence and incapacitation and the strategies of rehabilitation and prevention. These strategies address many of the causes of delinquency described in the second section.

I should note that this book does more than simply describe the major research on juvenile delinquency. It also describes how this research was carried out. That is, it describes how criminologists do such things as estimate the extent of delinquency, determine whether some factor causes delinquency, and determine whether some program or policy is effective at reducing delinquency. This information will not only increase your understanding of the delinquency research, but it will better enable you to evaluate the statements you hear about delinquency (and other topics) from friends, family, the media, politicians, and others. Further, this book encourages you to apply the delinquency research. It encourages you, for example, to use the leading theories of delinquency to explain the basic facts about delinquency and to evaluate programs for reducing delinquency. It also encourages you to apply the delinquency research to your own lives and to issues in the larger community.

I hope you find this book useful and I am most interested in hearing any comments you might have about it—including suggestions for improving the next edition. You can e-mail me at *bagnew@emory.edu* or write to me at Department of Sociology, 1555 Pierce Drive, Emory University, Atlanta, GA 30322.

Part I

The Nature and Extent of Delinquency

Chapter 1

What Is Delinquency and How Does It Differ From Adult Crime?

❖ ❖ ❖ ❖

"What is delinquency?" is a relatively easy question to answer. Juvenile delinquency refers to <u>violations of the criminal law by minors.</u> In most states, a minor is anyone under the age of 18. In some states, however, minors are defined as anyone under the age of 17 or even 16. So if a minor commits an act that would be a crime when committed by an adult, that minor has engaged in "juvenile delinquency" and may be considered a "juvenile delinquent." This definition, while correct, might lead you to believe that the only way delinquency differs from adult crime is in terms of age. Delinquent acts are committed by minors while crimes are committed by adults.

But juvenile delinquency differs from adult crime in a number of major ways besides the age of the offender. In particular, we tend to *view juvenile delinquents differently than adult criminals,* and we tend to *treat juvenile delinquents differently than adult criminals*—with an important exception that I will note. When I say "we," I refer to both the general public and the juvenile justice system.

This chapter is in three sections. First, I describe how we view juvenile delinquents differently than adult criminals. Second, I describe how our different views of delinquents and adult criminals have led us to treat them differently. I note, however, that there has been a recent trend to view and treat *certain* juvenile offenders—especially older, serious offenders—like adult criminals. Finally, I discuss the "invention" of juvenile delinquency. People did not always view and treat juvenile delinquents differently than adult criminals. For most of history, in fact, juveniles who broke the law were viewed and treated very much like adults who broke the law. I briefly discuss some of the factors that led society to view and treat juvenile delinquents differently.

We View Juvenile Delinquents Differently Than Adult Criminals

On the first day of my juvenile delinquency class I play a trick on my students. I pass out a description of a crime that has occurred: Someone walks into a bank, points a gun at a teller, and demands money. It is a toy gun, but the teller believes it is real and gives the bank robber several hundred dollars. The robber later spends most of the money on luxury items before being caught. I ask the students what the court should do to this robber. Unbeknownst to the students, the robber is described as a "7-year-old boy" in half the descriptions and a "32-year-old man" in the other half (the actual crime was committed by a 7-year-old boy).

After the students have considered the case for a few minutes, I ask for volunteers to tell me what they think should be done to the "bank robber." Some of the students describe what might be considered "mild" reactions on the part of the court: The robber should receive counseling, should be closely monitored for a period of time, should perform some community service, or the like. Other students describe what might be considered "tough" reactions on the part of the court; most commonly, they state that the robber should be locked up for several years. The students, of course, are confused by the responses of many of their classmates. Those with the 7-year-old robber

❖ ❖ ❖ ❖

wonder how some of their classmates could be so cold-hearted as to recommend years of imprisonment, while those with the 32-year-old robber think some of their classmates are far too "soft" on crime.

I eventually tell the students that they are working with two different case studies and that this age discrepancy is the major reason for their different reactions. I then try to justify the trick I have played by telling the students that their different reactions to the 7- and 32-year-old robbers illustrate a very important point about juvenile delinquency: We tend to view juvenile delinquents differently than adult criminals.

If a juvenile breaks the law, we generally view that person as *immature and in need of our guidance and help*. There is no precise definition of immaturity, but notions of immaturity usually include one or more of the following: The individuals did not know that what they were doing was wrong; they did not appreciate the harm that their actions might cause; they could not control themselves; or they were easily led astray by others.[1] They therefore do not deserve serious punishment. Rather, they need our help. So when a 7-year-old robs a bank, many students state that the major response of the court should be to provide that person with counseling. But if an adult breaks the law, we generally view that person as someone who *is responsible for his or her behavior and deserves to be punished*. So most students have no qualms about sending a 32-year-old who robbed a bank to prison for many years.

Many students take exception when I characterize juveniles in this way. They state that many juvenile offenders know exactly what they are doing and that these offenders should be punished just as severely as adults. They often describe some horrifying crime committed in the recent past by a juvenile, and they state that this juvenile surely deserves the most serious punishment the law can provide.

I realize that many people feel this way. Certain juvenile offenders—especially older juveniles who commit serious crimes—are not viewed as all that different from adult offenders. And the justice system is starting to treat these offenders like adult criminals. So when I say that we view juvenile delinquents differently than adult criminals, an important exception should be noted. We often view older, serious juvenile offenders like adult offenders. I will talk more about this exception shortly. Aside from this important exception, we still tend to view juvenile delinquents differently than adult criminals. I provide my students with a few additional examples to illustrate this point.

There is the case of a 6-year-old girl in Florida who got into a fight with her 7-year-old friend. The 6-year-old girl repeatedly hit her 7-year-old friend with a piece of wood, while an older boy held the 7-year-old's arms behind her back. The 7-year-old's nose was damaged and her dress was soaked with blood by the time she arrived home to her mother. Her mother, of course, was outraged and immediately called the police. For legal reasons that I will not describe, there was some discussion of trying the 6-year-old girl as an adult. If tried as an adult, she would face a maximum penalty of fifteen years in prison and a $10,000 fine. This story made the national news, and people were outraged that such a young girl might be so severely penalized. They felt that the 6-year-old did not know what she was doing and that she needed guidance and help much more than punishment. Imagine the reaction, however, if a 30-year-old woman had committed this crime. People would be demanding the severest of penalties.

To give another example, a 6-year-old boy in California was charged with savagely beating a month-old baby. He was accused of kicking, punching, and beating the sleeping baby with a stick, possibly causing permanent brain damage. The 6-year-old was said to have done this to seek revenge against the family of the baby for allegedly harassing him. I asked the students in my class how the court should respond to this boy. This is a savage crime, but the young age of the boy led many in the class to talk of his immaturity and to argue that he is in desperate need of guidance and help. Again, imagine the difference in reaction if a 30-year-old man were charged with this crime.

With the exception of older juveniles who commit serious crimes, we clearly tend to view juvenile delinquents differently than adult criminals. We view juvenile delinquents as immature and in need of guidance and help, while we view adult criminals as fully responsible for their behavior and deserving of punishment. To illustrate, one recent national poll found that only 21 percent of the public said that rehabilitation should be the most important sentencing goal for *adults*, but 50 percent said that it should be the most important sentencing goal for *juveniles*.[2]

We Treat Juvenile Delinquents Differently Than Adult Criminals

The difference in the way we *view* juvenile and adult offenders has led us to *treat* juvenile delinquents differently than adult criminals (with an important exception, to be noted). In particular, we have created a special set of laws that apply just to juveniles in order to more closely regulate their lives. We have created a special court for juvenile offenders, a court that places more emphasis on rehabilitation and less on punishment than does adult criminal court. And we have created special correctional programs for juveniles, programs that also focus more on rehabilitation and less on punishment—at least in theory.[3]

Special Laws for Juveniles: Status Offenses

Juveniles are delinquent if they commit any act whose violation by an adult would be a crime—acts like homicide, assault, rape, robbery, burglary, and larceny. However, in most states juveniles can be arrested and referred to juvenile court for certain acts that are legal for adults. These acts are called "status offenses," since they apply only to people with the status of juvenile.

The most common status offenses are running away from home, failure to attend school (truancy), refusing to obey parents (incorrigibility), drinking alcoholic beverages, violating curfew, and engaging in certain consensual sexual activities. These activities are illegal for juveniles in all or many areas, but they are legal for adults; for example, it is illegal for juveniles to stop attending school. They can be arrested and taken to juvenile court in most states if they do so. It is perfectly legal for you, however, to stop coming to class.

The state felt that it was necessary to regulate the lives of juveniles more closely than the lives of adults. Rather than intervening only when juveniles committed a crime, the state felt it necessary to intervene when juveniles gave indications that they might be heading down the "wrong path"—a path that might lead to crime. Status offense laws, then, are directly tied to the view of juveniles as immature and in need of guidance or direction.

These status offense laws were taken quite seriously until the late 1960s and early 1970s. Juveniles who committed status offenses were frequently arrested and referred to juvenile court. They were often formally processed by the court, and they could be "adjudicated," or judged, "delinquent" by juvenile courts in nearly every state. And status offenders were sometimes subject to severe punishments. In particular, about half the juveniles in correctional institutions were there for status offenses like running away and being incorrigible. Status offense laws were especially likely to be enforced against females. Females were (and are) more closely supervised than males, and their sexual behavior, in particular, is more closely regulated. Females who committed status offenses like disobeying parents, running away from home, drinking, and having sex were more likely than boys to be arrested, referred to the court, and sent to institutions for such offenses. There is some evidence that this is still the case today (see Chapter 20 for a fuller discussion).

Status offense laws came under heavy criticism during the 1960s and 1970s. They were often vague. What, for example, does it mean to be incorrigible? Virtually all juveniles disobey their parents at some point. Also, these laws often subjected juveniles who had not committed any criminal acts to severe penalties, such as confinement in an institution (where they were exposed to serious offenders and sometimes subject to physical and sexual assault). Further, there was evidence that poor, minority, and female juveniles were more likely to be punished for such offenses.

In response to such criticisms, most states developed "diversion" programs designed to divert status offenders from the juvenile court. Rather than being formally processed by the court, most status offenders were dealt with informally by the court or were referred to special programs outside the court. Status offenders who were processed by the juvenile court were no longer classified as "delinquents" in most states. Rather, they were classified as Children in Need of Supervision (CHINS), Persons in Need of Supervision (PINS), or similar labels. This new designation was partly designed to reduce the stigma of a delinquent label. The federal government passed a law in 1974 that strongly encouraged states to stop placing status offenders in institutions. And evidence suggests that this law was largely effective: There has been a dramatic decline in the number of status offenders confined in institutions. Finally, a few states went so far as to decriminalize status offenses. Status offenses could no longer result in arrest and referral to the juvenile court; rather, status offenses were dealt with by social service agencies.

Nevertheless, status offenses are still illegal in almost all states. About a half million status offenders are arrested each year, and about 150,000 are formally processed by the juvenile court. As indicated in Chapter 19, some status offenders still get confined in institutions. So while status offenses are not treated as severely today as in the past, they are still taken seriously in many cases.

A Special Court for Juveniles: Juvenile Court

Every state has created special courts for juvenile offenders. Juvenile court differs from adult court in several fundamental ways, with the differences between the two courts reflecting our different views of juvenile delinquents and adult criminals. The differences between juvenile court and adult court have diminished in recent years, but they are still substantial.

First, the goals of juvenile court are different from those of adult court. Adult court determines whether individuals are guilty of committing specific crimes and then punishes them if they are. Juvenile court was *not* set up to punish juveniles but rather to *guide and help them*. The court was supposed to act in "the best interests" of juveniles, providing them with the guidance and help that their parents should have provided. The court, in fact, was supposed to play the role of "superparent," assisting children whose parents had failed them. The goals of many juvenile courts have changed in recent years, with more courts coming to place an increased emphasis on punishing juveniles—especially older, serious offenders. Nevertheless, the juvenile court still places more emphasis on the goal of rehabilitation than does adult court. (This is not to say that the court always accomplishes or even tries to accomplish the goal of rehabilitation. As discussed later, there is often a large gap between goals and accomplishments.)

Second, the juvenile court focuses more on the *offender than on the offense*. Adult court focuses primarily on the offense(s) that the individual has committed. The punishment that individuals receive is based largely on their current and past offenses. Juvenile court is less concerned about punishing individuals for the specific offenses they have committed. Rather, it seeks to help juveniles. The court therefore focuses on the entire juvenile—not just the offense(s) that brought the juvenile to court. The court seeks to learn all it can about the juvenile, especially any personal, family, school, peer, or other problems the juvenile may have. And the actions that the court takes are supposed to address these problems—not simply respond to the juvenile's specific offense(s). Again, some changes are taking place in this area, with many juvenile courts putting more emphasis on the specific offenses that juveniles have committed and basing their response to juveniles largely on these offenses. Even so, there is still a substantial difference between juvenile and adult courts in this area.

Third, the juvenile court is *more informal and less adversarial* than adult court. Adult court provides accused individuals with numerous due process rights designed to protect them from being unfairly punished. These rights include the right to be represented by an attorney, the right to confront and cross-examine the witnesses against you, the right to proof beyond a reasonable doubt, and the right to a trial by jury. As a consequence of such rights, adult court is very formal and it is adversarial in nature—at least in theory. The prosecution and defense attorneys are pitted against one another, arguing their cases before a judge or jury. The juvenile court, however, initially provided juveniles with few due process rights. It was felt that such rights were unnecessary since the court sought to help rather than punish juveniles. Juveniles, then, did not need protection from unfair punishment. As a consequence, the juvenile court was more informal and less adversarial than adult court. Juveniles, for example, were not represented by attorneys. Often, the judge would simply talk with the juvenile—much like parents having a firm talk with their child. The judge might also question the police, witnesses, and others.

This informality has changed since the 1960s. In particular, a series of Supreme Court decisions have granted juveniles most—although not all—of the due process rights available to adults. The Supreme Court essentially argued that the juvenile court often fails to help the juveniles it processes and it often does punish them. They are sometimes confined in institutions, for example. They therefore deserve at least some of the due process protections available to adults. So juveniles now have such rights as the right to be represented by an attorney and to confront and cross-examine witnesses (see Chapter 19 for a fuller discussion). Juvenile court is now more formal and adversarial than it once was. But juveniles do not have all the rights available to adults; most notably, they lack the right to a trial by jury. Further, juveniles frequently waive their rights—sometimes with the encouragement of the juvenile court. In many courts, for example, less than half the juveniles are represented by an attorney. So while juvenile court has changed a great deal in recent decades, it is still less formal and adversarial than adult court—a difference that reflects the difference in goals between juvenile and adult court.

There are still other differences between juvenile and adult court. There are differences in the terminology employed. In juvenile court, the juvenile is not found "guilty" of a particular offense like robbery or burglary. The word "guilt" implies responsibility. Rather, the juvenile is "adjudicated" a "delinquent," regardless of the particular criminal offense(s) he or she committed. (In the case of status offenses, the juvenile is adjudicated a "Person in Need of Supervision" or whatever the label is for status offenders in that court.) Once adjudicated, the judge does not "sentence" the juvenile. A sentence implies punishment. Rather, the judge renders his or her "disposition."

Juvenile court hearings are generally closed to the public and the media to protect the juvenile from adverse publicity and stigma. Likewise, juvenile court records are generally unavailable to the public and media. Further, juveniles are usually able to "seal," or erase, their juvenile court records if they stay out of trouble for a certain period of time. These policies are beginning to change; the public and media are being given greater access to juvenile court hearings and records. Nevertheless, the privacy of juvenile offenders receives much more protection than that of adult offenders. Adult court hearings are open to the public, adult court records are available to the public, and adult court records remain for life except under certain very special circumstances. The Juvenile Court tends to view delinquent acts as the mistakes of immature children, and it wants to minimize the damage that might result from such mistakes. One way to do this is to protect the privacy of juvenile offenders and allow them to "erase" their records in certain cases.

There are also differences in the sentences given out by juvenile and adult courts. In particular, juvenile courts cannot impose the death penalty, and there are limits as to how long juvenile courts can confine juveniles. Most juvenile courts cannot confine juveniles beyond their twenty-first birthday. This age limit often angers people because it means that juveniles who commit serious crimes cannot be confined for more than a few years (unless they are transferred to adult court). There are still other differences between juvenile and adult court, and excellent summaries can be found in Bernard (1992) and Snyder and Sickmund (1999).

Special Correctional Programs for Juveniles

Finally, the view of juveniles as immature creatures in need of guidance and help has led us to develop special correctional programs for them. Juvenile correctional institutions protect juveniles from contact with adult criminals, who might exploit and corrupt them. And these institutions are more concerned with rehabilitation than with punishment. Unfortunately, juvenile institutions often do not live up to their stated aim of rehabilitation. Again, there is often a large gap between goals and accomplishments. Nevertheless, juvenile institutions place more stress on the goal of rehabilitation than do adult institutions. Juvenile institutions are not called "prisons" rather, they are called "youth development centers" or "training schools" or similar names that reflect their supposed emphasis on rehabilitation. A range of community-based programs designed to rehabilitate juveniles has also been developed. This is not to say that there is no concern with the rehabilitation of adult offenders, but rather that rehabilitation is a greater concern in the juvenile justice system.

In sum, we, the general public and the justice system, tend to view most juvenile delinquents differently than adult criminals and we tend to treat them differently as a result. As noted, however, our view of delinquents—especially older, serious offenders—is changing. And related to this, our treatment of delinquents—especially older, serious offenders—is starting to resemble our treatment of adult criminals.

Older, Serious Juvenile Offenders as an Exception

I earlier provided several examples of juvenile offending—a 7-year-old boy who robbed a bank, a 7-year-old girl who assaulted someone, and a 6-year-old boy who seriously assaulted an infant—and I asked how you would respond to these crimes. My examples, however, were carefully chosen. They were designed to get you to think about the immaturity of juveniles and their need for guidance and help. Let me next provide you with two additional examples of juvenile offending.

A husband, wife, and their two young children were driving home one evening. They stopped at a convenience store in a crime-ridden neighborhood to buy a soda. The wife got out of the car to purchase the soda while the husband and children remained in the car, with the engine running and lights on. The parking lot adjacent to the store was a popular location for drug sellers. A 13-year-old known in the neighborhood as "Little B" approached the husband and told him to turn off his car lights (which were illuminating the drug market). The husband refused. Little B felt that he had been "disrespected" in front of the older drug dealers. He got a rifle that he had hidden nearby and fired two shots into the car. The husband was killed in front of his two children. According to witnesses, Little B exclaimed that "This is still New Jack City!" referring to a movie about violent drug gangs.

My second example occurred one month after two juveniles shot thirteen other people to death at Columbine High School in Colorado. A 15-year-old juvenile entered the commons area at Heritage High School in Conyers, Georgia. The juvenile was carrying a 22-caliber sawed-off rifle, and he started shooting into a crowd of between 150 and 200 students. He hit six of the students, although none died. He ran out of the school. Two of his classmates chased him. He pulled out a .357 magnum handgun and fired at them but missed both. A letter was later found under the juvenile's bed. Part of it read:

> The one big question everybody is probably wondering is, Why? Well, for the sake of my brothers and sisters related to the Trenchcoat Mafia, that will have to remain a mystery to the public eye. I have been planning this for years, but I finally got pissed off enough to really do it (Stafford, 1999). (*Note:* The juveniles who killed thirteen others at Columbine High School were said to be part of a group known as the 'Trenchcoat Mafia.')

These two juveniles elicited a different reaction from the community and juvenile justice system than the juvenile offenders described earlier. With isolated exceptions, there was little talk of their immaturity and the need to guide and help them. Little B, in fact, was described in the media and by politicians as a "thug" and an "evil" in the city, among other things. Most people were outraged at the horrible crime he had committed and demanded that he be severely punished. Little B was tried as an adult and sentenced to life in prison. He will be eligible for parole in fourteen years. The second juvenile had not yet been tried as of the writing of this book. He did, however, have a "waiver" hearing, a hearing where a juvenile court judge determined whether he should be tried as a juvenile or an adult. If tried as a juvenile, he could receive a maximum of five years confinement in a juvenile institution. If tried as an adult, he could receive a maximum sentence of 351 years. His defense attorney argued that he was severely depressed and should be tried as a juvenile, but a headline in the local newspaper asked whether he was "Depressed or a cold killer?" (Farber and Stafford, 1999). The juvenile court judge decided that he should be tried as an adult.

These case studies illustrate an important point about the changing nature of juvenile delinquency: We are starting to view and treat older juveniles who commit serious crimes like adult offenders. There was a dramatic increase in serious juvenile violence from the mid-1980s to the early to mid-1990s. Further, many of the violent crimes committed by juveniles received massive publicity, like the shooting deaths that occurred at several schools throughout the United States. Many people came to feel that this violence was not the work of "immature" juveniles who needed guidance and direction but rather the work of "younger criminals" and "stone cold predators" (see Zimring, 1998). Also, many people came to feel that the juvenile court was not equipped to deal with such violence. In particular, they came to feel that such juveniles should be treated and punished like adults.

As a consequence, there has been a major movement in recent years to punish more severely older juveniles who commit serious crimes. Part of this movement has focused on increasing the severity of the punishments administered by the juvenile court, but its major thrust has focused on making it easier to try older juveniles who commit serious crimes in adult court. These issues are discussed more fully in Chapter 19. I simply want to emphasize the point that there is an important exception to my statement that we view and treat juvenile delinquents differently than adult criminals.

How Can We Explain the Invention of Juvenile Delinquency?

It may sound strange to speak of the "invention of juvenile delinquency." I do not mean to imply that juveniles did not commit delinquent acts in the past. Juveniles have always committed those acts we now label as "delinquent" and "status" offenses. In fact, there is good reason to believe that some of these acts, such as fighting, drinking alcohol, and engaging in sex, were much more common at certain points in the past than they are today (see Empey et al., 1999).

When I speak of the invention of juvenile delinquency, I refer to the special way that we view and treat juvenile delinquents. As discussed in the preceding pages, we tend to view delinquents as immature and in need of guidance and help. And we tend to treat juvenile offenders differently: They are subject to a special set of laws that apply only to juveniles, they are sent to a special court, and they are placed in special correctional programs. Compared to adult criminals, we place much more emphasis on their rehabilitation and much less on their punishment. We have not, however, always viewed and treated juvenile delinquents differently than adult criminals.

Juvenile offenders were viewed and treated very much like adult offenders until the 1800s. There were no separate correctional facilities for juveniles in this country until the early to mid-1800s. The first juvenile court did not appear until 1899, and it was not until 1945 that all states had juvenile courts. Many status offense laws are also of recent origin. Laws requiring school attendance, for example, did not emerge until the late 1800s and early 1900s in most places. Even the word "delinquent" was not used until the 1800s. So the special way that we view and treat juvenile delinquents is relatively new, having emerged in the last 100 to 200 years.

Criminologists have recently tried to explain the invention of juvenile delinquency—that is, why society and the law started to view and treat juvenile delinquents differently than adult criminals over the last 100 to 200 years. Space prevents me from providing a full answer to this question, but I will describe the key features of the answer that has emerged from the research.[4]

Changing Conception of Children

Part of the answer has to do with our *changing conception of children*. Children past the age of 6 or 7 were not viewed much differently than adults until a few hundred years ago. The fact that children were viewed as adults is reflected in paintings from the 1600s and before, where the children have adult features and are dressed and posed like adults. The children, in fact, look like miniature adults. Children were also treated like adults: They lived and slept in large rooms with adults, drank alcohol, engaged in sexual behavior (willingly and unwillingly), began work at an early age, and were subject to severe punishments if they misbehaved. In fact, children were routinely subjected to treatment that would be classified as abusive today. Children who broke the law were treated very much like adults who broke the law. They were tried in the same courts and given the same punishments, including the death penalty and confinement in the same institutions as adults. Very young children, however, were usually exempted from state punishments, and older children sometimes received lighter punishments than adults.

However, people's view of children began to change in the 1500s and 1600s. Children began to be seen as different from adults—as immature and dependent on adults for guidance and protection. There are a variety of reasons for this change. The decline in the death rate of children is viewed as a major factor. Prior to this time, perhaps as many as two-thirds of all children died before the age of 20. Partly as a consequence, parents did not form strong attachments to their young children—it was emotionally risky to do so since their children would likely die. Very young children were viewed with indifference, while older children were viewed as adults. The decline in the death rate, however, made it easier for parents to form close attachments to their children. As they formed such attachments, they were more inclined to view children as different from adults—as less developed and more in need of their special care and protection. Another factor contributing to this new view of children was the extension of education to broader segments of the population. Several factors increased the need for a formal education, including the increase in industry and trade and the invention of the printing press and subsequent spread of printed materials. Formal education also highlighted the immaturity and dependence of children because it widened the gap between what children know and what adults know. Still other factors can be listed, but the central point is that the new view of children paved the way for the invention of juvenile delinquency. As people came to view children differently than adults, they were more inclined to view and treat juvenile offenders differently than adult offenders.

Major Social Changes, Especially the Growth of Urban Slums

The new view of children, however, was not the only factor that led to the invention of juvenile delinquency. Also important were the *major social changes that occurred in the United States during the 1800s and early 1900s* (and in many other countries at the same or somewhat different times). The United States underwent a radical transformation during this time, moving from a largely rural to a largely urban society. Further, the urban areas that developed were populated by a large number of poor people, including many recent immigrants to the United States, and these areas were plagued by a range of problems, including crime. Before describing how these changes contributed to the invention of juvenile delinquency, let me first provide some more information on the nature of these changes.

At the end of the 1700s the United States was largely a rural society. In 1790, only 5.1 percent of the population lived in urban areas. There were only a few cities with populations over 2,500. By 1920, over 50 percent of the population lived in urban areas. Many cities experienced a tremendous increase in population over a very short period of time. Chicago, for example, had a population of 5,000 in 1840. By 1890, it had a population of 1 million. This rapid growth in urban populations was largely due to the industrial revolution. Technological advances were improving farming techniques, so fewer people were necessary to work the land. Many rural residents then moved to the city, hoping to find work in the newly emerging industries. Likewise, many foreign residents came to the United States hoping to find work in those industries. In fact, it is estimated that in 1920 about half the residents of major urban areas were immigrants or the children of immigrants.

Many of these people were poor and they were not always able to find work, or at least work that paid a decent wage. As a result, large slums began to appear. These slums suffered from a variety of problems: poor housing, overcrowding, sanitation problems, health problems, and much crime and vice. Many individuals became especially concerned about the children living in these slums. These children often spent much time on the streets, frequently stealing things and committing other crimes to survive. Their families and neighborhood residents seemed unable to control them, and there was concern that they were being corrupted by the "unwholesome" environment in which they lived. There were individuals, however, who felt that there was hope for these children. They believed the children were not yet fully developed, and with the proper guidance from adults they might be diverted from a life of crime.

There are two interpretations, however, about how this concern over poor children contributed to the invention of juvenile delinquency. The first interpretation argues that reformers were genuinely concerned about the plight of poor children growing up in the city. These reformers were primarily middle-class women, many of them involved with charity or social welfare organizations. They felt that slum children needed protection from the evils of city life and should have more guidance and direction than they were receiving. So they lobbied to get special laws passed, laws that would more closely regulate the behavior of these children (e.g., status offense laws like those requiring school attendance). They also lobbied for the creation of a special court and special correctional facilities that would provide these children with the protection and guidance they needed. According to this view, then, the invention of juvenile delinquency sprang from the *desire of middle-class reformers to help children, especially poor children in the city.*

A second interpretation argues that many upper-class people were disturbed by the large concentration of poor people—especially immigrants—in the city. They were concerned that these people—frequently referred to as the "dangerous classes"—might become a disruptive force in society. The upper class wanted to ensure that these people did not threaten their privileged position, and one way they did this was by exercising greater control over the children of the poor. They lobbied for laws requiring these children to attend school so that they would be properly socialized. They lobbied for other laws designed to more closely regulate the children's behavior. The juvenile court was the institution designed to enforce these laws, even if it meant removing the children from their parents. And juvenile institutions were designed to teach these juveniles proper discipline and respect for authority. According to this view, the invention of juvenile delinquency is due to the *desire of upper-class people to protect their privileged position in society.*

Which interpretation is correct? A number of historians and criminologists have examined what is called the "child-saving movement." That is, they have examined individuals and groups who worked to pass status offense laws and create a separate juvenile court and juvenile correctional institutions. Each state and major city in the United States had its own group of "child savers." Researchers have looked at whether the leaders of the child-saving movement were members of the middle or upper class. They have tried to examine the motives of the child savers on the basis of what they said and what they did. For example, do their statements indicate a genuine concern about the plight of children or do they simply express a desire to control poor children and thereby protect "society?" Were these children helped and protected or simply subject to greater control? Studies have examined the child-saving movements in such cities as Chicago, Los Angeles, New York, and Memphis (see the sources cited in note 4). Different studies reach different conclusions about which interpretation is correct, and there is no clear resolution of the issue yet. Perhaps both interpretations have some merit, with the invention of delinquency being partly motivated by a genuine concern for poor children and partly by a desire to control such children because of their perceived threat. In any event, it is important to remember that we did not always view and treat juvenile delinquents differently than adult criminals. Juvenile delinquency is a social invention.

Summary

You now know what juvenile delinquency is. It refers to violations of the criminal law (and sometimes status offense laws) by minors. You also know that we tend to view and treat juvenile delinquents differently than adult criminals—although older juveniles who commit serious crimes are something of an exception. Now that you know what delinquency is, I next want to examine the extent of delinquency and the characteristics of delinquents. Before doing that, however, I must give you information about how delinquency is measured.

Notes

1. *See* Feld, 1999; Rutter et al., 1998; Zimring, 1998.
2. Gerber and Engelhardt-Greer, 1996; also see Bernard, 1992; Empey et al., 1999; Feld, 1999; Howell, 1997a; Zimring, 1998.
3. *See* Bernard, 1992; Empey et al., 1999; Feld, 1998, 1999; Howell, 1997a; Snyder and Sickmund, 1999; Zimring, 1998.
4. For excellent overviews of this topic, see Bernard, 1992; Empey et al., 1999; Feld, 1999; and Howell, 1997a; also see Aries, 1962; DeMause, 1974; Finestone, 1976; Platt, 1969; Salerno, 1991; Schlossman, 1977; Shelden and Osborne, 1989; Sutton, 1988. ✦

Chapter 2

How Is Delinquency Measured?

❖ ❖ ❖ ❖   Now that you know what delinquency is, I want to answer two basic questions about it: How much delinquency is there in the United States, and is delinquency increasing? But before I can attempt to answer these questions (Chapter 3), I first have to discuss the different ways of measuring delinquency. As you will see, the way in which delinquency is measured often has a major impact on the conclusions we draw about the extent of delinquency and trends in delinquency. You might be groaning a bit right now, thinking "Oh no, I don't want to read some technical discussion about how to measure delinquency!" But bear with me; this information is important. A lot of what you hear about the extent of delinquency and trends in delinquency is wrong or misleading. This section will help you understand why.

There are three major ways of measuring the extent of and trends in delinquency: (1) "official" statistics from the police, juvenile court, and juvenile correctional agencies; (2) "self-report" data from juveniles, with juveniles being asked about the offenses they have committed; and (3) "victimization" data, with people being asked whether they have been the victims of various crimes. This chapter describes each of these methods and their advantages and disadvantages.[1]

Official Statistics—Especially Arrest Data From the Police

Official statistics include data from the police, the courts, and juvenile correctional agencies, that is, data from "official agencies" responsible for dealing with juvenile offenders. The most commonly used official statistics are *arrest data from the police*. Because only some of the juveniles arrested by the police are referred to juvenile court, and only some of the people referred to juvenile court are sent to juvenile correctional agencies, arrest data provide a more accurate indication of the extent of delinquency.

Each year the FBI collects data from the police and publishes these data in a volume called *Crime in the United States: The Uniform Crime Reports*. Copies are probably available in the reference department or government documents section of your library (also see the FBI's web site at *http://www.fbi.gov/*). This volume is divided into several sections. The first section contains information on the number of "crimes known to the police." As the name implies, these are crimes that the police know about, both crimes that have been reported to the police and crimes that the police have discovered on their own. The second section contains information on the number of crimes that have been "cleared" or solved by arrest. Contrary to the impression you might get from the media, most crimes are not cleared by arrest. In 1998, about 21 percent of the crimes known to the police were cleared by arrest. The third section contains information on the number of people who were arrested and the characteristics of these people, including the crimes they were arrested for and their age, sex, and race. Note that the number of crimes cleared by arrest is not equal to the number of people who are arrested. Sometimes multiple crimes might be cleared by a single arrest. For example, an individual may be arrested for several burglaries. And sometimes a single crime might be cleared by the arrest of many people. For example, several people may be arrested for a single burglary. Juveniles usually

commit their crimes in groups, and it is often the case that several juveniles are arrested for a single crime.

Information on the extent of delinquency and trends in delinquency comes from the clearance and arrest data. These data (unlike the crimes known to the police data) contain information on the age of the offender. So they allow us to estimate such things as the number of crimes committed by juveniles, the number of juveniles who are arrested, what they are arrested for, and whether juvenile arrests are increasing or decreasing. Most media reports regarding the extent of and trends in delinquency are based on this clearance and arrest data.

The FBI Crime Reports focus on what are known as "Part I," or "Index," offenses and "Part II" offenses. The Part I, or Index, offenses are eight relatively serious violent and property crimes. They include murder and non negligent manslaughter, forcible rape, robbery, aggravated assault, burglary, larceny-theft, motor vehicle theft, and arson. The FBI reports both "crimes known to the police" and clearance/arrest data on these offenses. The top half of Table 2.1 provides a definition of each of these offenses. Read these definitions and then try to answer the multiple-choice question below:

> Your roommate steals your TV from the living room of your apartment while you are attending class. Is this a:
>
> a. burglary
>
> b. larceny-theft
>
> c. robbery
>
> d. all of the above

The Part II offenses consist of twenty additional offenses as well as a category for "all other offenses." These offenses are listed in the bottom part of Table 2.1. Note that this list includes two status offenses: running away and curfew violation, and liquor law violations often involve the status offense of drinking under age. Arrests for all other status offenses are included in the "all other offenses" category. The FBI only reports arrest data for the Part II offenses.

Table 2.1   FBI Part I and Part II Offenses

Part I or Index Offenses

1. **Criminal homicide**: The willful (nonnegligent) killing of one human being by another. Deaths caused by negligence and justifiable homicides are excluded.

2. **Forcible rape**: The carnal knowledge of a female forcibly and against her will. Attempts to commit rape by force or threat of force are included. Statutory rapes (no force used and victim under age of consent) are excluded.

3. **Robbery**: The taking or attempting to take anything of value from the care, custody, or control of a person or persons by force or threat of force or violence and/or by putting the victim in fear.

4. **Aggravated assault**: An unlawful attack by one person upon another for the purpose of inflicting severe or aggravated bodily injury. This type of assault is usually accompanied by the use of a weapon or by means likely to produce death or great bodily harm. Simple assaults are excluded.

5. **Burglary**: The unlawful entry of a structure to commit a felony or a theft. Use of force to gain entry is not required.

6. **Larceny-theft**: The unlawful taking, carrying, leading, or riding away of property from the possession or constructive possession of another. It includes crimes like shoplifting, pocket picking, purse snatching, thefts from motor vehicles, thefts of motor vehicle parts and accessories, and bicycle thefts in which no force, violence, or fraud occurs. Embezzlement, con games, forgery, worthless checks, etc. are excluded.

7. **Motor vehicle theft**: The theft or attempted theft of a motor vehicle—includes automobiles, trucks, buses, motorcycles, motor scooters, snowmobiles, etc.

8. **Arson**: The willful or malicious burning or attempt to burn, with or without intent to defraud, a dwelling house, public building, motor vehicle or aircraft, personal property of another, etc.

Part II Offenses

Other assaults
Forgery and counterfeiting
Fraud
Embezzlement
Stolen property: buying, receiving, possessing
Vandalism
Weapons: carrying, possessing, etc.
Prostitution and commercialized vice
Sex offenses (except forcible rape and prostitution)
Drug abuse violations
Gambling
Offenses against family and children
Driving under the influence
Liquor laws
Drunkenness
Disorderly conduct
Vagrancy
All other offenses
Curfew and loitering law violations
Runaways

Source: Federal Bureau of Investigation (1998).

The data from the FBI have several advantages. They are collected from   ❖ ❖ ❖ ❖
police departments representing approximately 95 percent of the U.S. population. They have been collected since 1930, so they provide long-term information on trends in crime. And certain evidence suggests that the "crimes
known to the police" data provide a moderately accurate measure of the
extent of and trends in certain types of serious crime, particularly homicide
and *serious instances* of certain other crimes like robbery, burglary, and
motor vehicle theft (see Gove et al., 1985). But at the same time, the FBI data,
particularly the arrest data, have a number of problems.

Problems With Arrest Data

Arrest data greatly underestimate the extent of most forms of delinquency, and they may sometimes provide misleading information about
trends in delinquency. There are several reasons for this underestimation,
including the following:

Most delinquent acts do not become known to the police.. There are
three reasons for this. First, the police usually find out about a crime when
someone else—usually the crime victim—reports it to them. But surveys of
crime victims indicate that only about a third of all crime victimizations are
reported to the police. Not surprisingly, serious crimes are more likely to be
reported to the police than minor crimes. Serious crimes include those where
a weapon is used, the victim is injured, and/or there is a significant financial
loss. Crimes involving strangers are also more likely to be reported to the
police. And crimes against adults are more likely to be reported to the police
than crimes against juveniles (see Finkelhor and Ormond, 1999). Second,
many crimes do not have a "victim" in the usual sense of the word—that is,
someone who feels that he or she has been injured. I am referring to crimes
like drug use, gambling, and consensual sex. It is unlikely that the participants in these crimes will notify the police. And third, it is physically difficult
for the police to detect most crimes on their own. Obviously they cannot
detect crimes that occur in private, but they also have trouble detecting
crimes that occur in public. The police in a patrol car may pass a given spot on
their beat once or twice a day, if that much, so it is unlikely that they will come
upon a crime in progress. The police therefore do not even know about the
large majority of crimes that occur, especially the less serious crimes. As a
result, even the "crimes known to the police" data greatly underestimate the
extent of crime, with the exception of homicide and serious instances of a few
other crimes.

*Even when crimes become known to the police, the police do not catch
the offender in most cases.* As indicated in Chapter 18, the police are unlikely
to catch the offender unless they discover the offender at the scene of the
crime or someone can identify the offender to them; this is one reason why
they are more likely to catch offenders who commit violent crimes than those
who commit property crimes. Most violent crimes involve people who know
one another, so the victim can often identify the offender (or the police have a
good idea of who the offender might be). But for nonviolent crimes, which
constitute the vast majority of crimes, the police usually do not catch the
offender.

The police do not arrest most of the suspected offenders they catch. As you will learn in Chapter 18, the police have a lot of discretion over whether or not to arrest suspected offenders. They exercise that discretion by releasing most of the suspected offenders they encounter. Several factors influence whether the police make an arrest; the seriousness of the offense is most important. But other factors also have an impact. The attitude of the victim or complainant is quite important. Does the victim press for arrest? If so, the police will usually make an arrest. If the victim argues against arrest, the police will usually let the offender go. As discussed in Chapter 20, the characteristics of the offender—including race, class, and sex—often influence the likelihood of arrest. The characteristics of the police department are also important. Some police departments encourage officers to informally resolve criminal matters, while others encourage officers to make arrests (see Wilson, 1976). Also, police departments occasionally "crack down" on certain offenses, like drug crimes, prostitution, curfew violation, and truancy. The police are more likely to search for and arrest individuals committing such crimes during these crackdowns. For example, the transit police in the city of Atlanta recently instituted a crackdown against truancy, and as a result the number of juveniles apprehended for truancy increased by almost 200 percent over a two-year period.

Research has shown that only about 21 percent of the crimes known to the police are cleared by arrest. (The percentage varies by type of crime. In 1998, 69 percent of all murders and 59 percent of all aggravated or serious assaults were cleared by arrest, versus 14 percent of all burglaries and motor-vehicle thefts.)

Police data reported to the FBI are sometimes inaccurate. On top of all this, the police sometimes report inaccurate data to the FBI. Sometimes these inaccurate reports are the result of mistakes on the part of the police, and sometimes the police deliberately distort crime data in an effort to make themselves look good. One common way in which this distortion occurs is by "unfounding" crime reports. The police usually investigate crime reports by citizens to determine whether a crime has occurred and what type of crime has occurred, if any. If they feel that a crime has not occurred, they "unfound" the crime report. And that "crime" does not become part of the "crimes known to the police" data reported to the FBI. Some police departments have lowered their crime rates by unfounding a large percentage of the crimes reported to them. Or they have reclassified these crimes from more to less serious categories. For example, they may reclassify aggravated assaults as simple assaults or robberies as larcenies. The police in my home town of Atlanta were recently accused of wrongly unfounding a large number of crimes in 1996. An external audit found some support for this allegation. For example, Atlanta reported 392 rapes to the FBI in 1996. This represented an 11 percent *decrease* in rapes compared to 1995. The external audit, however, concluded that the Atlanta police wrongly unfounded 56 rapes in 1996. If these 56 rapes had been reported to the FBI along with the other rapes, the number of rapes in Atlanta would have *increased* 2 percent from 1995 (Martz, 1999). Other cities, like New York and Philadelphia, have also faced recent allegations of underreporting crime.

Summary

Arrest data, then, vastly underestimate the extent of delinquency. This underestimation is especially true for minor delinquency, which is less likely to become known to the police and is less likely to result in arrest. Further, arrest data may provide misleading information on trends in delinquency. Suppose, for example, that arrest data suggest an increase in juvenile delinquency over time. This increase could be due to a number of factors. Perhaps victims have become more likely to report crimes to the police. Perhaps complainants have become more likely to press for arrest (e.g., stores have become more likely to press for arrest in shoplifting cases). Perhaps police departments have become more likely to encourage officers to make arrests (e.g., many police departments are adopting "zero-tolerance" policing, where even minor violations of the law may result in arrest). Perhaps the police have cracked down on certain types of crime, like drug use or gun-related crimes. Perhaps the police are turning in more accurate crime reports (data suggest that crime reports have become more accurate in recent decades). Or perhaps juvenile delinquency really is increasing. It is sometimes the case that we cannot tell which factor or factors is responsible for a change in arrest rates.

Self-Report Data

Given the problems with arrest data, criminologists have tried to develop alternative ways to measure the extent of delinquency. The major alternative they have developed is self-report data. Self-report data is obtained by asking juveniles about the extent of their delinquency. Sometimes the juveniles are interviewed and sometimes they fill out questionnaires. Most self-report surveys focus on delinquency committed during the previous year, to minimize problems with memory. In almost all cases, self-report surveys are anonymous, or respondents are assured that their answers are confidential. A popular self-report measure of delinquency is shown in Table 2.2. Take a few minutes to answer the questions in this measure (although you should *not* record the answers in this book in case it gets lost or borrowed).

Self-report surveys of delinquency did not come into wide use until the 1960s, but they are now the major way that criminologists use to measure delinquency. The major advantage of self-report data is that it provides an estimate of all delinquency committed by juveniles, regardless of whether that delinquency is known to the police or has resulted in arrest. As a consequence, self-report data indicate that delinquency is far more extensive than arrest data suggest. But before I continue my discussion of self-report data, let me address a question that I know is on your mind.

How Do We Know That Juveniles Are Telling the Truth?

Most people have the same reaction to self-report surveys: How do researchers know that juveniles are telling the truth? They are asking juveniles whether they have engaged in a range of illegal behaviors, some of which are strongly condemned and subject to severe punishment. It is reasonable to think that many juveniles will underreport their delinquency. Researchers have tried to estimate the accuracy of self-report data in several

Table 2.2   A Popular Self-Report Measure of Delinquency

How many times in the last year have you:

1. Purposely damaged or destroyed property belonging to your *parents* or other *family members*.
2. Purposely damaged or destroyed property belonging to a *school*.
3. Purposely damaged or destroyed *other property* that did not belong to you (not counting family or school property).
4. Stolen (or tried to steal) a *motor vehicle*, such as a car or motorcycle.
5. Stolen (or tried to steal) something worth more than $50.
6. Knowingly bought, sold, or held stolen goods (or tried to do any of these things).
7. Thrown objects (such as rocks, snowballs, or bottles) at cars or people.
8. Run away from home.
9. Lied about your age to gain entrance or to purchase something (lied about your age to buy liquor or get into a movie).
10. Carried a hidden weapon other than a plain pocket knife.
11. Stolen (or tried to steal) things worth $5 or less.
12. Attacked someone with the idea of seriously hurting or killing him/her.
13. Been paid for having sexual relations with someone.
14. Had sexual intercourse with a person of the opposite sex other than your wife/husband.
15. Been involved in gang fights.
16. Sold marijuana or hashish ("pot," "grass," "hash").
17. Cheated on school tests.
18. Hitchhiked where it was illegal to do so.
19. Stolen money or other things from your *parents or other members of your family*.
20. Hit (or threatened to hit) a *teacher* or other adult at school.
21. Hit (or threatened to hit) one of your *parents*.
22. Hit (or threatened to hit) other *students*.
23. Been loud, rowdy, or unruly in a public place (disorderly conduct).
24. Sold hard drugs, such as heroin, cocaine, and LSD.
25. Taken a vehicle for a ride (drive) without the owner's permission.
26. Bought or provided liquor for a minor.
27. Had (or tried to have) sexual relations with someone against their will.
28. Used force (strong-arm methods) to get money or things from other *students*.
29. Used force (strong-arm methods) to get money or things from a *teacher* or other adult at school.
30. Used force (strong-arm methods) to get money or things from *other people* (not students or teachers).
31. Avoided paying for such things as movies, bus or subway rides, and food.
32. Been drunk in a public place.
33. Stolen (or tried to steal) things worth between $5 and $50.
34. Stolen (or tried to steal) something at school, such as someone's coat from a classroom, locker, or cafeteria, or a book from a library.
35. Broken into a building or vehicle (or tried to break in) to steal something or just to look around.
36. Begged for money or things from strangers.
37. Skipped classes without an excuse.
38. Failed to return extra change that a cashier gave you by mistake.
39. Been suspended from school.
40. Made obscene telephone calls (calling someone and saying dirty things).

Table 2.2   A Popular Self-Report Measure of Delinquency (continued)

How often in the last year have you used:

41. Alcoholic beverages (beer, wine, and hard liquor).
42. Marijuana or hashish ("grass," "pot," "hash").
43. Hallucinogens ("LSD," "mescaline," "peyote," "acid").
44. Amphetamines ("uppers," "speed," "whites").
45. Barbiturates ("downers," "reds").
46. Heroin ("horse," "smack").
47. Cocaine ("coke").

Source: Elliott and Ageton (1980).

ways. None of these ways are perfect, but taken together they provide a rough estimate of the accuracy of self-report data.

1. *Official record comparisons*. Most commonly, researchers compare the self-reported delinquent acts of respondents with their police or court records. They determine whether respondents report the offenses for which they have been arrested or convicted.[2] Failure of respondents to report such offenses suggests that self-report data are inaccurate. Reporting such offenses *suggests* that self-report data *may* be accurate. It does not, of course, prove that self-report data are accurate. People may admit to offenses for which they have been arrested or convicted but fail to report other offenses.

2. *Comparisons with peer, family, or school reports*. Certain researchers have estimated the accuracy of self-reports by determining whether respondents report the delinquent acts that their friends, parents, and/or teachers attribute to them (e.g., Gold, 1966). If they do not, that suggests that self-report data are inaccurate. If they do, that suggests that self-report data may be accurate.

3. *Lie-detector tests*. Certain researchers have used lie-detector tests or the threat of lie-detector tests to estimate the accuracy of self-report data (e.g., Clark and Tift, 1966; Hindelang et al., 1981). For example, juveniles in one study were interviewed about the extent of their delinquency. They were then interviewed again, but this time they were told that their answers would be evaluated using a "psychological stress evaluator" that detects dishonest responses. They were then asked a variety of questions, including the same questions they had previously been asked about the extent of their delinquency. The researchers then determined whether the juveniles changed their answers in the second interview.

4. *Comparisons with drug tests*. Researchers have estimated the accuracy of self-reports of drug use by comparing such reports to estimates of drug use obtained from urine, saliva, or blood tests (e.g., Akers et al., 1983).

5. *Comparisons between groups known to differ in their level of delinquency.* Researchers have also estimated the accuracy of self-reports by comparing the self-reported delinquency of groups known to differ in their level of delinquency. For example, they have compared the self-reported delinquency of institutionalized delinquents to that of high school students (e.g., Short and Nye, 1958). If there is little difference in self-reported delinquency between these groups, that suggests that self-report data are inaccurate. If the institutionalized delinquents have a higher level of self-reported delinquency, that suggests that self-report data may be accurate.

Again, none of these methods is perfect, but taken together they allow researchers to form a rough estimate of the accuracy of self-report data. Overall, they suggest that self-report data provide a *moderately* accurate estimate of the extent of delinquency. Most juveniles are reasonably honest in their responses, although there is some underreporting (and even a little over reporting) of delinquency. Most studies suggest that the amount of underreporting is not large; certain studies, however, suggest that it may be substantial (see Hindelang et al., 1981; Turner et al., 1998). Limited data suggest that this underreporting is greatest for serious offenses. That is, juveniles are more likely to conceal serious offenses than minor ones. And certain data suggest that black males are more likely to underreport the extent of their delinquency, although findings here are somewhat mixed.[3]

Problems With Self-Report Data

While self-report data appear to provide a moderately accurate estimate of the extent of delinquency, they do have some problems. One problem is that there are very few long-term, nationwide self-report surveys of delinquency. While the federal government collects data from police departments on an annual basis, the government has no comparable program for the collection of self-report data. Most self-report surveys are administered by university professors (who may receive government funding for their research). Their surveys usually focus on the extent of self-reported delinquency in a single city or region at one point in time. Only a few national self-report surveys have been done. As a result, estimates of the extent of self-reported delinquency in the U.S. and trends in such delinquency are somewhat limited.

A second problem is that self-report surveys often underestimate the extent of serious delinquency. One reason for this has already been indicated: Data suggest that respondents sometimes underreport serious delinquent acts. Three additional reasons for the underestimation of serious delinquency are described below. Some of the newest and best self-report surveys, however, have taken significant steps to obtain better estimates of serious delinquency. These steps are also described below.

Self-report surveys sometimes employ measures of delinquency that focus on minor offenses and employ vague response categories. The early self-report surveys and some recent self-report surveys employ questions identical or similar to the ones in Table 2.3. Take a moment to examine these questions. You will immediately notice that the questions focus on minor forms of delinquency. There is a reason for this. Most self-report surveys, especially the early surveys, examine samples of only a few hundred juveniles. Serious delinquent acts, like serious assaults and rapes, are not common, so only a small number of juveniles will report such acts in a sample of a few hundred. As a consequence, there are too few instances of these acts to allow any meaningful analyses. Many self-report researchers therefore focus on the more frequently occurring minor offenses.

Further, notice the response categories for each delinquency question ("no," "once or twice," "several times," "very often"). Respondents who commit an act ten times will probably select "very often," but so will respondents who commit an act a hundred times. The response categories do not distinguish offenders who commit an act a few times from those who commit an act scores or even hundreds of times. This lack of precision is a serious problem. Recent data indicate that there is a small group of high-rate offenders, each of whom commits hundreds of delinquent acts per year. These offenders account for a majority of all delinquent acts in some studies. But the response categories used in the survey shown in Table 2.3 do not provide an accurate count of the number of delinquent acts committed by these offenders. So not only do some self-report surveys focus on minor delinquency, they often provide an imprecise estimate of the extent of delinquency.

Many recent self-report surveys try to obtain accurate counts of the number of delinquent acts committed. Further, they obtain larger samples and focus on both minor and serious offenses. The self-report delinquency measure in Table 2.2 is an example of a measure that focuses on both minor and serious delinquency and that tries to accurately measure the number of times delinquent acts have been committed. This measure was developed by Elliott and associates and has served as a model for measures in many recent self-report studies (see Elliott and Ageton, 1980).

Table 2.3   An Early Self-Report Measure of Delinquency

Have You Ever:
1. Driven a car without a driver's license or permit?
   No___
   Once or twice ___
   Several times ___
   Very often ___
2. Skipped school without a legitimate excuse?
   Same response categories as above.
3. Defied your parents' authority (to their face)?
4. Taken little things (worth less than $2) that did not belong to you?
5. Bought or drank beer, wine, or liquor? (Include drinking at home.)
6. Purposely damaged or destroyed public or private property that did not belong to you?
7. Had sex relations with a person of the opposite sex?

Source: Nye (1958).

Juveniles often report trivial acts on self-report surveys—acts that would probably not be considered delinquent by law enforcement officials. Examples of trivial acts would be sipping a little wine at the dinner table with your parents' permission or playfully shoving one of your siblings. While juveniles might report these as underage drinking and minor assault, it is quite unlikely that law enforcement officials would see them as such.

Trivial events are most likely to be reported in response to questions about minor delinquent acts. In one study, over 75 percent of the minor assault reports were classified by the researcher as trivial (Elliott et al., 1989:15). Trivial events, however, are sometimes reported when respondents are questioned about serious delinquent acts like aggravated assault. Some researchers ask respondents a series of follow-up questions about the delinquent acts they report, in order to classify these acts as trivial or nontrivial. The trivial acts are then excluded from the estimates of delinquency. Many self-report researchers, however, do not do this follow-up. So, self-report surveys often focus on minor, even trivial offenses.

Self-report surveys <u>tend to under sample</u> the most serious delinquents. Self-report surveys are usually based on school or household samples. For example, a researcher might try to survey a sample of students from several schools in a city. Or a researcher might try to survey juveniles from a sample of households in a city. The researcher first selects the juveniles to survey and then tries to obtain their permission to conduct the interview or complete the questionnaire. It is usually necessary to obtain the permission of their parents or guardians as well.

These strategies have the advantage of reaching broad samples of juveniles—both those who have been arrested and those who have not. These strategies, however, most likely under sample the most serious delinquents, including those who commit the most offenses and those who commit very serious offenses. If you sample school students, you miss students who have dropped out of school, are suspended, or are truant. These students tend to be the more serious offenders. This under sampling is less of a problem if the researchers sample households, but even here they are likely to miss juveniles who live on the street or spend a lot of time on the street. Such juveniles tend to be more serious offenders (see Hagan and McCarthy, 1997a, 1997b). Further, there is reason to believe that the more serious offenders (and their parents) are less likely to agree to participate in the survey. In fact, it is often the case that 30 percent or more of the juveniles who are selected in the initial sample refuse to participate in the survey or cannot be reached. As a consequence, data suggest that self-report surveys under sample serious delinquents (see Cernkovich et al., 1985).

Self-report surveys do not, of course, miss serious offenders entirely (see Elliott, 1994). And some of the newer and better self-report surveys make a special effort to include serious offenders in their samples. For example, they over sample juveniles in neighborhoods that have high delinquency rates. Also, they screen juveniles before including them in the survey, making a special effort to detect and recruit serious offenders in their survey (see Thornberry et al., 1995). These surveys have shown some success in including serious offenders, but it is still the case that most self-report surveys probably under sample serious offenders.

In sum, *self-report data provide moderately accurate information on the extent of delinquency, especially the minor delinquency of juveniles in the general population*. There is reason to believe, however, that self-report data provide less accurate information on the extent of serious delinquency, partly because (1) serious offenses are more likely to be underreported, (2) measures of delinquency often focus on minor offenses and employ vague response categories, (3) respondents often report trivial acts, and (4) self-report surveys tend to under sample serious offenders. Again, however, some of the more recent self-report surveys have taken significant steps to overcome these problems.

Victimization Data

The problems with police data have also motivated criminologists to develop another way of estimating the extent of crime and delinquency: victimization data. Victimization data is obtained by asking people to report on their experiences as crime victims. Several victimization surveys were conducted in the 1960s, and the federal government started compiling victimization data on an annual basis in the early 1970s through the administration of the National Crime Victimization Survey. Each year people ages 12 and older in approximately 50,000 households throughout the United States are asked about their experiences as crime victims. These households are selected so as to be representative of all households in the United States. Data from the National Crime Victimization Survey allow researchers to estimate the total amount of crime and delinquency in the United States. These victimization data are published annually in a report titled *Criminal Victimization in the United States* or, more recently, *Criminal Victimization* (see Rennison, 1999; also look for victimization data on the web site of the Bureau of Justice Statistics: *http://www.ojp.usdoj.gov/bjs/*).

The respondents in the victimization survey are asked if they have been the victims of crime, including aggravated assault, simple assault, rape/sexual assault, robbery, burglary, motor vehicle theft, and larceny. (They are not, of course, asked if they have been the victims of homicide.) If they reply that they have been the victim of one of these crimes, they are asked a number of questions about this victimization. For example, they are asked whether they reported the victimization to the police and if not, why not. In 1998, only 38 percent of all victimizations were reported to the police; the most common reason for not reporting is that the victimization is a private or personal matter. Respondents are also asked if they saw the person(s) who victimized them. If so, they are asked about the age, sex, and race of this person(s), among other things. On the basis of their responses, researchers can estimate the number of victimizations committed by young people and trends in such victimization over time.

Like self-report data, victimization data provide information on both crimes that have come to the attention of the police and crimes that have not. They also provide much information on the experiences and characteristics of crime victims.

Problems With Victimization Data

There are, however, problems with using victimization data to estimate the extent of delinquency.

1. Victimization data only focus on a few violent and property crimes committed against individuals ages 12 and older. They do not provide any information on crimes such as drug use and on status offenses. They do not provide any information on crimes

committed against businesses—like shoplifting at department stores. And they do not provide any information on crimes committed against people less than 12 years of age.

2. Certain groups with high rates of criminal victimization are under sampled, such as homeless people, transients, and institutionalized persons.

3. There is evidence that many crime victims do not report their victimizations to the interviewers. There are a variety of reasons for this nonreporting, including memory loss and embarrassment. Data suggest that victimizations by family members, friends, and acquaintances are often not reported to the interviewer.

4. The victim often does not see the offender and so cannot estimate the offender's age. This is especially likely for property crimes. One study found that the victim only saw the offender in 6 percent of all burglaries and motor vehicle thefts and in 4 percent of all household larcenies (Hindelang, 1981). The victim, of course, does see the offender in most violent crimes. The victim, however, can only make a rough estimate of the offender's age. In particular, it is often hard to distinguish older juveniles from young adults.

For these reasons, victimization data are somewhat limited in the information they provide about the extent of and trends in delinquency. The discussion in Chapter 3 therefore draws primarily on arrest and self-report data. However, I will note certain relevant findings from victimization data. And I will also briefly discuss the extent to which juveniles are crime *victims*, as well as offenders.

Summary

There are three major ways to measure the extent of delinquency and trends in delinquency: arrest, self-report, and victimization data. Each has its advantages and disadvantages. With the exception of homicide, arrest data vastly underestimate the extent of delinquency and *may* provide misleading information on trends in delinquency. Arrest data are especially likely to provide misleading information on minor crimes, since these crimes are the least likely to be reported to the police and the least likely to result in arrest. Self-report data provide a better estimate of the extent of delinquency since they focus on all offenses, both those that have come to the attention of the police and those that have not. Self-report data, however, tend to focus on minor offenses committed in the general population. Estimates of the extent of serious delinquency are less accurate, for reasons indicated in the preceding paragraphs. Victimization data also attempt to measure both crimes that have come to the attention of the police and those that have not. But victimization data suffer from several problems; most notably, they focus only on a small number of crimes, and victims usually have not seen the offenders who committed the crime—with the exception of violent crimes.

As you can tell, measuring delinquency is not a simple matter. It is easy to produce estimates of the extent of delinquency and trends in delinquency, and we are exposed to such estimates on a regular basis in the media. Most estimates, however, are problematic for the reasons indicated here. The situation is not as bad as it might appear, however. We can often use our knowledge of these data sources to judge which provides the best estimate of the extent of delinquency or trends in delinquency in a particular situation. And sometimes the three data sources agree with one another.

Notes

1. For fuller discussions, see Bernard, 1999; Cernkovich et al., 1985; Elliott, 1982; Elliott and Ageton, 1980; Elliott et al., 1989; Farrington et al., 1996; Gove et al., 1985; Hindelang et al., 1979, 1981; Huizinga and Elliott, 1986; Jackson, 1990; O'Brien, 2000; Reiss and Roth, 1993; Rutter et al., 1998; Weis, 1986; Wells and Rankin, 1995.
2. *See* Farrington et al., 1996; Hindelang et al., 1981; Huizinga and Elliott, 1986.
3. *See* Farrington et al., 1996; Hindelang et al., 1981; Huizinga and Elliott, 1986; Weis, 1986. ✦

Chapter 3

How Much Delinquency Is There and Is Delinquency Increasing?

This chapter focuses on the two simple questions asked in the title: How much delinquency is there in the United States? Is delinquency increasing? Simple questions, however, often have complex answers. The complexity can be frustrating at times, but you will end up with a much fuller understanding of delinquency. I first focus on the extent of delinquency in the United States, presenting estimates from arrest, self-report, and victimization data. I then focus on trends in delinquency, again presenting estimates from arrest, self-report, and victimization data. These data sources do not always agree with one another, but I think there are some conclusions we can safely draw about the extent of and trends in delinquency.

I should warn you that any discussion in this area is going to contain a lot of numbers. I try to keep the numbers to a minimum, and I encourage you to focus on the central points that are being made and to avoid getting caught up in the specific numbers. Many of the numbers that follow come from the *Sourcebook of Criminal Justice Statistics* (Maguire and Pastore, 1999; also see *http://www.albany.edu/sourcebook/*). The *Sourcebook* publishes a wide range of data on crime from the FBI, self-report surveys, the National Crime Victimization Survey, and other sources. It is a great place to look if you ever want to know anything about the extent of crime, trends in crime, the characteristics of delinquents, or a range of other topics.

How Much Delinquency Is There?

How Many Juveniles Are Arrested and What Are They Arrested For?

As you know, arrest data vastly underestimate the extent of delinquency. Most delinquent acts do not come to the attention of the police, and acts that do come to the attention of the police usually do not result in arrest. This is especially true for minor crimes. Nevertheless, many juveniles are arrested each year (see Snyder, 1999).

Table 3.1 shows the *number of juvenile arrests* in 1998 broken down by type of crime. The top part of the table focuses on Part I or Index crimes, while the bottom part focuses on Part II crimes. Overall, there were about 2.6 million juvenile arrests. That number does not mean that 2.6 million *different* juveniles were arrested. Many juveniles were arrested more than once.

About 700,000 of these arrests were for Part I crimes. Note that arrests for property crimes are much more common than arrests for violent crimes. In fact, well over half of all Part I arrests are for larceny-theft. Larceny-theft, in fact, is the crime with the highest number of arrests. About 1.9 million arrests were for Part II offenses, with the most arrests being for "other assaults," drug abuse violations, curfew violations, disorderly conduct, running away, and liquor law violations.

Overall, note that the number of arrests tends to be higher for minor crimes than for serious crimes. For example, 2,100 juveniles were arrested for homicide and 5,300 were arrested for forcible rape. Over 400,000 were arrested for larceny-theft, however.

These data, while useful, may be a little difficult to interpret. One way to help interpret them is to look at *arrest rates*. Arrest rates show the number of

Table 3.1 The Number of Juveniles Arrested, 1998	
Total	2,603,300
Part I Offenses	
Murder and nonnegligent manslaughter	2,100
Forcible rape	5,300
Robbery	32,500
Aggravated assault	72,300
Burglary	116,000
Larceny-theft	417,000
Motor vehicle theft	54,100
Arson	9,000
Part II Offenses	
Other assaults	237,700
Forgery and counterfeiting	7,100
Fraud	11,300
Embezzlement	1,600
Stolen property (buying, receiving, possessing)	33,800
Vandalism	126,800
Weapons (carrying, possessing, etc.)	45,200
Prostitution and commercialized vice	1,400
Sex offenses (except forcible rape and prostitution)	15,900
Drug abuse violations	205,800
Gambling	1,600
Offenses against the family and children	10,200
Driving under the influence	21,000
Liquor law violations	157,300
Drunkenness	24,600
Disorderly conduct	183,700
Vagrancy	2,900
All other offenses (except traffic)	453,000
Suspicion	1,300
Curfew and loitering	187,800
Runaways	165,100

Source: Snyder (1999).

juvenile arrests *per 100,000 juveniles ages 10 to 17* in the population (very few juveniles under age 10 are arrested). Arrest rates are useful because they give us an idea of the probability that a juvenile will be arrested. The overall juvenile arrest rate was about 8,930 per 100,000 juveniles. In other words, there were about 8,930 juvenile arrests for every 100,000 juveniles ages 10 to 17 in the population (or about 8.9 arrests per 100 juveniles). The arrest rate for violent Part I offenses was about 394 per 100,000 juveniles (or 0.4 arrests per 100 juveniles). The arrest rate for Part I property crimes was about 2,130 per 100,000 juveniles (or about 2.1 arrests per 100 juveniles).

I want to add a note of caution: The fact that there were 2.6 million juvenile arrests does not mean that juveniles committed 2.6 million crimes. I earlier stated that juveniles usually commit their crimes in groups. As a consequence, several juveniles are often arrested for a single crime. For example, several juveniles might be arrested for a single act of vandalism. To estimate the number of crimes committed by juveniles, it is best to look at *the number* of crimes cleared by the arrest of juveniles. Clearance data allow us to estimate the number of *Part I crimes* committed by juveniles (clearance data are not reported for Part II crimes). While about 708,000 juveniles were arrested in 1998 for Part I crimes, only about 391,000 Part I crimes were cleared by the arrest of juveniles.

You know that arrest data vastly underestimate the extent of delinquency. Self-report data, discussed in the following section, provide a more accurate estimate of the extent of delinquency.

How Much Self-Reported Delinquency Is There?

I have the students in my juvenile delinquency course fill out a short survey on the first day of class. Among other things, the survey asks whether they have ever committed any of fourteen different delinquent acts as juveniles. Some of these acts are status offenses, like running away and truancy. Some are minor crimes, like petty larceny and trespassing. And some are more serious crimes, like burglary and robbery. The students are always shocked by the results. I typically find that anywhere from 90 to 100 percent of the students have committed at least one of the delinquent acts. And it is often the case that about half the class has committed at least seven of the fourteen delinquent acts. Keep in mind that these are largely upper-middle-class students who have done quite well in school. A high percentage of them will go on to become doctors, lawyers, and business managers. (Look at the self-report survey in Table 2.2 again; how many of the delinquent acts have you committed?) Self-report surveys typically find that 90 percent or more of all juveniles have engaged in at least some forms of delinquency—usually minor delinquency but often a few instances of more serious delinquency as well.

I do not, however, want you to think that I am picking on juveniles. Two criminologists recently conducted a self-report survey of crime among criminologists (Robinson and Zaitzow, 1999). They describe their motivation for doing such a survey by stating that "We were in an airplane on our way back from a recent American Society of Criminology meeting . . . [and] we overheard from the seats directly in front of us two criminologists discussing what they had taken (i.e., stolen) from the conference hotel." They began to wonder just how common crime was among criminologists. So they surveyed 522 criminologists from throughout the United States, most of whom had doctoral degrees and half of whom were faculty members at colleges and universities. The large majority of these criminologists had engaged in one or more crimes at some point in their lives. For example, 55 percent had committed theft, 22 percent had committed burglary, 60 percent had used illicit drugs, and 25 percent had physically attacked another person. Self-report data, then, indicate that delinquency (and crime) are common, even among students like yourselves and the faculty who teach you. Keep this in mind when you and I are examining topics like the causes of delinquency. To some extent, we are examining your (and my) behavior.

As indicated earlier, not many self-report surveys have been administered to juveniles *throughout the United States*. But a few such surveys exist. The most recent is the 1998 Monitoring the Future survey (see the *Sourcebook of Criminal Justice Statistics* at the web site identified earlier). The Monitoring the Future survey is administered to a sample of about 3,000 high school seniors throughout the United States each year. While the survey provides national data on the extent of self-reported delinquency, it does have certain problems. It focuses on high school seniors, thereby missing dropouts and students who were suspended or truant when the survey was administered. As indicated earlier, such juveniles are more likely to be serious offenders. It does not examine many delinquent offenses, especially serious offenses like homicide and rape. And it employs vague response categories. In particular, it uses the response category "5 or more times," so that researchers cannot distinguish someone who committed an act five times from someone who committed the same act 100 times. Nevertheless, the data in Table 3.2 provide you with an idea of the extent of delinquency in this group.

Note that certain forms of delinquency are quite common, particularly status offenses and minor forms of delinquency. For example, the large majority of high school seniors have drunk alcohol and have argued or fought with their parents in the past year (the status offense of "incorrigibility"). And a substantial percentage of students have engaged in petty theft and fighting. More serious forms of delinquency are less frequent but not uncommon. For example, about 14 percent of high school seniors reported that they "hurt someone badly enough to need bandages or a doctor" in 1998. Also note that the *rates* of self-reported offending are much higher than the *arrest rates* for comparable offenses.

The best self-report survey conducted on a national level is the National Survey of Youth (see Elliott et al., 1985). This survey was administered to a sample of 1,725 adolescents ages 11 through 17 throughout the United States in 1977. These adolescents were asked about the extent of their delinquency in 1976. The same group of adolescents was surveyed several additional times through the 1990s, but they, of course, turned from adolescents into adults as the surveys progressed. Elliott and his associates looked at a total of forty-seven delinquent acts, including status offenses, minor crimes, and serious crimes (see Table 2.2 for a list of these acts). They took care to precisely measure the number of times each act was committed, avoiding the use of vague response categories. They found that the average number of delinquent acts committed by a juvenile in 1976 was 52. As high as this number is, there is reason to believe that it might be somewhat higher today (see below, also see the trend data in Jensen and Rojek, 1998). So while FBI data indicate that there are 8.9 arrests per 100 juveniles, self-report data indicate that there are at least 5,200 self-reports of delinquency per 100 juveniles (52 x 100). And while arrest data indicate that there were 2.6 million juvenile arrests in 1998, self-report data suggest that the 30 million juveniles between age 10 and age 17 in the United States engaged in hundreds of millions of delinquent acts in 1998.

Again, self-report data indicate that most of these delinquent acts are status offenses and minor crimes. More serious crimes are less frequent, although they are not uncommon, particularly in certain subgroups. For example, Elliott (1994) found that 36 percent of 17-year-old black males and 25 percent of 17-year-old white males committed at least one serious act of violence over the course of a year. Serious acts of violence include aggravated assaults, robberies, and rapes; all involve some injury or the use of a weapon.

The large discrepancy between arrest data and self-report data highlights the fact that most delinquent acts do not come to the attention of the police or result in arrest. Dunford and Elliott (1984) used the National Youth Survey to explore the relationship between self-reported delinquency and arrest data. They classified youth according to the number of delinquent acts they self-

Table 3.2	The Extent of Self-Reported Delinquency Among High School Seniors, 1998					
During the last 12 months how often have you:	Not at all %	Once %	Twice %	3 or 4 times %	5 or more times %	Rate (no. of acts per 100 juveniles)
1. Argued or had a fight with either of your parents?	11.9	9.6	14.1	23.7	40.7	324.3
2. Hit an instructor or supervisor?	96.7	1.6	.8	.3	.6	7.3
3. Gotten into a serious fight in school or at work?	83.4	9.8	3.7	1.6	1.6	30.8
4. Taken part in a fight where a bunch of your friends were against another group?	79.4	10.3	5.1	3.0	2.2	42
5. Hurt someone badly enough to need bandages or a doctor?	85.6	7.9	3.1	1.7	1.7	28.6
6. Used a knife or gun or some other thing (like a club) to get something from a person?	95.7	2.2	.8	.5	.9	10.1
7. Taken something not belonging to you worth under $50?	68.8	13.2	7.4	4.9	5.7	74
8. Taken something not belonging to you worth over $50?	88.4	5.3	2.6	1.4	2.3	25.9
9. Taken something from a store without paying for it?	70.3	12.5	6.5	4.1	6.4	71.9
10. Taken a car that didn't belong to someone in your family without permission of the owner?	95.2	2.7	.9	.6	.7	12.1
11. Taken part of a car without permission of the owner?	94.9	2.5	1.2	.6	.8	11
12. Gone into some house or building when you weren't supposed to be there?	75.4	10.6	6.5	3.6	3.9	55.7
13. Set fire to someone's property on purpose?	97.1	1.1	.8	.2	.8	7.4
14. Damaged school property on purpose?	85.7	7.5	2.6	2.0	2.3	31.2
15. Damaged property at work on purpose?	92.7	3.3	1.6	.9	1.6	17.7
16. Used alcohol at least once in 1998?		74.3				
17. Used marijuana at least once in 1998?		37.5				

Source: The Monitoring the Future survey, as reported in the *Sourcebook of Criminal Justice Statistics* (http://www.albany.edu/sourcebook/).

reported in a two-year period and then examined the percentage of youth in each group who had been arrested at least once during the same two-year period. They found that the probability of arrest was quite low, even among youths who had committed a large number of offenses. For example, only 7 percent of the youths who self-reported between 101 and 200 delinquent acts were arrested. Only 19 percent of the youth who self-reported over 200 delinquent acts were arrested. Overall, the probability that a youth will be arrested for a given delinquent act is well under 1 percent. The probability of arrest is low even for those who commit serious offenses. For example, Elliott (1995) estimated that the probability of arrest for a serious violent offense (aggravated assault, rape, robbery) is about 2 in 100.

What can we conclude about the extent of delinquency according to self-report data? Delinquency is far more common than arrest data suggest. Most juveniles engage in delinquency. They generally commit status offenses and minor crimes, but serious crimes are not uncommon.

How Many Juveniles Are Victimized and How Many Victimizations Are Committed by Juveniles?

Victimization data provide another alternative to arrest data. As indicated earlier, victimization data tell a lot about crime victims. They have somewhat less to say about the number of victimizations committed by juveniles, largely because crime victims usually do not see the person who victimized them. Nevertheless, victimization data do provide some information about the number of violent crimes committed by juveniles.

Table 3.3 shows the number of victimizations experienced by U.S. residents ages 12 or older in 1998, as estimated by the National Crime Victimization Survey (see Rennison, 1999). About 31 million victimizations were reported in 1998, including 8.1 million violent victimizations and 22.9 million property victimizations. That amounts to about 3.7 violent victimizations and 21.7 property victimizations for every 100 people age 12 or older. As you can see, people are most often the victims of larceny-theft. Victimization data, like arrest and self-report data, indicate that property crimes are more common than violent crimes, and minor crimes are more common than serious crimes.

Table 3.3 The Number and Rate of Victimizations, 1998		
	Number	Rate (per 1,000 persons age 12 or older or per 1,000 households)
All crimes	31,307,000	
Rape/sexual assault	333,000	1.5
Robbery	886,000	4.0
Aggravated assault	1,674000	7.5
Simple assault	5,224,000	23.5
Personal theft*	296,000	1.3
Household burglary	4,054,000	38.5
Motor vehicle theft	1,138,000	10.8
Theft	17,703,000	168.1

*Includes pocket picking, purse snatching, and attempted purse snatching.
Source: Rennison (1999).

Who is most likely to be victimized? Who do you think is most likely to be victimized by crime: young or old, male or female, white or black, Hispanic or non-Hispanic, poor or rich?

Young people have higher rates of victimization than older people for violent crimes (data for most property crimes are reported for households rather than for individuals). Rates of victimization are highest for those between 16 and 19 years old, followed closely by those between 12 and 15. Rates of victimization generally decline with age and are lowest among those 65 or older. To illustrate, about 9 out of every 100 people between ages 16 and 19 were the victims of violence in 1998, a rate more than thirty times higher than those age 65 and over. As dramatic as this difference is, there are data suggesting that the National Crime Victimization Survey substantially underestimates the extent of victimization against young people. Data from other surveys suggest that about 25 of every 100 adolescents are the victims of violence each year and perhaps as many as 50 of every 100 are the victims of theft (Wells and Rankin, 1995).

Males have higher rates of victimization than females for violent crimes, with the exception of rape/sexual assault. About 4.3 of every 100 males were the victims of violence in 1998, versus about 3.0 of every 100 females. Females were about 14 times more likely than males to be the victims of rape/sexual assault. About 2.7 rapes, attempted rapes, or sexual assaults per 1,000 females were reported in 1998. These estimates, however, should be viewed with much caution. Data suggest that the National Crime Victimization Survey substantially underestimates the amount of rape and other violence against women. For example, the best survey data suggest that 15 to 20 percent of all females will be the victims of a completed or attempted rape at some point in their lives, with at least half of these rapes occurring before the age of 18 (see Tjaden and Thoennes, 1999). Most of the rapes and other violence against women are committed by "intimate partners" (current and former spouses, cohabiting partners, and dates or boyfriends). As indicated by Gove et al. (1985), intimate partner violence is much less likely to be reported in the National Crime Victimization Survey than is violence committed by strangers.

Blacks are somewhat more likely than whites to be victims of violence, with the exception of simple assault. About 4.2 of every 100 blacks were the victims of violence in 1998, versus about 3.6 of every 100 whites. Black households or households headed by blacks have higher rates of property crime than white households. About 5.5 of every 100 black households were burglarized, versus about 3.6 of every 100 white households. Hispanics and non-Hispanics are about equally likely to be the victims of violence, but Hispanic households are more likely to be the victims of property crime than non-Hispanic households. ("Hispanics" are defined as persons of Spanish-speaking origin; they may identify themselves as white, black, or members of other racial groups.)

People with lower incomes are more likely to be the victims of violence. About 6.4 of every 100 people in households with incomes of less than $7,500 were the victims of violence, versus about 3.3 of every 100 people in households with incomes of $75,000 or more. The relationship between household income and theft is mixed. About 5.5 of every 100 households with incomes lower than $7,500 were burglarized, versus 2.8 of every 100 households with incomes of at least $75,000. Households with higher incomes, however, were more likely to experience larceny-theft.

In sum, crime victims tend to be young, (possibly) male, black, Hispanic (for property crime), and poor (for violent crime).

How many victimizations are committed by juveniles? What does victimization data tell us about the number of crimes *committed* by juveniles? As indicated, crime victims are asked whether they saw the person(s) who victimized them. They rarely see the offender(s) in property crimes like larceny and burglary, but they almost always see the offender in violent crimes like assault, rape, and robbery. If victims saw the offender(s), they are asked to estimate that person's age. The information that victimization data provide about the extent of juvenile delinquency, therefore, is largely limited to violent crime (although see Hindelang, 1981, regarding property crime). Data from 1997 indicate that juveniles under 18 were involved in 27 percent of all serious violent victimizations, or about 830,000 acts of rape/sexual assault, robbery, and aggravated assault (Snyder and Sickmund, 1999). This estimate exceeds by several times the number of juvenile arrests for serious violent crimes or the number of violent crimes cleared by the arrest of juveniles. Victimization data show that violent crime among juveniles is far more extensive than arrest data indicate, although not as extensive as indicated by self-report data.

Summary

You have been presented with a lot of numbers and may be a little overwhelmed. Again, try not to get too caught up in all the numbers. Focus on the basic points being made by these numbers. These points include the following:

1. Arrest, self-report, and victimization data provide different estimates of the extent of delinquency in the United States. Arrest data provide the lowest estimates, and self-report data provide the highest. You should be able to explain why this is the case, drawing on the discussion of the advantages and disadvantages of each type of data.

2. Self-report data probably provide the most accurate estimate of the extent of delinquency. At least 90 percent of all adolescents engage in delinquency at some point, and, *on average*, juveniles commit at least 52 delinquent acts per year.

3. All three data sources indicate that minor offenses are more common than serious offenses and that property crime is more common than violent crime, although minor or simple assault is common.

Is Juvenile Delinquency Increasing?

As Bernard (1992) points out, most people think that juvenile delinquency is worse now than in the past. In fact, they often think of the past as the "good old days," a time when it was safe to walk the streets and juveniles almost never committed serious crimes like murder and rape. It is easy to understand why people feel this way. The media regularly report on the horrible crimes committed by juveniles. Occasionally, a crime like the shooting deaths of thirteen people at Columbine High School in Colorado captures the national attention for weeks or even months. But what do the data show? Is delinquency increasing, decreasing, or staying the same? Once more, we must examine arrest, self-report, and victimization data. As you will see, they sometimes disagree with one another regarding trends in delinquency. Nevertheless, an examination of these data sources will allow us to draw some tentative conclusions about trends in delinquency. My focus is on trends in delinquency since the early 1980s.

Are Juvenile Arrests Increasing?

When examining trends in juvenile arrests it is best to look at *arrest rates* rather than the *number of arrests*. Arrest rates are usually presented as the number of arrests per 100,000 juveniles in the population. Arrest rates have the advantage of controlling for changes in the size of the juvenile population. If there is an increase in the number of juveniles, the number of juvenile arrests will likely increase because there are more juveniles to be arrested. This will occur even if the typical juvenile is no more or less delinquent than before. For example, there was a dramatic increase in the number of juvenile arrests during the 1960s and early 1970s. But part of this increase was because there were more juveniles to be arrested. As a result of the post–World War II baby boom, the number of juveniles between 10 and 17 years of age increased from about 25 million in 1960 to over 33 million in 1975. The *arrest rate* is not influenced by changes in the size of the juvenile population, since it shows the number of arrests *per 100,000 juveniles*. Changes in the arrest rate, then, provide a better indication of whether juveniles are becoming more or less delinquent.

The graphs in Figure 3.1 show changes in the juvenile arrest rate for Part I violent crimes (homicide, aggravated assault, robbery, rape) and Part I property crimes (burglary, larceny, motor vehicle theft). Take a moment to look at these graphs.

These graphs suggest the following:

Property crime. The rate of property crime was reasonably stable from the early 1980s to 1995, hovering around 2,500 arrests per 100,000 juveniles between 10 and 17. The rate has declined to less than 2,000 since 1995. (When criminologists look at the specific types of property crime, discerning a trend gets more involved. The rate of larceny-theft, far and away the most common type of property crime, has been reasonably stable. The rate of burglary, however, has declined since the early 1980s. In fact, the 1998 burglary rate is about half the 1980 rate. The rate of motor vehicle theft increased markedly from 1983 to 1989 but has been dropping since 1991.)

Violent crime. The rate of violent crime arrests was reasonably stable from 1980 to 1988. It then increased by more than 60 percent between 1988 and 1994. This increase did much to draw attention to the juvenile crime problem, with the media running numerous stories about juvenile violence during this time. Violent crime arrests have been declining since 1994, with the 1998 rate just 13 percent higher than the 1988 rate. (This pattern tends to

Figure 3.1 Trends in the Juvenile Arrest Rate for Part I Violent and Property Crime

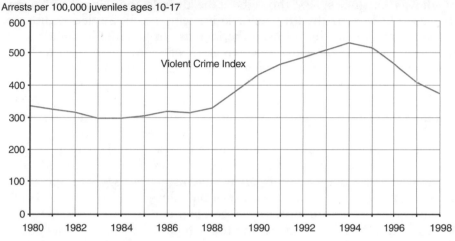

Arrests per 100,000 juveniles ages 10-17

Violent Crime Index

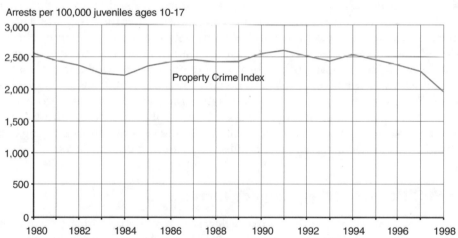

Arrests per 100,000 juveniles ages 10-17

Property Crime Index

Source: Snyder, 1999.

hold for most violent crimes, although the arrest rates for rape have been more stable than the rates for other violent crimes.)

I want to draw special attention to the crime of murder, since trends in the arrest rate for murder have been the subject of much discussion in the media and in the criminology literature.[1] The *juvenile* arrest rate for murder more than doubled between 1987 and 1993. This increase was especially dramatic because the arrest rate for murder among those over 25 declined during this period. Further, the increase in the juvenile arrest rate for murder was entirely due to an increase in gun-related murders. The juvenile arrest rate for nongun murders was stable. There has been much discussion about why the juvenile arrest rate for gun-related murders increased so dramatically during the late 1980s and early 1990s. Among other things, the increase has been attributed to the spread of crack cocaine during the mid- to late 1980s. Juveniles became heavily involved in the crack trade, and they often armed themselves for protection (you cannot call the police for protection if you are a crack dealer). So guns became more common among certain juveniles. This led other juveniles to feel that they had to carry guns for protection. The end result was that guns spread throughout the juvenile population, and disputes that used to be settled with fists or knives came to be settled with bullets. Other criminologists have linked the increase in juvenile homicides to the spread of gangs. As indicated in Chapter 13, gang members are much more likely to carry and use guns than are nongang members.

The juvenile arrest rate for murder then experienced a sharp decline from 1994 to 1998. In fact, it has returned to the same level it was in 1987. There has also been much discussion about the reasons for this decline and the more general decline in crimes of violence. The decline has been linked to a decline in crack use and the stabilization of crack markets (e.g., there are fewer territorial disputes between dealers). It has also been linked to such things as the improving economy, new policing methods (see Chapter 18), an increase in the certainty and severity of punishments (see Chapter 19), and the spread of prevention programs (see Chapter 22).

Overall, arrest data suggest the following about trends in delinquency since the early 1980s: (1) rates of property crime were stable until 1995, then declined; (2) rates of violent crime were stable through the late 1980s, increased substantially between 1988 and 1994, and have been declining since 1994. I have focused on Part I crimes. I should note that trends in Part II crimes are mixed. Among other things, there has been a dramatic increase in the arrest rates for drug abuse and curfew/loitering violations in the 1990s. There is good reason to believe, however, that much of the increase in curfew/loitering arrests reflects changes in the law and police practices. Many cities, for example, responded to the increase in juvenile violence by instituting curfews for juveniles or more strictly enforcing existing curfew laws.

Is Self-Reported Delinquency Increasing?

The Monitoring the Future survey described earlier provides information on trends in self-reported delinquency. Again, these data focus on high school seniors. They do not contain information on certain serious crimes, like murder and rape. Rather, they tend to focus on minor offenses or minor instances of more serious offenses (for reasons indicated above). Also, their use of the response category "5 or more times" means that they underestimate the extent of delinquency. Nevertheless, these data provide some indication of trends in delinquency—especially minor delinquency—among high school seniors throughout the United States (see Browning and Huizinga, 1999; Huizinga et al., 1998, for additional self-report data on trends in delinquency).

The graphs in Figure 3.2 shows trends in the rate of self-reported property crime and violent crime from 1980 to 1998. In particular, they show the number of property and violent crimes reported each year *per 100 high school seniors*. I focus on four property crimes: larceny under $50, larceny over $50, shoplifting, and auto theft (there is no good measure of burglary in the survey). And I focus on three violent crimes: serious assault, group fights, and robbery. Take a moment to examine the graphs in Figure 3.2. Focus on long-term trends, rather than short-term or year-to-year fluctuations in the delinquency rate. These short-term fluctuations may be due to chance, but substantial changes in the crime rate that last for several years likely reflect real changes. Jensen and Rojek (1998) and Osgood et al. (1989) have conducted similar analyses using earlier data from the Monitoring the Future survey.)

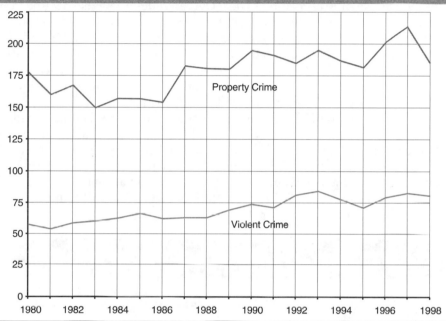

Figure 3.2 Trends in the Rate of Self-Reported Delinquency of High School Seniors (Rate = no. acts per 100 seniors)

Source: The Monitoring the Future survey, as reported in the *Sourcebook of Criminal Justice Statistics* (http://www.albany.edu/sourcebook/).

Property crime. The rate of property crime was generally stable during the early to mid-1980s but then increased by a modest amount during the late 1980s. The rate of property crime fluctuated during the 1990s, but then decreased after 1995. To illustrate, the average rate of property crime each year from 1980 to 1986 was 159.6 property crimes per 100 high school seniors. The average rate of property crime per year from 1987 to 1998 was 189.2 property crimes per 100 seniors. These data are somewhat at odds with arrest data, which suggest that rates for most property crimes were reasonably stable during the 1980s and 1990s.

Violent crime. The rate of violence was reasonably stable during much of the 1980s but then increased during the late 1980s. The rate of violence has fluctuated during the 1990s, but has generally remained at a high level. To illustrate, the average rate of violence each year from 1980 to 1988 was 59.6 violent acts per 100 high school seniors. The average rate of violence each year from 1989 to 1998 was 76.3 violent acts per 100 seniors. These data, like arrest data, indicate there was an increase in juvenile violence in the late 1980s. The increase in these data, however, is not as large as the increase in arrest data. Also, these data do not provide clear evidence for a decrease in juvenile violence in recent years.

Drug use. Figure 3.3 shows trends in drug use using data from the National Household Survey on Drug Use. These data, unlike the Monitoring the Future data, focus on juveniles 12 to 17 years old. Further, the survey is based on a sample of households and so is more likely to include dropouts and truants. The numbers in Figure 3.3 show the percentage of adolescents reporting any illicit drug use in the year indicated. Illicit drugs include marijuana, hashish, cocaine/crack, inhalants, hallucinogens, heroin, and the nonmedical use of prescription drugs. Overall, illicit drug use declined during the 1980s and early 1990s. In fact, the percentage of adolescents reporting illicit drug use in 1992 was less than half of what it was in 1979. Rates of illicit drug use then generally increased from 1992 to 1997, with a slight decrease in 1998. The Monitoring the Future data show similar trends in drug use among high school seniors. The increase in drug use during much of the 1990s attracted a lot of attention in the media and was a major issue in the 1996 Presidential campaign. This increase was the main reason behind the major anti-drug ad campaign recently launched by the federal government (see Office of National Drug Control Policy, 1999). The very recent decrease in drug use has been attributed to this ad campaign, among other things. I should note that the trends in drug use vary somewhat by type of drug (see Maguire and Pastore, 1999; Office of National Drug Control Policy, 1999).

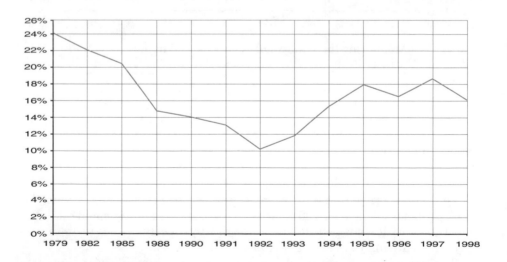

Figure 3.3   Trends in Self-Reported Illicit Drug Use Among Juveniles Ages 12-17 (Percentage using illicit drugs at least once in year indicated)

Source: The National Household Survey on Drug Abuse, as reported in the *Sourcebook of Criminal Justice Statistics* (http://www.albany.edu/sourcebook/).

In sum, self-report data suggest the following about trends in delinquency: (1) rates of property crime increased by a modest amount in the late 1980s and generally remained high throughout the 1990s; (2) rates of violence increased in the late 1980s and generally remained high throughout the

1990s; and (3) rates of illicit drug use decreased during the 1980s and early
1990s, generally increased from 1992 to 1997, and declined slightly in 1998.

Are Victimizations Committed by Juveniles Increasing?

We can use the National Crime Victimization Survey to estimate the rate of *violent* crime victimizations committed by juveniles ages 12 through 17. Data indicate that this rate decreased a modest amount from the early to mid-1980s, then increased substantially from the late 1980s to 1993. If we focus on serious violence, the rate increased from about 25 to 30 violent acts per 1,000 juveniles ages 10 through 17 in the early to mid-1980s to 42 violent acts per 1,000 juveniles in 1993. The rate, however, has dropped substantially since 1993. It was about 25 violent acts per 1,000 juveniles in 1998.[2] Paralleling these trends, the rate at which juveniles were *victimized* by violent crime increased substantially in the late 1980s and early 1990s but has declined since (Perkins, 1997; Snyder and Sickmund, 1999). So victimization data, like arrest data, indicate that the violent crime rate for juveniles was reasonably stable during the early to mid-1980s, increased in the late 1980s and early 1990s, and declined in recent years. Unfortunately, victimization data on trends in property crime by juveniles are largely lacking.

Summary

We began with a simple question: Is juvenile delinquency increasing? But, as you can see, the answer is anything but simple. The answer varies somewhat by type of crime and by data source. Nevertheless, there are some general conclusions we can draw:

Property crime. Arrest and self-report data disagree somewhat regarding trends in property crime. The strengths and weaknesses of both arrest data and the Monitoring the Future survey make it difficult to determine which is more accurate. But, at a minimum, I can safely state that rates of juvenile property crime have been somewhat stable since the early 1980s— with a modest increase in the late 1980s, and a decrease since 1995.

Violent crime. All three data sources indicate that rates of juvenile violence were generally stable in the early to mid-1980s and then increased substantially in the late 1980s and early 1990s. There are, however, some areas of disagreement. Arrest data show the largest increase in violence, followed by victimization data, then self-report data. Arrest and victimization data suggest that rates of juvenile violence have declined since 1994, while self-report data do not show clear evidence of a decline. I lean toward the arrest and victimization data when it comes to trends in *serious violence*. For reasons indicated above, arrest and victimization data probably do a better job of measuring serious violence. So I would conclude that serious violence increased dramatically in the late 1980s and early 1990s but is now in decline. I lean toward the self-report data for trends in less serious violence. That is, less serious violence increased during the late 1980s and early 1990s but perhaps not as much as arrest data suggest. Further, less serious violence may not have declined in the mid- to late 1990s.

Drug crimes. It seems safe to conclude that overall rates of illicit drug use declined substantially during the 1980s and early 1990s. Data from both the

National Household Survey on Drug Abuse and the Monitoring the Future
survey indicate such a decline. Arrest rates for drug abuse during this period
are relatively stable, but arrest rates for drug abuse are heavily influenced by
police practices as well as by true levels of drug abuse. It also seems safe to
conclude that rates of drug use increased substantially from about 1992 to
1997. Both self-report and arrest data are in agreement here. Self-report data,
however, suggest that rates of drug use declined slightly in 1998.

Notes

1. *See* Blumstein, 1995; Cook and Laub, 1998; Fox and Zawitz, 1999; National Institute of Justice, 1998a; Zimring, 1998.
2. Snyder and Sickmund, 1999; also see Federal Interagency Forum on Child and Family Statistics, 2000; Sickmund et al., 1997; Cook and Laub, 1998. ✦

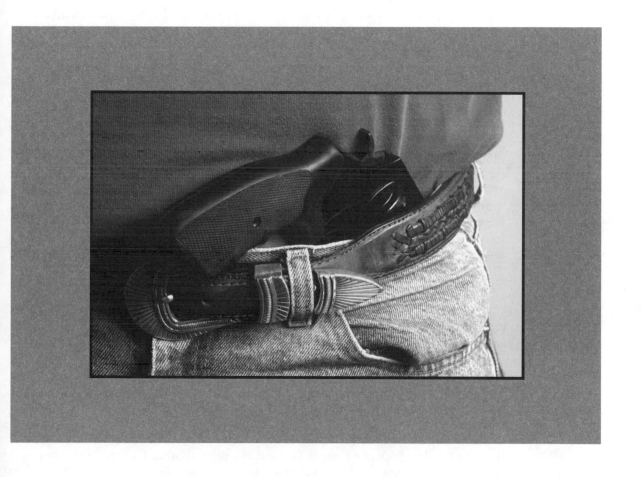

Chapter 4

Who Is Most Likely to Engage in Delinquency?

Suppose that you encountered a group of people, some young and some old, some male and some female, some white and some black, and some lower class and some middle class. Further, suppose that you wanted to divide this group in two: criminals on the one side and noncriminals (or less serious criminals) on the other. What characteristic would best allow you to do this: age, gender, race, or social class?

If you are like many people, you probably think that race and class do the best job of distinguishing criminals from non criminals. This view is often fostered by the media, which tend to portray crime as a problem that is concentrated in poor black communities. But in fact, age and gender do a far better job of distinguishing criminals from non criminals. In particular, adolescent males have crime rates that far exceed those of other groups. Of course, not all adolescent males engage in crime. While age and sex are strongly related to crime, the relationship is far from perfect. Nevertheless, age and sex are more strongly related to crime than class and race.

This chapter examines the *sociodemographic* characteristics of delinquents. I focus on the relationship between delinquency and social class, race, gender, and age. (Social class is usually measured in terms of the occupational prestige, education, and/or income of the juvenile's parents.) Once more, you will find that simple questions often have complex answers. This is especially the case when I ask whether lower-class juveniles are more delinquent than middle-class juveniles and whether blacks are more delinquent than whites. Also, you will find that arrest, self-report, and victimization data sometimes disagree about the characteristics of delinquents. I think that there are nevertheless a number of conclusions that can safely be drawn about the characteristics of delinquents, and I think that you will find some of these conclusions rather surprising, because I suspect that they will challenge your view of the typical juvenile delinquent.

Is Social Class Related to Delinquency?

Before I talk about social class in my juvenile delinquency course, I tell the students about a trait known as "tolerance of ambiguity." Some individuals have a low tolerance of ambiguity. That is, they have a strong need for definite, clear-cut answers. When they take a course, they want to be told what is right and what is wrong—no "ifs, ands, or buts." They get very uneasy, even upset, if they are told that the studies in an area contradict one another or that the relationship between certain factors depends on other factors. I mention this trait to you for a good reason: I want to warn you in advance. If you have a low tolerance of ambiguity, you might get a little uneasy with the following discussion on the relationship between social class and delinquency.

Most people assume that lower-class juveniles are more delinquent than middle-class juveniles. A large number of studies have tried to determine whether this is true, but these studies often contradict one another. In fact, you can find studies that support just about any position you like. Many studies find that lower-class juveniles are more delinquent than middle-class juveniles. Many studies find that lower-class and middle-class juveniles engage in about the same amount of delinquency. And a few studies even find that middle-class juveniles are more delinquent than lower-class juveniles. The conclusions that criminologists draw about the relationship between social class

and delinquency reflect these studies. Some prominent criminologists argue
that there is little or no relationship between class and delinquency, while
others argue that lower-class juveniles are more likely to engage in at least
some types of delinquency. So we ask a simple question: Are lower-class juveniles more delinquent than middle-class juveniles? The answer is anything
but simple.[1]

I want to help you make sense of the contradictory research on this topic.
The best way to do that is by providing you with a historic overview of the
research on the relationship between class and delinquency. At the end of this
overview, I'll draw two general conclusions about the relationship between
class and delinquency, one well supported by the data and the other more
tentative.

Early Studies Based on Arrest Data

Until the 1960s, the main way of measuring delinquency was through the
use of arrest data or police reports. Criminologists asked whether lower-class
juveniles were more likely to be arrested or come in contact with the police
than higher-class juveniles. The FBI does not provide any information on the
social class of arrested individuals. But researchers compared the juvenile
arrest rates of lower- and higher-class *communities*. And, less commonly, they
examined the arrest records of lower- and higher-class *juveniles*.

Virtually every study found that lower-class communities had much
higher arrest rates than higher-class communities (see the discussion on
communities in Chapter 14). Also, most studies found that lower-class juveniles were more likely to be arrested or have police reports than middle-class
juveniles (see especially Braithwaite, 1981). One of the best studies in this
area looked at all juveniles who were born in Philadelphia in 1958 *and* who
lived in Philadelphia from the ages of 10 through 17, a total of 27,160 juveniles. It was found that 42 percent of the lower-class males had a police
record, as compared to 24 percent of the higher-class males (Tracy, 1990).

On the basis of these studies, criminologists came to the conclusion that
social class was strongly associated with delinquency. In fact, criminology
textbooks from the 1960s and before often state that one of the most important and best-supported facts about delinquency is that it is concentrated in
the lower classes. This belief led criminologists to construct a number of theories to explain why delinquency was concentrated in the lower classes. And
billions of dollars were spent on the "War on Poverty" in the 1960s and early
1970s, partly on the assumption that poverty was a major cause of crime and
delinquency. Criminologists, however, experienced a major shock in the
1960s.

Early Self-Report Studies

Self-report surveys of delinquency came into wide use during the 1960s,
and most of these surveys found little or no relationship between social class
and delinquency. This result challenged a fundamental belief of most criminologists, as well as of policy makers and people in the general public. (Victimization data cannot be used to examine the relationship between social

class and delinquency, since crime victims are not asked to estimate the class of the people who victimized them.)

The finding that lower- and middle-class adolescents are equally delinquent seems to challenge our personal experiences. Lower-class neighborhoods, for example, seem unsafe to us, while middle-class neighborhoods seem quite safe. This finding also seems to challenge common sense. It is easy to think of reasons why lower-class adolescents should be more delinquent than middle-class adolescents, but difficult to think of reasons why lower- and middle-class adolescents should be equally delinquent. Nevertheless, numerous self-report studies during the 1960s and 1970s found little or no relationship between class and delinquency. Further, some evidence suggested that the relationship between social class and arrest rates was becoming weaker over time (Tittle et al., 1978). As a consequence, many criminologists came to feel that class was unrelated to delinquency. A major review article published in 1978, in fact, was titled "The Myth of Social Class and Criminality" (Tittle et al., 1978).

If class is unrelated to delinquency, how can one account for the findings from arrest data? It was said that arrest data were biased. Only a small number of delinquent offenses were reported to the police and, of those, only a small number resulted in arrest. It was claimed that offenses committed by lower-class juveniles were more likely to come to the attention of the police and were more likely to result in arrest. (Chapter 20 discusses the evidence on police discrimination against lower-class juveniles.)

Likewise, if class is unrelated to delinquency, how can one account for the perception that lower-class juveniles are more delinquent? A fascinating study by Chambliss (1973) suggests why perceptions regarding the relationship between social class and delinquency may be wrong. Chambliss examined two groups of adolescent males in a high school: the "Saints" and the "Roughnecks." The middle-class Saints were well liked and respected by their teachers and members of the community. In fact, the Saints included some of the top students in the school. The lower-class Roughnecks were disliked and seen as delinquents by their teachers and community residents. Chambliss, however, discovered that the two groups were about equally delinquent. Why, then, were they perceived so differently? Chambliss lists three reasons. First, the delinquency of the Saints was *less visible*. The Saints went to great lengths to hide their delinquency; for example, their greater access to cars allowed them to commit many of their delinquent acts in remote locations. Second, the Saints had a *better demeanor*: They were respectful and apologetic when caught doing something wrong. The Roughnecks, however, were often hostile. As a consequence, people tended to assume that the Saints were basically "good kids" who would occasionally "sow their wild oats," while the Roughnecks were "troublemakers." Finally, people were simply *biased* in favor of the Saints and against the Roughnecks, this bias reflecting their beliefs about what lower-class and middle-class people are like. This bias, in turn, influenced their perceptions of the two groups—what they noticed and how they interpreted what they noticed.

Finally, if class is unrelated to delinquency, how can we account for all the good reasons linking class to delinquency? A recent study presents data indicating that while higher-class juveniles are *less* likely to engage in delinquency for some reasons, they are *more* likely to engage in delinquency for other reasons (Wright et al., 1999a). For example, higher-class juveniles are less likely to engage in delinquency because they have less need for money. But higher-class juveniles are more likely to engage in delinquency because they have greater "social power"; that is, they are better able to avoid detection and are better able to resist the efforts of others—teachers and police, for example—to punish them. These effects tend to cancel one another out, so one finds that social class has little relationship to delinquency.

By the late 1970s many criminologists were stating that there was little or no relationship between social class and delinquency. Several criminologists, however, challenged this conclusion.

Criticisms of the Early Self-Report Studies

Some criminologists said that the early self-report studies suffered from several problems and that these problems account for their failure to find any relationship between social class and delinquency.[2]

First, the early self-report studies *focused on minor delinquent acts*. That is, they used measures that focus on status offenses and minor delinquent acts like petty theft and simple assault. Many of these studies, for example, employed the measure of delinquency shown in Table 2.3. Or if the studies did consider serious acts, these acts were not examined separately. Rather, the researchers created general scales that measured the extent to which adolescents engage in *both* minor and serious delinquency. The more frequently occurring minor offenses have a much greater influence on counts of delinquency than the less frequently occurring serious offenses (see Elliott and Huizinga, 1983:153–154). The early self-report studies, then, do not tell us anything about the relationship between class and *serious* delinquency. They simply suggest that class is unrelated to *minor* delinquency. It may be that class is related to serious delinquency. In this area, some criminologists note that arrest data contain a higher portion of serious offenses than self-report data. This may be why arrests are typically related to social class, while self-reports of delinquency are not.

Second, the early self-report studies often used delinquency measures with *truncated response categories*, like "five or more times." So someone who commits an act five times is included in the same category as someone who commits the act 100 times. Again, this is a serious problem because there is a small group of high-rate offenders who commit an enormous number of delinquent acts. The early self-report surveys, however, did not accurately measure the delinquency of these high-rate offenders. These high-rate offenders, committing scores or even hundreds of delinquent acts, are not distinguished from juveniles committing only a few delinquent acts. It may be that the lower class has more high-rate offenders than the middle class. And if the delinquency of these high-rate offenders was accurately measured, one might well find that the lower class engages in more delinquency than the middle class.

Third, the early self-report studies often *failed to examine very poor juveniles*. Many of the early self-report studies examined only a few hundred juveniles from one or a few schools; there are not enough very poor juveniles in these studies to examine separately. In other cases, researchers fail to distinguish the very poor juveniles from other groups. For example, the very poor are combined with the working class. It may be that delinquency is higher among the very poor, but that there is no difference in delinquency between the working and middle classes. So it is important to examine the very poor separately, and criminologists have started to experiment with different methods for better identifying the very poor. For example, they focus on juveniles whose parents receive welfare benefits or whose parents have been unemployed for long periods (see Brownfield, 1986; Farnworth et al., 1994).

The Later Self-Report Studies

Several criminologists have conducted self-report studies that attempt to correct for some or all of the problems discussed in the preceding section. Perhaps the most prominent of these studies are the analyses of the National Youth Survey (NYS) conducted by Elliott and associates (Elliott and Ageton, 1980; Elliott and Huizinga, 1983). The NYS was described earlier. It examines both minor and serious delinquency. It accurately measures the number of delinquent acts that juveniles commit. And Elliott and associates distinguish lower-class juveniles from both working- and middle-class juveniles. What do their analyses of the NYS data reveal about the relationship between social class and delinquency? Their major findings are as follows:

1. There are few or no class differences in most types of minor delinquency. Table 4.1 reports the average number of delinquent acts committed by lower-, working-, and middle-class juveniles for several types of delinquency. Note that the averages are quite similar for the minor types of delinquency.

2. The lower class is more likely to engage in serious delinquency. As indicated in Table 4.1, the average number of violent crimes committed by a lower-class juvenile is about four times as high as the average number committed by a middle-class juvenile. The average number of property crimes committed by a lower-class juvenile is about twice as high as the average number committed by a middle-class juvenile.

3. The reason that lower-class juveniles have a higher average rate of serious delinquency is that there are more high-rate offenders in the lower class. For example, 2.8 percent of the lower-class juveniles commit more than 55 serious violent acts per year, whereas only 0.8 percent of the middle-class juveniles commit more than 55 violent acts per year. This point is very important. The lower class has a higher average rate of serious crime *not* because the typical lower-class juvenile is more involved in serious crime than the typical working- or middle-class juvenile. *Most lower-class juveniles commit very few serious crimes*. Rather, most of the serious crimes are committed by a small group of high-rate offenders. These high-rate offenders make up only a very small proportion of the lower class, but these high-rate offenders are two to three times more common in the lower class than in the middle class. And that is why the *average* rate of serious crime is higher in the lower class.

Table 4.1	Average Number of Self-Reported Delinquent Acts Committed by Lower-, Working-, and Middle-Class Juveniles in 1976			
	Violent Crimes	Property Crimes	Public Disorder Crimes	Status Offenses
Lower Class	12	14	14	14
Working Class	8	9	16	14
Middle Class	3	7	14	16

Note: Violent crimes include sexual assault, aggravated assault, simple assault, and robbery. Property crimes include vandalism, burglary, auto theft, larceny, stolen goods, fraud, and joyriding. Public disorder crimes include carrying a concealed weapon, hitchhiking, disorderly conduct, drunkenness, panhandling, making obscene phone calls, and marijuana use. Status offenses include runaway, sexual intercourse, alcohol use, and truancy.
Source: Elliott and Ageton (1980).

These findings provide some support for the critiques of the early self-report surveys. They demonstrate that it is important to examine serious delinquency separately from minor delinquency; to accurately count the number of delinquent acts that are committed; and to pay special attention to the very poor. When these steps were taken, Elliott and his associates found a relationship between class and *serious* delinquency. At the same time, they found little or no relationship between class and minor delinquency.

There have been several attempts to replicate the findings of Elliott and associates. That is, other researchers have examined serious delinquency separately from minor delinquency, have accurately measured the extent of delinquency, and/or have focused on the very poor. Unfortunately, not all of these attempts at replication have reached the same conclusions as Elliott and associates. Certain studies, in particular, have found that social class is unrelated to both serious and minor delinquency (e.g., Weis, 1987). Other studies tend to support the work of Elliott and associates, although some studies find that social class has only a *moderate* association with serious delinquency.[3]

Summary

You can see why there is still some confusion in the field about the relationship between social class and delinquency. Again, we began with a simple question, but the answer turns out to be quite complex. Nevertheless, I believe that there are some general conclusions that can be drawn about the relationship between social class and delinquency.

1. There seems little doubt that social class is largely unrelated to minor delinquency. Virtually all self-report studies come to this conclusion. Arrest data tend to focus on more serious delinquency, so they are of limited relevance here.

2. It is *likely* that social class is moderately related to serious delinquency, with lower-class juveniles having higher average rates of such delinquency. The average rates of serious delinquency may be higher in the lower class because there are more high-rate of-

fenders in the lower class—*not* because the typical lower-class juvenile is more delinquent than the typical working- or middle-class juvenile. Most of the better self-report studies suggest a relationship between class and serious delinquency, as do most studies based on arrest data. Further, there is little doubt that lower-class *communities* have higher rates of serious crime. As Braithwaite (1981:37) points out, "it is hardly plausible that one can totally explain away the higher risks of being mugged and raped in lower-class areas as a consequence of the activities of middle-class people who come into the area to perpetrate such acts."

Is Race Related to Delinquency?

As with social class, the data on race and delinquency are somewhat contradictory, but there are some conclusions that criminologists can more or less safely draw. My focus will be on blacks and whites because most data deal with these groups. Unfortunately, there are much less data on other races and ethnic groups, although this imbalance is beginning to change.

I first describe what arrest, self-report, and victimization data have to say about the relationship between race and delinquency. I then draw two general conclusions about the relationship. And I finish by discussing whether the relationship between race and serious delinquency is explained by race-related differences in social class.[4]

Arrest Data

Arrest data indicate that blacks are more likely to engage in most forms of delinquency than whites, with a few exceptions. In 1998, blacks made up about 15 percent of the juvenile population and whites made up about 79 percent (most Hispanics were classified as white). Blacks accounted for 26 percent of all juvenile arrests and 30 percent of all juvenile arrests for Part I offenses. They were especially likely to be arrested for serious violent crimes, accounting for 49 percent of murder arrests, 39 percent of rape arrests, 54 percent of robbery arrests, and 37 percent of aggravated assault arrests. Blacks were less likely to be arrested for property crimes, although they were still disproportionally arrested for such crimes. For example, they accounted for 26 percent of all larceny-theft arrests.

I should note that race differences in arrest rates have declined in recent decades. In 1960, the juvenile arrest rate for Part I crimes was 3.1 times higher for blacks than for whites. Today, it is 2.3 times higher. This decline reflects the fact that the arrest rate for whites has been increasing faster than that for blacks, although there are certain exceptions such as homicide and drug arrests.

Criticisms of Arrest Data

Arrest data suggest that blacks are more likely to engage in most forms of delinquency, especially serious violence, but arrest data, as you know, have a number of problems. Only a small percentage of the crimes that are committed come to the attention of the police, and only a small percentage of these crimes result in arrest. Perhaps crimes committed by blacks are more likely to come to the attention of the police and result in arrest. The data in this area are somewhat complex, but they suggest that blacks who commit a given offense are more likely to be arrested than whites who commit the same offense (see Chapter 20 for a full discussion). As a consequence, it is important to examine the relationship between race and delinquency using self-report and victimization data. These data sources have the advantage of measuring delinquent acts that do and do not result in arrest.

Self-Report Data

There are certain dangers in using self-report data to study the relationship between race and delinquency. As indicated earlier, *some* evidence suggests that black males may be more likely than other groups to underreport their delinquency in self-report surveys. Nevertheless, it is instructive to examine what self-report data say about the relationship between race and delinquency.

Most early self-report surveys find that there is little or no relationship between race and delinquency. Blacks and whites are about equally delinquent. As you know, however, the early self-report surveys suffer from a number of problems: a focus on minor offenses, the use of truncated response categories, and the under sampling of serious offenders.

Later self-report surveys that correct for these problems find a more complex relationship between race and delinquency, a relationship similar to that found for social class and delinquency. These studies include the National Youth Survey, described earlier, and studies in Seattle, Denver, Rochester, and Pittsburgh.[5] The results of these studies may be summarized as follows:

1. Blacks and whites report similar levels of minor delinquency.

2. Blacks are more likely to engage in serious delinquency, *although not nearly to the extent reported in arrest data*. For example, Elliott et al.'s (1989) analysis of the 1976 National Youth Survey found that blacks had a rate of serious assault about two and one-half times higher than the white rate. Arrest data, however, suggest that the black rate for serious assault is about five times higher than the white rate.

3. The average rate of serious crime among blacks is higher because there are more high-rate offenders among blacks (see Elliott and Ageton, 1980). This point requires emphasis: Blacks have a higher rate of serious crime *not* because the typical black is more criminal than the typical white. Most blacks commit no or very few serious crimes. Rather, most serious crimes are committed by a small group of high-rate offenders. These high-rate offenders make up only a small proportion of black juveniles, but they are about twice as common among blacks as among whites.

Victimization Data

There is no victimization data on the relationship between social class and delinquency, but such data have been collected for race. Crime victims are asked to identify the race of the person or persons who victimized them. Such data are limited, however, since victims usually see the offender only in violent crimes. Nevertheless, victimization data suggest that blacks are disproportionately involved in violent crime. In particular, a recent study of crime victims found that 39 percent of all juvenile offenders were reported to be black.[6] The involvement of blacks in certain crimes is not as high as suggested by arrest data, but it is higher than that suggested by self-report data.

Data also indicate that black juveniles are more likely than white juveniles to be crime *victims*, especially the victims of serious violence. Black juveniles, for example, are about five times as likely as white juveniles to be the victims of homicide. In fact, homicide is now the leading cause of death among blacks between ages 15 and 24. Criminologists know that most crimes are *interracial*: Blacks tend to victimize other blacks and whites tend to victimize other whites. The fact that blacks have much higher victimization rates for serious violence suggests that they have higher offending rates as well.

Is Race Related to Delinquency?

I think we can safely draw the following conclusions about race and delinquency:

1. There is little or no relationship between race and minor delinquency. Self-report surveys consistently find little relationship between race and minor delinquency. Arrest and victimization data are less relevant here, since they tend to focus on more serious delinquency.

2. Blacks are more likely than whites to engage in serious delinquency, especially serious violence. The relationship between race and serious delinquency, however, is probably not as strong as suggested by arrest data. Arrest data, victimization data, and most of the better self-report surveys indicate that blacks are more involved in serious delinquency, although self-report data and to a lesser extent victimization data suggest that arrest data exaggerate the involvement of blacks in such delinquency. The greater involvement of blacks in serious delinquency may reflect the fact that there are more high-rate offenders among blacks.

Are Race Differences in Serious Delinquency Explained by Social Class?

Given the history of discrimination in this country, it should come as no surprise that race and social class are related. Blacks are *more likely* to be members of the lower class than whites (although most blacks are *not* members of the lower class). As discussed, lower-class individuals are more likely to engage in serious delinquency than higher-class individuals. So it is reasonable to ask whether blacks are more likely to engage in serious delinquency because they are more likely to be in the lower class.

Researchers have examined this issue by comparing the delinquency of lower-class blacks to that of lower-class whites and by comparing the delinquency of middle-class blacks to that of middle-class whites. Class is usually measured in terms of family income, parents' occupational prestige, and/or parents' education. If social class explained the higher rate of serious delinquency among blacks, we would expect that lower-class blacks and whites would have similar levels of serious delinquency. Likewise, we would expect that middle-class blacks and whites would have similar levels of delinquency.

The data suggest that social class explains *some but not all* of the association between race and serious delinquency. For example, comparisons find that lower-class blacks are still more likely to engage in serious delinquency than lower-class whites, but race differences in delinquency are reduced somewhat when the researchers take account of class.

Researchers, however, have recently pointed out that the life circumstances of poor blacks are often quite different from those of poor whites. Most notably, poor blacks are much more likely than poor whites to live in high-poverty *communities,* that is, communities where a high percentage of the other people are poor. More than 4 of 10 poor blacks lived in high-poverty communities in 1990, versus about 1 of 10 poor whites. These high-poverty communities suffer from a range of problems, such as an absence of jobs, a high percentage of single-parent families, inferior schools, and few conventional role models. As Sampson and Lauritsen (1997:338) state, "even given the same objective socioeconomic status, blacks and whites face vastly different environments in which to live, work, and raise their children." Blacks are more likely to live in high-poverty areas for several reasons, including the effects of past and present discrimination in housing and jobs. So it is misleading to simply compare poor blacks to poor whites. One must also take account of the type of community in which they live.[7]

A few studies have attempted to take account of community context. That is, they have attempted to compare blacks and whites who live in high-poverty communities, as well as blacks and whites who live in higher-class communities. Such comparisons are difficult to make, since it is hard to find more than a few whites who live in high-poverty communities. But limited data suggest that race differences in delinquency are substantially reduced when researchers take account of the types of communities in which blacks and whites live.[8] More research is needed in this area, but we may *tentatively* conclude that much—perhaps all—of the race difference in serious delinquency is explained by the fact that blacks are more likely to be poor and to live in high-poverty communities, which suffer from a host of problems that are conducive to delinquency (see Chapter 14).

Is Age Related to Delinquency?

The data on social class, race, and delinquency are complex and frustrating. The data on the relationship between age and delinquency, however, are fairly straightforward. Arrest, self-report, and victimization data generally agree with one another in this area.[9]

Crime rates are highest for people in mid- to late adolescence. The graphs in Figure 4.1 show the relationship between age and the arrest rates for Part I property crimes and Part I violent crimes. Arrest rates for property crime peak at age 16 and then decline rapidly. A 16-year-old, for example, is almost three and one-half times more likely to be arrested for a property crime than a 26-year-old. Arrest rates for violent crime peak at age 18 and then decline somewhat more slowly. An 18-year-old, for example, is almost twice as likely to be arrested for a violent crime as a 28-year-old. Self-report and victimization data tend to show similar patterns. Although not illustrated in a graph, rates of illicit drug use tend to peak in the late teens and early 20s, but the peak varies somewhat by type of drug (e.g., inhalant use peaks in the early to mid-teens). There is little doubt, then, that most crime peaks during mid- to late adolescence.

Figure 4.1   The Relationship Between Age and Arrest Rates for Property and Violent Crime, 1998

Property Crime

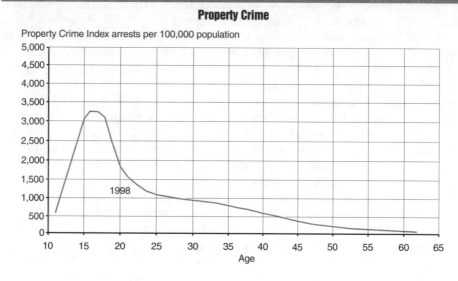

Violent Crime

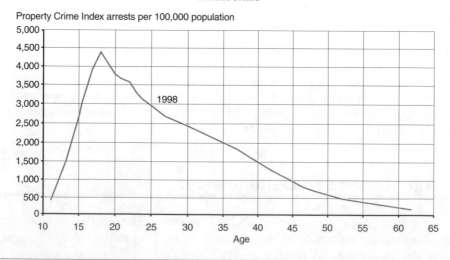

Source: Snyder, 1999.

Crime rates may peak during adolescence because there are a fixed number of criminals who increase their rate of offending during adolescence. Or they may peak because there is an increase in the number of criminals during adolescence; that is, new criminals appear. What do the data show? Do criminals start committing more crimes during adolescence or is there an increase in the number of criminals during adolescence? The data tend to favor the latter explanation. The peak in crime rates during adolescence is largely due to the fact that many juveniles start committing crimes when they become adolescents. Most of these juveniles then stop committing crimes when they become adults, or at least they substantially reduce their level of offending. Criminologists have recently devoted much attention to explaining these patterns, and you should ask yourself the following questions:

1. Why do so many juveniles start committing criminal acts when they become adolescents?

2. Why do most of these adolescent offenders stop committing criminal acts when they become adults?

I will address these questions later in the book, and they are also addressed in the references cited in note 9.

I should note that the relationship between age and crime is somewhat different for females and for blacks. Female offending, especially violence, tends to peak at a slightly earlier age than male offending. And blacks are much less likely than whites to stop offending when they become adults. Elliott (1994), for example, used data from the National Youth Survey to study blacks and whites who had committed serious violent crimes as juveniles. He found that the blacks were almost twice as likely as the whites to continue committing such offenses in their twenties. Elliott and others explain this finding by arguing that blacks have more difficulty obtaining decent work when they enter adulthood. In the words of Steffensmeier and Allan (1995b:103):

> In the inner cities of this nation, where the labor market for young adults is dominated by marginal jobs with low hours, low pay, high turnover, and limited benefits and opportunities for advancement, the other goals of conventional life—marriage, family, community involvement—are more difficult to attain, and the proportion of the population still attracted to illegitimate alternatives will be greater.

Is Gender Related to Delinquency?

The data on the relationship between gender and delinquency are also fairly straightforward, although there are a few areas of disagreement between the different data sources. Let me begin, however, with the areas of agreement.

Arrest, self-report, and victimization data (where applicable) agree on the following facts about gender and delinquency: Males have a higher rate of delinquency than females. Gender differences in delinquency are greatest for serious violent and property crimes. They are lowest for minor crimes and status offenses, with males and females having similar rates of involvement in certain minor crimes and status offenses. Males have higher rates of delinquency because there are more male than female delinquents and because male delinquents commit more offenses than female delinquents. In particular, there are more male than female high-rate offenders. I elaborate on some of these points below. I also point to a few key areas where arrest and self-report data disagree.[10]

Arrest Data

Arrest ratios. Overall, about three males are arrested for every female who is arrested. The ratio of male to female arrests is highest for serious violent and property crimes. For example, males are about twelve times more likely to be arrested for murder, ten times more likely to be arrested for robbery, and eight times more likely to be arrested for burglary. Sex ratios are lowest for minor crimes and status offenses. For example, males are about twice as likely to be arrested for larceny and simple assault. Females are more likely than males to be arrested for only one offense: running away (58 percent of runaway arrests are females). (I discuss the higher female arrest rate for running away in Chapter 20, when examining gender discrimination in the juvenile justice system.)

What crimes are males and females arrested for? Males generally commit more crimes than females, but do males commit different types of crime than females? The preceding discussion might lead you to believe that males commit serious crimes, whereas females commit less serious crimes. This belief is not correct. Consider the four crimes for which male and female juveniles are most frequently arrested. For males, 18 percent of all arrests are for "all other offenses" (including status offenses like incorrigibility); 14 percent are for larceny-theft; 9 percent are for drug abuse violations; and 9 percent are for simple assaults. For females, 21 percent of all arrests are for larceny-theft; 16 percent are for "all other offenses"; 14 percent are for running away; and 10 percent are for simple assaults. Thus, both males and females are most often arrested for minor crimes. Only 5 percent of male arrests and 2.7 percent of female arrests are for serious violent crimes. And only 7.8 percent of male arrests and 3.1 percent of female arrests are for the serious property crimes of burglary and motor-vehicle theft. Further, males and females tend to be arrested for many of the same minor crimes—larceny-theft, "all other offenses," and simple assault.

Trends in male and female delinquency. Even though males are generally more likely to be arrested than females, the proportion of all arrests accounted for by females has been increasing over time. In 1967, females accounted for 13 percent of all juvenile arrests for Part I offenses. Today, females account for 27 percent of all Part I arrests. This increase has occurred for both violent and property crimes, although the bulk of the increase comes from increases in the crime of larceny-theft. Arrest rates have generally been increasing faster for females than for males. For example, male arrest rates for property crime have been generally stable over the last decade, but female rates have slowly increased. And while both male and female rates of violence increased from the late 1980s to mid-1990s, the increase was greater for females (except for the crime of homicide).

Self-Report Data

Self-report data also find that males have higher rates of delinquency than females, with gender differences in delinquency being greatest for serious crimes and lowest for minor crimes and status offenses. Self-report data also indicate that while males generally commit more delinquent acts than females, males and females tend to commit similar types of delinquent acts. Females, for example, steal, fight, and use drugs—but less frequently than males. There are, however, some areas in which self-report data are at odds with arrest data.

Gender ratios in delinquency. While self-report surveys indicate that males are generally more delinquent than females, such surveys often find that gender differences in delinquency are not as large as indicated by arrest data. Arrest data find that there are three male arrests for every female arrest, whereas self-report surveys often find that there are about two male reports of delinquency for every female report. This difference can be at least partially accounted for by the self-report surveys' focus on minor offenses and minor instances of more serious offenses. As just indicated, gender differences in delinquency are lowest for minor offenses. Even so, there is still some uncertainty over whether gender differences in particular types of delinquency are as large as those revealed by arrest data.[11]

Trends in male and female delinquency. Self-report surveys do not indicate that female delinquency is increasing faster than male delinquency.[12] The limited self-report data we have on trends in delinquency suggest that the gender ratio in delinquency has been fairly stable since the late 1960s. This has led some researchers to question the accuracy of arrest data; they claim that the increase in female arrests may reflect changes in police practices or the behavior of those who report crimes to the police (e.g., the police have become more likely to arrest females over time). On the other hand, self-report data on trends in delinquency are not very good, for reasons discussed earlier. Also, victimization data suggest that female crime has increased faster than male crime in recent years (Jensen and Rojek, 1998).

Summary

Overall, the following conclusions can be drawn about the relationship between gender and delinquency:

1. There is little doubt that males generally have higher rates of delinquency than females, with gender differences in delinquency being greatest for serious violent and property crimes. Males have higher rates of delinquency because there are more male than female offenders and because male offenders commit more offenses than female offenders.

2. While males commit *more* offenses than females, males and females tend to commit similar types of offenses. Contrary to certain stereotypical views, female offending is not limited to a few sex-related offenses. Females, like males, fight, steal, use drugs, and engage in other delinquent acts. They just do so less than males.

3. There is some evidence that female delinquency is increasing faster than male delinquency, so that the gender difference in delinquency is becoming smaller (although it is still large). The increase in female delinquency, however, may not be as large as indicated by arrest data.

Are There Different Types of Delinquents?

We have been talking about delinquents and nondelinquents, with an occasional reference to high-rate and serious offenders. As you might imagine, though, dividing juveniles into delinquents and nondelinquents is a bit simplistic. There are many types of delinquents. As mentioned earlier, for example, delinquents differ greatly in their frequency of delinquency. Some delinquents commit only a few offenses each year, while others commit hundreds—thus, we have low-rate and high-rate delinquent offenders.

Criminologists are now devoting much attention to the identification of different types of delinquents. As you will see, this is an important task. The factors that cause juveniles to become one type of delinquent may differ from those that cause them to become another type. For example, the factors that cause juveniles to become low-rate offenders may differ from those that cause them to become high-rate offenders. Also, the existence of different types of delinquents has important implications for society's efforts to control delinquency. For example, we may want to focus our control efforts on high-rate offenders since they commit so many delinquent acts. Further, high-rate offenders may require different types of intervention programs than low-rate offenders.

This section briefly reviews the research on the different types of delinquents. While criminologists still have much to learn in this area, some generally accepted conclusions can be drawn about the types of delinquent offenders.[13]

An Overview of the Research on the Different Types of Delinquents

Researchers try to classify delinquents into different types on the basis of such things as their frequency of offending, the types of offenses they commit, and when they start and stop offending. The major research in these areas is reviewed below.

How many offenses do juveniles commit? Both arrest and self-report data indicate that juveniles vary a great deal in the frequency of their delinquency. Self-report surveys typically find the following: A small percentage of juveniles—10 percent or less in most studies—refrain from delinquency. A much larger percentage of juveniles—a majority in all studies—commit a small to moderate number of delinquent offenses each year. And a small percentage of juveniles commit an enormous number of offenses each year. The relative size of this high-rate group depends on the cut-off point that is used, but it is usually about 5 to 15 percent of all juveniles.

For example, Dunford and Elliott (1984) examined the frequency of offending using self-report data from the National Youth Survey. They found that about 11 percent of the juveniles did not report any delinquent acts over a two-year period. About 34 percent reported one to ten delinquent acts during this period. About 41 percent reported 11 to 100 acts. About 8 percent reported 101 to 200 delinquent acts (one to two delinquent acts per week). And about 6.5 percent reported 200 or more delinquent acts (at least two delinquent acts per week).

In some studies, the high-rate offenders account for a majority of all delinquent offenses and for the large majority of serious delinquent offenses. For example, a major study in Philadelphia found that 7.5 percent of the juvenile males accounted for 61 percent of all juvenile arrests, including 61 percent of the homicide arrests, 65 percent of the aggravated assault arrests, 76 percent of the forcible rape arrests, and 73 percent of the robbery arrests (Tracy et al., 1990). Clearly, then, at a minimum, one can distinguish high-rate offenders from lower-rate offenders.

What types of offenses do juveniles commit? Criminologists once assumed that juveniles specialized in particular types of crimes. For example, it was argued that some juveniles specialized in property crimes like larceny and burglary, others specialized in violent crimes, and still others specialized in drug use and sales (e.g., Cloward and Ohlin, 1960). Recent data suggest that there is some specialization in juvenile offending—but not nearly as much as previously believed. A *minority* of juvenile offenders may specialize in particular types of crime (see Farrington et al., 1988), but *most juveniles* who commit more than a few offenses tend to commit a variety of offenses. They do not specialize in particular types of crime. (Specialization is more common among adult offenders.)

Data, however, suggest that some offenders commit primarily minor offenses while others commit a mixture of minor and serious offenses. (It is rare for an offender to commit *only* serious offenses; individuals who commit serious offenses usually commit minor offenses as well.) In particular, the large majority of juvenile offenders commit a range of minor offenses, plus the occasional serious offense. A much smaller percentage of juvenile offenders commit a range of both minor and serious offenses. Even though most offenders commit a variety of offenses, it is possible to distinguish between offenders who commit primarily minor crimes and those who commit both minor and serious crimes. And several researchers have distinguished minor from serious offenders.

An analysis of data from the 1976 National Youth Survey found that about 8.6 percent of the juveniles could be classified as "serious" offenders, meaning that they had committed at least three Part I or serious offenses during 1976. These serious offenders accounted for more than three-fourths of all the Part I offenses, and they also committed a large number of minor crimes and status offenses. Most of the remaining juveniles committed a small to moderate number of minor crimes and status offenses (Dunford and Elliott, 1984; Elliott et al., 1989).

When do juveniles start to commit delinquent acts and when do they stop? Studies in this area find much variation among offenders. Some offenders *start* committing delinquent acts in childhood, while others wait until late adolescence or beyond. And some offenders *stop* committing crimes in adolescence, while others continue to offend well into the adult years. The most common pattern is for offenders to start committing crimes in late childhood to mid-adolescence and to stop committing crimes in late adolescence. Individuals who follow this pattern have been described as "adolescent-limited" offenders, since their offending is largely limited to their adolescent years (see Moffitt, 1993, 1997). These adolescent-limited offenders are largely responsible for the fact that rates of offending peak during mid- to late adolescence (see the discussion on age and crime).

There is a much smaller group of offenders who begin to engage in delinquent or "antisocial" behavior as young children. They lie, steal, cheat, and engage in aggressive behavior at an early age; their parents and others commonly describe them as "troublesome" or "difficult." Studies suggest that these individuals are more likely to offend at high rates, to commit serious offenses, and to continue offending as adults than juveniles who start committing delinquent acts at a later age. In fact, the "early onset" of delinquency is one of the best predictors of the frequency, seriousness, and duration of offending. I should note, however, that the early onset of delinquency does not guarantee that a person will have problems later in life. For example, only about half of the juveniles with an early onset of delinquency become adult offenders. Nevertheless, there is a small group of individuals who offend from early childhood well into adulthood. These individuals have been referred to as *"chronic"* offenders, and they may be distinguished from the adolescent-limited offenders.

Are there any patterns to juvenile offending over the life course? Juveniles vary a good deal in the frequency of their offending, the seriousness of their offending, and the ages at which they start and stop offending. Despite this variation, there are certain common patterns in juvenile offending over the life course.

First, studies suggest that there is a general tendency to move from less serious to more serious offending. For example, minor delinquency like petty theft and status offending tends to precede more serious delinquency like burglary and aggravated assault. And alcohol use tends to precede marijuana use, which tends to precede hard drug use. Most juveniles, of course, do not advance all the way from minor to serious offending. Most remain at the level of minor offending. But those who engage in serious offending usually begin their careers with minor offending.

Second, studies suggest that there is a general tendency for the *frequency* of offending to increase during early to mid-adolescence and to decrease during late adolescence and adulthood. This behavior pattern is especially true for adolescent-limited offenders. It is less true for chronic offenders, but recent data suggest that even chronic offenders increase their level of offending somewhat during adolescence (see D'Unger et al., 1998).

What Are the Different Types of Delinquents?

As indicated, juvenile offenders differ in terms of the frequency of their offending, the seriousness of their offending, and the ages at which they start and stop offending. Researchers have drawn on these differences to describe the major types of delinquent offenders. Some descriptions focus on the frequency of offending, distinguishing low-rate from high-rate offenders. Some focus on the seriousness of offending, distinguishing minor from serious offenders (or serious violent offenders). Some focus on the duration of offending, distinguishing adolescent-limited from chronic offenders. And some descriptions focus on two of the above dimensions—the frequency and duration of offending, for example (D'Unger et al., 1998; also see Loeber et al., 1991). It is probably best, however, to classify offenders using all three dimensions. Although these dimensions are related to one another (e.g., high-rate offenders are more likely to be serious offenders), the relationship is not perfect (e.g., certain high-rate offenders commit only minor crimes).

Some researchers are beginning to classify offenders using all three dimensions. At one extreme, we have high-rate, serious, chronic offenders. Data suggest that only a small percentage of juveniles fall into this group: perhaps 5 percent or so of the juvenile population. Nevertheless, this small group is an important one, given the enormous amount of crime, especially serious crime, they commit. At the other extreme, we have low-rate, minor, adolescent-limited offenders. Between these two extremes there are several groups. It is unclear what percentage of juveniles fall into each of these groups. The answer depends, in part, on the type of data used (arrest versus self-report) and the definitions employed for high-rate, chronic, and serious offending. For example, how many delinquent acts must juveniles commit each year before they rate classification as high-rate offenders?

In any event, it is important to keep in mind that there are different types of delinquent offenders. These types will come up again when I discuss the causes of crime. Some evidence suggests that the causes of high-rate, serious, chronic offending differ somewhat from the causes of less extreme types of offending. These types will also come up when I discuss strategies to control delinquency. In particular, there has been a major movement to crack down on the more extreme types of delinquents, especially those who commit serious crimes.

Summary

We can draw the following major conclusions about the characteristics of delinquents:

1. Males have higher rates of delinquency, especially serious delinquency, than females. There are more male offenders, and male offenders offend at higher rates than female offenders.

2. Rates of delinquency peak in mid- to late adolescence and decline rapidly thereafter. This peak and decline occurs largely because there is an increase in the number of offenders during adolescence, but data also suggest that rates of offending increase during adolescence as well.

3. Lower-class juveniles are more likely to engage in serious delinquency than higher-class juveniles. This difference exists because there are more high-rate offenders in the lower class. There is little or no relationship between class and minor delinquency.

4. Blacks are more likely to engage in serious delinquency, especially violent delinquency, than whites. Again, data suggest that this difference occurs because there are more high-rate offenders among blacks. There is little or no relationship between race and minor delinquency.

5. Juveniles differ a great deal in the frequency, seriousness, and duration of their offending.

The next section of the book focuses on the causes of delinquency. I will try to explain the basic facts about delinquency presented in this chapter and Chapter 3. Most notably, I will try to explain why some juveniles commit more delinquent acts, commit more serious delinquent acts, and offend for longer periods than other juveniles. I will also try to explain why certain groups have higher rates of delinquency than other groups. Why, for example, are males more delinquent than females?

Notes

1. For selected studies and overviews of the research in this area, see Braithwaite, 1981; Elliott and Ageton, 1980; Elliott and Huizinga, 1983; Farnworth et al., 1994; Hagan, 1992; Harris and Shaw, 2000; Heimer, 1997; Hindelang et al., 1979, 1981; Tittle and Meier, 1990; Tittle et al., 1978; Wright et al., 1999a.
2. *See* Brownfield, 1986; Elliott and Ageton, 1980; Farnworth et al., 1994; Hagan, 1992; Hindelang et al., 1979, 1981; Thornberry and Farnworth, 1982.
3. *See* Brownfield, 1986; Farnworth et al., 1994; Loeber, Farrington, Stouthamer-Loeber, Moffitt, and Caspi, 1998.
4. For selected studies and overviews of the research on race and delinquency, see Elliott and Ageton, 1980; Elliott et al., 1989; Hagan and Peterson, 1995; Harris and Shaw, 2000; Hawkins, Laub, and Lauritsen, 1998; Hindelang, 1978; Hindelang et al., 1981; Huizinga and Elliott, 1987; Lauritsen and Sampson, 1998; Sampson and Lauritsen, 1997.
5. *See* Elliott and Ageton, 1980; Elliott et al., 1989; Farrington et al., 1996; Hindelang et al., 1981; Huizinga and Elliott, 1987; Kelley et al., 1997; Office of Juvenile Justice and Delinquency Prevention, 1999a; Peeples and Loeber, 1994.
6. *See* Snyder and Sickmund, 1999:192; also see Hindelang, 1981; Tonry, 1995.
7. For a fuller discussion of these issues, see Chapter 14 in this text and Hawkins, Laub, and Lauritsen, 1998; Lauritsen and Sampson, 1998; Sampson and Lauritsen, 1997; Sampson and Wilson, 1995.
8. *See* Peeples and Loeber, 1994; also see Krivo and Peterson, 1996; Sampson, 1985, 1987.
9. For overviews and selected studies, see Cook and Laub, 1998; Elliott, 1994; Elliott et al., 1989; Farrington, 1986, 1994; Greenberg, 1977, 1985; Hirschi and Gottfredson, 1983; Huizinga, 1995; Kelley et al., 1997; Le Blanc and Loeber, 1998; Osgood et al., 1989; Rowe and Tittle, 1977; Sampson and Laub, 1993; Snyder, 1998; Snyder and Sickmund, 1999; Steffensmeier and Allan, 1995b, 2000; Steffensmeir et al., 1989; Warr, 1993.
10. For overviews and selected studies on gender and delinquency, see Canter, 1982; Chesney-Lind and Shelden, 1998; Daly, 1998; Elliott et al., 1989; Federal Bureau of Investigation, 1998; Hindelang et al., 1981; Jensen and Rojek, 1998; Kelley et al., 1997; Poe-Yamagata and Butts, 1996; Steffensmeier, 1993; Steffensmeier and Allan, 1996, 2000.
11. Compare Canter, 1982; Chesney-Lind and Shelden, 1998; Elliott, 1994; Hindelang et al., 1981; Jensen and Rojek, 1998.
12. *See* Canter, 1982; Chesney-Lind and Shelden, 1998; Steffensmeier, 1993; also see Jensen and Rojek, 1998.
13. For overviews and selected studies in this area, see Cohen and Villa, 1996; D'Unger et al., 1998; Dunford and Elliott, 1984; Elliott et al., 1989; Farrington, 1986, 1994; Howell, 1997a; Howell, Krisberg, and Jones, 1995; Huizinga, 1995; Kelley et al., 1997; Le Blanc and Loeber, 1998; Loeber, Farrington, and Waschbusch, 1998; Moffitt, 1997; Piquero et al., 1999; Sampson and Laub, 1993a; Thornberry et al., 1995; Tolan and Gorman-Smith, 1998; Visher, 2000. ✦

Part II

The Causes of Delinquency

Chapter 5

What Is a Theory and How Do We Test Theories?

The next twelve chapters focus on what is probably the most frequently asked question about delinquency: Why do they do it? Numerous theories try to explain why some juveniles break the law.[1] Chapters 6 through 8 focus on the three leading theories of delinquency: strain theory, social learning theory, and control theory. Chapter 9 gives you some experience in applying these theories (e.g., using them to explain why crime rates peak in adolescence). Chapters 10 through 15 examine research derived from or at least compatible with these theories. This research examines a range of factors that influence delinquency, including individual traits, family factors, school factors, peer groups and gangs, religion, work, the mass media, guns, and drugs. Chapter 16 attempts to pull all the previous material together by discussing the possibility of constructing a general, or integrated, theory of delinquency.

But before I describe these theories and the research derived from them, I use this chapter to address three basic questions. First, what is a theory? Second, why is it important to study theories of delinquency? And third, how do we go about testing theories or testing ideas derived from them? In particular, how do we determine whether some factor causes delinquency? I then conclude by listing three points for you to keep in mind when reading the subsequent chapters on the causes of delinquency.

What Is a Theory?

A theory is an attempt to explain something or describe the causes of something. Most of you probably already have theories of delinquency in mind. You may believe, for example, that poverty causes delinquency or that poor parental supervision causes delinquency (or that several factors cause delinquency). The delinquency theories that we will examine simply represent the efforts of criminologists to explain delinquency.

When criminologists develop theories of delinquency, however, they draw not only on their own experiences and creative abilities (as you do, when you develop your theories). They also draw on previous theories and research regarding delinquency. Their theories, then, are based on a large body of information. Further, the theories they develop are tested, and the results of such tests are used to develop still better theories or explanations of delinquency.

What Are the Basic Parts of a Theory?

Theories usually have several parts. Let us take the following simple theory as an illustration: Child abuse causes delinquency. Abuse makes children angry, and they often take this anger out on others through delinquency.

First, this theory lists what it is that we want to explain. In our case, we want to explain juvenile delinquency. In particular, we want to explain why some juveniles are more delinquent than others. The delinquency theories described in this book are rather general: They attempt to explain why some juveniles and why some groups are more likely to engage in a wide range of delinquent acts, including violent acts, property crimes, drug offenses, and status offenses. Some delinquency theories are more narrow in focus. For example, they attempt to explain particular types of delinquency, like drug abuse.

Second, the theory lists what we believe to be the cause of juvenile delinquency: child abuse. In the language of social research, child abuse is our *independent variable* and juvenile delinquency is our *dependent variable*. Delinquency is said to *depend* on child abuse. Most theories of delinquency are more complicated than our simple theory and list several independent variables or causes of delinquency. (A variable is anything that can vary. Sex is a variable, since one can be male or female. Income, education, and beliefs regarding violence are also variables.) Theories of delinquency also sometimes discuss the relationship between these independent variables. For example, they argue that income influences beliefs regarding violence.

Third, the theory explains *why* the independent variable causes delinquency. In particular, we claim that child abuse causes delinquency because it angers the child, who then strikes out at others. You can probably think of other reasons why child abuse might cause delinquency. Child abuse, for example, may teach children that violence is an appropriate way to deal with one's problems. Or child abuse may reduce the child's respect and affection for parents, thereby making it difficult for parents to properly raise their children. The leading theories of delinquency often share many of the same independent variables in common; these theories are most sharply distinguished from one another in terms of their description of *why* these independent variables cause crime (see Agnew, 1995a).

Many crime theories also have a fourth part. In the preceding example, we claim that child abuse causes delinquency. Studies provide some support for this theory: Abused children are somewhat more likely than non abused children to engage in delinquency (see Chapter 11). But not all abused children have high rates of delinquency. Child abuse increases the likelihood of delinquency, but it does not result in delinquency in all cases. Many theories try to specify the conditions under which a variable like child abuse is most likely to cause delinquency.

The simple theory we stated did not do this. We might, however, argue that child abuse is most likely to cause delinquency when the child is also having problems at school (Zingraff et al., 1994). Certain theories list those factors that influence the likelihood that their independent variables will cause delinquency. Such factors are sometimes called *conditioning variables*, since they specify the conditions under which the independent variables are most likely to cause delinquency (see Cullen, 1984, for an extended discussion of conditioning variables in crime theory).

You now know the basic parts of a theory, and I'll make reference to them in the descriptions of strain, social learning, and control theory that follow.

Why Is It Important to Study Theories of Delinquency?

It is important to study theories for several reasons. First, these theories can help explain the "basic facts" about delinquency that were discussed in previous chapters. Most notably, they can help explain why certain individuals and groups are more likely to engage in delinquency. Why, for example, are males more delinquent than females?

Second, most of the *research* on the causes of delinquency is guided by these theories or can be interpreted in terms of them. These theories are basically "educated guesses" about why juveniles engage in delinquency. Most of the research conducted by criminologists—like surveys and observational studies—represents an attempt to test and extend these theories. Chapters 10 through 15 describe this research.

Third, these theories can help society prevent and control delinquency. These theories point to the major causes of delinquency, and prevention and control programs are more likely to be successful to the extent that they target these causes. Chapters 18 through 22 describe a number of successful programs that are based on or compatible with these theories.

Finally, these theories can help us better understand our own behavior and the behavior of those around us. As discussed in Chapter 3, most of us have committed at least minor delinquent acts. And most of us know individuals who have committed delinquent acts and live in communities where delinquency is a problem.

How Do We Test Theories of Delinquency (or Determine Whether Some Factor Causes Delinquency)?

As indicated, theories are basically "educated guesses" about what causes delinquency. That is, they describe factors that *may* cause delinquency. It is therefore important that we test theories to determine if they are true. But how do we go about determining if some factor really does cause delinquency? For example, how do we determine whether child abuse causes delinquency? This question is not only relevant to the causes of delinquency, but to all areas where causal statements are made. It is relevant to many of the other courses you are taking and to your daily lives. You are constantly exposed to causal statements like the following: TV violence causes crime; second-hand smoke causes cancer; and welfare causes laziness. The discussion that follows will not only help you better understand the research on the causes of delinquency, but it will help you better judge the accuracy of these sorts of claims.

The Scientific Method

Suppose you believe that child abuse causes delinquency. That is your theory of delinquency. You may have good reason to believe that this theory is correct. It may be supported by your personal experiences; perhaps you know someone who was abused and they turned out to be delinquent. The theory may make much sense to you; you can think of many good reasons why abuse might lead to delinquency. The theory may be held by other people whom you respect. It is, nevertheless, still important to test the theory. Personal experiences do not provide a sufficient basis for judging the accuracy of our theory. Even though you may know an abused individual who turned out to be delinquent, that does not prove that abuse causes delinquency. It may be that abused and nonabused individuals are equally likely to engage in delinquency; you just happen to know one of the abused individuals who engages in delinquency. It is dangerous to generalize from this one individual to all abused individuals. Also, the fact that this theory makes sense to us or is supported by others does not mean that it is correct. Many people, for example, believe that low self-esteem is a major cause of delinquency, and this belief makes much sense to them. The data, however, suggest that self-esteem has little or no effect on delinquency (Blackburn, 1993; Jang and Thornberry, 1998).

How, then, do we determine whether our theory that abuse causes delinquency is correct? We test our theory against *data* gathered from juveniles. Social and behavioral scientists have developed a number of guidelines for us to follow in this process: guidelines for collecting and analyzing data. These guidelines form the core of the "scientific method," and they describe the steps that we should follow in order to provide an *accurate* test of our theories. A brief overview of these guidelines is provided below (see Babbie, 1995; Champion, 2000 for fuller discussions).

Carefully define your independent and dependent variables. The first step in testing our theory involves carefully defining our independent and dependent variables (remember, the independent variable is what causes the dependent variable). For our theory, we must carefully define what we mean by abuse and delinquency. For example, does abuse constitute only physical aggression, or does it also include such things as inappropriate sexual contact, verbal harassment, and physical neglect (e.g., the failure to provide adequate food, clothing, medical care, and shelter)? Suppose we decide to limit our definition of abuse to physical aggression. What constitutes such aggression? If a parent softly spanks her or his child for a misdeed, is that aggression? If not, what is the dividing line between physical contact that is abusive and contact that is not abusive? As you can see, it is sometimes difficult to carefully define variables. Nevertheless, it is important: We cannot test our theory that abuse causes delinquency unless we can precisely define abuse and delinquency. For the purposes of our example, let us define abuse as any deliberate act of physical violence against the child (see English, 1998, for a discussion of efforts to define child abuse).

In evaluating any piece of research, you should carefully examine the definitions of all variables: Are these variables precisely defined and do the definitions seem reasonable? For example, you might criticize the definition of abuse that I just presented. This definition excludes acts that many people would define as abusive, such as verbal abuse, physical neglect, and certain forms of sexual behavior. Further, it includes certain acts that many people would not define as abusive, such as spanking.

Decide how to gather data to test your belief or theory. Second, you must decide how you will gather data to test your belief or theory. Criminologists gather data from juveniles in three major ways. As you will see, each method has certain advantages and disadvantages.

Surveys. The most common way is by *surveying* juveniles. Surveys involve asking people questions. We either interview them or have them fill out questionnaires. For our theory, we might ask a sample of juveniles how many times their parents deliberately hit them in the last year and how many times they have engaged in certain delinquent acts in the last year. We would then have data on the extent of their abuse and delinquency. We could use this data to *begin* to explore whether abuse causes delinquency. In particular, we could determine whether abused juveniles are more likely to engage in delinquency than nonabused juveniles.

Surveys have the advantage of allowing us to study a large number of juveniles. Further, if we select these juveniles carefully, we can ensure that they are representative of all juveniles. At the same time, there is the danger that some juveniles may not provide accurate answers to our questions. They may forget some of the things that they have done or that others have done to them. Also, they may lie to us in an effort to make themselves look good.

Experiments. Criminologists also collect data by doing *experiments* on juveniles. In an experiment, you do something to a group of people and then observe the consequences. For example, you reward them for aggression and then observe whether they act in a more aggressive manner.

As discussed in Chapter 17, properly conducted experiments are a good way to determine if something causes something else. Many laboratory experiments, however, have been criticized as artificial. Conditions in the lab may not adequately reflect conditions in the real world, so when someone behaves a certain way in the lab, it does not necessarily mean that he or she will behave the same way in the outside, or "real," world. For example, a laboratory experiment may reveal that juveniles often respond to violent cartoons by hitting an inflated doll in a playroom. This behavior, however, does not necessarily mean that they respond to violent cartoons in the *real world* by hitting other *people*. Further, ethical considerations often prevent social scientists from doing experiments on the causes of delinquency. For example, we would not want to abuse a group of juveniles and then determine whether they become more delinquent. Likewise, we would not want to create conditions of poverty, broken homes, or poor grades to study such alleged causes of delinquency. Such ethical considerations are why experiments are used less often than surveys when studying the *causes* of delinquency. Experiments are more often used to determine whether programs are successful at *reducing* or *preventing* delinquency, and we will discuss them further in Chapter 17. Nevertheless, experiments are sometimes used to study the causes of delinquency. For example, numerous experiments have investigated the impact of media violence on juveniles. Juveniles are exposed to media violence (e.g., a clip from a violent TV show), and researchers then observe the consequences of this exposure on their behavior (e.g., are they more aggressive to a toy clown in the playroom).

Observational Studies. Finally, criminologists collect data by *observing* juveniles. Criminologists sometimes go out into the community and observe juveniles first-hand in an effort to study the causes of delinquency. They typically supplement their observations with intensive interviews with the juveniles and others. Criminologists have conducted a number of major observational studies, most of which focus on the effect of gangs and community characteristics on delinquency.[2]

Observational studies provide a much more detailed picture of social life than is provided by surveys and experiments. Researchers directly observe juveniles over an extended period of time and have long conversations with them. As a consequence, they get a fuller picture of the circumstances in which juveniles live and the factors that influence their behavior. Also, since the researcher directly observes juveniles, observational studies are less affected by the fact that juveniles are sometimes unable or unwilling to provide accurate answers to questions.

❖ ❖ ❖ ❖

At the same time, observational studies have certain limitations. It is difficult for a criminologist to observe more than a small number of juveniles. There may also be limits to what can be observed. Most families, for example, would probably be reluctant to have a researcher in their homes observing them. Further, the presence of the observer might change the behavior being observed. Parents might be reluctant to abuse their kids, and juveniles might be reluctant to commit delinquent acts if there is an observer present. Finally, the observers' biases may influence what they observe and how they interpret what they observe. Techniques have been developed to minimize these problems, but they are nevertheless important limitations. It is for these reasons that observational studies are less common than survey research. Even so, observational studies have provided criminologists with important information about the causes of delinquency—information that would have been difficult or impossible to obtain with surveys and experiments.

Each method of collecting data, then, has its own special set of advantages and disadvantages. Ideally, researchers should study the causes of delinquency using all three methods when feasible and ethical.

Develop measures of your independent and dependent variables. Since most research on the causes of delinquency employs surveys, I will focus on survey research for the remainder of this discussion. Once you have decided to conduct a survey, you need to decide how you will measure your variables. That is, you need to decide what *questions* you will ask the juveniles in your sample to measure variables like child abuse and delinquency. You want to make sure that your questions reflect the definitions you have developed. At the same time, you want to make sure that your questions will be properly understood by your respondents, many of whom may be young and of limited intellectual ability. In some cases, it is an easy matter to develop questions. For example, if you want to measure a variable like age, you can simply ask juveniles, "How old are you?" In other cases, it is much more difficult to develop good questions. For example, how do you measure a variable like "self-control" (defined in Chapter 8)? This variable has several components, including impulsivity, insensitivity, and a preference for risk-taking. Researchers have measured self-control by asking respondents whether they agree with a series of questions, such as "I often act on the spur of the moment without stopping to think"; "I try to look out for myself, even if it means making things difficult for other people"; and "Sometimes I will take a risk just for the fun of it" (see Grasmick et al., 1993). Responses to these questions are then used to develop an overall measure of self-control.

Textbooks on social research, like Babbie (1995), and Champion (2000), provide guidelines for researchers to follow in developing good measures. In evaluating a piece of research, you should ask yourself whether there are any potential problems with the measures employed. As you may recall from earlier chapters, one major issue in delinquency research involves the way delinquency is measured. Many researchers measure delinquency using arrest data. Arrest data, however, suffer from several problems, including the fact that they overlook the vast majority of delinquent acts, which do not come to the attention of the police. As a consequence, most criminologists studying the causes of delinquency now rely on self-report measures of delinquency. Such measures are not problem-free, but if properly constructed they are generally thought to provide a better indicator of delinquency. Researchers, however, place greatest confidence in findings that hold for both self-report *and* arrest measures. We can be more confident, for example, that child abuse really does cause delinquency if it affects both self-reported delinquency *and* arrests. Fortunately, both the research based on arrest data and the research based on comparable self-report measures have generally produced similar results about the causes of delinquency, although there are some exceptions.

Select a sample of juveniles to survey. There are about 30 million juveniles between age 10 and age 17 in the United States. Fortunately, it is not necessary to survey all of them. If researchers carefully select a sample of one or two thousand juveniles, they can accurately generalize from this sample to all juveniles in the United States. If the researchers find, for example, that abused juveniles are more delinquent than nonabused juveniles in this sample, they can be reasonably confident that they would find the same thing if they surveyed all 30 million juveniles in the United States. Researchers must, however, carefully select their sample so that it is *representative* of all juveniles in the United States. What do I mean by "representative"? I mean that the characteristics of the juveniles in our sample should be similar to those of all juveniles in the United States The two groups should be proportionately similar in terms of delinquency and all the potential causes of delinquency—including variables like class, race, sex, and age. How do we ensure that our sample is similar to or representative of all juveniles? The best way to do this is to collect a *random sample*.

A random sample is collected such that each juvenile in the population has *an equal chance of being selected*. For example, imagine that we put the names of all juveniles in the United States in an enormous hat. We then thoroughly mixed the names up and had a blindfolded person pull out 2,000 names. We would have a random sample, and we could be reasonably sure that the juveniles in this sample were similar to or representative of all juveniles in the United States. Researchers do not collect random samples in quite this manner; rather, they have developed more sophisticated techniques for randomly sampling juveniles from a population (see Babbie, 1995; Champion, 2000). Unfortunately, it is often difficult for researchers to collect random samples of juveniles—even random samples of juveniles from a single city. There is no list containing the names of every juvenile in the United States (or in cities or states within the United States). Even if there were such a list, it is often hard to locate certain juveniles, and if you do locate them, they may refuse to participate in your survey.

As a consequence, most studies of delinquency are based on samples that are not quite representative of all juveniles or that are of questionable representativeness. For example, researchers commonly collect random samples of students from high schools (e.g., they select every twentieth student on the rolls from all the high schools in a city or from a random sample of high schools in the United States). As indicated earlier, however, many juveniles have dropped out of school, are suspended, or are absent from school the day the survey is administered. This absenteeism is especially likely to be true of lower-class juveniles and serious delinquents. Also, many students refuse to participate in the survey, or their parents refuse to allow them to participate. So the final sample of students is not representative of all juveniles. As a consequence, criminologists have to be cautious when generalizing from their sample to all juveniles. In fact, some researchers have claimed that the use of unrepresentative samples—including school samples—has led scientists to draw some inaccurate conclusions about the causes of delinquency (e.g., Bernard, 1984; Hagan and McCarthy, 1997a, 1997b). The extent to which the sample is unrepresentative obviously depends on the particular survey, and some of the more recent surveys on juvenile delinquency have gone to great lengths to select more representative samples of juveniles. In particular, they have made a special effort to make sure that serious delinquents are included in the sample (see Thornberry et al., 1995). In any event, when you are evaluating a piece of survey research, you should ask whether the sample is representative of the population from which it is drawn. And if it is not representative, how might that lack affect the results? (Good researchers will usually address these issues in their research reports.)

Analyze the data you have collected. Once researchers have developed their measures and selected their sample, they administer the survey. Most delinquency surveys today contain hundreds of questions (remember, it may take several questions to measure a single variable) and are administered to as many as 2,000 or more juveniles. Researchers enter all the data they have collected into a computer and then analyze this data using certain statistical techniques. Before researchers can conclude that some independent variable like child abuse causes delinquency, they must demonstrate *four* things: The independent variable is *associated* with delinquency; the *association is not due to chance*; *the association is not due to third variables*; and *the independent variable precedes delinquency in time*. These are the four conditions for making causal statements. Let me describe each of them in turn (see Hirschi and Selvin, 1967, for a fuller discussion).

Association. Before we can say that our independent variable causes delinquency, we must first demonstrate that our independent variable is associated, or correlated, with delinquency. For example, before we can say that child abuse causes delinquency, we must demonstrate that abused juveniles are higher in delinquency. This requirement makes sense. If child abuse causes delinquency, then we would expect abused juveniles to be *more* delinquent than nonabused juveniles. (This is an example of a *positive* association: A high score on our independent variable is associated with a *higher* level of delinquency. This positive association is illustrated in Figure 5.1A; as the level of abuse increases, the level of delinquency also increases.) To give another example, suppose we argue that school grades cause delinquency: Those with higher grades have more to lose by engaging in delinquency and should therefore be lower in delinquency. If this argument is correct, school grades should be associated with delinquency: Those with high grades should be *less* delinquent than those with low grades. (This is an example of a *negative* association: A high score on our independent variable is associated with a *lower* level of delinquency. This negative association is illustrated in Figure 5.1B; as grades increase, the level of delinquency decreases.)

It is important to emphasize that most associations are far from perfect. Do not expect to find that all abused juveniles are delinquent and that all non abused juveniles are not delinquent. Instead, you might find that 30 percent of all abused juveniles are high in delinquency compared to 17 percent of all nonabused juveniles. Delinquency is caused by a large number of variables, most of which have small to moderate associations with delinquency. So when you read that low grades or broken homes are associated with delinquency, you should *not* assume that all or even most juveniles with low grades or from broken homes are delinquent (or that all juveniles with high grades or from intact homes are nondelinquent). What you can safely assume is that juveniles with low grades and juveniles from broken homes are somewhat more likely to engage in delinquency than juveniles with high grades and juveniles from intact homes.

Figure 5.1   Examples of a Positive Association and a Negative Association

5.1A   A Positive Association Between Child Abuse and Delinquency

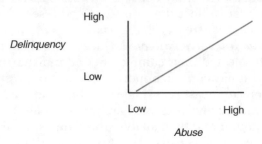

5.1B   A Negative Association Between Grades and Delinquency

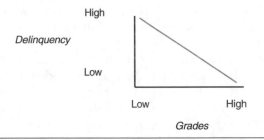

Most of the statistics employed by researchers summarize the association between the independent and dependent variables. These statistics usually tell the researcher how much delinquency increases or decreases when the independent variable increases by a certain amount. For example, they might tell the researcher that juveniles commit an average of five fewer delinquent acts every time school grades increase by one unit (from D to C, C to B, etc.). See Babbie (1995), and Champion (2000) for an overview of such statistics.

Association not due to chance. Suppose we find that child abuse and delinquency are associated, with abused juveniles being more delinquent than nonabused juveniles. Does that mean that child abuse causes delinquency?

It does not. The association may be due to chance. For example, suppose you randomly sample ten students from your school. You find that 40 percent of the blue-eyed students in your sample are delinquent, whereas only 20 percent of the brown-eyed students are. So there is an association between eye color and delinquency. But this association may be due to chance. If you surveyed *all* the students at your school, you might find that eye color is unrelated to delinquency (e.g., 30 percent of the blue-eyed students are delinquent and 30 percent of the brown-eyed students are delinquent). But, by chance, your sample of ten happened to include too many blue-eyed delinquents and too few brown-eyed delinquents. The fact that two variables are associated does not prove that one causes the other; the association may be due to chance.

The likelihood that a given association is due to chance becomes smaller as the sample size increases. Larger samples generally produce more accurate results, although increases in sample size beyond 2,000 or so juveniles only produce small increases in accuracy (see Babbie, 1995, for a discussion of factors affecting the accuracy of sample results, including sample size). Also, if you have collected a random sample, you can estimate the probability that any association you find is due to chance. For example, you can say that the probability that the association between child abuse and delinquency is due to chance is less than 1 in 20 (5 percent) or less than 1 in 100 (1 percent). Researchers state that such associations are "statistically significant."

Association not due to third variables. Now suppose that we have demonstrated that child abuse and delinquency are associated and that it is unlikely that this association is due to chance. Can we now say that child abuse *causes* delinquency? I'm afraid the answer is still "no." The association between child abuse and delinquency may be caused by a third variable that is causally prior to both of the original variables.

Let me provide an example from actual research. Criminologists have found that there is an association between IQ and delinquency: People with low IQs are higher in delinquency. Further, it is quite unlikely that this association is due to chance. Does that mean that low IQ causes delinquency? Many criminologists argue that it does not. They claim that the association between IQ and delinquency is *not* due to the fact that low IQ *causes* delinquency. Rather, it is due to the fact that both IQ and delinquency are caused by the same third variable. In particular, they claim that the third variable, social class, affects both IQ and delinquency (see Figure 5-2). Lower-class people have lower IQs and are higher in delinquency. That is why low IQ is associated with high delinquency—not because low IQ causes delinquency but because both IQ and delinquency are caused by the same third variable, social class. (Try to think of another example where the association between two variables may be caused by a third variable. Hint: A popular example involves the following three variables: number of storks in an area, area birthrate, and urban/rural location—see Babbie, 1995).

Figure 5.2 It Has Been Argued That the Association Between IQ and Delinquency Is Caused by the Third Variable of Social Class.

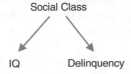

Social Class

IQ   Delinquency

Before we can argue that the independent variable in our theory causes delinquency, we must also demonstrate that the association between our independent variable and delinquency is not caused by a third variable. How do we do this? Let us continue with the example. Again, many criminologists argue that people with low IQs are more likely to be delinquent because they are more likely to be lower class, not because they have low IQs. Likewise, they argue that people with high IQs are less likely to be delinquent because they are more likely to be higher class, not because they have high IQs. If these arguments are correct, the association between IQ and delinquency should disappear if we examine just lower-class people. That is, IQ should be unrelated to delinquency in a sample of lower-class people: Lower-class people with low IQs should be about as delinquent as lower-class people with high IQs. Likewise, the association should disappear if we examine just higher-class people: Higher-class people with low IQs should be about as delinquent as higher-class people with high IQs. If IQ is no longer associated with delinquency when we examine lower-class people separately from higher-class people, that finding suggests that the original association between IQ and delinquency is caused by social class and we can no longer claim that IQ causes delinquency.

What if the association does not disappear? What if we find that lower-class people with low IQs are more delinquent than lower-class people with high IQs, and that higher-class people with low IQs are more delinquent than higher-class people with high IQs? This finding means that the association between IQ and delinquency is *not* caused by the third variable of social class. And, in fact, that is what researchers have found: IQ is still associated with delinquency even when the analysis is limited to lower-class people only or to higher-class people only (e.g., Hirschi and Hindelang, 1977).

Researchers, then, determine whether the association between an independent variable and delinquency is caused by a third variable by "controlling" for the third variable, or "holding it constant." We examined the association between IQ and delinquency separately for each category of social class—lower and higher. If the association disappears, that suggests that it was caused by our third variable. (I realize that these arguments may be difficult for some of you to follow. I encourage you to consult with your classmates and to try to come up with examples of your own; also see the discussion in Hirschi and Selvin, 1967:73–87.)

When you are evaluating a piece of research, you should ask yourself whether any of the reported associations might be caused by a third variable. Is there some causally prior third variable that might account for the association between the independent variable and delinquency? Are there any third variables, for example, that might account for the association between child abuse and delinquency? Most researchers will try to anticipate third variables that might account for the associations they report and then control for them. This is not always done, however, for a variety of reasons.

Correct causal order. Suppose you find that child abuse is associated with delinquency, the association is not due to chance, and it appears that it is not caused by a third variable. Can you now state that child abuse causes delinquency? If not, why not?

It may be that the association between child abuse and delinquency exists because *delinquency causes child abuse*. Juveniles who engage in delinquent acts may upset their parents, and the upset parents may react by striking their children. Much recent data, in fact, suggest that the behavior of juveniles often has a large effect on how others treat them, including how their parents treat them. Children who are difficult to raise, for example, are more likely to be rejected and elicit negative reactions from their parents (see Rutter et al., 1998:171–174).

Before we can say that child abuse causes delinquency, we must demonstrate that the abuse preceded the delinquency in time. That is, the abuse came first and the delinquency followed. This is usually accomplished by conducting a *longitudinal* survey. We survey the same group of juveniles over time. For example, during our initial survey we ask a sample of juveniles about the extent of their delinquency and whether their parents hit them. Then we survey the same group of juveniles one year later, once again asking them about the extent of their delinquency. These two surveys allow us to determine whether abused juveniles engage in more *subsequent* delinquency than nonabused juveniles.

It is difficult to do longitudinal surveys of this type, since it is often hard to keep track of a large group of juveniles over time. Much research on the causes of delinquency suffers from the fact that it is not longitudinal in nature (such research is said to be "cross sectional," since it looks at juveniles at one cross-section in time). Nevertheless, several excellent longitudinal surveys of delinquency have been conducted or are now in progress (e.g., Elliott et al., 1985; Thornberry et al., 1995). One interesting finding to emerge from these studies is that variables sometimes have a *reciprocal* effect on one another. For example, research suggests that associating with delinquent peers and delinquency are reciprocally related. Associating with delinquent peers causes delinquency, and delinquency causes a juvenile to associate with delinquent peers (see Chapters 7 and 13).

Summary

Determining whether your beliefs or theories about the causes of delinquency are correct is not an easy matter. There are a number of guidelines that should be followed when collecting and analyzing data, but it is often difficult to follow them all, and sometimes the research on the causes of delinquency is suspect as a result. Perhaps a variable is not well defined or measured. Perhaps an unrepresentative sample is employed. Perhaps there is a failure to control for relevant third variables. Perhaps the research is not longitudinal in nature. Given these problems, criminologists sometimes need to be cautious when making causal statements. I will try to indicate when that is the case in the discussions that follow. At the same time, there are some areas in which they can make causal statements with some confidence. Certain areas have been well researched, and a range of studies have come to similar conclusions. Criminologists do not like to place too much faith in a single study. But if a number of different studies agree—especially well-conducted studies that use different measures and samples—we are more confident in our conclusions.

Some Important Points to Keep in Mind When Studying the Causes of Delinquency

The next several chapters discuss the causes of delinquency. I describe the three leading theories of delinquency, beginning with strain theory, and then I describe the research based on or compatible with these theories, like the research examining the effect of individual traits, family factors, school factors, and peer groups on delinquency. Before discussing the causes of delinquency, however, I want to list three important points for you to keep in mind as you read these chapters.

First, delinquency is caused by a wide range of factors. This phenomenon will become apparent in the chapters that follow. The point that delinquency is caused by a range of factors may sound obvious, but it is common for politicians and people in the general public to blame delinquency on one or a few factors. Most recently, there has been much talk about how delinquency is caused by mass media violence and a lack of religion (or the absence of school prayer). Not only does such talk ignore the many other causes of delinquency, but media violence and the lack of religion are *not* among the most important causes of delinquency (see below).

At the most general level, delinquency is caused by both *individual traits* and various features of *the social environment*. Individuals with certain traits—like an irritable temperament or low intelligence—are more likely to engage in delinquency than other individuals. Likewise, individuals in certain environments, like abusive families or poor communities, are more likely to engage in delinquency. Most factors only have small to moderate effects on delinquency, but a few factors have larger effects. I will try to provide some indication of the relative importance of the different factors, although doing so is difficult at times because of a lack of good research (i.e., studies that examine large, representative samples of juveniles; employ good measures; examine a wide range of causes; and are longitudinal).

Second, most of the causes of delinquency are related to one another. For example, individuals with traits conducive to delinquency are more likely to be in environments conducive to delinquency. So irritable juveniles are more likely to be in bad family environments (in part because they upset and overwhelm their parents). And individuals in bad family environments are more likely to associate with delinquent peers and belong to gangs. It is difficult to keep track of all the relationships between the causes of delinquency, but I will try to give you a rough sense of how these causes are related in the chapters that follow. And I try to provide a summary of such relationships in Chapter 16 when I discuss the possibility of constructing an integrated or general theory of delinquency.

Third, not only are the causes of delinquency related to one another, but they may sometimes condition the effect of one another on delinquency. For example, many criminologists now argue that individual traits and the social environment condition the effect of one another on delinquency. Let me provide a couple of illustrations. While irritable individuals are more likely to engage in delinquency, not all irritable individuals are delinquent. It is argued that irritable individuals are most likely to become delinquent when they are in certain environments, such as abusive families. Likewise, while the residents of poor communities are more likely to engage in delinquency, not all such residents are delinquent. It is argued that the residents of poor communities are most likely to engage in delinquency when they possess certain traits, such as irritability. There has not been much research on such conditioning effects, although the limited research that has been done is generally supportive of such effects. In particular, certain data suggest that delinquency is most likely among individuals who possess traits like irritability or low intelligence *and* are in environments conducive to delinquency, like abusive families or poor communities.[3] I discuss such conditioning effects further in Chapter 16.

Please keep the above points in mind when reading the following chapters. While I often discuss the causes of delinquency in isolation from one another, these causes usually work together to produce delinquency.

Notes

1. For recent overviews, see Akers, 1997; Cullen and Agnew, 1999; Shoemaker, 2000; Vold et al., 1998.
2. *See* Anderson, 1990, 1999; Campbell, 1984; Hagedorn, 1988; Moore, 1991; Padilla, 1992; Sullivan, 1989.
3. *See* Brennan et al., 1995; Brennan and Raine, forthcoming; Denno, 1990; Farrington, 1996b; Fishbein, 1996; Moffitt, 1990, 1993, 1997; Moffitt et al., 1997; Raine, 1993; Raine, Brennan, and Farrington, 1997; Raine, Brennan, Farrington, and Mednick, 1997; Rutter, 1997; Rutter et al., 1998; Tibbetts and Piquero, 1999; Wilson and Herrnstein, 1985; Wright et al., 1999b. ✦

Chapter 6

Strain Theory: Does Strain or Stress Cause Delinquency?

❖ ❖ ❖ ❖   According to strain theory, when juveniles experience strain or stress, they become upset, and they *sometimes* engage in delinquency as a result. They may engage in delinquency to reduce or escape from the strain they are experiencing. For example, they may engage in violence to end harassment from others; they may steal to reduce financial problems; or they may run away from home to escape abusive parents. They may also perform delinquent acts to seek revenge against those who have "wronged" them. And they may engage in illicit drug use in an effort to feel better.

Many of the delinquent acts that you may have committed or came close to committing can probably be explained using strain theory. You experienced some type of strain or stress; most probably, someone did something to you that you did not like. Perhaps someone insulted you or did not give you something you wanted. You became angry and frustrated as a result, and you thought about or actually committed some delinquent act. For example, studies indicate that a large number of violent acts start off with one person insulting another or otherwise doing something that the other person does not like.[1]

There are several versions of strain theory, the most prominent being those of Merton (1938, 1968), Cohen (1955), Cloward and Ohlin (1960), Greenberg (1977), Elliott et al. (1979), Agnew (1992), and Berkowitz (1993). Each version basically tries to do two things: describe the major types of strain that lead to delinquency and describe the conditions under which strain is most likely to lead to delinquency. All strain theorists recognize that strain usually does *not* lead to delinquency. As a consequence, such theorists describe those "conditioning variables" that influence the likelihood of that strain will result in delinquency. Rather than describe each version of strain theory, I will present a generic version that incorporates the central arguments of the major strain theories, although this generic theory draws most heavily on Agnew's (1992) general strain theory.

What Are the Major Types of Strain?

Researchers often measure strain by presenting juveniles with lists of strainful events and conditions and asking them which events/conditions they have experienced.[2] Certain of these lists contain over 200 items, including things like parents divorcing, parents arguing or fighting, a close friend dying or becoming seriously ill, not being selected for a much-wanted extracurricular activity, disagreements with teachers, disagreements with friends, breaking up with a romantic partner, and money problems. Theorists have tried to categorize these types of strain in various ways and to list the types of strain that are most strongly related to delinquency. Two general categories of strain have been linked to delinquency: the failure to achieve your goals and the loss of positive stimuli/presentation of negative stimuli.

The Failure to Achieve Your Goals

All strain theorists argue that a major type of strain is the failure to achieve your goals. They argue that many adolescents place special emphasis on certain goals and that the failure to achieve these goals contributes to much delinquency. These goals include money, status/respect, and autonomy from adults.

Money. Certain strain theorists argue that money is the central goal in the United States (see especially Merton, 1968; Cloward and Ohlin, 1960). All people, poor as well as rich, are encouraged to work hard so that they might make a lot of money. Further, money is necessary to buy many of the things people want, including the necessities of life and all those luxury items to which most people are regularly exposed. Money is said to be important for adolescents as well as for adults, since adolescents need money for such things as clothing, social activities, and automobiles (see Greenberg, 1977). Many adolescents, however, are not able to obtain the money they need through legal channels, such as parents and work. This inability is especially true of poor adolescents, but it may also be true of many middle-class adolescents. As a consequence, such adolescents experience strain and they may attempt to get money through illegal channels, such as theft, selling drugs, and prostitution.

Studies provide some support for this argument. Criminals and delinquents often report that they engage in income-generating crime because they want money but cannot easily get it any other way.[3] The fact that some delinquents report monetary strain, however, does not prove that such strain is a cause of delinquency. Many individuals who experience monetary strain do *not* engage in delinquency. Many of you, for example, have probably been in situations where you wanted more money than you had, yet you did not engage in crime. Criminologists must demonstrate that people who are high in monetary strain *are more likely* to engage in delinquency than people low in such strain (see the discussion of "association" in Chapter 5). Surprisingly, only a few studies have tried to do this, and most suffer from serious problems.[4] Some data, however, suggest that crime is more common among people who are dissatisfied with their monetary situation; such dissatisfaction is higher among lower-class people and people who state that they want "a lot of money."[5] So there is *limited* support for the idea that monetary strain is related to delinquency. More research is needed in this area, however.

Status/respect. Closely related to the desire for money is the desire for status and respect (see Cohen, 1955). People want to be positively regarded by others and they want to be treated respectfully, which at a minimum involves being treated in a just or fair manner (see Agnew, 1992). Data suggest that anger is often the result of disrespectful or unjust treatment (Agnew, 1992). Although people have a general desire for status and respect, the desire for *"masculine status"* is said to be especially relevant to delinquency.[6]

There are class and race differences in views about what it means to be a "man," although most such views emphasize traits like independence, dominance, toughness, competitiveness, and heterosexuality (see Messerschmidt, 1993). Most male juveniles experience difficulties in their desire to be viewed and treated as a man, particularly given the emphasis of the school system on docility and submission (see Greenberg, 1977; Messerschmidt, 1993). Certain juveniles, however, experience special difficulties in this area, especially lower-class and minority group members.[7] Such juveniles may attempt to "accomplish masculinity" through delinquency. They may engage in delinquent acts to demonstrate that they possess traits like toughness, dominance, and independence. And they may attempt to coerce others into giving them the respect they believe they deserve as "real men." In this connection, they may adopt a tough demeanor, respond to even minor shows of disrespect with violence, and occasionally assault and rob others in an effort to establish a tough reputation. There have been no large-scale tests of this idea, although several studies provide support for it.[8]

Autonomy from adults. Several researchers have argued that a major goal of most adolescents is to achieve autonomy from adults.[9] Autonomy may be defined as power over oneself—the ability to resist the demands of others and engage in action without the permission of others. Adolescents are often encouraged to be autonomous by others—parents and teachers, for example. They are granted more autonomy in certain spheres of life, which may increase their desire for autonomy in other spheres. And they come to desire autonomy as they physically and socially mature. Adults, however, often deny adolescents the autonomy they desire. Although adolescents have more autonomy than children, their behavior is still subject to much control; a broad range of behaviors are prohibited or restricted. Most notably, adolescents find their desire for autonomy frustrated in the school system with its extensive regulations and emphasis on authoritarian styles of teaching (see Greenberg, 1977). Parents may also continue to restrict the freedom of adolescents. The denial of autonomy may lead to delinquency for several reasons: Delinquency may be a means of asserting autonomy (e.g., sexual intercourse or disorderly behavior), achieving autonomy (e.g., stealing money to gain financial independence from parents), or venting frustration against those who deny autonomy.

Some data support these arguments. Adolescents often demand greater autonomy from parents and teachers and they frequently clash with these individuals over issues involving autonomy. Such issues include doing chores, clothing, appearance, schoolwork, interpersonal relations, and rules for such things as bedtime and curfew (see Agnew, 1997). Only one study has examined the relationship between autonomy and delinquency. Agnew (1984) found that adolescents with a strong need for autonomy were higher in delinquency and that one of the reasons for their behavior was that they were angrier and more frustrated.

Strain, then, may result from the failure to achieve one's goals. I have listed three goals that are said to be important to most adolescents: money, status/respect, and autonomy from adults. Strain may also result from the failure to achieve other goals, and any test of strain theory should attempt to determine what goals the people being examined consider important. For example, one goal that many college students consider important is good grades. And many college students experience strain when they find that they are unable to achieve this goal through legal channels—like studying. I have the students in my juvenile delinquency course fill out a survey on the first day of class; among other things, I ask them what grade they would *ideally like* to get in my class and what grade they *realistically expect* to get. Not surprisingly, almost all the students state that they would ideally like to get an "A" (sometimes one or two students with more modest ambitions state that they would like a "B"). Such ideal goals have something of the utopian in them and probably are not taken seriously by many students. I find, however, that roughly 70 percent of the students state that they realistically expect to get an "A." The percentage of students who actually end up getting an "A," however, is usually between 25 and 30 percent. Many students thus experience strain and, although I have not tested this idea, I suspect that some of these students respond to such strain with deviance, such as cheating on exams or excessive alcohol use.

Loss of Positive Stimuli/Presentation of Negative Stimuli

The types of strain described above all involve what might be called *"nonevents."* The juvenile wants or expects something—like money or popularity or autonomy—but does not get it. The second major category of strain involves negative *events* or conditions. Juveniles lose something they value (positive stimuli) or are presented with noxious or negative stimuli. For example, the juvenile may break up with a boyfriend or girlfriend; a relative or close friend may die or move away; someone may take something from the juvenile; or someone may insult or physically assault the juvenile. In short, people treat the juvenile in a negative manner—in a way that she or he does not like. Such negative treatment may upset or anger the juvenile and, as indicated above, delinquency may be the result.

Several studies have asked juveniles about the types of events that anger or upset them (see Agnew, 1997, for an overview). The answers inevitably focus on interpersonal problems, typically interpersonal problems with parents, siblings, teachers, friends, and romantic partners. Juveniles report that they became angry or upset because these others insulted them, physically assaulted them, disciplined or sanctioned them when they did not deserve it, pressured them, overburdened them, got into conflicts with them, or rejected them. Studies have found that many of these negative events and conditions increase the likelihood of delinquency.[10]

In particular, delinquency has been linked to child abuse and neglect, criminal victimization, physical punishment by parents, negative relations with parents, negative relations with teachers, negative school experiences, negative relations with peers, neighborhood problems, and a wide range of stressful life events like the divorce or separation of parents, parental unemployment, and changing schools. Certain of the studies also indicate that these factors affect delinquency partly because they increase the adolescent's level of anger/frustration.

What Impact Does Strain Have on the Juvenile?

Strainful events and conditions make people feel bad—angry, frustrated, depressed, anxious, or the like. These negative feelings, in turn, create pressure for corrective action. You feel bad and want to do something about it. Anger and frustration, especially, energize the individual for action, create a desire for revenge, and lower inhibitions. There are several possible ways to cope with strain and with these negative emotions, *only some of which involve delinquency*.

Adolescents may cope by *cognitively reinterpreting* the strain they experience so as to minimize its impact. Agnew (1992) lists three major cognitive coping strategies, summarized in these phrases: "It's not that important." "It's not that bad." "I deserve it." Imagine, for example, an individual who is unable to achieve his or her monetary goals. This individual may minimize the failure to obtain enough money by claiming that money is not that important, perhaps claiming that other goals, such as good grades, are more important. Or this individual may come to exaggerate the amount of money they have, claiming that they really have enough money to satisfy their needs, or this individual may state that they are to blame for their lack of money. This may not reduce feelings of depression, but it is likely to reduce anger at others. All these cognitive coping strategies reduce the likelihood that individuals will react to strain with delinquency.

Adolescents may also employ *behavioral* coping strategies, attempting to act in ways that reduce the strain they are experiencing. Certain of these strategies may involve nondelinquent behavior. Adolescents, for example, may get a job to earn money; they may avoid the peers who harass them; or they may negotiate with the teachers who frustrate them. Other behavioral strategies for reducing strain, as indicated earlier, involve delinquency (e.g., stealing money or attacking the peers who harass you).

Finally, adolescents may engage in *emotional* coping. Rather than trying to reduce strain or cognitively reinterpret it, they act directly on the negative emotions that result from strain. They may attempt to reduce their negative emotions through nondelinquent strategies like exercise, deep breathing, listening to music, or other relaxation techniques. Or they may employ delinquent strategies, such as the use of illegal drugs.

The existence of these different coping strategies, some involving delinquency and some not, raises a major question for strain theorists.

Why Are Some Juveniles More Likely to Cope With Strain Through Delinquency?

Strain theorists have argued that several factors influence whether or not people will respond to strain with delinquency (see Agnew, 1992, forthcoming).

Strain is more likely to lead to delinquency when it *involves areas of life that the individual considers important*. For example, financial problems are more likely to result in delinquency among individuals who attach high absolute and relative importance to money (i.e., they state that money is very important to them and that it is more important than other goals). Likewise, challenges to masculinity are more likely to result in delinquency among individuals who attach great importance to their masculine identity. If strain affects a central area of a person's life, it will be more difficult to ignore it or define it away using the cognitive strategies described in the preceding section.

Strain is more likely to lead to delinquency among individuals with *poor coping skills and resources*. Some individuals are better able to legally cope with strain than others. For example, they may have the verbal skills to negotiate with peers and adults, or they have a high level of "self-efficacy," believing that they have the ability to solve their problems. A variety of factors influence an individual's ability to legally cope (without turning to delinquency), including financial resources, intelligence, problem-solving skills, interpersonal skills, and self-efficacy.

Strain is more likely to lead to delinquency among individuals with *few conventional social supports*. Family, friends, and others often help us cope with our problems, providing advice, direct assistance, and emotional support. Such help or support reduces the likelihood of delinquent coping.

Strain is more likely to lead to delinquency when juveniles are in *situations where the costs of delinquency are low and the benefits are high*. Delinquency is therefore more likely when juveniles are in situations where the probability of being caught and punished is low and the rewards of delinquency are high. For example, people are more likely to respond to financial strain with theft if they encounter an open cash register and no one is around.

Finally, strain is more likely to lead to delinquency among *individuals who are disposed to delinquency*. The individual's disposition to engage in delinquency is influenced by a number of factors. As discussed in Chapter 10, certain individual traits, like irritability and impulsivity, increase the disposition for delinquency. Another key factor is whether the individual blames his or her strain on the deliberate behavior of someone else. Such blame makes the individual feel *angry*, which increases the likelihood of delinquency. Other factors include the individual's beliefs regarding delinquency and his or her fear of punishment. Some individuals do not believe that delinquency is wrong, and they have little fear of punishment by others. They are therefore more disposed to respond to strain with crime (see Chapter 8 on control theory). Finally, individuals are more disposed to delinquency if they hold beliefs that justify delinquency; if they have been exposed to delinquent models; and if they have been reinforced for delinquency in the past (see Chapter 7 on social learning theory). This is especially likely to be the case if the individual has delinquent friends.

A variety of factors, then, may influence whether individuals respond to strain with delinquency. Unfortunately, there has not been much research on the extent to which these factors condition the impact of strain, and the research that has been done has produced mixed results.[11]

Summary

At core, strain theory is rather simple: Strain makes you upset and you *may* respond with delinquency. As you can see, however, this rather simple idea has been the subject of much elaboration. In particular, there has been much discussion of the major types of strain that contribute to delinquency and the factors that condition the effect of strain on delinquency. The data provide some support for strain theory, although certain parts of the theory have not been well tested. A fair amount of data indicate that many negative events and conditions involving the loss of positive stimuli or the presentation of negative stimuli increase the likelihood of delinquency. There is less data, however, on whether the inability to achieve the goals of money, status/respect, and autonomy contributes to delinquency. Likewise, there are little data on whether the effect of strain on delinquency is conditioned by the factors listed above. Strain theory, then, might be described as a promising theory with some support.

Notes

1. *See* Felson, 1993; Felson and Steadman, 1983; Lockwood, 1997; Luckenbill, 1977.
2. *See* Compas, 1987; Kohn and Milrose, 1993; Williams and Uchiyama, 1989.

3. *See* Anderson, 1990; Jankowsi, 1995; MacLeod, 1987; Padilla, 1992; Sullivan, 1989.

4. *See* Agnew, 1994a, 1995b; Agnew et al., 1996; Burton and Cullen, 1992.

5. *See* Agnew, 1994a:423–426; Agnew et al., 1996; Burton and Dunaway, 1994; Wright et al., 1999a.

6. *See* Agnew, 1997; Anderson, 1994, 1999; Greenberg, 1977; Majors and Billson, 1992; Messerschmidt, 1993.

7. *See* Anderson, 1994, 1999; Greenberg, 1977; Majors and Billson, 1992; Messerschmidt, 1993.

8. *See* Anderson, 1994, 1997, 1999; Fagan, 1998; Majors and Billson, 1992; Messerschmidt, 1993.

9. *See* Agnew, 1997; Greenberg, 1977; Moffitt, 1993, 1997.

10. *See* Agnew, 1985a, 1992, 1997, forthcoming; Agnew and Brezina, 1997; Agnew and White, 1992; Baron and Hartnagel, 1997; Brezina, 1998; Hagan and McCarthy, 1997a; Hoffmann and Cerbone, 1999; Hoffmann and Miller, 1998; Landau, 1998; Mazerolle and Piquero, 1997, 1998; Paternoster and Mazerolle, 1994.

11. *See* Agnew, forthcoming; Agnew and White, 1992; Hoffmann and Cerbone, 1999; Hoffmann and Miller, 1998; Hoffmann and Su, 1997; Mazerolle and Piquero, 1997; Paternoster and Mazerolle, 1994. ✦

Chapter 7

Social Learning Theory: Do Individuals Learn to Be Delinquent From Others?

Social learning theory says that juveniles *learn* to engage in delinquency, primarily through their association with others. They are reinforced for delinquency; they learn beliefs that are favorable to delinquency, and they are exposed to delinquent models. As a consequence, they come to view delinquency as something that is desirable or at least justifiable in certain situations. The primary version of social learning theory in criminology is that of Akers, and the description that follows draws heavily on his work (Akers, 1985, 1997, 1998; also see Bandura, 1973, 1986). Akers' theory, in turn, represents a reformulation and elaboration of Sutherland's differential association theory (see Matsueda, 1988; Sutherland et al., 1992).

According to social learning theory, juveniles learn to engage in delinquent behavior in the same way they learn to engage in conforming behavior: through association with or exposure to others. Primary or intimate groups like the family and peer group have an especially large impact on what people learn. In fact, association with delinquent friends usually emerges as the best predictor of delinquency, other than prior delinquency.[1] People also learn how to behave through their association with others at their school, job, religious institution, neighborhood, and other settings. Further, people do not have to be in direct contact with others to learn from them; for example, they may learn from observing people in the media.

Most of social learning theory involves a description of the mechanisms by which people learn from others to engage in delinquency. According to the theory, other individuals teach us to engage in delinquency by (1) reinforcing our delinquency, (2) teaching us beliefs favorable to delinquency, and (3) providing delinquent models for us to imitate. I describe each of these learning mechanisms below.

The Differential Reinforcement of Delinquency

Other individuals may teach us to engage in delinquency through the reinforcements and punishments they provide for our behavior. Delinquent behavior is more likely to occur when it (a) is frequently reinforced and infrequently punished; (b) results in large amounts of reinforcement (e.g., a lot of money, social approval, or pleasure) and little punishment; and (c) is more likely to be reinforced than alternative behaviors.

These three factors—*the frequency, amount, and relative probability of reinforcement/punishment*—are easy to understand if you think of a concrete example. Let's begin with the *frequency* of reinforcement and punishment. This simply means that juveniles are more likely to commit a delinquent act like fighting if they are frequently reinforced and seldom punished for fighting. Juveniles who win most of their fights and receive praise from their friends are more likely to fight than juveniles who lose most of their fights and are ridiculed. We tend to repeat behaviors that are reinforced and avoid those that are punished. As for the *amount* of reinforcement and punishment, juveniles who receive *a lot* of reinforcement and *little* punishment for fighting are more likely to fight than juveniles who receive little reinforcement and much punishment. The *relative probability of reinforcement* refers to the likelihood that delinquent acts will be reinforced relative to other behaviors. For example, juveniles who get into conflicts with others might resolve these conflicts through fighting or through negotiation. They are more likely to choose fighting if fighting is more likely to result in reinforcement than negotiation. The term "differential reinforcement" means simply that different behaviors have different probabilities of being reinforced. We are more likely to engage in behaviors with the highest probabilities of reinforcement. I encourage you to think of additional examples involving the frequency, amount, and relative probability of reinforcement/punishment.

Positive and Negative Reinforcement

Reinforcement may be positive or negative. In *positive reinforcement*, the behavior results in something good—some positive consequence. This consequence may be in the form of money; the pleasurable feelings associated with drug use; attention from parents; approval from friends; or an increase in social status. For example, suppose you shoplift a video game with your friends. Your friends congratulate you for the theft and you spend the afternoon playing the game with them. The approval of your friends and the pleasure you get from playing the game function as positive reinforcers for your shoplifting. In *negative reinforcement*, a behavior results in the removal of something bad—a punisher is removed or avoided. For example, suppose your friends have been calling you a coward because you refuse to use drugs with them. You eventually take drugs with them, after which time they stop calling you a coward. Your drug use has been negatively reinforced.

Punishment

Reinforcement increases the likelihood that a behavior will be repeated, and punishment reduces the likelihood that a behavior will be repeated. Like reinforcement, punishment may be either positive or negative. *Positive punishment* involves the presentation of something bad. For example, you engage in a delinquent act and your parents spank you or verbally reprimand you. *Negative punishment* involves the removal of something good. For example, your parents punish your delinquency by reducing your allowance or prohibiting you from watching your favorite TV show.

The Sources of Reinforcement and Punishment

Our behavior is reinforced and punished by family members, friends, teachers, neighborhood residents, and others, although family members and friends are the major sources of reinforcement and punishment for juveniles. People may also engage in *self*-reinforcement and punishment. Individuals usually adopt or internalize standards for their behavior from others—parents, for example. They may then evaluate their own behavior using these standards, praising themselves when they meet these standards and criticizing themselves when they do not (see Akers, 1998: 72–75; Bandura, 1973:207–221, 1986:335–389).

According to social learning theory, some individuals are more likely to be reinforced for delinquency than others. Sometimes this reinforcement is *deliberate*. For example, the parents of aggressive children often deliberately encourage and reinforce aggressive behavior outside the home (Anderson, 1994; Bandura, 1973). Anderson (1994:86) states that *some* families in inner-city communities tell their children that they should respond to provocations with aggression. Further,

> Many parents actually impose sanctions if a child is not sufficiently aggressive. For example, if a child loses a fight and comes home upset, the parent might respond, "Don't you come in here crying that somebody beat you up; you better get back out there and whup his ass. I didn't raise no punks! Get back out there and whup his ass. If you don't whup his ass, I'll whup your ass when you come home." Thus the child obtains reinforcement for being tough and showing nerve.

At other times, the reinforcement for delinquency is less deliberate (see Patterson et al., 1989; Patterson et al., 1992). Two common scenarios will illustrate what I mean. First, a mother repeatedly asks her son to clean up his room. The son ignores her. The mother eventually starts to yell at and threaten her son. The son yells back at his mother and then slams the door to his room and locks it. The mother, exasperated with her son's behavior, leaves. Without intending to do so, the mother has just negatively reinforced her son's belligerent behavior. Second, a father takes his daughter to the supermarket. The daughter says she wants a candy bar at the check-out line, but the father refuses. The daughter repeatedly asks for the candy bar, but the father continues to refuse. Eventually, the daughter is screaming for the candy bar and attempting to hit her father. Everyone is now watching and the embarrassed father gives his daughter the candy bar. The daughter stops screaming and eats the bar. In this instance, the father has positively reinforced his daughter's screaming and hitting by giving her a candy bar. Also, the daughter has negatively reinforced the father for giving in to her demand (she stopped screaming after she got the candy bar).

Some individuals are also in environments where *conventional behaviors are not reinforced*. Many parents, for example, often ignore or otherwise fail to reinforce the conventional behavior of their children (Patterson et al., 1989; Patterson et al., 1992). For example, they ignore a child who brings home good grades or displays good manners at a social function, rather than praising him or her. In some cases, conventional behaviors may even be punished. For example, behaviors like studying or cooperating with teachers are punished in certain peer groups. And "inmates" in juvenile institutions often reinforce behaviors like fighting and punish behaviors like cooperating with the staff.

According to social learning theory, individuals in these types of environments should be more likely to engage in delinquency, since we tend to repeat behaviors that are reinforced and avoid those that are punished.

Intermittent Reinforcement

Delinquents, of course, are rarely reinforced for every delinquent act they commit. Only some of their delinquent acts are reinforced. For example, it may be the case that only every third or fourth delinquent act, on average, results in significant reinforcement. This type of schedule is referred to as an *intermittent schedule of reinforcement* (as opposed to a continuous schedule of reinforcement, in which every act is reinforced). Such intermittent schedules, however, are usually sufficient to maintain a behavior. (For example, witness the behavior of slot machine players: They continue to pour money into the machine even though they are only occasionally reinforced.) In fact, behaviors that are reinforced on an intermittent schedule are *more* difficult to eliminate than those reinforced on a continuous schedule. As Bandura states, "behavior that has been reinforced on a thin unpredictable schedule is exceedingly difficult to extinguish because one's efforts are sustained by the belief that the actions will eventually prove successful" (1973:186).

Discriminative Stimuli

Juveniles usually find that their delinquency is more likely to be reinforced in some situations than in others. For example, smoking marijuana *with your friends* may result in much reinforcement, including the approval and companionship of your friends. Smoking marijuana in front of your *parents*, however, may result in far more punishment than reinforcement. Individuals soon learn to distinguish between situations in which delinquency is likely to be reinforced and those in which it is likely to be punished. They do so based on *"discriminative stimuli,"* such as the presence of friends or parents. Juveniles, of course, are most likely to commit delinquent acts in situations where the probability of reinforcement is highest.

Research on the Reinforcement and Punishment of Delinquency

Numerous studies have examined the effect of reinforcement and punishment on delinquency and aggression.[2] Experimental studies have focused on the effects of reinforcing or punishing aggressive behavior. For example, children might be rewarded with praise or with marbles for hitting a toy clown. These experiments usually indicate that such reinforcement or punishment has a strong effect on subsequent aggression (which might be measured by how often the child continues to hit the toy clown). Surveys and observational studies have examined the impact of reinforcement and punishment on various types of delinquency. In one well-known survey, for example, Akers and his colleagues asked a sample of adolescents a series of questions about the reinforcements and punishments they received for drug and alcohol use.[3] The researchers asked, for example, about the positive and negative sanctions that friends and parents have applied (or would apply) to the respondent for using drugs. Such sanctions ranged from encouraging drug use to turning the adolescents in to the authorities. They also asked about the effects that alcohol and drugs have on the respondent, with responses ranging from mostly bad to mostly good. Such studies also tend to find that reinforcement and punishment have an important effect on behavior.

Beliefs Favorable to Delinquency

Other individuals may not only reinforce our delinquency, they may also teach us beliefs favorable to delinquency. Most individuals, of course, are taught that delinquency is bad or wrong. They eventually accept or "internalize" this belief, and they are less likely to engage in delinquency as a result. For example, suppose I were to ask you why you do *not* burglarize houses or rob people. You would probably reply that burglary and robbery are wrong. This value is what you have been taught all your life—by parents, friends, and others—and you have come to believe it. Some individuals, however, learn beliefs that are favorable to delinquency, and they are more likely to engage in delinquency as a result.

When I speak of "beliefs favorable to delinquency," I do *not* mean that some people believe that serious delinquent acts like burglary and robbery are *generally good or acceptable*. Very few people, including delinquents, generally approve of serious delinquent acts.[4] Surveys and interviews with juveniles suggest that beliefs favoring delinquency fall into three categories, and data suggest that each type of belief increases the likelihood of delinquency.[5]

Generally Approve of Minor Delinquency

Some juveniles *generally approve of or hold neutral attitudes toward certain minor forms of delinquency*, such as sexual intercourse between consenting adolescents; certain forms of gambling, truancy, and curfew violations; and certain forms of alcohol and "soft" drug use. For example, a nationwide survey of high school seniors in 1998 found that 27.9 percent believed that using marijuana should be "entirely legal" (see the *Sourcebook of Criminal Justice Statistics* at *www.albany.edu/sourcebook.html*). Presumably, these seniors generally approve of marijuana use. Many additional juveniles have a *neutral attitude* toward delinquent acts like marijuana use. That is, they neither approve nor disapprove of these acts. This neutral attitude does not directly encourage delinquency, but it increases its likelihood because the attitude fails to restrain delinquency (see the discussion of control theory in Chapter 8).

Conditionally Approve of Delinquency, Including Some Serious Delinquency

Some juveniles *conditionally approve of, justify, or excuse certain forms of delinquency, including some serious delinquent acts*. These juveniles believe that delinquency is generally wrong but that some delinquent acts are excusable, justifiable, or even desirable *in certain conditions*. Many juveniles, for example, will state that fighting is generally wrong but that it is justified if you have been insulted or provoked in some way. In a study employing data from a national sample of adolescents, I found that 16 percent of the respondents believed that "if people do something to make you really mad, they deserve to be beaten up" (Agnew, 1994b). Another study found that 18 percent of arrested males and 34 percent of gang members agreed that "it is okay to shoot someone who disrespected you" (Decker et al., 1997). Yet another study found that 28 percent of inner-city high school students and 61 percent of inmates in juvenile institutions agreed that it is "okay to shoot someone who hurts or insults you" (Sheley and Wright, 1995). Several theorists have argued that certain groups in our society—especially lower-class young minority males—are more likely to define violence as an acceptable response to a wide range of provocations and insults. They claim that this "subculture of violence" is at least partly responsible for the higher rate of violence in these groups. Data in this area are somewhat mixed, but recent studies suggest that males, young people, and possibly lower-class people and people from poor neighborhoods are more likely to hold beliefs favorable to violence. There is less evidence for a relationship between race and beliefs favorable to violence.[6]

Sykes and Matza (1957) argue that the excuses and justifications employed by juveniles assume five basic forms, each of which specifies the conditions in which crime is justified/excused.

1. Denial of responsibility: Delinquents claim that delinquency is justifiable or excusable when a person is not responsible for his or her behavior (e.g., "I was drunk and didn't know what I was doing" or "My parents abused me and I can't help myself").

2. Denial of injury: Delinquents claim that delinquency is justifiable or excusable when no one is harmed by it (e.g., "Insurance will cover the loss" or "I was just borrowing the car").

3. Denial of the victim: Delinquents claim that delinquency is justifiable when the victim deserves it (e.g., "The store owner is dishonest" or "She started it by insulting me").

4. Condemnation of the condemners: Delinquents claim that delinquency is justifiable or excusable when those who condemn you also engage in questionable behavior (e.g., "All the cops and politicians are crooked" or "My parents drink and that's just as bad as using marijuana").

5. Appeal to higher loyalties: Delinquents claim that delinquency is justifiable when it serves some higher purpose ("I did it to help my friends" or "to protect my turf").

Other researchers have listed additional justifications and excuses.[7] Not all juveniles accept such justifications/excuses, but those who do are more likely to engage in delinquency.

Many of us employ such justifications/excuses when we engage in deviant acts, minor or otherwise. Suppose, for example, you wake up one morning and do not feel like going to class. You may believe that cutting class is generally bad, but you tell yourself that in your case it is justified because you are not feeling well (a form of "denial of responsibility"). What other sorts of justifications/excuses do students employ for cutting class and for other forms of deviance like cheating on exams (see Agnew and Peters, 1985; McCabe, 1992)? Do these justifications/excuses fall into the categories described by Sykes and Matza or are additional categories necessary?

General Values Conducive to Delinquency

Some juveniles hold certain *general values that are conducive to delinquency*. These values do not explicitly approve of or justify delinquency, but they make delinquency appear a more attractive alternative than might otherwise be the case. Theorists have listed three general sets of values in this area.[8] The first is an attraction to "excitement," "thrills," or "kicks." The desire for excitement can be satisfied through legitimate as well as illegitimate means, but criminal activities hold a special appeal since they have the added element of danger—of "experimenting with the forbidden."

Individuals who value excitement, then, are more likely to find crime an attractive alternative in a given situation. The second value involves a disdain for hard work and a desire for quick, easy success. Many delinquents, for example, are said to have "grandiose dreams of quick success." Crime, of course, would have an obvious appeal to those who place a low value on hard work and a high value on money and pleasure. Finally, delinquents are said to place a high value on toughness—on being "macho." Macho includes being physically strong, being able to defend yourself, not letting others "push you around," and showing bravery in the face of physical threat. Such individuals will clearly view delinquent activities like fighting in a more favorable light than people without those values.

Where Do the Beliefs Favorable to Delinquency Come From?

Juveniles learn the beliefs favorable to delinquency from others, including family members, friends, community residents, and the media. Data suggest that delinquent friends are an especially important source of such beliefs.[9] Also, juveniles often come to adopt such beliefs *after* engaging in delinquency.[10] In particular, juveniles who engage in delinquency—for whatever reason—often find it advantageous to adopt such beliefs. Such beliefs allow them to neutralize whatever guilt they might feel and to reduce the likelihood of punishment by others (which is why young children often try to convince their parents that the victims of their delinquency deserved it). Once such definitions are adopted, however, they make further delinquency more likely since they define delinquency in a favorable light or at least allow a juvenile to justify or excuse delinquent behavior.

The Imitation of Delinquent Models

People's behavior is not only a function of their beliefs and the reinforcements and punishments they receive, but also of the behavior of those around them. In particular, people often imitate or model the behavior of others, especially when they have reason to believe that such imitation will result in reinforcement. It is perhaps for this reason that we are most likely to imitate a model when we "like or respect the model, see the model receive reinforcement, see the model give off signs of pleasure, or are in an environment where imitating the model's performance is reinforced" (Baldwin and Baldwin, 1981:187). Data from a wide range of studies demonstrate the importance of modeling (see Akers, 1997, 1998; Bandura, 1973, 1986). A large number of experimental studies, for example, have exposed individuals to aggressive models and then observed the impact of such exposure on the subjects' behavior. Such studies typically demonstrate an increase in aggression.

I should note that some people may *inadvertently* model delinquent or aggressive behavior for juveniles, just as they inadvertently reinforce delinquency/aggression. Parents, for example, may punish aggression in their children by spanking or beating them, or parents who smoke or drink may warn their children about the dangers of drug use. In each case, the parents are modeling the type of behavior they wish to stop in their child. Such modeling increases the likelihood of delinquency in the child.[11]

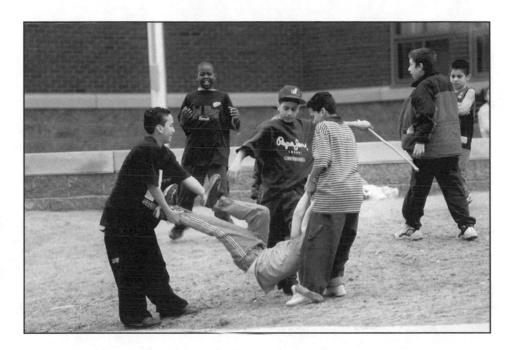

We do not have to be in direct contact with the models we imitate. In fact, a good deal of research has focused on the extent to which juveniles model the aggressive behavior of those in the media, especially television. The media often show glamorous characters engaging in frequent and extreme forms of violence. Such characters often receive much reinforcement and little punishment for their aggression. As Bandura (1973:101) states, "the modern child has witnessed innumerable stabbings, shootings, stompings, stranglings, muggings and less blatant but equally destructive forms of cruelty before [he/she] has reached kindergarten age." The negative impact of media violence is discussed in Chapter 14.

Summary

Social learning theory has much support. Data indicate that people in our environment have a strong impact on whether we become delinquent and that this impact is partly explained by the effect these people have on our beliefs regarding delinquency, the reinforcements and punishments we receive, and the models we are exposed to. Social learning theory and control theory, described in Chapter 8, are the leading explanations of delinquency (Ellis and Walsh, 1999).

Notes

1. *See* Akers, 1998; Elliott et al., 1985; Elliott and Menard, 1996; Gorman and White, 1995; Huizinga et al., 1998.
2. For overviews, see Akers, 1985, 1997, 1998; Bandura, 1973; Patterson et al., 1992.
3. *See* Akers et al., 1979; also see Akers, 1998; Krohn et al., 1985; Patterson et al., 1992; Thornberry et al., 1994.
4. *See* Matza, 1964; Short and Strodtbeck, 1965; Agnew, 1994a.

5. *See* Agnew, 1994b, 1995b; Akers, 1998; Akers et al., 1979; Heimer, 1997; Markowitz and Felson, 1998; Thornberry et al. 1994; Zhang et al., 1997.

6. *See* Anderson, 1994, 1999; Cao et al., 1997; Fagan, 1998; Heimer, 1997; Markowitz and Felson, 1998; Sampson and Dartusch, 1999; Wolfgang and Ferracuti, 1982.

7. *See* Bandura, 1990; Conklin, 1992; Minor, 1981.

8. *See* especially Matza and Sykes, 1961; also see Agnew, 1995b; Curtis, 1974; England, 1960; Miller, 1958; Vaz, 1967.

9. *See* Agnew, 1995b; Akers, 1998; Heimer, 1997; Matsueda and Heimer, 1987; Thornberry et al., 1994, 1998; Warr and Stafford, 1991.8-28-00

10. *See* Agnew, 1995b; Heimer, 1997; Thornberry et al., 1994; Zhang et al., 1997.

11. *See* Bandura, 1986; Heimer, 1997; Patterson et al., 1992. ✦

Chapter 8

Control Theory: Do Weak Controls Result in Delinquency?

Strain and social learning theorists ask: "Why do juveniles engage in delinquency?" They then focus on the factors that push or entice juveniles into committing delinquent acts. Control theorists, in contrast, begin with the question "Why do juveniles *conform*?" Unlike strain and social learning theorists, control theorists take the existence of delinquency for granted. They argue that all people have needs and desires that are more easily satisfied through delinquency than through legal channels. For example, it is much easier to steal money than to work for it. So in the eyes of control theorists, delinquency requires no special explanation; it is usually the most expedient way for people to get what they want. These theorists argue that rather than explaining why people engage in delinquency, we need to explain why they do not.

This argument may strike you as odd. Most of us take conformity for granted and feel that delinquency is in need of explanation. If you observe the behavior of very young children, however, you begin to appreciate the argument of control theorists. When these children want something, they simply take it, whether it belongs to them or not. When they get angry, they often hit and shove others. And when their verbal skills are sufficiently developed, they often lie and deceive others. Their behavior, however, usually does not impress us as odd; they are simply trying to satisfy their needs and desires in the most direct, expedient way possible. Control theorists ask why most older juveniles and adults do not do the same.

Why Do Juveniles Conform (and Sometimes Deviate)?

According to control theorists, people do not engage in delinquency because of the controls or restraints placed on them. While strain and social learning theory focus on the factors that push or lead the individual into delinquency, control theory focuses on the factors that restrain the individual from engaging in delinquency.

Let me provide some examples of these controls or restraints. Each year I ask the students in my juvenile delinquency class the following question: "Why are you not a delinquent?" (or, in some cases, "Why are you a delinquent?"). Students then write their responses on a sheet of paper. Here are some examples of the most common types of responses: "I know the difference between what's right and wrong." "My parents raised me to respect the laws and follow them." "I was disciplined by my parents." "It's at odds with my belief in right and wrong, which comes from my religion." "I feel too guilty when I do something wrong." "Because I am afraid of getting caught." "My family would be greatly disappointed." "My parents would disown me." "My parents would kill me." "I'm worried about what my friends would think or say." "The consequences could somehow affect my college career and my other career goals." "I have many plans for the future and delinquency may hinder or destroy my future." "It would look bad on my resume." "I have more to lose than to gain from being delinquent." "I can control my anger instead of resorting to violence when I am in a conflict."

These responses nicely illustrate many of the controls or restraints that prevent people from engaging in delinquency (at least frequent or serious delinquency). We do not engage in delinquency because we believe it is wrong and because we fear that we will be caught and sanctioned in some way. We might get arrested, hurt people we care about, jeopardize our education and future career, and so on. Our beliefs and fear of sanctions, then, act as controls or restraints on our behavior: They help explain our conformity.

Control theory argues that people differ in their level of control, or in the restraints they face to delinquency. Some individuals are high in control; for example, they believe that delinquency is very wrong and that they would be heavily sanctioned if they committed a delinquent act. They would upset their beloved parents; their friends would leave them; they would lose their scholarship to college; they would ruin their chances of getting into law school; and so on. According to control theory, such individuals should be less likely than others to engage in delinquency.

Other individuals, however, are low in control; for example, they believe that delinquency is only a little bit wrong and that they would *not* be heavily sanctioned if they committed a delinquent act. They do not care what their parents think about them; their friends would not leave them; they have no scholarship to lose; and they have no plans for going to law school. According to control theory, such individuals should be more likely to engage in delinquency. Nothing is holding them back from delinquency, and so they are *free* to pursue their wants and desires in the most expedient way possible, which often involves delinquency. So if they see something they want, they may steal it.

How Is Control Theory Similar to and Different From Social Learning Theory?

If you have been following this discussion closely, you may have noticed that there is some overlap between control theory and social learning theory. Social learning theory not only has a lot to say about the factors that *cause* delinquency, it also has a lot to say about the factors that *prevent* delinquency. In this area, both control theory and social learning theory argue that delinquency is less likely when it is sanctioned or punished and when conformity is reinforced. Individuals may be sanctioned by others, like parents and school officials, and they may sanction themselves if they believe that delinquency is wrong. Both theories, then, focus on the extent to which delinquency is prevented through sanctions. There is, however, a crucial difference between the theories.

Social learning theory also focuses on the extent to which delinquency is *motivated* through modeling, beliefs, and reinforcement. Some individuals are said to have a relatively strong motivation for delinquency because they have been exposed to delinquent models, have learned beliefs favorable to delinquency, and have been reinforced for delinquency. Social learning theory, then, is broader than control theory since it focuses on both the factors that prevent delinquency *and the factors that motivate it*. Theorists like Akers (1985) and Conger (1976) have argued that social learning theory is a more powerful theory as a result and that it is capable of incorporating control theory.

Control theorists, however, argue that it is not important to examine the motivation for delinquency. They claim that the motivation for delinquency is more or less equally strong for everyone: that we all have unfulfilled wants and desires that would more easily be satisfied through delinquency. Delinquency is said to be largely a function of differences in the level of control. As the leading control theorist has stated: "control theories assume that the potential for asocial conduct is present in everyone, that we would all commit delinquent acts were we not somehow prevented from doing so. . . . The important differences between delinquents and non delinquents are not differences in motivation; they are, rather, differences in the extent to which natural motives are controlled."[1]

What Are the Major Types of Control (or Restraints to Delinquency)?

Control theories basically describe the major types of control or the major restraints to delinquency. The leading control theory is that of Hirschi (1969), who lists four types of social control. Major versions of control theory have also been developed by Reiss (1951), Toby (1957), Nye (1958), Reckless (1961), Matza (1964), Briar and Piliavin (1965), Kornhauser (1978), Gottfredson and Hirschi (1990), and Sampson and Laub (1993a). Rather than describing the different types of control in all of these theories, I will present a generic version of control theory that draws from them.

This generic theory lists three major types of control, with each type having two or more components. The first type is *direct control*, which refers to the efforts of others to directly control the juvenile's behavior by (a) setting rules for the juvenile, (b) monitoring the juvenile's behavior, (c) sanctioning the juvenile for rule violations and delinquency, and (d) reinforcing the juvenile for conventional behavior. The second type of control or restraint is the juvenile's *stake in conformity*, which refers to things that the juvenile might lose by engaging in delinquency. Juveniles with a lot to lose should be less likely to engage in delinquency. Stake in conformity is a function of the juvenile's (a) emotional attachment to conventional others and (b) actual or anticipated investment in conventional activities (like getting an education). The third type of control is *internal control*, which refers to the juvenile's efforts to restrain himself or herself from delinquency. Internal control is a function of the juvenile's (a) beliefs regarding delinquency and (b) ability to exercise self-control, as indexed by several personality traits. Control is highest, then, when others try to control the juvenile's behavior, when the juvenile has a lot to lose by engaging in delinquency, and when the juvenile tries to control his or her own behavior.

Direct Control

When most people think of control, they think of direct control: someone watching over the juvenile and sanctioning him or her for deviance. Such control may be exercised by parents, school officials, neighborhood residents, police, and others. Parents, however, are the major source of direct control, given their long-standing and intimate relationship with the juvenile. Direct control has four components: setting rules, monitoring behavior, sanctioning deviance/delinquency, and reinforcing conventional behavior.

Setting rules. Direct control is enhanced to the extent that parents and others provide the juvenile with clearly defined rules that prohibit delinquent behavior and that limit the opportunities and temptations for delinquency. These rules may specify who the juvenile associates with; for example, parents may forbid or strongly discourage their children from associating with juveniles who seem prone to delinquency. The rules may specify where the juvenile can and cannot go; for example, some parents may forbid their children from spending time in unsupervised locations, such as the street. The rules may specify the activities in which juveniles can and cannot engage; for example, some parents may forbid their children from attending unsupervised parties. The rules may specify what the juvenile can and cannot have; for example, parents may limit the spending money of their children or refuse to allow them to dress in a certain way. These rules may also specify time restrictions for the juvenile; for example, parents frequently impose curfews on their children.

Monitoring. Direct control involves more than just setting rules. It also involves monitoring juveniles' behavior to ensure that they comply with the rules and do not engage in delinquency. Monitoring may be direct or indirect. In direct monitoring, the juvenile is under the direct surveillance of a parent or other conventional "authority figure." In indirect monitoring, the parent or authority figure does not directly observe the juvenile but makes an effort to keep tabs on what the juvenile is doing. The parent, for example, may ask the juvenile where he or she is going, may periodically phone him or her, may ask others about the juvenile's behavior, or the like. Juveniles obviously differ in the extent to which their behavior is monitored. In some cases, a parent meets the juvenile when he or she arrives home from school and the juvenile is seldom out of the sight of adults. In other cases, the juvenile's parents are seldom at home, or the juvenile spends much time on the street or in other locations where monitoring by conventional adults is minimal.

Setting rules and monitoring behavior should restrain delinquency: The rules prohibit delinquency and limit the temptations and opportunities for delinquency, while monitoring increases the likelihood that rule violations/delinquency will be detected. Several studies have examined the relationship between setting rules, monitoring, and delinquency, with most such studies focusing on parents.[2] These studies tend to find that higher levels of rule setting/monitoring are associated with moderately lower levels of delinquency, although certain data suggest that *overly strict* parents may be ineffective or that they may even increase delinquency (perhaps for reasons related to strain theory).

Sanctioning delinquency. Parents and others may closely supervise the child—setting rules and monitoring behavior—but they may fail to effectively sanction delinquency/deviance when it occurs. Direct control, then, is enhanced to the extent that delinquency/deviance is effectively sanctioned. What do I mean by "effectively sanctioned"? Effective sanctions are *consistently applied*. Studies indicate that the failure to punish and the inconsistent use of punishment contribute to delinquency. Effective punishments are also *fairly applied*; that is, the child is punished only when he or she deserves it and the punishment fits the offense (e.g., the child is not severely punished for trivial infractions). Further, effective punishments are *not overly harsh*. Data suggest that punishments using physical violence and verbal abuse are not effective; in fact, they tend to increase delinquency.[3] Such punishments may create "fear and resentment" in the child and "break the bonds of respect" between parent and child (Sampson and Laub, 1993a: 68, 73). Many researchers recommend punishments like verbally condemning the act and explaining why it is wrong; time out; withdrawal of privileges; and requiring the juvenile to perform certain tasks (e.g., Patterson and Gullion, 1977; Straus, 1994).[4]

Reinforcing conventional behavior. Parents and others should not only sanction delinquency but should also reinforce conventional behaviors that compete with or provide alternatives to the delinquency. For example, suppose your child frequently resorts to violence when he or she gets into disputes with others. You should not only punish your child for such violence, you should also teach the child how to resolve disputes through verbal means, and you should reinforce them when they do so.

Stake in Conformity

The efforts of others to directly control juveniles' behavior are a major restraint to delinquency. These efforts, however, are more effective with some juveniles than with others. For example, all juveniles are subject to more or less the same direct controls at school: the same rules, the same monitoring, and the same sanctions if they deviate. Yet some juveniles are very responsive to these controls, while others commit deviant acts on a regular basis. There are several reasons for this difference, but one fundamental reason is that some juveniles have *more to lose* by engaging in deviance. These juveniles have what has been called a high "stake in conformity," and they do not want to jeopardize that stake by engaging in deviance/delinquency (see Toby, 1957). For example, imagine two students: one has an "A" average and dreams of going to Harvard, and the other has a "D" average and dreams of dropping out of school. Who do you think is going to be more responsive to the threat of school sanctions?

An individual's stake in conformity—what a person stands to lose by engaging in delinquency—functions as another major restraint to delinquency. Those with a lot to lose will be more fearful of being caught and sanctioned and so will be less likely to engage in delinquency. A stake in conformity has two components: (1) emotional attachment to conventional others and (2) the actual or anticipated investment in conventional society.

Emotional attachment to conventional others. If we have a strong emotional attachment to conventional others, like parents and teachers, we have more to lose by engaging in delinquency. Our delinquency may upset people we care about, cause them to think badly of us, and possibly disrupt our relationship with them. For example, many of the students in my juvenile delinquency class report that they do not engage in delinquency because they do not want to hurt their parents or cause their parents to think badly of them. People's emotional bond to conventional others, then, is one major component of their "stake in conformity."

Studies generally confirm the importance of this bond.[5] Individuals who report that they love and respect their parents and other conventional figures are usually lower in delinquency. Individuals who do not care about their parents or others have less to lose by engaging in delinquency and so are more "free" to act on their desires. The association between emotional attachment and delinquency, however, is usually small to moderate in size. I should note an attachment to *delinquent* others does not reduce delinquency, since delinquency is not likely to jeopardize the relationship with these others. Attachment to delinquent others often increases delinquency, as one would expect from social learning theory.[6]

Actual or anticipated investment in conventional activities. A second major component of a person's stake in conformity is her or his investment in conventional society. Most people have put a lot of time and energy into conventional activities, like "getting an education, building up a business, [and] acquiring a reputation for virtue" (Hirschi, 1969:20). And they have been rewarded for their efforts in the form of good grades, material possessions, a good reputation, and the like. Juveniles may also expect their efforts to reap certain rewards in the future; for example, they may anticipate getting into college or professional school, obtaining a good job, and living in a nice house. In short, they have a large investment—both actual and anticipated—in conventional society. They do not want to jeopardize that investment by engaging in delinquency. Once again, they have too much to lose. Studies usually indicate that delinquency is moderately lower among juveniles who like school, are doing well in school, and have high educational and occupational expectations.[7]

Internal Control

Imagine that you had the opportunity to steal something that you wanted but could not afford. Imagine further that you were certain that you would not be caught and sanctioned. Would you do it? Some of you will say "yes"; the absence of direct controls and the feeling that you have nothing to lose are enough to result in your delinquency. Others, however, will say "no." That is because you are high in internal control: *You* are able to *restrain yourself* from committing delinquency. Your level of internal control is a function of your beliefs regarding delinquency and your level of self-control. Internal control is obviously important, since we all sometimes find ourselves in situations where we are tempted to engage in crime and the probability of external sanction is low.

Beliefs regarding delinquency. Most people believe that delinquency is wrong, and this belief acts as a major restraint to the performance of delinquent acts. The extent to which people believe that delinquency is wrong is at least partly a function of their level of direct control and their stake in conformity. Did their parents provide them with a clear set of rules that condemned delinquency? Did their parents monitor their behavior and punish delinquency? Such actions serve to teach children that delinquency is wrong. Were the children strongly attached to their parents? Such attachment increases the likelihood that the children will adopt parental beliefs. Finally, do they have a large investment in conventional society? People are more likely to accept conventional beliefs when it is to their advantage to do so.

Individuals who are low in direct control and have a low stake in conformity are less likely to believe that delinquency is wrong. Rather, such individuals often have an *amoral orientation* to delinquency: They believe that delinquency is neither good nor bad. As a consequence, their beliefs do not *restrain* them from engaging in delinquency. Their beliefs do *not* propel or push them into delinquency; they do not believe that delinquency is good. Their amoral beliefs simply *free* them to pursue their needs and desires in the most expedient way. Unlike social learning theorists, most control theorists argue that few people define delinquency as good or acceptable. Rather then being *taught* that delinquency is good, control theorists argue that some juveniles are simply *not taught that delinquency is bad*.

Studies suggest that juveniles do differ in the extent to which they condemn delinquency. Most juveniles define delinquent acts, especially serious acts, as generally wrong. A significant minority of juveniles, however, have a somewhat amoral view of delinquent acts. For example, a national sample of adolescents was asked, "How wrong is it for someone your age to hit or threaten to hit someone without any reason?" Seven percent of the respondents replied "a little bit wrong," while 93 percent said "wrong" or "very wrong." Individuals with amoral beliefs are somewhat more likely to engage in delinquency (Hirschi, 1969; Kornhauser, 1978). (Studies, however, also suggest that many juveniles do have beliefs favorable to delinquency, as described in the chapter on social learning theory.)

Self-control. Several types of control or restraints to delinquency have been listed in the preceding pages, including direct control, stake in conformity, and beliefs regarding delinquency. Some individuals, however, are less responsive to these controls than others. These individuals have trouble restraining themselves from acting on their immediate desires. For example, if someone provokes them, they are more likely to get into a fight. Or if someone offers them drugs at a party, they are more likely to accept. They do not stop to consider the long-term consequences of their behavior. Rather, they simply focus on the immediate, short-term benefits or pleasures of the delinquent act. In the words of Gottfredson and Hirschi (1990:87), they are more "vulnerable to the temptations of the moment." Such individuals are said to be low in "self-control."

Self-control is indexed by several personality traits. According to Gottfredson and Hirschi (1990:90), "people who lack self control will tend to be impulsive, insensitive, physical (as opposed to mental), risk-taking, short-sighted, and nonverbal."[8] Many of these traits are discussed in Chapter 10. Certain researchers claim that the major cause of low self-control is "ineffective child-rearing." In particular, low self-control is more likely to result when parents do not establish a strong emotional bond with their children, do not properly supervise their activities, and do not sanction them for delinquency. As discussed in Chapter 10, certain theorists also claim that some of the traits characterizing low self-control have biological as well as social causes. Several recent studies have examined the relationship between self-control and delinquency and have found that people with low self-control are more delinquent.[9]

Summary

Control theory asks why juveniles conform rather than why they deviate. And it says we conform because of the controls or restraints placed on our behavior. In particular, conformity is most likely when others attempt to directly control our behavior, when we have a large stake in conformity, and when we are able to control our own behavior. Conversely, delinquency is most likely when these forms of control are low or absent. In such cases, individuals are free to satisfy their needs and desires in the most expedient way— which is often through delinquent acts. The data are generally supportive of control theory, and, as indicated earlier, control and social learning theories are the leading explanations of delinquency.

Notes

1. *See* Hirschi, 1977:329; also see Kornhauser, 1978:46–50; Agnew, 1993.
2. *See* Browning and Huizinga, 1999; Burton et al., 1995; Farrington, 1996a; Hagan, 1989; Hawkins, Herrenkohl, Farrington, Brewer, Catalano, and Harachi, 1998; Huizinga et al., 1998; Loeber, Farrington, Stouthamer-Loeber, and Van Kammen, 1998; Loeber and Stouthamer-Loeber, 1986; Nye, 1958; Patterson et al., 1992; Sampson and Laub, 1993a; Snyder and Patterson, 1987; Thornberry et al., 1998; Wells and Rankin, 1988; Wright and Wright, 1995.
3. *See* Agnew, 1983; Loeber and Stouthamer-Loeber, 1986; Nye, 1958; Patterson et al., 1992; Sampson and Laub, 1993a; Snyder and Patterson, 1987; Straus, 1994; Wells and Rankin, 1988; Wright and Wright, 1995.
4. For additional information on the factors influencing the effectiveness of punishment, see Bandura, 1973:222–227; Quay, 1983; and Snyder and Patterson, 1987; see Patterson and Gullion, 1977, for a child training manual.
5. *See* Costello and Vowell, 1999; Hirschi, 1969; Jang, 1999; Loeber and Stouthamer-Loeber, 1986; Rankin and Kern, 1994; Sampson and Laub, 1993a; Wright et al., 1999b; Wright and Wright, 1995; see Kempf, 1993, for an overview.
6. *See* Agnew, 1991b; Conger, 1976; Jensen and Brownfield, 1983.
7. *See* Costello and Vowell, 1999; Hawkins and Lishner, 1987; Hirschi, 1969; Jang, 1999; Kempf, 1993; Maguin and Loeber, 1996; Sampson and Laub, 1993a; Thornberry et al., 1998; Wright et al., 1999b.
8. *See* Cohen and Villa, 1996; Grasmick et al., 1993; Longshore et al., 1996.
9. *See* Burton et al., 1998; Evans et al., 1997; Grasmick et al., 1993; LaGrange and Silverman, 1999; Le Blanc, 1993; Longshore, 1998; Piquero and Tibbetts, 1996; Polakowski, 1994; Wood et al., 1993; Wright et al., 1999b. ✦

Chapter 9

Reviewing and Applying the Major Delinquency Theories

This section began by asking: "Why do they do it?" It then examined the three leading explanations of why juveniles break the law: strain theory, social learning theory, and control theory. The best way to review these theories is to list their major independent variables and their explanations of *why* these independent variables cause delinquency.

An Overview of Strain, Social Learning, and Control Theories

Strain theory focuses on two major categories of strain: goal blockage and the loss of positive stimuli/presentation of negative stimuli. The experience of strain leads to negative emotions like anger and frustration, and individuals *may* turn to delinquency in an effort to cope with strain and these emotions. Delinquency may allow them to reduce or escape from their strain, seek revenge against those who have wronged them, or manage their negative emotions (through illicit drug use).

Social learning theory focuses on the extent to which individuals associate with others who reinforce delinquency, present beliefs favorable to delinquency, and model delinquent behavior. These activities lead individuals to believe that delinquency is a desirable or at least justifiable response in certain situations.

Control theory focuses on the extent to which individuals are subject to direct control, have a stake in conformity, and are able to exercise internal control. The absence of such controls *frees* individuals to satisfy their needs and desires in the most expedient way possible, which is often through delinquent acts.

Each theory presents a different image of the delinquent. In strain theory, the individual is seen as angry and frustrated, beset with a variety of problems or strains and unable to cope through legal channels. In social learning theory, the individual is presented as someone who believes that delinquency is a desirable or justifiable response in her or his particular situation. Control theory presents the individual as unrestrained, free to satisfy his or her needs and desires in the most expedient way possible.

All three theories have some support, with control and social learning theories dominating the literature. I should emphasize, however, that these theories continue to be tested and revised. They are not "engraved in stone." Rather, they are ongoing creations. In fact, both control theory and strain theory have been subject to major modifications in the past decade.[1]

Each theory partly explains why individuals engage in delinquency. One theory may sometimes be more relevant to a particular individual or group than the other theories. For example, you may know a delinquent individual who appears to be high in control and low in strain. This person's delinquency may best be explained in terms of social learning theory: Perhaps their delinquency is frequently reinforced and seldom punished; perhaps they accept certain beliefs that justify their delinquency; or perhaps they have had much exposure to delinquent models. Strain or social control theory, however, may provide the best explanation of delinquency for someone else. In most cases, all three theories probably have some relevance to the explanation of delinquency.

A complete explanation of delinquency, therefore, should draw on strain, social learning, and control theory. Given this fact, you might ask about the possibility of combining these theories into a more general theory of delinquency. In this area, I noted that there is some overlap between control and social learning theory; both focus on the extent to which delinquency is prevented through punishment. Many criminologists have, in fact, tried to develop integrated theories of crime that combine all or some of these theories. (This issue is discussed further in Chapter 16.)

What Are Some of the Other Theories of Delinquency?

While strain, social learning, and control theory are the dominant theories of delinquency, there are many other important theories. They include labeling theory, conflict theory, feminist theory, subcultural deviance theory, social disorganization theory, institutional-anomie theory, routine-activities theory, rational-choice theory, and several biopsychological theories of crime.[2] Most of these theories, however, can be viewed as extensions or elaborations of the three theories treated in this book.

To illustrate, social disorganization theory focuses on several community characteristics that contribute to crime, like poverty and high rates of family disruption (or a high percentage of single-parent families). This theory, however, is an extension of control theory (as well as of strain and social learning theory, to a lesser extent). Social disorganization theory basically argues that such community characteristics reduce the level of control to which individuals are subject. Communities with high levels of family disruption, for example, are said to exercise less control over neighborhood youth (Sampson and Groves, 1989). At its core, then, social disorganization theory explains crime in terms of the controls to which individuals are subject. It simply points to the ways in which community-level variables affect such controls. The key ideas of this theory are discussed in Chapter 14, in the section on communities and delinquency.

To give another illustration, routine-activities theory argues that crime is most likely when three factors converge: *motivated offenders* come together with *suitable targets* in the *absence of capable guardians* (i.e., police, neighbors, homeowners). The likelihood of this convergence is a function of a person's everyday, or routine, activities. For example, an increasing percentage of women have entered the workforce over the last few decades and so have undergone a fundamental change in their routine, or everyday activities: They now leave home and go to work on a regular basis. As a consequence, homes are more often left unprotected during the day, and women are more often in public places. Both of these changes increase the likelihood that motivated offenders will encounter suitable targets in the absence of capable guardians (see Cohen and Felson, 1979). This theory represents an extension of social learning and control theory, since it basically points to some of the factors that influence the likelihood that offenders will be reinforced rather than punished for crime. That is, it points to factors that influence whether motivated offenders will encounter suitable targets in the absence of capable guardians. The key ideas of this theory are discussed in Chapter 15.

Similar arguments can be made regarding most of the other major theories. As a final illustration, consider the biopsychological theories of such individuals as Eysenck (1977), Wilson and Herrnstein (1985), and Moffitt (1993). These theories also represent extensions of strain, social learning, and/or control theory. They point to individual traits that influence the likelihood that people will experience strain, find crime rewarding, and be deterred by punishment. Such traits are said to be a function of biological and social factors.

Most theories, then, ultimately explain crime in terms of the mechanisms outlined by strain, social learning, and control theories. This is not to deny the importance of these additional theories; they direct attention to a range of important variables that were not considered in the original versions of strain, social learning, and control theories. As such, they represent important extensions of these theories. Nevertheless, the variables identified by these theories affect crime because they influence the individual's level of strain or reaction to strain, the reinforcements and punishments associated with crime, and the individual's level of control. (The key variables in these additional theories are discussed in Chapters 10 through 16.)

Applying Strain, Social Learning, and Control Theory

You should be sure you that you understand and can *apply* the major delinquency theories. These theories are tools for you to use. As indicated earlier, they can help you understand the "basic facts" about delinquency, the research on the causes of delinquency, and efforts to control delinquency. These theories are also relevant to your own lives: They can help you understand your own behavior and the behavior of those around you.

Perhaps a fitting way to end the discussion of these theories is with some examples of how they might be applied. Let us begin by applying these theories to one of the basic facts about delinquency presented in Chapter 4.

Why Are Adolescents More Criminal Than Children and Adults?

As described in Chapter 4, most forms of crime peak during adolescence. That is, adolescents are more likely to engage in crime than either children or adults. How might we explain this major fact about crime using strain, social learning, and control theory?[3]

Strain theory. A strain theorist might explain adolescents' greater propensity for crime by arguing that adolescents experience greater strain (see Agnew, 1997; Greenberg, 1977). Adolescents actively pursue a number of goals that are often difficult for them to achieve through legitimate channels, such as attaining money and autonomy. Children are not as interested in these goals, and adults are better able to achieve them through legitimate channels. Adolescents also live in a relatively larger and more demanding social world than children and adults, which increases the likelihood that they will be negatively treated by others. They leave elementary school and enter larger, more impersonal, and more diverse secondary schools. They spend more time away from home, especially in the evenings and on weekends. Also, there are increases in the size of their peer group, their contact with the opposite sex, the level of intimacy they experience with same- and opposite-sex peers, and the level of association with delinquent peers. This dramatic increase in the size and complexity of their social world is itself likely to be stressful. But it also increases the likelihood of negative treatment, since the adolescents are interacting with many more people—often in unsupervised settings. As adolescents become adults, however, their social world begins to narrow again, and they have more control over the nature of this world (for example, they have some choice over where they live and work). Some data support the argument that adolescents experience more strains or stressors than children and adults (see Agnew, 1997).

Also, a strain theorist might argue that adolescents are less able to cope with strain through legal channels. Children are usually under the protection of adults, who cope on their behalf and provide them with much social support. This protection frequently ends at adolescence, however, with adolescents being expected to handle their own problems. Unfortunately, adolescents have little experience at coping, and they may feel reluctant to turn to adults for assistance. Also, adolescents have little power. They are "compelled to live with their family in a certain neighborhood; to go to a certain school; and, within limits, to interact with the same group of peers and neighbors" (Agnew, 1985a:156). If any of these contexts is aversive, there is often little that adolescents can do to legally cope. Finally, adolescents are often more disposed to delinquency. They are more likely to associate with delinquent peers, for example, who provide delinquent models, teach beliefs favorable to delinquency, and reinforce delinquency. For all these reasons, then, adolescents are also more likely to cope with strain through delinquency than are children or adults.

Social learning theory. Social learning theory focuses on who the juvenile associates with and the extent to which these others teach beliefs favorable to delinquency, model delinquency, and reinforce delinquency. Data suggest that adolescents are much more likely to associate with delinquent peers than are children or adults. For example, one study based on a national sample of adolescents found the following: at age 11, approximately 9 of 10 respondents reported that none of their friends had used alcohol during the past year; at age 18, this figure had fallen to approximately 1 in 10 (Warr, 1993; also see Elliott and Menard, 1996). Similar, although less dramatic, figures were reported for other forms of delinquency. Further, adolescents spend more time with their peers, place more importance on peer activities, and are more loyal to their peers than are children and adults. The increased importance of delinquent peers may help explain the peak in crime during adolescence.

In particular, adolescents are more likely than children or adults to associate with others who teach beliefs favorable to delinquency, model delinquent behavior, and reinforce delinquency. Also, adolescents may be less involved in relationships where conformity is reinforced and delinquency is punished. The adolescent is less tied to her or his family than the child and less than adults who form families of their own. Secondary schools may provide less control over behavior than smaller, more personal elementary schools and less control than adults' places of employment. Also, the sanctions administered by the juvenile justice system are less severe than those administered by the adult criminal justice system. Data suggest that much of the association between age and crime is explained by such changing associations (see Warr, 1993, 1998).

Control theory. Control theory would explain the adolescent peak in crime by arguing that adolescents are less subject to various types of control than are children and adults. Adolescents are less subject to direct control by the family and school system than are children. Adolescents spend more time away from their family than children, and the larger, more impersonal nature of most secondary schools reduces the effectiveness of direct controls. Adolescents are also subject to less direct control than adults. Adults often spend much time with family members, and spouses often take a keen interest in the behavior of their partners. Further, adults are subject to the direct controls associated with work. Data, in fact, suggest that delinquent adolescents who get decent jobs and enter satisfying marriages experience dramatic reductions in their delinquency.[4] Finally, the adult criminal justice system imposes more severe sanctions than does the juvenile justice system.

Adolescents may also have a lower stake in conformity. They may be less strongly bonded to family members than are children and adults, and their investment in conventional society is lower than that of most adults. There is also some evidence to suggest that adults are higher in internal control, including beliefs condemning crime.[5]

It is possible to list additional reasons for the adolescent peak in delinquency, but the preceding arguments should give you an idea of the ways in which these theories can be applied.

Why Is Child Abuse Related to Delinquency?

The three theories have inspired a great deal of research on the causes of delinquency. Several criminologists have drawn on these theories to argue that child abuse causes delinquency (see Brezina, 1998). And the data do, in fact, suggest that the victims of abuse are somewhat more likely to engage in delinquency (see Chapter 11). How might we explain this connection in terms of strain, social learning, and control theory?

A strain theorist would obviously argue that child abuse is a major type of strain, involving the presentation of negative stimuli. Such abuse may anger the child, and the child may turn to delinquency in an effort to end or reduce the abuse (e.g., running away from home, assaulting the abuser); seek revenge against the abuser or related targets; or manage the negative feelings that result from abuse (perhaps through drug use).

A social learning theorist would argue that abuse increases the likelihood of violence since it models violence and implicitly teaches the child that violence is an appropriate way to deal with problems. Also, abuse by parents may undermine their influence on the child. The child may avoid or ignore parents, thus reducing their effectiveness as models, instructors, and sanctioning agents. If this retreat from parents is accompanied by an increase in the time spent with peers, the child may also come to experience reinforcement for delinquency.

A control theorist would argue that abuse may decrease all three forms of control. Abused children may try to escape or withdraw from parents, thus reducing direct control. Abuse may reduce the child's emotional bond to his or her parents. It may also interfere with the child's performance in school, thereby reducing the child's investment in conventional society (see Zingraff et al., 1994). Finally, abuse may reduce the effectiveness of parents in transmitting anti-delinquent beliefs and in instilling self-control.

Summary

You should test your knowledge of these theories by applying them to additional examples. For example, how would these theories explain the fact that males are more delinquent than females or that lower-class individuals are more involved in serious delinquency than higher-class individuals?[6] How would they explain some of the other research findings on the causes of delinquency, such as the fact that people from larger families are somewhat more likely to be delinquent or that juveniles with low grades in school are more delinquent? Finally, what recommendations would these theories make for controlling/preventing delinquency?

Notes

1. *See* Agnew, 1992; Gottfredson and Hirschi, 1990; Sampson and Laub, 1993a.
2. *See* Akers, 1997; Cullen and Agnew, 1999; Shoemaker, 1996; Vold et al., 1998, for summaries.
3. For attempts to explain the relationship between age and crime, see Agnew, 1997; Farrington, 1986; Greenberg, 1977, 1985; Moffitt, 1993, 1997; Rowe and Tittle, 1977; Sampson and Laub, 1993a; Steffensmeier and Allan, 1995b, 2000; Thornberry, 1997; Warr, 1993, 1998.
4. *See* Sampson and Laub, 1993a; Wright et al., 1999b; also see Warr, 1998.
5. *See* Burton et al., 1998; Le Blanc, 1993; Markowitz and Felson, 1998.
6. For examples of how these theories have been applied to these issues, see Broidy and Agnew, 1997; Chesney-Lind and Shelden, 1998; Cohen, A., 1955; Jensen and Eve, 1976; Leonard, 1982; Steffensmeier and Allan, 1996, 2000; Thornberry, 1987. ✦

Chapter 10

Individual Traits: What Impact Do Individual Traits Have on Delinquency?

❖ ❖ ❖ ❖   Chapters 6 through 9 described the three leading theories of delinquency. These theories have inspired social scientists to do a great deal of *research* on the causes of delinquency. In particular, criminologists have devoted much effort to testing these theories or testing ideas derived from them. Criminologists have also conducted much research on the causes of delinquency that was not inspired by the three theories. Nevertheless, most of that research can be interpreted in terms of the theories.

This chapter begins to describe the research on the causes of delinquency. The focus is on *individual traits* that increase the likelihood of delinquency. Although most of these traits were suggested by versions of control, learning, and strain theory, certain traits were suggested by other theories or simply emerged from exploratory research. The effect of all of these traits on delinquency, however, can be explained in terms of strain, social learning, and control theories. After listing these traits, I then examine why some individuals are more likely than others to possess them.

Are Juveniles With Certain Traits More Likely to Engage in Delinquency?

Think back to some of the people you knew before college—not just your friends but others as well—and think about the ways these people differed from one another. They probably differed in terms of intelligence—some were smart and some were not so smart. Some may have been easy-going and friendly, while others were "touchy" or "irritable." Some may have liked excitement or adventure—even risky, dangerous activities—while others preferred safer activities. Some may have been impulsive, engaging in activities without much thought for the consequences, while others were more thoughtful and reflective. Some may have been socially skilled, getting along well with people, while others had problems in social relations. People often differ in the traits they possess. By "traits," I mean relatively stable ways of perceiving, thinking about, and behaving toward the environment and oneself (see Blackburn, 1993). For example, if a person regularly acts without thinking, we can say this person possesses the trait of impulsivity.

Research indicates that people with certain traits are more likely to engage in delinquency. In certain cases, the research linking these traits to delinquency is reasonably good. In other cases, the research suffers from one or more problems. Most of these problems were described in Chapter 5, such as the use of poor measures; the use of small, unrepresentative samples; the failure to control for relevant third variables; and the failure to conduct longitudinal studies.[1] Nevertheless, there has been enough good research for us to safely state that certain traits increase the likelihood of delinquency.

At the same time, certain cautions are in order. There is some indication that many of these traits are most relevant to the explanation of high-rate, chronic, serious offending.[2] That is, many of these traits help explain why some juveniles become high-rate, chronic, serious offenders, but they do not help explain why some juveniles become low-rate, less serious, adolescent-limited offenders (see the discussion of "types of delinquents" in Chapter 4). The latter type of offending, which most people engage in, may be more a function of the social environment. Also, none of these traits *perfectly* explains delinquency. So do not assume, for example, that all juveniles with low IQs are delinquent and that all juveniles with high IQs are nondelinquent. The traits under discussion simply increase the probability that juveniles will engage in delinquency, perhaps only slightly in some cases. The following paragraphs present a list of traits that may have a causal impact on delinquency. I try to provide some indication of whether the research linking these traits to delinquency is strong or weak.

As you review this list, ask yourself how you might best measure each trait. For example, ask yourself what questions you might ask juveniles (or their parents or teachers) to determine whether they are high or low in each trait. This exercise will help increase your understanding and memory of each trait. Also, ask yourself how you might explain the effect of each trait on delinquency using strain, social learning, and control theory. (I provide brief discussions in this area.)

Low Verbal IQ

Much data suggest that individuals with low IQ scores are more likely to engage in delinquency.[3] This finding is true whether criminologists use self-report or official measures of delinquency. It is true when researchers control for third variables like social class and race. For example, researchers find that IQ is associated with delinquency when they limit their analysis to whites only and to blacks only. Also, it is true in longitudinal as well as cross-sectional studies. Data suggest that it is primarily a person's *verbal IQ score* that affects delinquency. (One's total IQ score is made up of two components: verbal and performance. The verbal IQ score reflects several subtests, measuring such things as general factual knowledge, vocabulary, memory, abstract thinking, and social comprehension and judgment. All these subtests are administered orally and require oral answers. The performance IQ score reflects several other subtests, which measure such things as attention to detail, visual puzzle solving, and maze completion. Manual rather than oral responses are required.) Individuals with low verbal scores have trouble expressing themselves, remembering information, and thinking abstractly.

How might we explain the effect of low verbal IQ on delinquency? A strain theorist would argue that low IQ leads to increased strain, making it more difficult for juveniles to achieve goals like educational success and increasing the likelihood of negative relations with teachers, peers, and others.[4] Low verbal IQ is also associated with problem-solving ability, so individuals with low verbal scores might be less able to cope with strain through legitimate channels (Moffitt, 1990). Social learning theorists argue that low verbal IQ reduces the likelihood that individuals will be reinforced for conventional behavior, like school work. Low IQ is also said to promote a concern for immediate rewards, which makes crime more appealing since it often results in immediate gratification. Further, it has been argued that low IQ affects a person's level of moral reasoning, so those with low verbal scores will be less likely to condemn crime (see Wilson and Herrnstein, 1985). Control theorists argue that low IQ leads to poor school performance and negative attitudes toward school, thereby weakening one's stake in conformity.[5]

Also, low IQ may lead to offending because it reduces the individual's ability to foresee the consequences of offending and to exercise self-control.[6]

Learning Disabilities

Learning disabilities are distinct from low IQ. As Raine (1993:235) points out, learning disabilities refer to "those situations in which a child fails to develop to the level that would be expected given his or her intellectual ability." Learning disabled children often have above average IQs. Several studies suggest that learning disabilities, especially reading disabilities, contribute to delinquency.[7] The relationship between learning disabilities and delinquency can be explained in many of the same ways used to explain the effect of low IQ.

Hyperactivity/Impulsivity/Attention Deficit

Numerous studies suggest that hyperactivity/impulsivity/attention deficit (HIA) contribute to delinquency.[8] These three factors tend to occur together, and individuals high in HIA display the following characteristics: They are overactive for their age—they frequently fidget, have trouble remaining seated, engage in excessive talking, and tend to "bounce around" in a given space. They act quickly without thinking, are more concerned with immediate than future rewards, and tend to engage in reckless behavior. They have trouble concentrating and are easily distracted. HIA is generally apparent in early childhood, often before the age of 2.

How might we explain the effect of HIA on delinquency? A strain theorist would argue that individuals with HIA are more likely to upset others, including parents, teachers, and peers. These others may then treat the HIA individual in a negative manner, thereby increasing the individual's level of strain. Also, individuals with HIA may be more likely to sort themselves into strainful environments, such as delinquent peer groups. Further, HIA individuals may be less able to cope with strain through conventional means. A social learning theorist would argue that individuals with HIA are less deterred by the threat of punishment and are more attracted to the immediate rewards associated with crime (see Wilson and Herrnstein, 1985). In particular, they are less likely to think about the negative consequences of their behavior, especially if such consequences are delayed, as punishment often is. They are more likely to focus on the immediate rewards that often result from crime, like money and positive feelings. A control theorist would argue that HIA individuals are lower in self-control and therefore less likely to be restrained by their beliefs regarding crime, their stake in conformity, and direct controls. Also, HIA individuals are probably less likely to believe that crime is wrong, to have a stake in conformity, and to be subject to direct controls. For example, individuals with HIA are less likely to get along well with parents and obtain good grades in school, which means that they will have a lower stake in conformity.

Sensation Seeking

❖ ❖ ❖ ❖

Closely related to HIA is the trait of sensation seeking. Certain data suggest that delinquents have a greater need than nondelinquents for stimulation, "thrills," or "excitement." As a consequence, delinquents are more easily bored than others and they often take social and physical risks to achieve the stimulation they desire.[9] The effect of sensation seeking on crime is easily explained in terms of strain theory. Delinquents crave stimulation but are sometimes unable to obtain it through legitimate channels, so they turn to crime. A social learning theorist would argue that the trait of sensation seeking makes crime more rewarding since crime often involves risky and exciting behavior (see Wilson and Herrnstein, 1985). A control theorist would argue that sensation seeking is one element of low self-control (Gottfredson and Hirschi, 1990). (At this point, you are probably beginning to appreciate a comment that I made at the beginning of Chapter 5. Strain, social learning, and control theory are distinguished less by the independent variables they focus on and more by their explanation of *why* these independent variables cause delinquency.)

Reduced Ability to Learn From Punishment

Certain studies suggest that delinquency is associated with the reduced ability to learn from punishment. As discussed earlier, the punishment of delinquent acts normally reduces the likelihood that such acts will be repeated in the future. Individuals come to associate the delinquent act with punishment; as a result, they become fearful or anxious when they later contemplate committing the act again. This fear response is equivalent to one's "conscience," and it acts as a restraint to delinquency. Some individuals, however, appear less able to learn from punishment than others. As a consequence, they are less fearful or anxious when contemplating delinquent acts. Related to this finding, there is some evidence that delinquents may be oversensitive to rewards, often focusing on the pursuit of rewards and ignoring actual and potential punishments.[10] These traits are obviously most relevant to social learning and control explanations of delinquency, both of which deal with the effect of punishment on delinquency.

Irritability

Several studies suggest that delinquents—particularly aggressive delinquents—are more irritable than nondelinquents. That is, they are sensitive to a wider range of stressors; their emotional reaction to given stressors is more intense; and they are more inclined to respond to stressors in an aggressive manner.[11] Such individuals score higher on scales with questions like "I think I am rather touchy" and "I feel like a powder keg ready to explode." This trait often emerges early in life; young children who possess it are often said to have a "difficult temperament." This trait is obviously relevant to strain theory. Individuals high in irritability will more often experience strain, will have stronger emotional reactions to strain, and will be more likely to respond to strain with delinquency. How might social learning and control theory explain the effect of this trait on delinquency?

Insensitivity to Others/Low Empathy

It has been argued that delinquents are less likely to be aware of the distress experienced by others and to feel bad about that distress, even if they have caused it. So delinquents are less likely to feel guilty when they harm others. Evidence regarding the association between this trait and delinquency is somewhat mixed, but it tends to suggest that there is a relationship between empathy and delinquency.[12] How might one explain the effect of this trait on delinquency using strain, social learning, and/or control theories?

Interpersonal Problem-Solving Skills/Social Skills

Several criminologists have argued that delinquents are less likely to possess certain social and problem-solving skills, and that this accounts for the difficulties that delinquents sometimes have in interacting with others and in dealing with the problems that arise from such interaction. These skills include the following:

1. The ability to accurately perceive what is happening in your social environment, including the "messages" being sent by other people. For example, some juveniles may have difficulty determining when other people are angry, or they may mistakenly believe that other people are trying to deliberately harm them.

2. The ability to generate effective solutions to problems that arise. Generating a solution requires determining the different options available in the situation, evaluating the likely consequences of these options, and selecting an appropriate solution, one that does not involve delinquency and that will be effective in dealing with the problem.

3. Implementing the solution that is selected. Implementation requires a range of social skills. Certain of these skills—things like eye contact, gesturing, posture, and facial expression—are called "micro-skills." Other, more complex skills—like holding a conversation and being assertive—are called "macro-skills."

Evidence suggests that delinquents may be deficient in at least some of these skills. Delinquents (1) are more likely to perceive the social world in a hostile manner; in particular, they are more likely to attribute hostile intentions to the benign or ambiguous acts of others; (2) generate fewer possible solutions to interpersonal problems; (3) are less likely to anticipate the negative consequences of the solutions they do generate; and (4) more often choose ineffective/aggressive solutions. Delinquents may also be deficient in certain social skills, such as maintaining eye contact and conversational skills. It is important to emphasize, however, that not much research has been done in this area and that not all studies indicate that delinquents are deficient in social and problem-solving skills. Dodge and his associates have been leading researchers in this area.[13]

How might one explain a relationship between social/problem-solving skills and delinquency? Strain theory would argue that individuals with deficient skills are more likely to believe that others are deliberately mistreating them. Also, their limited social skills increase the likelihood that they will have trouble getting along with others. As a consequence, such individuals should be higher in strain. Further, their limited skills should increase the likelihood that they will respond to strain with delinquency. How might social learning and control theory explain the association between social/problem-solving skills and delinquency?

Moral Reasoning and Moral Beliefs

Moral reasoning refers to the principles that one uses to judge the rightness or wrongness of conduct. Kohlberg (1976) has argued that there are three stages of moral reasoning, each being divided into an early and a late level. At the preconventional stage, individuals are essentially amoral: they focus on avoiding punishment and satisfying their own needs. Conduct is judged to be "right" if it allows individuals to avoid punishment and get what they want. At the conventional stage, individuals focus on gaining social approval from others through conformity and, later, on abiding by the law and meeting obligations to others. At the postconventional stage, individuals focus on living by certain universal moral principles emphasizing justice, human rights, and dignity. Individuals are said to progress from one stage to the next as they develop. The first stage characterizes children and a minority of adolescents and adults. Most adolescents and adults are at the second stage, and a minority of adults reach the third stage. It has been argued that delinquents exhibit developmental delays in moral reasoning; delinquents are more likely to be operating at the preconventional stage of moral reasoning. Limited data provide some support for this argument.[14]

The principles that one uses to make moral judgments are related to, but distinct from, the content of one's moral beliefs. As indicated in Chapters 7 and 8, delinquents are more likely to hold beliefs that favor delinquency or that are amoral, neither approving nor disapproving of delinquency. The effect of moral reasoning and moral beliefs on delinquency is best explained using social learning and control theory.

How Are These Different Traits Related to One Another?

A variety of traits, then, are said to contribute to crime and delinquency—particularly high-rate, chronic, serious delinquency. Such traits include low verbal IQ, learning disabilities, hyperactivity/impulsivity/attention deficit, sensation seeking, reduced ability to learn from punishment, irritability, insensitivity/low empathy, limited social/problem-solving skills, immature moral reasoning, and beliefs favorable to delinquency/amoral beliefs. Criminologists have argued that many of these traits are closely associated with one another. That is, they tend to cluster in individuals. In fact, some of these traits may have a causal impact on others. Low IQ, for example, has been said to contribute to impulsiveness, immature moral reasoning, and deficient problem-solving skills.

Several criminologists have developed lists of traits that they believe cluster. Perhaps the best-known list is composed of the traits that characterize the "psychopath." The psychopath is said to possess several of the traits just listed, including impulsivity, sensation seeking, an inability to learn from punishment, irritability, and insensitivity/low empathy (see Blackburn, 1993;

Lykken, 1995, 1996; many researchers now distinguish between different types of psychopaths, most notably between primary and secondary psychopaths). Another very popular list of traits that are said to cluster together is provided in Gottfredson and Hirschi's (1990) description of individuals who are low in self-control. These traits were briefly described in Chapter 8 and also include many of the traits just listed.

Studies suggest that many of these traits do cluster together, although there is still some uncertainty about whether they cluster into one or more groups and about the specific traits that fall into each group (see Caspi et al., 1994; Cloninger, 1987, for recent examinations of this issue). Nevertheless, it is clear that individuals with certain traits are more likely to engage in delinquency. In particular, criminologists are fairly confident that traits such as low verbal IQ, learning disabilities, HIA, irritability, and moral beliefs contribute to delinquency. Research regarding the other traits discussed in this chapter is more limited or somewhat mixed, but there is some reason to believe that these traits may also contribute to delinquency. At this point, however, you are probably beginning to wonder why individuals differ on these traits.

Why Are Some Individuals More Likely Than Others to Possess These Traits?

Evidence suggests that most of these traits are a function of biological factors and the social environment. I will first discuss the ways in which biological factors may contribute to these traits and will then discuss the role of the social environment.

Biological Factors

Evidence suggests that there may be a genetic component to crime and that crime may sometimes result from certain types of biological harm, such as that caused by birth complications, head injury, and exposure to toxic substances such as lead. Researchers, however, do not claim that these factors lead directly to crime. For example, there is no gene for crime. Rather, it is usually claimed that genetic factors and biological harm may create a predisposition for crime by influencing the likelihood that individuals will develop traits like those mentioned in the preceding section. Such factors are usually said to influence the development of these traits through their effect on the central nervous system (the brain and spinal cord) and the autonomic nervous system (which controls the heart rate and gland secretions, among other things, and influences the emotional reaction to stimuli).

Genetic inheritance of crime. Studies suggest that there is a genetic component to crime.[15] That is, crime is inherited to some extent. Researchers have tried to estimate the extent of genetic inheritance using two major methods: twin studies and adoption studies. Twin studies compare identical twins to fraternal twins. Identical twins are genetically identical, while fraternal twins are about 50 percent genetically alike on those genes that vary among people (see Raine, 1993:54). It is assumed that twins, whether identical or fraternal, are exposed to the same environmental influences. If crime is genetically inherited, we would expect that identical twins would be more similar in criminal behavior than fraternal twins. Most studies indicate that this is the case. Twin studies, however, suffer from certain problems. Most notably, evidence suggests that identical twins—because of their similar appearance—are treated more alike than fraternal twins. This factor, rather than their identical genes, may explain their greater similarity in criminal behavior.

Adoption studies overcome this problem to some extent, although such studies are not problem free. Adoption studies focus on children who were separated from their biological parents early in life. The traits of these children are compared to the traits of their biological parents. If a tendency to commit crime is inherited, there should be more crime among adopted children whose biological parents are criminal than among adopted children whose biological parents are not criminal. Most data suggest that this is the case. For example, one large study in Denmark found the following: When neither adopted nor biological parents were criminal, 13.5 percent of the adopted boys had criminal convictions; when adoptive parents were not criminal and the biological parents were, 20 percent of the adopted boys had criminal convictions (Raine, 1993).

Although the evidence suggests that the tendency to commit crime is inherited to some degree, it is difficult to precisely specify the extent to which the tendency is inherited; genetic factors *may* be as important as environmental factors for some types of crimes and offenders. At the same time, certain cautions are in order (see Brennan et al., 1995; Raine, 1993). The extent to which crime is inherited may vary by type of crime (e.g., violent versus property) and type of offender (e.g., male versus female). Evidence suggests that juvenile delinquency may be less heritable than adult crime, although genetic factors *may* play an influential role in the explanation of high-rate, chronic delinquency (Raine, 1993:73–76). Finally, both twin and adoption studies suggest that genetic inheritance only partly explains crime, environmental factors also play an important role in the explanation of crime. In particular, these studies suggest that crime is most likely when the individual possesses a biological predisposition for crime and is in an environment conducive to crime. For example, crime is most likely when the individual has *both* biological and adoptive parents who are criminal.

Biological harm and crime. A person's biological state is a function both of the environment and genetic inheritance. Data suggest that at least certain types of criminal behavior may be influenced by the biological harm caused by these environmental factors: (1) the mother's poor health habits during pregnancy, including poor nutrition and alcohol and drug use; (2) certain types of delivery complications; (3) exposure to toxic substances such as lead; (4) diet; and (5) head injury.[16] The research in these areas often suffers from one or more of the problems listed in Chapter 5, such as the failure to control for relevant third variables or to conduct longitudinal studies. Nevertheless, the data as a whole suggest that certain types of biological harm may contribute to at least some crime.

The central and autonomic nervous systems. The mechanisms by which genetic inheritance and biological harm contribute to crime are not fully understood. Most researchers in the area, however, suggest that such factors contribute to crime through their effect on the central and autonomic nervous systems. A number of possible effects have been explored, the most popular of which include the following: Genetic factors and biological harm may contribute to dysfunctions in the frontal lobe of the brain, which is involved in abstract thinking, planning, the self-monitoring of behavior, and behavioral inhibition (Moffitt and Henry, 1989; Raine, 1993:105). These factors may also contribute to dysfunctions in the left hemisphere of the brain; such dysfunctions have been linked to low verbal IQ scores. And these factors may affect the autonomic nervous system; with data suggesting that criminals are under aroused. That is, criminals show less emotional response to stimuli (they are "physiologically 'drowsy' " in the words of Bartol and Bartol, 1986:69). This underarousal is reflected in their lower skin conductance (i.e., criminals sweat less in response to stimuli), lower resting heart rate, and slower alpha brain waves. As indicated below, this underarousal may contribute to traits such as HIA.

Researchers are now investigating the ways in which genetic inheritance and biological harm may affect the central and autonomic nervous systems. For example, recent data suggest that some of these factors may result in reduced levels of serotonin, a neurotransmitter (Berman et al., 1997; Moffitt et al., 1997). Neurotransmitters allow for communication between brain cells and so underlie all of our behavior, thoughts, perceptions, emotions, and the like. Reduced serotonin may lower one's level of inhibition, contributing to such traits as impulsivity and the reduced ability to learn from punishment.

Biological factors and traits conducive to crime. Genetic factors and certain types of biological harm, then, may increase the likelihood of crime through their effect on the central and autonomic nervous systems. There is still the question, however, of why "dysfunctions" in the central and autonomic nervous systems may lead to crime. The most commonly advanced theory is that such dysfunctions increase the likelihood that individuals will develop traits conducive to crime, such as low IQ, HIA, and irritability. There is some evidence for this line of argument.[17] In particular, there is good evidence of a genetic effect on many of the traits discussed here. Much evidence, for example, suggests that genetic inheritance has a substantial effect on one's IQ and on HIA—an effect perhaps equal to or greater than the effect of the environment (Plomin and Petrill, 1997; Rutter et al., 1998). There is also good evidence that many of the traits listed are influenced by biological harm, such as birth complications and exposure to lead. Lead poisoning, for example, has been linked to such traits as learning disabilities and hyperactivity (Denno, 1990). Further, many of these traits have been linked to dysfunctions in the central and autonomic nervous systems.[18] Dysfunctions in the frontal lobe may contribute to such traits as HIA, irritability, the reduced ability to learn from punishment, insensitivity/low empathy, difficulties in problem solving, and immature moral reasoning. Underarousal in the autonomic nervous system has been linked to HIA, sensation seeking, and the inability to learn from punishment. Individuals who are underaroused are less affected by punishment, and it takes more to stimulate them, which may cause them to become easily distracted, overly active, and in greater need of thrills/excitement. The extent of biological influence likely differs from trait to trait, although biological influences have been demonstrated or alleged for all of the traits discussed, with the possible exception of beliefs conducive to crime (and even this trait may be indirectly affected by those biological factors that affect traits like IQ and moral reasoning).

Environmental Factors

The traits discussed are also a function of the individual's social environment, and most criminologists place great emphasis on the early family environment of the child.[19] Several features of the family environment are said to affect at least some of the traits (most of these features are discussed in Chapter 8). In particular, children are said to be less likely to develop traits such as impulsivity, low empathy, and beliefs favorable to crime if parents do the following: (1) Develop a strong emotional bond with their children; (2) provide clear rules for behavior; (3) monitor behavior; (4) consistently sanction deviance in an appropriate manner; and (5) model and reinforce conventional behavior. Also important are the resources and amount of stimulation provided to the child. Data suggest that social class, in particular, has a strong effect on at least some of the individual traits listed (e.g., Meich et al., 1999). Further, programs that attempt to compensate for childhood deprivation often lead to changes in these traits. For example, data indicate that children from deprived environments experience a boost in IQ when they are placed in programs that provide intellectual stimulation—certain types of preschool programs, for example (Ramey and Ramey, 1995).

Traits, then, are a function of the environment as well as of biological factors. It should be noted, however, that it is often difficult to separate out the effects of environmental and biological factors in a precise manner. Many types of biological harm are a function of the social environment—like one's social class. Lower-class individuals, for example, are more likely to be exposed to lead and to have poor prenatal care (Denno, 1990). At the same time, biological factors may shape one's social environment. Children with dysfunctions in their central and autonomic nervous systems, for example, may be more difficult for parents to raise. They may be more likely to elicit negative reactions from their parents, including harsh discipline and abusive behavior. Further, environmental and biological factors may condition the effect of one another on the traits discussed (see the discussion of conditioning effects at the start of Chapter 5). For example, biological factors like genetic inheritance or birth complications may be *more* likely to produce the above traits if the individual is in a poor family environment. Likewise, a poor family environment may be more likely to produce these traits if the individual has a genetic predisposition for such traits or has experienced certain types of biological harm. The important point to remember is that there is evidence suggesting that most of these traits are a function of both biological and environmental factors (see Rutter et al., 1998, for a fuller discussion of these issues).

Summary

Evidence suggests that juveniles with certain traits are more likely to engage in delinquency, especially high-rate, chronic, serious delinquency. These traits include low verbal IQ, learning disabilities, hyperactivity/impulsivity/attention deficit, sensation seeking, the reduced ability to learn from punishment, irritability, insensitivity/low empathy, poor problem-solving and social skills, immature moral reasoning, and amoral beliefs or beliefs favorable to delinquency. Many of these traits tend to cluster in the same people, although there is still some uncertainty about whether they cluster into one or more groups and which traits fall into each group. And, as just discussed, data suggest that these traits are a function of both biological and environmental factors.

The effect of these traits on delinquency can be explained in terms of strain, social learning, and control theories. With respect to strain theory, these traits influence the individual's exposure to strain, emotional reaction to strain, and likelihood of coping with strain through delinquency. For example, HIA individuals are more likely to elicit negative reactions from others. Irritable individuals are more likely to become upset when they are treated badly. And individuals with poor problem-solving skills are more likely to cope with strain through delinquency. With respect to social learning theory, these traits influence the extent to which individuals experience reinforcement and punishment for both conventional behavior and crime. People with low IQs, for example, are less likely to receive good grades for conventional behaviors like doing school work. Impulsive individuals are more likely to be reinforced by the immediate rewards associated with crime (and less likely to be reinforced by the delayed rewards often associated with conventional behavior). These traits also influence the likelihood that individuals will form positive relationships with conventional role models, like parents and teachers. Further, these traits influence or directly measure the extent to which individuals hold beliefs favorable to delinquency. With respect to control theory, these traits influence the extent to which individuals are subject to, aware of, and care about direct controls (e.g., some individuals are less influenced by the punishments administered by parents, teachers, and others). These traits influence the extent to which individuals develop a stake in conformity (e.g., low IQ individuals are less likely to do well in school; irritable individuals are less likely to form close attachments to others). Finally, these traits influence or directly measure the individual's level of internal control, including beliefs opposed to delinquency and self-control.

Applying the Research on Individual Traits

Knowledge of these individual traits is of little value unless you can also apply this knowledge. Following the practice established in Chapter 9, you should ask yourself how these traits can be used to explain the basic facts about delinquency described in Chapters 3 and 4. As illustrations, let us explore how these traits might help us explain why some juveniles become high-rate, chronic, serious offenders and why males are more delinquent than females.

How Can Traits Help Us Explain Why Some Juveniles Become High-Rate, Chronic, Serious Offenders?

As indicated at the end of Chapter 4, a small group of juveniles commit a high number of offenses over much of their lives, including many serious offenses. It is important to understand the behavior of these offenders since they account for a large share of all delinquency, especially serious delinquency. Certain data suggest that these offenders are more likely to possess the traits under discussion than other juveniles. Many of these traits develop early in life and are relatively stable over the life course. This stability helps explain the chronic, high-rate offending of these individuals. In particular, these traits can help explain their offending in several ways.[20]

❖ ❖ ❖ ❖

First, these traits increase the likelihood that juveniles will respond to a given situation with delinquency. For example, they increase the likelihood that juveniles will respond to a provocation with aggression or that they will respond to an unguarded piece of property with theft. This increased likelihood of a delinquent response can be explained in terms of strain, social learning, and control theories, as indicated above.

Second, juveniles with these traits are more likely to elicit negative reactions from others in particular situations. Individuals with these traits are not pleasant people, and they often exasperate and irritate their parents, teachers, and peers. As a consequence, they are more likely to be avoided or treated in a negative manner by others. This negative treatment also increases the likelihood they will engage in delinquency over the life course (for reasons largely related to strain theory).

Third, individuals with such traits are more likely to be in environments that are conducive to delinquency, such as problem families, delinquent peer groups, and slum communities; there are several reasons for this. Many of the traits described are partly inherited, so children with these traits are more likely to have parents with the same traits. Also, many of these traits are partly caused by the social environment, so once again children with these traits are more likely to be in undesirable environments. Finally, these individuals help create or select themselves into environments that are conducive to crime. Their interactions with family members may deteriorate to the point where emotional bonds are broken and they are subject to harsh discipline or receive no discipline at all. They may alienate teachers and perform badly in their course work. Conventional peers may reject them, and so they may associate with delinquent peers. Their location in these negative environments further contributes to their delinquency (for reasons related to strain, social learning, and control theory). Further, these negative environments serve to maintain and perhaps strengthen the negative individual traits. Such individuals, then, become firmly entrenched in delinquency.

Such individuals are not necessarily trapped in their delinquent lifestyles. Some of them are able to escape from delinquency, although the escape often requires a dramatic change in their lives—a good marriage to a conventional spouse, a stable job, entrance into the military, or participation in certain rehabilitation programs.[21]

How Can Traits Explain the Fact That Males Are More Delinquent Than Females?

As discussed in Chapter 4, males are more likely to engage in most forms of delinquency than females, especially serious delinquency. One might explain this difference by arguing that males are more likely to possess those individual traits conducive to delinquency. Although the data are limited and sometimes mixed, there is some evidence that males are more likely than females to be high in HIA, sensation seeking, irritability, and beliefs favorable to delinquency. Males are also lower in empathy, concern for others, and certain problem-solving skills.[22] Further, males may be more likely to possess clusters of traits that have been shown to be related to delinquency, such as psychopathy and low self-control.[23] Recent data suggest that the greater delinquency of males is partly due to such differences in individual traits.[24]

It is not clear how much biological factors or environmental factors account for sex differences in the above traits and delinquency. Some researchers argue for the importance of biological factors. Among other things, they point out that (1) sex-related differences in temperament have been noted at birth (e.g., newborn females are more likely to smile and cling to their mothers); (2) sex differences in physical aggression/crime emerge very early in life; and (3) historical and cross-cultural studies consistently find that males are more involved in most forms of physical aggression and crime (although the extent to which males are more involved varies over time and between societies). The precise biological causes of such sex differences, however, are unclear. The most commonly advanced explanation has to do with sex differences in the level of testosterone, a hormone that stimulates the development of masculine characteristics. Evidence linking testosterone to aggression, however, is mixed.[25]

Other researchers argue that sex differences in traits and aggression/crime are best explained in terms of the social environment. They argue that males are treated differently than females from birth onward and that such differences in treatment are largely responsible for sex differences in traits and crime/aggression. Much data, in particular, suggest that males and females are socialized differently by family members and others. Among other things, females are more likely to be socialized to be submissive and dependent on others, empathetic with others, and supportive of others. Females are more often exposed to models that exhibit these behaviors, are taught beliefs conducive to these behaviors, and are more likely to be reinforced for these behaviors. Males, by contrast, are more likely to be socialized to be aggressive/assertive, independent, and competitive with others. As a consequence of such differences in socialization, males may be more likely to possess many of the traits that contribute to delinquency, such as sensation seeking, a low ability to learn from punishment, low empathy, irritability, and moral beliefs favorable to delinquency.

Notes

1. *See* Gottfredson and Hirschi, 1990; Moffitt, 1990; Caspi et al., 1994.
2. *See* Bartusch et al., 1997; Moffitt, 1993, 1997; Moffitt et al., 1994; Rutter et al., 1998.
3. *See* Bartusch et al., 1997; Blackburn, 1993; Denno, 1990; Farrington, 1996b, 1998; Hirschi and Hindelang, 1977; Loeber, Farrington, Stouthamer-Loeber, Moffitt, and Caspi, 1998; Moffitt, 1990, 1997; Moffitt et al., 1994; Rutter et al., 1998; Wilson and Herrnstein, 1985.
4. *See* Loeber, Farrington, Stouthamer-Loeber, Moffitt, and Caspi, 1998; Moffitt, 1990; Wilson and Herrnstein, 1985:171.
5. *See* Denno, 1990; Hirschi and Hindelang, 1977; Rutter and Giller, 1983.
6. *See* Farrington, 1996b; Moffitt, 1990; Wilson and Herrnstein, 1985.
7. *See* Blackburn, 1993; Hawkins and Lishner, 1987; Raine, 1993.
8. *See* Bartusch et al., 1997; Blackburn, 1993; Caspi et al., 1994; Denno, 1990; Hawkins, Herrenkohl, Farrington, Brewer, Catalano, and Harachi, 1998; Hollin, 1992; Farrington, 1996b, 1998; Loeber, Farrington, Stouthamer-Loeber, Moffitt, and Caspi, 1998; Moffitt, 1997; Pepler and Slaby, 1994; Pulkkinen, 1986; Rowe et al., 1995; Rutter et al., 1998; Taylor, 1986; White et al., 1994; Wright et al., 1999b.

9. *See* Caspi et al., 1994; Farrington, 1996b; Loeber, Farrington, Stouthamer-Loeber, Moffitt, and Caspi, 1998; White et al., 1985.

10. *See* Baron and Richardson, 1994; Blackburn, 1993; Fonseca and Yule, 1995; Lykken, 1996; Moffitt, 1990; Raine, 1993; Wilson and Herrnstein, 1985.

11. *See* Agnew, 1997; Baron and Richardson, 1994; Berkowitz, 1993; Caspi et al., 1994; Glueck and Glueck, 1950; Loeber, Farrington, Stouthamer-Loeber, Moffitt, and Caspi, 1998; Pepler and Slaby, 1994; Rowe et al., 1995.

12. *See* Blackburn, 1993; Loeber, Farrington, Stouthamer-Loeber, and Van Kammen, 1998; Wilson and Herrnstein, 1985.

13. *See* Dodge and Schwartz, 1997; also see Agnew, 1997; Baron and Richardson, 1994; Blackburn, 1993; Hollin, 1992; Pepler and Slaby, 1994; Rutter et al., 1998; Slaby and Guerra, 1988.

14. *See* Bartol and Bartol, 1986; Blackburn, 1993; Jennings et al., 1983; Raine, 1993; also see Bandura, 1986.

15. For excellent overviews, see Brennan et al., 1995; Carey and Goldman, 1997; Farrington, 1998; Fishbein, 1996; Raine, 1993; Rutter et al., 1998.

16. *See* Brennan et al., 1995; Denno, 1990; Hawkins, Herrenkohl, Farrington, Brewer, Catalano, and Harachi, 1998; Raine, 1993; Rutter et al., 1998; Tibbetts and Piquero, 1999.

17. *See* Bartol and Bartol, 1986; Brennan et al., 1995; Buikhuisen, 1988; Denno, 1990; Farrington, 1996b, 1998; Fishbein, 1996; Hollin, 1992; Moffitt, 1990; Raine, 1993; Rutter et al., 1998; Wilson and Herrnstein, 1985.

18. *See* Lykken, 1996; Moffitt and Henry, 1989; Moffitt, 1990; Raine, 1993.

19. *See* Bartol and Bartol, 1986; Blackburn, 1993; Gottfredson and Hirschi, 1990; Pulkkinen, 1986; Wilson and Herrnstein, 1985.

20. *See* Agnew, 1997; Caspi et al., 1989; Moffitt, 1993; Howell and Hawkins, 1998; Meich et al., 1999; Rutter et al., 1998; Sampson and Laub, 1993a; Wright et al., 1999b.

21. *See* Sampson and Laub, 1993a; Warr, 1998; Wright et al., 1999b.

22. *See* Bartol and Bartol, 1986:120; Berger, 1989; Broidy and Agnew, 1997; Gilligan and Attanucci, 1988; Hagan et al., 1979; Hagan et al., 1996; Heimer, 1996; Mears et al., 1998; Morash, 1983; Rowe et al., 1995; Rutter et al., 1998; Slaby and Guerra, 1988; Steffensmeier and Allen, 2000; Taylor, 1986; White et al., 1985.

23. *See* Bartol and Bartol, 1986; Burton et al., 1998; LaGrange and Silverman, 1999.

24. *See* Burton et al., 1998; Gottfredson and Hirschi, 1990; LaGrange and Silverman, 1999; Rowe et al., 1995.

25. For further information on biological explanations of gender differences in crime, see Archer and McDaniel, 1995; Berkowitz, 1993; Blackburn, 1993; Denno, 1990; Fishbein, 1996; Olweus, 1986; Raine, 1993; Rutter et al., 1998; Widom and Ames, 1988; and Wilson and Herrnstein, 1985. ✦

Chapter 11

The Family: What Impact Does the Family Have on Delinquency?

❖ ❖ ❖ ❖   Chapter 10 concluded that certain individual traits increase the likelihood of delinquency, especially high-rate, chronic, serious delinquency. Delinquency is also caused by the individual's social environment. Individuals in certain types of environments are more likely to engage in delinquency—for reasons explained by strain, social learning, and control theories. Environmental pressures are especially important for individuals who possess traits conducive to delinquency, but they also lead many "normal" individuals to engage in delinquency.

This chapter begins to examine the effect of the social environment on delinquency. In particular, I ask what types of families increase the likelihood of delinquency. Chapter 12 examines the effect of school experiences and characteristics on delinquency. Subsequent chapters then focus on the effect of delinquent peer groups, gangs, religion, work, the mass media, the larger community, and situational characteristics.

The Effect of the Family on Delinquency

All major delinquency theories argue that the family plays a central role in determining whether juveniles engage in delinquency. The family—perhaps more than any other social group—influences: (1) the juvenile's level of and reaction to strain; (2) whether the juvenile learns to conform or deviate; and (3) the control to which the juvenile is subject. The family sometimes has a direct effect on delinquency, and it sometimes has an indirect effect through its influence on such things as the juvenile's individual traits, school performance, and selection of friends. Many criminologists have gone so far as to claim that juvenile delinquency is largely a function of the juvenile's family experiences (e.g., Gottfredson and Hirschi, 1990; Patterson et al., 1989). Several states have even passed laws that hold parents responsible for the criminal behavior of their children in certain circumstances. These laws are seldom enforced, but a Michigan couple was recently fined $1,200 for not controlling their 16-year-old son. The son had been arrested for burglarizing several homes and having a 4-foot marijuana plant in his bedroom. According to the verdict, the couple had failed to properly supervise their son after his earlier arrests for burglarizing churches and for attacking his father with a golf club (see Murphy and Healy, 1999).

What does the research say about the influence of the family? Are family factors a major cause of delinquency? You've already been exposed to the family research in Chapters 6 through 8, where I discussed the evidence on strain, social learning, and control theories. Much of the research on the family has been directly guided by these theories. As a consequence, portions of the following discussion will sound familiar. The research on the family and delinquency has focused on four major aspects of the family. The first aspect is *family structure*, which has to do with the size and composition of the family; it is commonly argued, for example, that "broken homes" cause delinquency. The second aspect is *parental and sibling deviance*, which has to do with the extent to which parents and siblings engage in crime and deviant behavior. The third aspect is *the quality of family relationships*, which has to do with the emotional ties between family members and how well family members get along with one another. It is commonly argued, for example, that juveniles who love and respect their parents are less delinquent. The fourth aspect is *parental socialization*, which has to do with the extent to which parents teach their children to conform or to deviate. In particular, do parents provide clear rules, monitor behavior, sanction deviance, instruct and model conformity, and reinforce conformity. I present here the major research findings in each of these four areas. As before, I will try to give you some sense of the findings that are fairly well established and those that are more tentative.

Family Structure

Are Juveniles From Broken Homes More Delinquent?

An "intact" home is typically defined as one in which both natural parents are present. "Broken homes" are defined as all other homes. Researchers sometimes distinguish between different types of broken homes, such as homes in which only the natural mother is present and homes in which there is a natural mother and a stepfather.

Many criminologists, politicians, and others argue that broken homes are a major cause of delinquency. The alleged impact of broken homes is usually explained in terms of the leading delinquency theories. Juveniles in broken homes are said to be under more strain, partly because of the conflict associated with the breakup and partly because of the financial and other problems that often follow the breakup. Juveniles in broken homes are said to be subject to less control; among other things, the breakup is said to disrupt the emotional bond between juveniles and their parents, reduce the ability of parents to exercise effective supervision, and have a negative impact on the juveniles' school performance. Finally, it is said that juveniles in broken homes are less exposed to conventional role models and more likely to fall prey to delinquent peers, who encourage delinquent behavior.

These arguments have taken on a special urgency in recent years, given the large percentage of juveniles who now live in broken homes. The percentage of children living in broken homes has more than doubled since 1970—with 32 percent of all children living in a broken home in 1999 (23 percent of all children live with their natural mothers, 4 percent with their natural fathers, and 4 percent with neither their natural mothers nor fathers). About 23 percent of white, non-Hispanic children live in broken homes, versus 37 percent of Hispanic children and 65 percent of black children. Much of the increase in the number of broken homes comes from increases in the number of unmarried women and in the birth rate of unmarried women (unmarried women accounted for 18 percent of all births in 1980 versus 33 percent of all births in 1998). Children in broken homes are more likely to suffer from a range of problems, most notably poverty. In 1998, 9 percent of the children in married-couple families were living in poverty versus 46 percent of the children in female-headed families (see Federal Interagency Forum on Child and Family Statistics, 2000, or their web site at *http://www.childstats.gov*). But are broken homes a major cause of delinquency?

The data on broken homes and delinquency are mixed. Some studies find that juveniles from broken homes engage in about the same amount of delinquency as juveniles from intact homes, while other studies find that juveniles from broken homes are somewhat more likely to engage in delinquency. Studies based on official data, like arrest statistics, tend to find that broken homes are more strongly related to delinquency than studies based on self-report data. The reason for this difference may be that police and court officials are more likely to arrest and process juveniles from broken homes than similarly delinquent juveniles from intact homes. They may believe that there is a greater need to assist or control juveniles from broken homes. In addition, broken homes generally have a stronger effect on status and minor offenses—especially family-related offenses like running away—than on serious offenses. When one considers the data as a whole, the best conclusion is that *broken homes have a small to moderate effect on delinquency*. The best overview of the research on broken homes and delinquency concluded that "the prevalence of delinquency in broken homes is 10 to 15 percent higher than in intact homes" (Wells and Rankin, 1991:87).

This conclusion is based on a simple comparison of broken homes and intact homes. You may wonder whether some types of broken homes have a bigger effect on delinquency than other types. For example, does it make a difference whether the home was broken by a divorce or separation versus the death of one of the parents? Since divorces and separations are often preceded by much conflict, we might expect that homes broken by divorce/separation would be more strongly related to delinquency. The data provide some support for this view, suggesting that homes broken by divorce/separation have a stronger association with delinquency.

You may also wonder whether delinquency is more or less likely in mother-only homes (the most common type of broken home) versus mother/stepfather homes (the next most common type). Some argue that remarriage may increase delinquency since it may lead to conflict between the stepfather and children. The data in this area are mixed; overall, they suggest that delinquency is about equally likely in each type of broken home. Other types of broken homes (e.g., natural father only) are less common and have not been well studied. Data also suggest that broken homes have similar effects on males and females, on whites and blacks, and on people who experienced the breakup at a young age and those who experienced it at an older age.[1]

Overall, then, broken homes have a *small to moderate* effect on delinquency. Limited data suggest that this effect is at least partly due to the fact that broken homes have an effect on the quality of family relationships and parental socialization.[2] The fact that broken homes have only a small to moderate effect on delinquency may surprise you, but much data indicate that the structure of the family (e.g., broken versus intact) is much less important than the behavior and attitudes of family members. To paraphrase Van Voorhis et al. (1988), what places a juvenile at risk for delinquency is not so much coming from a broken home as coming from a bad home. While broken homes have an effect on the behavior and attitudes of family members, there are many broken homes with good relationships and many intact homes with poor relationships. A broken home with good relationships is less likely to result in delinquency than an intact home with bad relationships.

Does the Mother's Employment Outside the Home Increase Delinquency?

Until recently, it was the norm for fathers to work outside the home and for mothers to assume major responsibility for child care. In 1950, only 16%

of all children had working mothers. There has been a dramatic increase in female labor force participation in recent years however, and close to 70% of all mothers with dependent children work today (Vander Ven et. al. 1998). As a consequence, some criminologists have asked whether the mother's employment outside the home increases delinquency. (Criminologists have not asked whether the father's employment increases delinquency.) It has been argued that the mother's employment outside the home may increase the likelihood of delinquency for several reasons. Among other things, it may reduce maternal supervision of the child and weaken the emotional bond between the mother and child. Data, however, suggest that the mother's employment outside the home has little effect on these factors, and that there is little or no relationship between delinquency and the mother's employment.

Are Teenage Mothers More Likely to Have Delinquent Children?

About 10 percent of all females between ages 15 and 19 become pregnant each year, and about half of these bear children. (About one-third have abortions; the others miscarry.) That amounts to approximately half a million teenagers who give birth each year. More than 175,000 of these teenage mothers are 17 or younger. I should note, however, that the rates of pregnancy, birth, and abortion among teenagers have been declining since the mid-1990s.

A recent study compared mothers who gave birth at age 17 and under to mothers who had their first birth at ages 20 or 21 (which is two to three years younger than the average age at first birth). Even after background factors like race/ethnicity and class were controlled, it was found that the teenage mothers obtained less education, had larger families, were more likely to be single parents, were more likely to live in poverty, and were more likely to obtain welfare or public assistance. Further, the children of these teenage mothers were more likely to (1) be born prematurely and be of low birth weight (which increases the likelihood that they will develop traits like hyperactivity); (2) be physically abused, neglected, or abandoned; (3) have trouble in school; and (4) become teenage mothers themselves (Maynard, 1997). Given such findings, one might expect that the children of teenage mothers will be more delinquent. The data tend to suggest that this is the case, although the effect of teenage motherhood is moderate in size.[4]

Teenage fathers have not received as much research attention as teenage mothers, although recent data suggest that delinquents are much more likely to become teenage fathers than nondelinquents. Further, there is some indication that teenage fathers increase rather than decrease their level of delinquency after their child is born (Thornberry et al., 2000). While the impact of teenage fathers on the delinquency of their children has not been well studied, there is good reason to expect that teenage fathers increase the likelihood of delinquency. As Thornberry et al. (2000:7) state, "Teen fathers are unlikely to be in a position to provide financial, emotional, or other parental support for their children, and in this regard can be considered poor role models. Their legacy to their children is likely to be one of socioeconomic disadvantage, poorer health, and poorer education, among other hardships."

Are Juveniles From Large Families More Delinquent?

Data suggest that juveniles from large families are slightly more likely to engage in delinquency, even after variables like class are controlled.[5] The reasons for the relationship between family size and delinquency are not entirely clear, but some evidence suggests that the following factors may play a role. Parental supervision is less adequate in large families. There are more children to supervise, and sometimes as a consequence child-rearing responsibilities are delegated to inexperienced siblings. Juveniles in large families are less attached to school and do less well in school. Strain or tension may be higher in large families, because of a number of factors: greater likelihood of overcrowding; the stretching of financial resources; and the competition among siblings for limited resources, such as material objects and attention or affection from parents. Finally, juveniles in large families are more likely to be exposed to delinquent siblings. (Once again, then, we explain the effect of family variables using control, strain, and social learning theory.)

Parental and Sibling Crime/Deviance

Are Juveniles With Criminal or Deviant Parents and Siblings More Likely to Be Delinquent?

The research on parental criminality and delinquency is easy to summarize. Juveniles with a criminal parent or parents are more likely to be delinquent. The likelihood is even greater if the parent has multiple convictions and if the convictions occurred after the juvenile was born. Also, juveniles with deviant parents (e.g., those with alcohol or drug problems or personality problems) are more likely to be delinquent. Having a criminal or deviant parent is a better predictor of delinquency than the family structure variables described above, but it is not as strongly related to delinquency as the family relationship and socialization variables discussed below.[6]

It is easy to think of reasons why parental criminality and deviance are associated with delinquency. One might draw on social learning theory and argue that criminal parents are more likely to model crime, to reinforce crime, and to teach values that favor crime. Limited data, however, suggest that this argument is too simplistic. Criminal parents seldom commit crimes with their children, and they usually disapprove of their children's crime.

Social learning theory, however, may still be of some relevance. While criminal parents may not model or directly encourage crime, they may model aggressive behavior and encourage their children to be tough and good fighters. Also, data suggest that control theory at least partly explains the relationship between parental crime/deviance and delinquency (Sampson and Laub, 1993a). Criminal/deviant parents are less likely to establish a strong emotional bond with their children, properly supervise their children, or use effective disciplinary techniques. In particular, they are more likely to be erratic, threatening, and harsh or punitive in their discipline. Further, the children of criminal/deviant parents perform less well in school. Strain theory may shed some light on the relationship as well, since criminal/deviant parents may be more likely to engage in abusive behaviors and get into conflicts with one another and other family members. All of these effects reflect the fact that criminal/deviant parents are more likely to lack the skills and traits necessary to be effective parents and spouses. Finally, the effect of criminal/deviant parents on delinquency may be partly genetic (see Rowe and Farrington, 1997). That is, criminal/deviant parents may pass on a predisposition for traits conducive to delinquency (see Chapter 10).

Not only are juveniles with criminal parents more likely to be delinquent, but so are juveniles with delinquent siblings.[7] In fact, having a delinquent sibling is about as strongly associated with the juvenile's delinquency as having a criminal parent. Since juveniles in the same family are exposed to similar family influences, it is not surprising that siblings tend to exhibit similar levels of delinquency. Data, however, suggest that this similarity is not simply a function of exposure to similar family influences. Delinquent siblings will often socialize one another in ways that increase the likelihood of crime; for example, they may provide models for delinquency, reinforce delinquency, and teach beliefs conducive to delinquency.

The Quality of Family Relationships

Family structure and parental/sibling crime affect delinquency largely through their effect on family relationships—how well family members get along and the extent to which the juvenile is socialized for conformity versus deviance. In this section and the next, I consider family relationship variables related to delinquency. These variables tend to be more strongly related to delinquency than the family structure and parental/sibling crime variables just discussed. First, I consider the quality of family relationships and then parental socialization.

Are Juveniles With 'Warm' or Close Relationships With Their Parents Less Delinquent?

Much data suggest that delinquency is lower among juveniles who have a close or warm relationship with their parents. This closeness or warmth involves several related dimensions.[8]

Parental rejection of or indifference to the juvenile. Delinquency is lower when parents love their children and express this love through their actions. Such parents talk with their children, engage in pleasurable activities with them, express interest in them, and provide them with comfort and support. Parents who do not do these things—who reject or ignore their children—are more likely to have delinquent children. In fact, parental rejection is one of the strongest family correlates of delinquency. If parents do not love their children and are unwilling to invest time and effort in them, parents are unlikely to earn their children's love or effectively socialize them.

Attachment of juvenile to parents. Delinquency is lower when juveniles have a strong emotional bond or attachment to their parents. Attachment to parents is usually measured by asking juveniles how much they love and respect their parents, care about them, identify with and want to be like them, feel close to them, or engage in intimate communication with them. Not surprisingly, attachment to parents is closely related to parental rejection of the juvenile, although parental attachment and parental rejection are distinct concepts (see Sampson and Laub, 1993a). Data suggest that attachment to parents is associated with lower delinquency, although the association is often modest in size. Attachment to mother and father have similar effects, although individuals who are attached to two parents are lower in delinquency than those attached to one (which partly explains why delinquency is higher among juveniles from single-parent homes; see Rankin and Kern, 1994).

Attachment may prevent delinquency for reasons related to control, social learning, and strain theories. Most notably, attachment functions as a form of control. Juveniles who are attached to their parents do not want to do anything to upset their parents. That is, they have a greater "stake in conformity." Further, juveniles who are attached to their parents will be more likely to model parental behavior, accept parental beliefs, and respond to parental sanctions. Among other things, this reduces the likelihood that juveniles will fall under the influence of delinquent peers. (It should be noted that while attachment to conventional parents reduces delinquency, attachment to criminal or deviant parents does not reduce delinquency and may even increase it; see Foshee and Bauman, 1992; Jensen and Brownfield, 1983). Finally, juveniles attached to their parents will likely find their home to be a less stressful place.

Family conflict. Parental rejection and parental attachment are closely related to, but distinct from, family conflict. Juveniles may reject and be rejected by their parents, but family conflict may nevertheless be low. Family members, for example, may ignore one another or spend little time together. Data suggest that delinquency is lower in families with little conflict. This includes conflict between spouses and between parents and juveniles. Such conflict may assume a number of forms: frequent quarreling, expressions of disapproval, nagging, scolding, threatening, and the like. Family conflict, of course, may be caused by the delinquent or troublesome behavior of the juvenile. Data, however, suggest that conflict also has a causal effect on delinquency. It may weaken the emotional bond between parents and the juvenile, disrupt efforts to socialize the juvenile, expose the juvenile to aggressive models and beliefs, increase the likelihood of association with delinquent peers, and increase the level of strain to which the juvenile is subject.

Child abuse. The quality of family relationships may sometimes deteriorate to the point that the child is being abused. Researchers have examined the impact of several types of child abuse on delinquency, especially physical abuse, sexual abuse, and neglect (failure to provide adequate food, shelter, medical care, affection/attention). In 1997, over 3 million cases of abuse were reported to authorities. Over 1 million of these cases were substantiated, representing a rate of 15 per 1,000 children. Twenty-two percent of these cases involved physical abuse, 8 percent sexual abuse, 54 percent neglect, 4 percent emotional abuse, and 12 percent other types of maltreatment (Wang and Daro, 1998). It is widely acknowledged that most cases of abuse are *not* reported to authorities. Researchers have tried to estimate the full extent of abuse by surveying parents, juveniles, and community professionals like doctors and school officials. For example, a 1995 Gallup Poll of 1,000 parents estimated that 3 million children each year are *physically abused*, representing a rate of about 44 per 1,000 children. English (1998) provides an excellent overview of the extent and consequences of child abuse.

❖ ❖ ❖ ❖

Early studies on the relationship between child abuse and delinquency suffered from a number of methodological problems, such as the use of small, nonrepresentative samples; cross-sectional designs; and questionable measures of both abuse and delinquency. There is some indication that these studies may have exaggerated the effect of abuse on delinquency, leading many people to conclude that abuse is a very strong predictor of delinquency. More recent studies, however, have begun to overcome such problems. These studies suggest that abuse increases the likelihood of delinquency by a *moderate* amount. Contrary to popular opinion, most abused individuals do not become serious delinquents. There is some indication that different types of abuse may have different effects on delinquency, with data suggesting that neglect may have a stronger effect on delinquency than other types of abuse.

It appears that many children are able to escape at least some of the negative consequences of abuse; researchers are now investigating this topic. For example, abuse is less likely to lead to delinquency among those who receive social support from others and do well in school.[9]

I discussed why abuse increases the likelihood of delinquency at the end of Chapter 9 (also see Brezina, 1998).

Parental Socialization

While it is important for parents to establish a warm or close relationship with their children, it is also important for them to teach their children to engage in conventional behavior and avoid delinquency. I have already discussed some of the steps parents must take in this area when I described social learning and control theories in Chapters 7 and 8. Parts of this discussion will be familiar to you as a consequence.

What Should Parents Do to Teach Their Children to Avoid Delinquency?

Provide clear rules for behavior. Parents must provide their children with a clear set of rules that specify what behaviors are unacceptable and that restrict opportunities to engage in deviance. Such rules, for example, may specify who the children can and cannot associate with, where they can and cannot go, what TV shows they can and cannot watch, and what time they should be home at night. As indicated in Chapter 8, such rules should not be overly strict. Overly strict rules may increase delinquency, perhaps for reasons related to strain theory.

Monitor the juvenile's behavior. Parents must monitor their children's behavior to ensure that they comply with the rules the parents have set down. Monitoring may be direct or indirect. Direct monitoring involves the parents' direct observation of the juvenile. Indirect monitoring may involve talking to the juvenile on a regular basis about their activities, talking with the juvenile's teachers and others, and keeping track of what the juvenile is doing—including how well they do their schoolwork and the character of their friends. Patterson et al. (1992:63) state that the "parents of antisocial children have little information about where their children are, who they are with, what they are doing, or when they will be home."

Consistently sanction the juvenile for rule violations. Such sanctions should not be too harsh or punitive. In particular, some evidence suggests that parents' verbal abuse and physical punishment may increase their children's delinquency (see Chapter 8). Recommended types of sanctions include the loss of privileges, the imposition of chores, clear expressions of disapproval, reasoning, and—for younger children—time out.

These parental actions not only provide direct control over the juvenile, but they also increase the juvenile's level of internal control. They lead to the internalization of beliefs that condemn delinquency. When rule violations are consistently followed by sanctions, the juvenile soon becomes anxious or nervous at the thought of doing something wrong, which means that the rules have been "internalized," or the juvenile has developed a "conscience." These actions also cause the juvenile to develop some measure of self-control (see Chapter 8). Data indicate that delinquency is lower in families where parents take these actions; in fact, they are among the most important family variables.[10]

Employ effective techniques for resolving problems/crises. All families occasionally confront problems that threaten to disrupt members' relations with one another. It is important for family members to develop effective techniques for resolving these problems. Otherwise, such problems may interfere with the ability of parents to effectively socialize their children and may increase the level of strain or stress in family members. Families with delinquent children are more likely to employ poor problem-solving techniques: family members tend to blame one another when problems arise, they get angry and argue with one another, and they spend less time trying to define the problem and evaluate effective solutions.

The following model for effective problem solving has been suggested: "(1) The problem should be clearly stated in neutral terms; (2) the other person paraphrases to show that he or she has heard the problem correctly; (3) brainstorm a list of possible solutions; (4) choose a solution through a process of negotiation (compromise), and write a contract that describes the terms of the agreement, the positive consequences for following the agreement, and the negative consequences for violating it" (Patterson et al., 1992:78).

Data on the relationship between delinquency and family problem-solving techniques is sparse, but limited data suggest a weak relationship (see Patterson et al., 1992).

Disciplinary styles. Data from Patterson and his associates suggest that the families of delinquent children frequently fall into one of two types. In the first type, supervision and discipline are *lax*. Parents do not define many objectionable acts as deviant; they do not closely monitor the juvenile; and they seldom punish deviant/delinquent acts.

In the second type, parents frequently punish or threaten to punish, but such punishment is ineffective because it is inconsistently applied. In particular, parents engage in what Patterson (1982) calls "*nattering*." They are quick to condemn even the most trivial deviant acts, and they regularly nag, scold, lecture, and issue commands to the juvenile. Occasionally, they may "explode" and physically abuse the juvenile. On most occasions, however, the parents fail to back up their verbal reprimands with meaningful, nonviolent punishments. In the words of Patterson (1982:225), "they tend to . . . natter, but they do not confront. They do not say, 'No.' They do not say, 'Stop that behavior here and now.'" So the parents complain a lot about the child's behavior, but the child is only occasionally punished for his or her misdeeds.

Often, a negative pattern of interaction develops between family members. Parents treat the child in an aversive way—for example, by threatening or scolding. The child responds by arguing or threatening. The situation escalates, with the parent and child threatening and insulting one another in a series of responses. Eventually, one of the family members—often a parent— backs down. The parent's backing down serves to negatively reinforce the juvenile's aversive behavior. In certain cases, the juvenile's aversive behavior may even be positively reinforced, often by attention from the parents. The juvenile's aggressive behavior, then, is inconsistently punished and frequently reinforced. The constant battles between family members have other negative effects. They reduce the emotional bonds between parent and child and the amount of time that family members spend interacting. This decrease in emotional bonds and interaction further reduces parents' control and makes it more difficult for them to effectively socialize the child. Antagonism between family members also creates a high level of strain and anger, which further increases the likelihood of aggression and delinquency.

What Should Parents Do to Teach Their Children to Engage in Conventional Behavior?

The socialization process has two sides. Parents not only need to teach their children to refrain from delinquency, they also need to teach them how to engage in conventional behavior. In particular, they need to teach their children social, academic, and problem-solving skills. Such skills are necessary if juveniles are to do well in school, become involved in conventional peer groups, and resolve any problems that arise with peers and others in a nondelinquent manner. The failure to teach such skills may result in school failure, rejection by conventional peers, and association with delinquent peers.[11]

Such skills are taught in several ways. Parents provide *direct instruction* (e.g., teaching children the alphabet, telling juveniles what they should do if they get into a dispute with a friend). Parents *model* these skills; for example, parents may model effective problem-solving skills when disputes arise between family members. Parents provide *opportunities* for juveniles to practice these skills; the parents should choose such opportunities so juveniles have a reasonable chance of successfully exhibiting the skill. And parents *reinforce* juveniles when they successfully employ these skills.

At the same time, juveniles often face problems or demands that they are not equipped to handle. In such cases, it is important for parents to provide support and assistance. Such support may assume several forms: emotional support, in which parents comfort or reassure the juvenile; informational support, in which parents provide advice on what to do or help clarify issues; and instrumental support, in which parents provide the juvenile with money, goods, or direct assistance. In some cases, parents may have to act on behalf of their children, functioning as their advocates.

The activities described in the preceding paragraphs are sometimes referred to as "positive parenting." There has not been much research on the relationship between these activities and delinquency, but limited data suggest that their absence is associated with delinquency. For example, data suggest that the parents of delinquent children are less likely to reinforce conventional behavior.[12]

Summary

Most people believe that the family has a major impact on delinquency. The data suggest that they are right in this belief. Many people, however, are misinformed about what aspects of the family are most strongly related to delinquency. They believe, for example, that delinquency is caused by mothers who work or by parents who do not spank their children. The data suggest that these arguments are wrong.

We considered four sets of family variables, those having to do with family structure; parental and sibling crime; the quality of family relationships; and parental socialization. Certain variables, like mothers' employment, appear to have little or no effect on delinquency. Other variables have a small to moderate effect on delinquency, such as broken homes, teenage parents, and family size. Still other variables have a moderate effect on delinquency: parental and sibling crime, attachment of juvenile to parent, family conflict, and child abuse. The most important family variables are parental rejection of the child and the nature of parental efforts to socialize the child against delinquency. The effect of other variables, such as parental efforts to teach the child conforming behavior, are less clear.

Data suggest that our ability to explain delinquency is substantially improved when we consider several family variables together.[13] In particular, data suggest that delinquency is *least* likely when the quality of family relationships is good *and* parents attempt to socialize children against delinquency (they set clear rules, monitor behavior, and consistently sanction deviance). This style of parenting has sometimes been called *warm and authoritative* (or warm but firm). Parents have a warm or close relationship with their children, but at the same time they have clear rules, which they enforce. Delinquency is most common among the children of parents who employ *warm and lax* and *cold and lax* styles of parenting.[14]

There is some evidence that family variables are more important during childhood and early adolescence than during mid- to late adolescence.[15] As children develop, they become more autonomous from parents and more subject to peer and community influences. Also, a person's predisposition to delinquency often forms early in life (see Patterson et al., 1992:22–27). Once it is formed, the family may come to exercise less influence over the juvenile.

I explained the effect of family variables on delinquency using strain, social learning, and control theories. In most cases, the effect of a particular family variable can be explained using two or all of these theories. One can argue, for example, that child abuse increases juveniles' level of strain, reduces their level of control (e.g., attachment to parents), and teaches them to engage in aggression (e.g., models aggression).

Why Do Some Parents Employ Poor Parenting Practices?

❖ ❖ ❖ ❖

Several related explanations for poor parenting practices can be given. First, some parents may lack the traits necessary to be successful parents. For example, they may be easily irritated and have little concern for the welfare of others, including their children. This may partly explain why criminal parents are more likely to be poor parents.[16]

Second, some parents may lack the knowledge to be effective parents. Perhaps they never experienced good parenting when they were children, so they do not know how to be good parents themselves. In this area, Patterson (1986) found that the poor disciplinary practices of grandparents were associated with the antisocial behavior of both their children and *grandchildren*. Some evidence suggests that the grandparents failed to teach their children effective disciplinary techniques, and this partly accounts for the antisocial behavior of the grandchildren (Patterson et al., 1992). Also, family training programs that teach parents good parenting skills have shown signs of success. That is, parents enrolled in such programs are often able to reduce the delinquency of their children. (Chapter 22 contains more information on such programs.)

Third, some parents may have "difficult" children, who possess traits like hyperactivity, attention deficit, impulsivity, and irritability. Children with such traits can challenge even the best of parents. Such parents may come to dislike their children and may even stop trying to "parent" them in an effort to avoid conflict and gain some measure of peace. Data suggest that difficult children do have an adverse effect on parenting practices.[17] Also, if traits like impulsivity are genetically based, difficult children may be more likely to have parents who are ill equipped to care for them. The most demanding children, then, may be matched with the least able parents.

Fourth, many parents may experience strains or stressors that make it difficult for them to employ good parenting practices. In this area, poor parenting practices have been linked to low socioeconomic status, unemployment, drug and alcohol use, divorce, teenage motherhood, large family size, and family violence.[18] Also, an observational study revealed that mothers were more likely to engage in poor parenting practices on days when they experienced high stress (Patterson et al., 1989).

Many of these risk factors often converge, and poor parenting appears most likely when unskilled parents facing numerous stressors attempt to raise difficult children.

Notes

1. For overviews and selected studies on broken homes and delinquency, see Farrington, 1996a, 1996b; Gove and Crutchfield, 1982; Henggeler, 1989; Hirschi, 1995; Hollin, 1992; Johnson, 1986; Loeber, Farrington, Stouthamer-Loeber, and Van Kammen, 1998; Loeber and Stouthamer-Loeber, 1986; Matsueda and Heimer, 1987; Nye, 1958; Rankin, 1983; Rankin and Wells, 1994; Rebellon, 1999; Rosen, 1985; Rutter et al., 1998; Sampson and Laub, 1993a; Simons et al., 1993; Thornberry et al., 1998; Wells and Rankin, 1991; Wilson and Herrnstein, 1985; Wright and Wright, 1995.

2. *See* Jang and Smith, 1997; Matsueda and Heimer, 1987; Rankin and Kern, 1994; Rankin and Wells, 1994; Rebellon, 1999; Rutter et al., 1998; Sampson and Laub, 1993a; Snyder and Patterson, 1987; Van Voorhis et al., 1988.

3. *See* Farrington, 1995; Loeber and Stouthamer-Loeber, 1986; Vander Ven et. al., 1998, Wells and Rankin, 1988; Wright and Wright, 1995.

4. *See* Furstenberg et al., 1987; Grogger, 1997; Loeber, Farrington, Stouthamer-Loeber, and Van Kammen, 1998; Maynard and Garry, 1997; Moore et al., 1997; Rutter et al., 1998.

5. *See* Farrington, 1995, 1996a; Fischer, 1984; Hirschi, 1995; Hollin, 1992; Loeber and Stouthamer-Loeber, 1986; Patterson et al., 1992; Rutter et al., 1998; Sampson and Laub, 1993a; Tygart, 1991; Wells and Rankin, 1988.

6. For overviews and recent research in this area, see Canter, 1982; Farrington, 1995, 1996a, 1996b; Henggeler, 1989; Loeber and Stouthamer-Loeber, 1986; Rowe and Farrington, 1997; Rutter and Giller, 1983; Sampson and Laub, 1993a; Snyder and Patterson, 1987; Wilson and Herrnstein, 1985; Wright and Wright, 1995; Wu and Kandel, 1995.

7. *See* Farrington, 1995; Hollin, 1992; Loeber and Stouthamer- Loeber, 1986; Rowe and Farrington, 1997; Rowe and Gulley, 1992; also see Sampson and Laub, 1993a.

8. For overviews and recent studies in this area, see Burton et al., 1995; Canter, 1982; Cernkovich and Giordano, 1987; Conger et al., 1992, 1994; Gove and Crutchfield, 1982; Henggeler, 1989; Hollin, 1992; Jang and Smith, 1997; Loeber and Stouthamer-Loeber, 1986; Matsueda and Heimer, 1987; McCord, 1991; Nye, 1958; Rankin and Kern, 1994; Rankin and Wells, 1990; Rosen, 1985; Sampson and Laub, 1993a; Snyder and Patterson, 1987; Thornberry et al., 1998; Wells and Rankin, 1988; Wilson and Herrnstein, 1985; Wright and Wright, 1995.

9. For overviews and recent studies, see Hirschi, 1995; Rutter et al., 1998; Siegel and Senna, 1997; Smith and Thornberry, 1995; Widom, 1989, 1997; Wilson and Herrnstein, 1985; Wright and Wright, 1995; Zingraff et al., 1993; Zingraff et al., 1994.

10. For overviews and selected studies, see Burton et al., 1995; Cernkovich and Giordano, 1987; Conger et al., 1995; Farrington, 1996a, b; Gove and Crutchfield, 1982; Henggeler, 1989; Hirschi, 1995; Hollin, 1992; Jang and Smith, 1997; Loeber, Farrington, Stouthamer-Loeber, and Van Kammen, 1998; Loeber and Stouthamer-Loeber, 1986; Matsueda and Heimer, 1987; McCord, 1991; Nye, 1958; Patterson, 1982; 1986; Patterson et al., 1989; Patterson et al., 1992; Rankin and Wells, 1990; Sampson and Laub, 1993a; Synder and Patterson, 1987; Thornberry et al., 1998; Wells and Rankin, 1988; Wright and Wright, 1995.

11. *See* Patterson, 1982; Patterson et al., 1989; Patterson et al., 1992; Snyder and Patterson, 1987.

12. *See* Cullen's, 1994, discussion of social support and crime; Catalano and Hawkins, 1996; Cullen and Wright, 1996; DuBow and Reid, 1994; Nye, 1958; the work of Patterson and associates cited.

13. *See* Loeber and Stouthamer-Loeber, 1986; Snyder and Patterson, 1987; Wright and Wright, 1995.

14. For a fuller discussion, see Henggeler, 1989; Loeber and Stouthamer-Loeber, 1986; McCord, 1991; Snyder and Patterson, 1987; Wilson and Herrnstein, 1985.

15. *See* Agnew, 1985b; Jang, 1999; Jang and Smith, 1997; Loeber and Stouthamer-Loeber, 1986; Sampson and Laub, 1993a; Thornberry, 1987, 1996; Thornberry et al., 1991, 1998.

16. *See* Patterson et al., 1992; Rutter et al., 1998; Sampson and Laub, 1993a; Snyder and Patterson, 1987.

17. *See* Jang and Smith, 1997; Moffitt, 1997; Patterson, 1982; Rutter, 1985; Rutter et al., 1998; Sampson and Laub, 1993a; Wilson and Herrnstein, 1985.

18. *See* Conger et al., 1992, 1994, 1995; Larzelere and Patterson, 1990; Moore et al., 1997; Patterson, 1982, 1986; Patterson et al., 1989; Patterson et al., 1992; Rutter et

al., 1998; Sampson and Laub, 1993a; Simons et al., 1993; Snyder and Patterson, 1987; Thornberry et al., 1998; Tygart, 1991. ✦

Chapter 12

The School: What Impact Does the School Have on Delinquency?

❖ ❖ ❖ ❖   There are good reasons for expecting the school to have an effect on delinquency. Most juveniles spend a great deal of time in school, and school experiences may have a significant impact on their level of strain, their level of control, and the extent to which they learn delinquent or conventional behavior. Many juveniles do poorly in school and come to dislike or even hate it. School becomes a source of strain for them, it exercises little control over them, and it provides a context for associating with other dissatisfied, often delinquent, adolescents. Schools, then, may contribute to delinquency in several ways.

I first discuss the effect of the juvenile's *school experiences* on delinquency. It is easy to describe the *association* between school experiences and delinquency. As you might expect, delinquents are more likely to (1) perform poorly in school; (2) be less involved in school activities; (3) dislike school; (4) have poor relations with teachers; (5) have lower educational goals; and (6) have higher rates of misbehavior in school. What is less clear, however, is the extent to which these experiences cause delinquency. As discussed below, some researchers argue that the association between school experiences and delinquency is caused by third variables and by the causal effect of delinquency on school experiences. Others disagree, claiming that school experiences do have a causal effect on delinquency.

What Types of School Experiences Contribute to Delinquency?

I describe the *association* between school experiences and delinquency below.[1]

1. *Academic performance*. Delinquents tend to have lower grades, score lower on tests measuring academic achievement, are more likely to be placed in special education classes or on noncollege tracks, and are more likely to be held back. One overview of the research in this area concluded that children with poor academic records (grades of F or D) were about twice as likely to engage in delinquency as children with good academic records (grades of C or above) (Maguin and Loeber, 1996).

2. *School involvement*. Delinquents are less likely to participate in school activities, spending less time on homework and in extracurricular activities (see Agnew and Petersen, 1989; Osgood et al., 1996).

3. *Attachment to school*. Delinquents are more likely to dislike school and to feel that school is irrelevant to them. For example, they are more likely to state that they do not like school, that they resent the restrictions at school, that school is boring and a waste of time, and that they would rather be elsewhere.

4. *Relations with teachers*. Delinquents are more likely to report that they dislike their teachers and have unpleasant relations with them. For example, they are more likely to state that their teachers often lose their tempers, make negative comments, and talk down to students (see Agnew, 1985a).

5. *Educational/occupational goals*. Delinquents have lower educational and occupational goals. For example, they desire less education than nondelinquents and they expect to receive less education. Delinquents are also more likely to drop out of school. Recent data, however, suggest that dropping out of school has little effect on subsequent delinquency in most cases. In certain cases, dropping out may lead to an increase or a decrease in delinquency, depending on such things as the reason for dropping out and the social class of the dropout (see Krohn et al., 1995; Jarjoura, 1993, 1996).

6. *School misbehavior*. Finally, delinquents are more likely to violate school rules. In particular, they are more likely to cut classes, be truant from school, and violate other rules.

Do School Experiences Cause Delinquency?

The association between the above school experiences and delinquency is often modest in size, but few criminologists would dispute that such an association exists. What is in dispute, however, is the meaning of this association (for overviews, see Maguin and Loeber, 1996; Wilson and Herrnstein, 1985). Some researchers suggest that school experiences have little *causal effect* on delinquency. The association between school experiences and delinquency is said to occur because both school experiences and delinquency are caused by the same third variables, in particular, early family experiences and individual traits like intelligence and hyperactivity/impulsivity/attention deficit. This argument has some support. Data suggest that early family experiences and individual traits have a causal effect on both school experiences and delinquency; there is also some evidence that when family experiences and traits are taken into account, the association between school experiences and delinquency is reduced and, in some studies, eliminated.[2] Further, some researchers argue that delinquency may cause negative school experiences, which would also help explain the associations reported above. The data also provide some support for this position.[3] So the association between school experiences and delinquency does not necessarily mean that school experiences cause delinquency. Rather, school experiences and delinquency may be caused by the same third variables, or delinquency may have a causal effect on school experiences.

Other researchers acknowledge the foregoing arguments but claim that school experiences still have some causal effect on delinquency. (You should test your knowledge of the leading delinquency theories by using them to explain why the school experiences listed above might cause delinquency.)[4] The debate over whether school experiences do have a causal effect on delinquency has important policy implications. If school experiences have a causal effect, then programs designed to improve school experiences should reduce delinquency. But if the association between school experiences and delinquency reflects third variables or the causal effect of delinquency on school experiences, such programs would have little effect. The resolution of this debate requires that researchers examine the effect of school experiences on *later* delinquency and take account of, or "control for," relevant third variables. Unfortunately, such research is scarce. As a consequence, the debate over whether school experiences have a causal effect on delinquency continues.[5]

My own tentative reading of the data is that school experiences have a modest causal effect on delinquency. The effect is often demonstrated in longitudinal studies that control for at least some relevant third variables, such as class, family characteristics, and prior delinquency.[6] Studies that control for individual traits such as impulsivity or irritability, however, are less common. Further, programs designed to improve school experiences often reduce delinquency.

Why Do Some Juveniles Have Negative School Experiences?

Since school experiences may have a modest effect on delinquency, it is important to ask why some juveniles have negative school experiences. I have already mentioned certain potential factors. First, individuals with certain traits, like low intelligence and hyperactivity/impulsivity/attention deficit, are more likely to have negative school experiences. Such individuals have more trouble satisfying the academic demands of school and conforming to school requirements, such as remaining seated and attending to the teacher.[7]

Second, many of the family factors listed in Chapter 11 (such as family size, parental criminality, parental rejection, and poor discipline) affect school experiences.[8] Such factors reduce the likelihood that parents will equip their children with the skills and attitudes necessary to do well in school; that parents will effectively monitor their child's school activities; and that parents will assist their children with schoolwork (see Weishew and Peng, 1993).

Third, misbehavior and delinquency affect school experiences. That is, data suggest that misbehavior has a causal effect on at least certain school experiences, like academic performance. Children who misbehave are less attentive to the teacher and spend less time on school tasks, among other things.[9]

Fourth, school experiences are affected by a range of background factors, including socioeconomic status, sex, race, residential mobility (i.e., frequent moving), and the type of community the juvenile lives in.[10] Juveniles from communities with high levels of poverty and family disruption, for example, are more likely to have negative school experiences (see Chapter 14). The effect of these background factors on school experiences is indirect; that is, they affect school experiences through their effect on the juvenile's individual traits and behavior, family and other interpersonal experiences, and the type of school the juvenile attends.

Finally, as discussed next, certain school characteristics have an effect on school experiences and delinquency. That is to say, it does make a difference what type of school a child attends.

School Characteristics and Delinquency

Students in certain schools are much more likely to engage in delinquency, both within school and without, than students in other schools. The students in some schools, for example, have official rates of delinquency (e.g., court appearances per 100 students) more than sixty times greater than that of students in other schools (Farrington, 1996a). I should note that contrary to certain media accounts, most schools do *not* have a major problem with serious violence or theft. Crimes involving serious injury or major financial losses are rare in most schools, although minor crimes do occur on a regular basis. Data from the 1997 National Crime Victimization Survey indicate that there were about 4 acts of violence in school per 100 students between ages 12 and 18. Most of these acts, however, were minor. There was about one act of serious violence (rape/sexual assault, robbery, aggravated assault) per 100 students, and school-age children have less than a one in a million chance of being killed at school. Serious violence is much more likely to occur away from school than at school. There were about 6 thefts at school per 100 students between ages 12 and 18. Most such thefts were minor. Further, evidence suggests that school crime is *not* increasing.[11] As Gottfredson and Gottfredson (1985:167) state, "much of the 'victimization' that occurs in schools involves minor indignities: smart-ass remarks or gestures, one boy forcibly asking another for a quarter, a notebook lifted from someone's desk." I do not mean to minimize the violence and crime that does occur in schools. As we are painfully aware, serious acts of violence do happen. And certain schools, particularly schools in poor urban areas, do suffer from high rates of serious crime and violence. Further, the minor crime and violence that occurs can have a devastating impact on many of its victims, particularly those who are chronically victimized.

Data suggest that school differences in delinquency are largely a function of differences between the students who attend the schools and the communities in which the schools are located. Delinquency rates are higher in schools that have a higher percentage of students who are less able, poor, male, and members of minority groups. Delinquency rates are also higher in schools that are located in urban communities with high rates of crime, poverty, unemployment, and female-headed households. However, when researchers take account of student and community characteristics, they find that school characteristics do have a small to modest association with delinquency rates—especially rates of within-school delinquency.

Several studies have focused on the association between school characteristics and in-school delinquency rates. One such study, for example, examined data from over 600 junior and senior public high schools in the United States (see Gottfredson and Gottfredson, 1985). Another examined data from a national sample of 1,051 schools that had eighth-graders in 1988 (Weishew and Peng, 1993). These studies are not in full agreement with one another, and there is some evidence that the findings vary by grade level and by type of delinquency (e.g., theft versus violence, delinquency directed at teachers versus that directed at students). Nevertheless, there are some tentative conclusions that can be drawn about those school characteristics associated with in-school delinquency rates.[12]

The characteristics of low-delinquency or effective schools are similar to the characteristics of effective families—both tend to be "warm but firm." In particular, there is some evidence that rates of in-school delinquency tend to be lower in:

1. *Small schools with good resources*. Delinquency tends to be lower in smaller schools and schools where the average teacher in-

structs a smaller number of different students. It is also lower in schools where teachers are provided with the materials and equipment they need to teach. Drawing on the leading delinquency theories, why do you think school size and resources might be important (recall our discussion of family size and delinquency)?

2. *Schools with good discipline.* Delinquency is lower in schools where there are clear rules for behavior and these rules are consistently enforced in a fair manner. Schools with unclear or ambiguous rules have higher rates of delinquency, as do schools that fail to enforce their rules. This finding does not mean that schools should severely punish minor infractions. In fact, there is some evidence that overly punitive discipline contributes to higher rates of delinquency. Certain studies, for example, suggest that delinquency rates are higher in schools that use physical punishment and that make frequent use of punishment (note the parallels with the family research here). It is best to spot disruptive behavior early and deal with it in a firm but appropriate manner. In particular, there are techniques for responding to disruptive behavior that are not overly punitive and that do not disrupt teaching activities. This early but firm response may prevent more serious problems from developing; problems that may call forth frequent and punitive disciplinary responses.

3. *Schools that provide opportunities for student success and praise student accomplishments.* Delinquency tends to be lower in schools that actively involve students in the learning process and that increase the opportunities for students to succeed, including students who do not plan to attend college. Certain teaching techniques that help accomplish these goals are described in Chapter 22. Further, delinquency tends to be lower in schools where teachers praise student accomplishments. As indicated in the discussion of the family, it is important both to punish delinquency *and* to reinforce conventional behavior.

4. *Schools with high expectations for students.* Delinquency is lower in schools with high standards for success, where the teachers have high expectations for their students and make rigorous but not unrealistic work demands on them.

5. *Schools with pleasant working conditions for students.* Delinquency is lower in schools where teachers have positive attitudes toward students and show concern for them. Such concern is shown by a teacher meeting with students who are having problems and by a teacher attempting to create a pleasant physical space for students to work (e.g., cleaning up trash and graffiti, providing attractive decorations).

6. *Schools with good cooperation between the administration and teachers.* Delinquency is lower in schools where administrators and counselors keep teachers informed of disciplinary problems and support or assist teachers in their disciplinary efforts. This

cooperation probably makes it easier for schools to develop and   ❖ ❖ ❖ ❖
effectively enforce a clear set of rules.

I should note that private schools generally have lower rates of delinquency than public schools, even after one takes account of differences between the students who attend private and public schools. Some evidence suggests that this difference arises because private and public schools differ on many of the characteristics just listed. Based on their extensive analysis of public and private schools, Coleman et al. (1982:102–103) state, "the Catholic schools are the strictest in discipline; the other private schools are somewhat less strict and appear to nurture the student to a greater degree (as evidenced by perceived teacher interest). The public schools, taken as a whole, are neither strict nor do they nurture the student. In addition, they are least often regarded by their students as fair in the exercise of discipline." Further, private schools are more academically demanding than public schools.

Taken as a whole, these data suggest that the schools with the lowest rates of delinquency are firm on the one hand; they have clear rules that are uniformly enforced and they are academically demanding. On the other hand, they are "warm"; they treat students in a fair manner; teachers are interested in students, provide opportunities for success, and praise student accomplishments; and school staff attempt to create a pleasant environment for the students.

It is easy to explain the effect of these school characteristics in terms of strain, social learning, and control theories. Schools with these characteristics should create less strain. They are more pleasant; students get along better with their teachers and presumably with other students (since student misbehavior is less tolerated). They are fairer. And students are more likely to achieve their success goals. The students in such schools are also subject to greater control. In particular, they are subject to more direct control; they are more likely to form an emotional attachment to teachers and an investment in conventional activities; and they may even be more likely to internalize beliefs condemning delinquency and develop some measure of self-control. Finally, drawing on social learning theory, one could argue that these schools are more likely to punish delinquency and reinforce conformity, teach conventional beliefs, and provide exposure to conventional models. Such schools may also be less likely to provide exposure to delinquent others, since the schools would discourage the formation of delinquent peer groups.

Notes

1. For overviews and recent studies, see Agnew, 1985a; Cernkovich and Giordano, 1992; Hawkins and Lishner, 1987; Jarjoura and Triplett, 1997; Jenkins, 1997; Maguin and Loeber, 1996; Sampson and Laub, 1993a; Thornberry et al., 1998; Wiatrowski and Anderson, 1987; Wiatrowski et al., 1981; Wiatrowski et al., 1982; Wilson and Herrnstein, 1985.
2. *See* Krohn et al., 1995; Maguin and Loeber, 1996; Wiatrowski and Anderson, 1987; Wiatrowski et al., 1982; Wilson and Herrnstein, 1985:267.
3. *See* Hawkins and Lishner, 1987; Krohn et al., 1995; Thornberry, 1996; Thornberry et al., 1998.
4. *See* Hawkins and Lishner, 1987; Maguin and Loeber, 1996; Wilson and Herrnstein, 1985.

5. *See* Jarjoura, 1993, 1996; Krohn et al., 1995; Maguin and Loeber, 1996; Wiatrowski et al., 1982.

6. *See* Loeber, Farrington, Stouthamer-Loeber, and Van Kammen, 1998; Maguin and Loeber, 1996; Sampson and Laub, 1993a; Thornberry, 1996; Thornberry et al., 1998.

7. *See* Maguin and Loeber, 1996; Sampson and Laub, 1993a; Wiatrowski et al., 1981.

8. *See* Jenkins, 1997; Patterson, 1986; Sampson and Laub, 1993a; Patterson et al., 1992.

9. *See* Hawkins and Lishner, 1987; Patterson, 1986; Patterson et al., 1989; Patterson et al., 1992; Thornberry, 1996; Thornberry et al., 1998.

10. *See* Alexander, 1997; Jenkins, 1997; Maguin and Loeber, 1996; Sampson and Laub, 1993a.

11. *See* Kaufman et al., 1999; also see Anderson, 1998; Elliott et al., 1998; Kopka, 1997; Lawrence, 1998; McDermott, 1993; Toby, 1995.

12. For overviews and recent studies, see Catalano and Hawkins, 1996; Coleman et al., 1982; Elliott et al., 1998; Gottfredson and Gottfredson, 1985; Hawkins and Lishner, 1987; Hellman and Beaton, 1986; Lawrence, 1998; Rutter et al., 1998; Rutter et al., 1979; Weishew and Peng, 1993; Welsh, Greene, and Jenkins, 1999; Wilson and Herrnstein, 1985; also see Alexander, 1997. ✦

Delinquent Peers and Gangs: What Impact Do Delinquent Peer Groups and Gangs Have on Delinquency?

❖ ❖ ❖ ❖   As juveniles enter adolescence, the peer group comes to occupy a central—in many cases *the central*—place in their lives. Adolescents start spending much more time with their peers; they attach more importance to their peers; and they are more strongly influenced by their peers (Thornberry et al., 1998, Warr, 1993). It is no surprise, then, that most adolescents who commit delinquent offenses do so in the company of peers. One study, based on a nationally representative sample of adolescents, found that 73 percent of delinquent offenses were committed in a group. For example, 91 percent of all burglaries and alcohol violations were committed in a group, 79 percent of all drug violations, 71 percent of all assaults, 60 percent of all acts of vandalism, 49 percent of all acts of truancy, and 44 percent of all thefts (Warr, 1996). Other studies produce somewhat different percentages, but most show that a majority of all delinquent acts are committed with peers.

Drawing on such data, many criminologists argue that the peer group has a major effect on an individual's delinquency. In particular, they claim that associating with delinquent peers is a major cause of delinquency. They most often draw on social learning theory when making this argument. As indicated in Chapter 7, delinquent peers are said to reinforce the adolescent's delinquency, model delinquent behavior, and present values conducive to delinquency. This chapter examines the impact of delinquent peers on delinquency. First, I focus on the impact of delinquent peers in general. I then examine the impact of a particular type of delinquent peer group that has received much attention in the media: the gang.

What Impact Do Delinquent Peers Have on Delinquency?

Is associating with delinquent peers an important cause of delinquency? Cross-sectional data indicate that juveniles with delinquent friends are much more likely to engage in delinquency. In fact, having delinquent friends is typically the strongest correlate of delinquency. But as you know, the fact that delinquent friends and delinquency are associated does *not* mean that having delinquent friends *causes* delinquency. Both of these variables may be caused by the same third variable(s). In particular, it has been argued that individual traits (e.g., impulsivity), family problems, and negative school experiences cause delinquency on the one hand and association with delinquent peers on the other. It has also been argued that the association is due to the fact that delinquency causes one to associate with delinquent peers. Most people prefer to associate with people who are like them, so delinquents may choose to associate with fellow delinquents ("birds of a feather flock together"). Until recently, it was not clear *why* having delinquent peers was associated with delinquency.

Data now suggest that the association between delinquent peers and delinquency is *partly* due to the causal effect of delinquent peers on delinquency. Several longitudinal studies have found that associating with delinquent peers leads to an increase in subsequent delinquency, even when other variables are controlled. In fact, associating with delinquent peers is often the best predictor of subsequent delinquency (other than the juvenile's level of prior delinquency). Research also indicates that the association is *partly* due to the fact that delinquent peers and delinquency are caused by the same third variables, such as negative family experiences. Further, delinquency has a causal effect on delinquent peers; that is, delinquent individuals are more likely to select fellow delinquents as friends.[1]

A recent study by Elliott and Menard (1996) sheds light on the relationship between delinquent peers and delinquency. Their data suggest that the progression from no delinquency to serious delinquency typically proceeds in the following manner: (1) juveniles associate with mildly delinquent peers *before* they engage in delinquency; (2) this peer association leads to minor delinquency; (3) this minor delinquency leads to association with more delinquent peers; (4) this association leads to more serious delinquency, and so on. Not all juveniles move as far as serious delinquency, and some juveniles do not complete these steps in the order shown. Some juveniles, for example, may engage in delinquency *before* associating with delinquent peers. Nevertheless, this pattern is the most common pattern of progression. It illustrates that delinquent peers and delinquent acts are reciprocally related to one another; each has a causal effect on the other.[2]

Under What Conditions Are Delinquent Peers Most Likely to Cause Delinquency?

Recent data suggest that the effect of delinquent peers on delinquency is not the same in all circumstances. The effect of delinquent peers is greatest when the juvenile likes these peers and spends a lot of time with them. It is greatest when these peers hold beliefs conducive to delinquency, approve of the juvenile's delinquency, and pressure the juvenile to engage in delinquency. And it is greatest when the juvenile is not strongly attached to or closely supervised by parents. The effect of delinquent peers may also be greater for certain types of offenses, like drug use.[3] These conditional effects should not be too surprising; they are easily explained by social learning and other theories. For example, social learning theory states that we are more likely to model someone's behavior if we like that person, are frequently exposed to her or his behavior, and are infrequently exposed to competing behaviors.

What Are Delinquent Peer Groups Like?

Only a small percentage of delinquent peer groups are gangs. The term "delinquent group," in fact, is somewhat misleading. Most "delinquent groups" are better described as *friendship groups* that occasionally engage in delinquency. This will become apparent as I comment on the *types of delinquency committed by these groups*, the *size and composition of the groups*, and the *quality of relations between group members*.

Types of delinquency. Delinquent peer groups usually only engage in minor delinquency on an occasional basis, although a significant percentage of groups engage in more frequent and serious delinquency. Warr (1993), for example, found that by mid- to late adolescence a majority of adolescents had close friends who engaged in minor forms of deviance such as marijuana and alcohol use, cheating, and petty theft. Less than 20 percent, however, had friends who engaged in serious offenses such as burglary, theft over $50, or selling hard drugs.[4]

Size and composition. The groups that engage in delinquency are usually small. The typical size is two to four juveniles, with the groups getting smaller in size as juveniles age. By mid- to late adolescence, the typical offending group consists of only two or three juveniles. (Adults, unlike juveniles, are most likely to commit their offenses alone.) These small groups are subsets of larger groups or cliques of youth (but usually not gangs). Juveniles seldom commit offenses with the same person(s) all the time; rather, they will usually commit offenses with different members of these larger groups or cliques. In this area, Warr (1996:16) states that "it is important to distinguish between *offending groups* (groups that actually commit delinquent acts) and *accomplice networks* (the pool of potential co-offenders available to the adolescent)." Warr found that the average size of accomplice networks was about seven, with the more delinquent youths having larger networks.

Group members are usually similar in terms of age and sex. Most such groups are made up of males. And membership in such groups peaks at ages 15 to 18. I should note that while males are most likely to offend with males and females are most likely to offend with females, female offenders are more likely to be a part of mixed-sex groups than are males.

One person in the group will usually suggest or instigate the offense (the "instigator"). Instigators are most often the same age as or a little older than the other group members(s), and they usually have a little more delinquent experience than the others. While the instigator is usually the same sex as the others in the group, females are more likely to report male instigators than males are to report female instigators (see Giordano, 1978; Warr, 1996). Most juveniles who have committed at least a few delinquent offenses report that they have played the role of both instigator and follower. They will often play the role of instigator with one set of friends and follower with another.

Quality of relations between group members. Some researchers have argued that the members of delinquent groups have poor relations with one another. One researcher describes the relations as "cold and brittle" (Hirschi, 1969). In particular, it is said that group members are not very attached to one another and that they frequently exploit one another. Other researchers, however, claim that the members of delinquent groups have great affection for and loyalty to one another. The latter image is often presented in films about gangs, with the classic example being *West Side Story*.

Recent data suggest that the quality of peer relations varies a lot from delinquent group to delinquent group, but that overall the relations in delinquent groups are *similar* to those found in conventional groups (see especially Agnew, 1991b; Giordano et al., 1986). One of the best studies in this area found that the members of delinquent groups spend as much time with one another as the members of conventional groups, have similar levels of caring and trust, are more likely to share private thoughts, are more influenced by one another, and find their friendships more rewarding in certain ways (Giordano et al., 1986). Reflecting these facts, the members of delinquent groups usually report that they are close friends or friends with one another (Warr, 1996). The members of delinquent groups, however, are also more likely to report conflict with one another than are members of conventional groups (Giordano et al., 1986).

Why Are Individuals in Delinquent Groups More Likely to Engage in Delinquency?

❖ ❖ ❖ ❖

As indicated, social learning theory is most often used to explain the effect of delinquent peers on a juvenile's delinquency. Data indicate that delinquent peers affect delinquency by reinforcing the juvenile's delinquency, providing delinquent models, and fostering beliefs that are conducive to delinquency. The data, however, also suggest that these are not the only mechanisms by which delinquent peers cause the juvenile to engage in delinquency. In particular, most studies find that delinquent peers affect delinquency even after one takes account of reinforcement, modeling, and beliefs (although the measures employed in such studies are often poor).

Some individuals have argued that delinquent peers may also affect delinquency for reasons related to social control theory (see Agnew, 1995a). In particular, having deviant friends may reduce the juvenile's fear of social sanctions. The support provided by delinquent friends may reduce the fear of retaliation and condemnation by others. Also, witnessing one's friends engage in delinquency without sanction may reduce the fear of official or police sanctions (see Johnson, 1979; Meier et al., 1984). Delinquent peers may also affect delinquency for reasons related to strain theory (see Agnew, 1995a). Delinquent peers may experience more conflict with one another and with others in the community. Further, membership in delinquent peer groups may close off certain legitimate opportunities. These effects may increase the strain of group members. Still other explanations have been offered for the effect of delinquent peers, although most are related to the leading delinquency theories.[5]

Why Are Some Juveniles More Likely to Get Involved With Delinquent Peers Than Others?

It has been argued that juveniles with some of the individual traits listed in Chapter 10 are more likely to get involved with delinquent peers. Some of these traits, like irritability and poor social skills, increase the likelihood that juveniles will be rejected by conventional peers. And some of these traits, like hyperactivity and sensation seeking, increase the appeal of delinquent groups. Juveniles with a strong need for thrills and excitement, for example, will probably be more attracted to the activities of delinquent groups. There has not been much research on the effect of individual traits on membership in delinquent groups, but limited data suggest that at least some of these traits increase the likelihood of membership in delinquent groups. For example, individuals with poor social skills and beliefs conducive to delinquency appear more likely to associate with delinquent peers.[6]

Most of the family variables that promote delinquency also increase the likelihood of membership in delinquent peer groups. In fact, evidence suggests that one of the major ways in which these family variables affect delinquency (perhaps the major way) is by increasing the likelihood that juveniles will associate with delinquent peers. Factors like large family size, parental criminality, parental rejection, low parental attachment, and poor parental supervision have all been shown to increase the likelihood of association with delinquent peers.[7] Likewise, certain data suggest that many of the negative school experiences described in Chapter 12 increase the likelihood of association with delinquent peers.[8]

Finally, as indicated, data suggest that delinquent behavior itself increases the likelihood of association with delinquent peers. This effect may reflect the fact that delinquents *prefer* to associate with other delinquents. It may also reflect the fact that conventional peers are reluctant to associate with delinquents, compelling them to associate with one another.

What Impact Do Gangs Have on Delinquency?

While the most common type of delinquent peer group is the simple friendship group, several authors have pointed to additional types of delinquent or law-violating groups, with the street gang receiving the most attention. This section addresses several basic questions about street gangs: What is a street gang and how common are such gangs? What effect do gangs have on crime and delinquency? What are gangs like, and why do some individuals join gangs and some communities develop gangs?[9]

Before proceeding, however, it is important to emphasize that it is difficult to talk about gangs in general. Gangs often differ greatly from one another. Gangs in one city, for example, may be large, highly organized, and heavily involved in drug sales. Gangs in another city may be small, loosely organized, and have little or no involvement in drug sales. The gangs *within a particular city* may also differ from one another. These differences are related to a number of factors, including the race/ethnic and sex composition of the gangs. For example, studies in certain cities report that Hispanic gangs are more concerned with issues of honor and protection of turf than other gangs. Perhaps because of this, they have higher rates of violence than other gangs. Black gangs are said to be more heavily involved in illegal methods of generating income, especially drug sales. Asian gangs are said to be less territorial, more highly organized, and more involved in property crimes like extortion and home invasions.[10] Certain other differences between gangs are described in what follows.

What Is a Street Gang?

There is no generally agreed-upon definition of a street gang. As will become apparent in the discussion that follows, this clash of definitions has created a number of problems. For example, it is difficult to talk about the extent of gangs if there is no generally accepted definition of gangs. Two cities may have similar gang problems, but officials in one city may employ a narrow definition of gangs and claim they have few gangs, while officials in the other city may employ a broad definition and claim they have many.

The most popular definition of gangs, and the one favored in this text, is that offered by Klein (1971:13): A gang is "any identifiable group of youngsters who (a) are generally perceived as a distinct aggregation by others in their neighborhood, (b) recognize themselves as a denotable group (almost invariably with a group name), and (c) have been involved in a sufficient number of delinquent incidents to call forth a consistent negative response from neighborhood residents and/or law enforcement agencies." The dividing line between a delinquent peer group and a gang may sometimes be fuzzy, but gangs are distinguished by their stronger group identity and their relatively strong involvement in delinquency.

Certain researchers have offered more elaborate definitions of gangs. They state, for example, that gangs have territories or turfs they protect and that they have formal organizational structures (e.g., they have official positions like president, vice-president, and war counselor). Many of the groups commonly thought of as gangs, however, are loosely organized at best and they do not claim territories that they protect (Asian gangs, for example often do not claim territories).

Other researchers have objected to Klein's definition of gangs because it equates gangs with illegal behavior.[11] In particular, they point out that researchers cannot examine whether gangs cause delinquency if they *define* gangs as delinquent groups. These researchers employ broader definitions of gangs that do not include involvement in delinquency. Their definitions, however, are so broad that they include many groups not commonly thought of as gangs, such as certain sports clubs and church groups. Further, Klein's definition does allow us to study the impact of gang membership on individual delinquency (does joining a gang lead to an increase in individual delinquency?) and the relationship between gang characteristics and gang crime (are gangs with certain characteristics more likely to engage in crime or certain types of crime?).

For these reasons, I favor Klein's definition. It should be noted, however, that even Klein's definition may include some groups not commonly thought of as gangs. As Bursik and Grasmick (1993) point out, *certain* fraternities on many college campuses may well fit Klein's definition of a gang.

How Common Are Gangs?

Most estimates of the extent of gangs are obtained by surveying police and sometimes other officials in samples of cities around the United States (for an overview, see Curry and Decker, 1998). The estimates from these surveys should be regarded with caution. Not all jurisdictions are surveyed; many jurisdictions do not respond to the surveys; and police estimates of the number of gangs and gang members may be biased. Police departments employ different definitions of gangs. Further, many police departments deny that they have a gang problem, particularly in the initial stages of the problem (see Klein, 1995). Some police departments, however, may exaggerate their gang problem—perhaps to secure more funding (see Curry et al., 1996). Nevertheless, data suggest that gangs are widespread, present in most major cities and many smaller areas throughout the United States.

The most comprehensive survey examining the extent of gangs was carried out by the National Youth Gang Center (*www.iir.com/nygc*)—an agency recently created by the U.S. Department of Justice. The 1998 survey of the Youth Gang Center was mailed to 3,018 police and sheriff's departments across the country, including departments in all major cities and suburban areas and a randomly selected sample of departments in small towns and rural areas (Moore and Cook, 1999). Of the 2,668 departments that responded to the survey, 48 percent reported gang activity. On the basis of the survey results, it was estimated that there were 28,700 gangs with 780,000 gang members in 1998. Most large cities and suburban areas reported gang problems, and gangs were also reported in many small cities and rural communities. Data, however, suggest that the gang problem is small in most areas, with fewer than ten gangs and 500 gang members being reported (Klein, 1995). Not surprisingly, large cities are more likely to report the existence of gangs and serious gang problems. Los Angeles and Chicago appear to have the most serious gang problems.

Several self-report studies have examined the extent of gang membership in selected cities, like Denver and Rochester. In most such studies, juveniles are simply asked whether they belong to a gang, although a series of follow-up questions are sometimes asked to make sure that the group really does qualify as a gang. These surveys of *urban* youth suggest that about 5 to 15 percent of adolescents belong to gangs in a given year, and 8 to 30 percent of all adolescents belong to gangs *at some point during adolescence.*[12] Gang membership, then, is somewhat common, but only a minority of adolescents belong to gangs at any point in time, even in urban areas known to have gang problems.

Are Gangs Becoming More Common?

Much data suggest that gangs have become more common in recent decades. Miller (1982) estimated that there were about 2,300 gangs with 98,000 members in 286 jurisdictions *in the late 1970s*. Estimates during the 1980s and 1990s showed a steady increase in the number of gangs, gang members, and cities with gang problems (see Curry and Decker, 1998; Klein, 1995). While such estimates should be regarded with caution, there is good reason to believe that the number of gangs, gang members, and gang cities did increase significantly in the last twenty years. Data from the 1998 National Youth Gang Survey, however, suggest that the number of gangs and gang members may be starting to stabilize or decline slightly. In particular, there was a slight decline in the number of gangs and gang members from 1996 to 1998.

It is sometimes claimed that the rapid growth in number of gangs between the 1970s and 1990s resulted from a plan on the part of certain gangs to increase their influence. Members of these gangs, it is said, deliberately move to other cities with the intention of setting up gang chapters in these cities, thereby increasing their share of the drug trade and other illegal activities. It is easy to understand the basis of this belief, since the gangs in many cities often adopt the names of well-known gangs or gang federations from other cities, such as the Bloods and Crips from Los Angeles or the People and Folks from Chicago. Recent data, however, suggest that the spread of gangs is *not* the result of a deliberate plan by gang members from certain cities. Most gangs appear to be homegrown, although these gangs will often adopt the names and symbols of well-known gangs in a copycat phenomenon. When members of gangs like the Bloods and Crips do move to a new city, it is usually because their families have decided to move, not because they are involved in a deliberate effort to spread gangs (see Howell, 1998a; Klein, 1995, for a fuller discussion). I discuss possible reasons for the rapid increase in homegrown gangs below.

What Effect Do Gangs Have on Crime and Delinquency?   ❖ ❖ ❖ ❖

How much crime and delinquency is gang related? It is not possible at present to give a precise answer to this question. Most cities do not attempt to calculate the proportion of all crimes that are gang related. Cities that do attempt such calculations usually focus only on homicide and maybe a small number of other serious crimes. Further, these cities often employ different methods to determine if a crime is gang related. Los Angeles, for example, classifies a crime as gang related if the offender or victim is a known or suspected gang member. Chicago, however, only classifies a crime as gang related if the *motive* for the crime is gang related (e.g., revenge against another gang, protection of turf). If this more restrictive definition were used in Los Angeles, the number of homicides classified as gang related would be cut by half in that city (see Klein, 1995; Maxson and Klein, 1990).

Data, however, suggest that a sizeable share of all crime, particularly serious crime, is gang related in certain cities. In 1994, gang members were suspects or victims in 44 percent of all homicides in Los Angeles. In that same year, 32 percent of all homicides had gang-related motivations in Chicago (see Maxson and Klein, 1996; Howell, 1999). Certain other cities report similar percentages.

Recent self-report studies also indicate that gang members account for a large share of crime, especially serious crime, in certain cities. In Denver, gang members made up 14 percent of all adolescents in high-crime communities, but they accounted for 79 percent of all serious violent crimes and 71 percent of all serious property crimes committed by adolescents (Huizinga et al., 1998). In Rochester, 30 percent of the juveniles belonged to a gang at some point during their high school career, but these juveniles accounted for 65 percent of all delinquent acts, including 86 percent of all serious delinquent acts, 69 percent of all violent acts, 68 percent of all property crimes, 70 percent of all drug sales, and 61 percent of all drug use (Thornberry and Burch, 1997). In Seattle, 15 percent of all juveniles belonged to gangs, but these gang members committed 58 percent of all delinquent acts (Battin et al., 1998).

While we cannot precisely estimate the share of all delinquency committed by gang members in the United States, it is clear that gang members commit a substantial share of all delinquency—perhaps the majority of all serious delinquency—in certain cities. These data, along with other data reported below, indicate that gangs should be a central focus of delinquency control/prevention efforts.

What types of crime do gang members commit? Gang members engage in a wide variety of delinquent and criminal acts, both serious and minor. While gang members are disproportionately involved in all forms of crime, their disproportionate involvement is greatest for serious and violent offenses. In this area, it should be noted that there has been a dramatic increase in lethal violence among gang members. In 1980, 633 gang-related homicides were reported in all major gang cities. In 1995, just two cities—Los Angeles and Chicago—reported over 1,000 gang homicides. There are a number of reasons for this increase in lethal violence, including the spread of guns among juveniles. Conflicts between juveniles are more likely to result in death when guns are involved. Data indicate that gang members are more likely than other juveniles to own and carry guns, including automatic, high-powered guns.[13] Most acts of gang violence involve acts of revenge or turf disputes, and members of other gangs are far and away the most frequent targets of gang violence. Contrary to certain media accounts, gang violence is usually *not* related to the drug trade (see Howell, 1999).

Certain myths regarding gang crime should be addressed. First, some individuals have the impression that gang members spend most of their time engaged in crime. Although gang members do commit a lot of crime, they spend the vast majority of their time simply hanging around—talking and waiting for something to happen. Partying is perhaps their second most frequent activity. When gang members do engage in crime, they commit far more minor than serious crime, something that is true of delinquents in general.

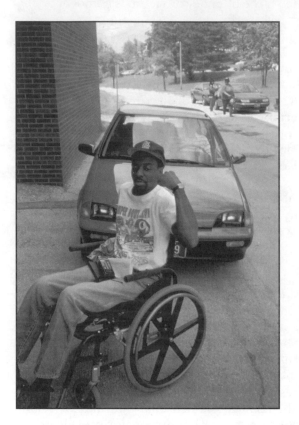

Second, many commentators claim that street gangs control drug sales in the United States Recent data suggest that this belief is mistaken. Many gang members do engage in drug sales—a majority in some studies. And gang members are more likely to engage in drug sales than nonmembers. But street gangs do not control drug sales (including crack sales) in the United States. Most drug sales are not conducted by gang members, and when gang members do sell drugs, they usually do so as individuals and on a sporadic basis. It is true that *some* street gangs have been become heavily involved in drug sales, especially in recent years. This involvement is more often true of black gangs, many of whom have become involved in crack sales, but these street gangs by no means control drug sales in the United States.[14] (It should be noted that drug sales in a community may be controlled by *drug gangs*. *Drug* gangs, however, are distinct from *street* gangs. Drug gangs are smaller, made up of older members, better organized, and focused on drug sales. Drug gangs sometimes employ the members of street gangs; Klein, 1995.)

Third, it should again be emphasized that gangs are not all alike. Among other things, they differ from one another in terms of the extent and nature of their delinquency. Based on a study of three communities, Fagan (1989) describes four types of gangs: (1) social gangs, whose members engage in high levels of alcohol and marijuana use but otherwise engage in little delinquency and other drug use, (2) party gangs, whose members engage in high rates of drug use and drug sales but otherwise engage in little delinquency (their drug sales help support their drug use); (3) serious delinquent gangs, whose members engage in a wide range of serious and minor delinquent acts but have little involvement in drug sales and serious drug use; (4) "organization" gangs, whose members are heavily involved in delinquency, drug sales, and drug use. Other researchers have reported similar types of gangs (see Shelden et al., 1997; see Klein, 1998, for another recent typology of gangs).

Does gang membership cause delinquency? It is well established that gang members commit more delinquent acts, especially serious delinquent acts, than nonmembers. In fact, both official and self-report data suggest that gang members have rates of offending that are several times higher than non-members.[15] Further, recent data indicate that gang members also have much higher rates of delinquency than juveniles with delinquent friends.[16] This association, of course, does not mean that gang membership causes delinquency. The association may simply arise because delinquents are more likely to join gangs or because both gang membership and delinquency are caused by the same third variables. Recent data provide some support for these arguments: Delinquent individuals are more likely to join gangs than nondelinquent individuals, and both gang membership and delinquency are caused by many of the same third variables. At the same time, data indicate that *individuals experience a dramatic increase in delinquency after they join a gang and a dramatic decrease after they leave the gang.* Further, the higher offending rates of gang members appear to hold even when a range of third variables are taken into account.[17] These important data suggest that there is something about the gang itself that leads to an increase in offending.

As with peer groups, the effect of gangs on offending can be explained in terms of social learning, strain, and control theories. With respect to social learning theory, researchers report that gang members hold values conducive to delinquency, such as toughness, achieving quick success, and backing up fellow gang members. Gang members spend much time talking about their delinquent exploits and occasionally modeling delinquent behavior. And gang members frequently reinforce delinquent behavior and punish certain forms of conventional behavior. With respect to strain theory, gang members frequently get into conflicts with one another, the members of rival gangs, the police, and others. Such conflicts often lead to acts of retaliation or revenge. With respect to control theory, gang members may feel better able to resist or escape the sanctions of others. The gang may also reduce the attachment of members to conventional others and institutions.[18]

What Are the Characteristics of Gang Members?

Gang members tend to be *poor and live in lower-income, urban communities,* although gangs exist in some working-class and even middle-class areas.

Gang members are *predominantly male.* The best data suggest that between 20 and 40 percent of gang members are female.[19] Self-report data show a greater percentage of female gang members than official estimates, which likely reflects the fact that the police are less likely to notice female gang members and keep official statistics on them. Some police departments, for example, have a policy of not counting females as gang members (Curry and Decker, 1998:98; Esbensen et al., 1999).

Most gang members are *young, typically teenagers.* Gang members tend to range in age from 12 to 30, with the average age being in the 17 to 20 range.

There has been an increase in the number of younger and especially older gang members in recent years. More and more adults are maintaining their gang membership, with some gang members in their 40s and even 50s. In the past, juveniles would quit or drift out of the gang as they got jobs and formed families. There has, however, been a massive loss of manufacturing jobs in inner-city communities, and it has become more difficult for the young adults in such communities to find decent work. As a consequence, many of these young adults elect to maintain their gang ties—particularly since the gang provides opportunities for obtaining money through illegal channels.

Most gang members belong to *minority groups*. According to one recent estimate based on a survey of law enforcement agencies, 34 percent of gang members are black, 46 percent are Hispanic, 12 percent are white, and 6 percent are Asian.[20] These numbers probably underestimate the percentage of white gang members because there is a tendency in law enforcement *not* to classify many white law-violating groups as street gangs. This includes groups such as Skinheads and Stoners (who emphasize heavy metal music, satanic themes, and drug use). Certain self-report studies have found the percentage of white gang members to be greater than 12 percent, although these studies still indicate that minorities are disproportionately involved in gangs (Esbensen et al., 1999; Esbensen and Osgood, 1997).

During the early 1900s most gang members were white. They were often the children of recent immigrants to the United States—such as Italian, Polish, and Irish immigrants (see Thrasher, 1927, for a classic discussion of such gangs in Chicago). These ethnic groups were the ones that populated the poor inner-city communities, the communities in which gangs are most common. As these groups moved up the economic ladder, they were replaced by blacks migrating from the rural South, Hispanics from Mexico and other areas, and Asians. Unfortunately, it will be more difficult for today's inner-city residents to move up the economic ladder—for reasons discussed later.

How Are Gangs Organized or Structured?

Gangs are often portrayed as highly organized groups. It is said that they have well-defined roles, such as President, Vice-President, War Counselor, and Treasurer; that they have well-defined goals and extensive rules that members are supposed to follow, with these goals and rules being specified in written constitutions or other documents; that they have hundreds or even thousands of members, with smaller gangs being organized into larger gang confederations; and that they are highly cohesive, with members expressing great loyalty to one another and to the larger group. It is true that *some* gangs are like this, particularly the older, larger gangs that exist in cities like Chicago and Los Angeles. *Most* gangs, however, do not fit this model.

Most gangs are loosely organized (see especially Klein, 1995). They do not have well-defined roles. There is often a distinction between core members and fringe members, with the fringe members including "wannabes." Wannabes are individuals—often younger juveniles—who want to join or become more involved with the gang. Certain of the core members may function as leaders on occasion, but the leaders may shift from occasion to occasion and no one may claim to be the leader of the gang. The gang may also be divided into age groups (e.g., Pee Wees, Juniors, Seniors, Ancients), although this age division is becoming less common. In most gangs, however, members divide up into a number of informal cliques or subgroups—and crimes are often committed with the members of these cliques.

There are few well-defined goals or rules for members to follow, beyond the goals and rules that characterize many gang *and nongang* youth in inner-city communities (e.g., be tough, do not "squeal" or "rat" to authorities). The membership of a gang often changes a good deal over time; self-report studies indicate that most gang members belong to the gang less than a year. Most estimates of gang size are in the 25 to 250 range. The gang itself is not highly cohesive. Some researchers have noted that there is often more conflict between members of the same gang than between members of different gangs. Several observers, in fact, have pointed out that what binds gang members together is not so much their respect and affection for one another, as it is their conflict with external groups like other gangs and the police.

What Are Female Gangs Like?

Female gangs are less common than male gangs, and most of the female gangs that exist are associated with male gangs (e.g., the "Vice Queens" are associated with the "Vice Kings"). There are, however, some independent female gangs and some gangs that include both male and female members. Certain researchers claim that these latter types of gangs are becoming more common, although there are no good data in this area.

The impression is sometimes given that the female gangs are largely subservient to male gangs, with female gang members being sexual objects to be used by the male gang members. Studies, however, suggest that the members of female gangs exercise a good deal of control over their own affairs. And while both male and female gang members may engage in much sexual behavior, the members of female gangs sanction indiscriminate sexual behavior. Further, the delinquent behavior of female gang members is not simply sexual in nature. Female gang members engage in a wide range of delinquent acts, including aggressive acts (although they engage in such acts less frequently than male gang members). Studies suggest that their involvement in delinquency is more strongly influenced by their association with female than with male gang members (i.e., females are not simply being led into delinquency by males). It should be noted, however, that female gang members are not as delinquent as male gang members.

Females join gangs for many of the same reasons that males join. They often have friends or relatives in the female gang or in the male gang associated with the female gang. And the gang is seen as a solution to the problems they face. Many of these problems are shared with males, like class and race discrimination. Data, however, suggest that there are two problems with special relevance to female gang members. First, some data indicate that female gang members are more likely than male gang members to have experienced problems like abuse at home. They may join the gang in an effort to cope with such problems: the gang makes it easier to escape from home life and may function as a surrogate family. In this area, some data suggest that females are more likely to join gangs in an effort to form close, family-like ties with their peers; males are more likely to join because they are attracted to the "action" associated with the gang (see Esbensen et al., 1999). Second, female gang members may join gangs as a partial escape from the gender oppression they encounter or anticipate encountering in the future.

Campbell (1990:172–173) describes the gender oppression that many lower-income females will likely encounter: (1) "a future of meaningless domestic labor with little possibility of educational or occupational escape," (2) "subordination to the man in the house," (3) "responsibility for children," and (4) "the social isolation of the housewife." According to Campbell (1990:172), the gang "represents for its members an idealized collective solution to the bleak future that awaits." That is, the gang represents a source of fun and excitement, although Campbell notes that gang members tend to exaggerate the positive side of gang life and minimize the negative.

Such findings do not mean that female gang members hold "liberated" views and that the gang is an effective solution to the problems they face. Female gang members often hold traditional gender role attitudes in many areas (although they are more accepting of the use of violence by females). As Chesney-Lind et al. state, "girls' gang life is certainly not an expression of 'liberation,' but instead reflects the attempts of young women to cope with a bleak and harsh present as well as a dismal future" (1996:203). Further, female gang members often find that they confront a range of problems when they join the gang, including physical and sexual abuse by the male gang members, many of whom hold sexist attitudes.[21]

Why Do Some Juveniles Join Gangs?

Juveniles give a variety of reasons for joining gangs. Some are *social* in nature. They have friends in the gang with whom they like to socialize. They see the gang as a source of fun and excitement (e.g., the gang holds a lot of parties and helps them meet romantic partners). They like the support, companionship, and sense of belonging they get from the gang. The gang is like a family for them. Some of the reasons relate to a desire for a *positive identity and status*. The gang makes them feel important, powerful, respected, and feared by others. Some of the reasons reflect a desire for *security or protection from others*. They believe the gang provides them with protection from rival gang members and others. They may also believe that the gang provides protection for the neighborhood and that it is their duty or responsibility to join. Finally, individuals may join for reasons of *financial gain*. They believe that the gang will help them make money through activities like drug selling, robbery, and burglary. Individuals are forced to join gangs in some cases, but such forced entry is uncommon. Most individuals join gangs because they believe that it will benefit them in some way.

By the time juveniles decide to join the gang, they have usually been hanging around with gang members for a while. They typically go through an initiation ceremony, which may involve being "jumped in" or "beatin' in" by other gang members (that is, enduring a beating by other gang members). The initiation might also involve the commission of a crime.

As mentioned earlier, most gang members leave the gang within a year. There are a variety of reasons for leaving: witnessing the death or injury of a friend, being the direct victim of violence, being sent to a correctional institution, getting a job, having children, getting married, burnout from frequent arrests, or simply "maturing out" with age. The gang itself may also break up (see Decker and Lauritsen, 1996, for a discussion of leaving the gang). Contrary to certain accounts, most individuals are able to leave gangs without suffering serious reprisals from other gang members.

Applying the theories. At a deeper level, one can explain why individuals join gangs in terms of strain, social learning, and control theories. Individuals may join gangs in an effort to cope with their strain. In many cases, they may be unable to achieve their goals through legitimate channels. Most commonly, they cannot make enough money through legitimate work or obtain the respect they feel they deserve. The gang may be seen as a way to make money through illegitimate channels or to achieve status and respect (see Cloward and Ohlin, 1960; Cohen, 1955). Their strain may also result from the loss of positive stimuli or the presentation of negative stimuli. Juveniles, for example, may be neglected or abused by family members; the gang may allow them to escape from their family, and it may function as a surrogate family, albeit an imperfect one. Juveniles may be harassed by others in their school or community. The gang may be seen as a source of protection from such harassment. Juveniles may feel that their lives are rather dull or boring and the gang may be seen as a source of excitement. In addition, the gang may be seen as a vehicle for rebelling or retaliating against individuals and groups who have mistreated the juvenile.

The experience of strain, however, does not guarantee that individuals will join a gang. Strained individuals are more likely to join gangs if they have friends who are gang members and if they live in communities where gang members are respected and reinforced for gang membership. In such cases, strained individuals will be exposed to attractive models who are gang members, will likely be exposed to beliefs favoring gang membership, and will likely conclude that gang membership has certain benefits for them.

Strained individuals with exposure to appealing gang members, however, may still not join gangs. Their parents or others may prevent them from doing so. And they may be concerned about the possible costs of gang membership. Among other things, gang membership may hurt their relations with parents and others, interfere with their schoolwork, and jeopardize their future career goals. Gang membership, then, is more likely when juveniles are low in direct control (e.g., are not well supervised by parents) and have a low stake in conformity (e.g., they dislike their parents, are doing poorly in school, and have low aspirations for future success).

If these arguments are correct, we would expect gang members to differ from nonmembers in a number of ways. Gang members should be more likely to possess traits that contribute to strain, low control, and a propensity to find delinquency reinforcing. Such traits include low intelligence, impulsiveness, irritability, and poor social skills. Gang members should be more likely to experience the family problems described in Chapter 11, such as poor parental supervision, parental rejection, and abuse. Gang members should be more likely to experience the types of school problems described in Chapter 12, such as poor grades, low attachment to teachers, and dropping out. Gang members should be more likely to have had friends who were gang members *before they joined the gang*. And gang members should be more likely to experience the types of strain described above.

Case studies of gang members provide some support for these arguments. Such studies usually report that juveniles join gangs partly because they are experiencing one or more types of strain; that juveniles knew gang members before they joined the gang; and that juveniles were low in at least certain types of control before they joined the gang. Some studies also suggest that gang members are likely to possess the individual traits listed in the preceding paragraph, although there is more disagreement about this point. These cases studies, however, suffer from certain problems. Most notably they usually examine only a small number of gang members, and they seldom compare gang members to nongang members. It may be the case, for example, that nongang members in the community are just as high in strain and low in control as gang members.

A few studies have *surveyed* gang *and* nongang members in an effort to overcome these problems. Gang members are then compared to nonmembers in the same community. Sometimes a distinction is made between nonmembers who have engaged in certain types of delinquent offenses ("nongang delinquents") and those who have not ("nongang nondelinquents"). These studies focus on some but not all the variables listed here (e.g., they often fail to measure certain types of strain and certain individual traits).

The results of these studies are generally supportive of the above arguments; gang members usually differ from nondelinquents in the ways described. Some studies, however, find only minimal differences between gang members and "nongang *delinquents*." Part of the explanation for this similarity may be that many of the delinquents in the high-crime communities studied drift in and out of gangs. As a consequence, many of the "nongang delinquents" may be former gang members or may join gangs in the future. In any event, we may conclude that there is some support for the strain, social learning, and control theory explanations of gang membership.[22]

Why Do Some Communities Develop Gangs?

Strain, social learning, and control theories help explain why *some individuals* in a community join gangs. In this section, I want to draw on these

same theories to explain why gangs are more likely to develop in *some communities*. In particular, why are gangs most likely to develop in lower-income, urban communities?

The answer is that these communities are more likely to foster low levels of control and high levels of strain. As a consequence, the juveniles in these communities frequently hang out on the street together, have little to lose by engaging in crime, and have problems for which the gang might be seen as an effective solution. It is little wonder, then, that gangs are more likely to appear in these communities. Let me elaborate.

These communities foster low control in several ways (see Chapter 14 for a full discussion). At a basic level, the residents of these communities have few resources and are struggling to deal with their own problems. Many are single mothers trying to raise families on limited incomes. These communities also tend to have high rates of residential mobility; that is, people move into and out of the community on a frequent basis. Recent immigrants to the city often settle in these communities because they cannot afford to live elsewhere, and such immigrants often struggle to adapt to urban life. Other residents move out of the community as soon as they can afford to. As a consequence of these factors, community residents lack the skills and resources to assist one another (e.g., to help juveniles do well in school or secure adequate jobs). Residents are also less likely to have close ties to their neighbors or to care about their community. Many, in fact, plan on leaving the community as soon as they are able. The residents are consequently less likely to get involved in community affairs, like sanctioning neighborhood delinquents. Further, residents are less likely to join organizations that might help them obtain such things as better schools and recreational programs. The end result is that the juveniles in these communities are not well supervised, are not strongly attached to conventional adults, and do not have a strong investment in school or their future careers.

Such communities also foster high levels of strain. Juveniles in these communities are poor and have little prospect for earning a decent living through legitimate channels. Among other things, adults have not prepared them well for school; the schools are not very responsive to their needs; and adults are not able to help them find decent jobs. The juveniles in these communities are subject to a range of additional strains: They are more likely to experience family disruption and the strains associated with such disruption, such as family conflict. They are more likely to live in dense, overcrowded, and substandard housing. They are more likely to get into conflicts with others, partly because they often live in close contact with others and are in competition for scarce resources. They are more likely to experience racial and ethnic discrimination (minorities are much more likely to reside in such communities). As a consequence, these juveniles not only are low in social control, but they are also high in strain. And, in the words of Cohen (1955), they are in the market for a solution to their problems.

Juveniles in these circumstances are ripe for gang involvement. Several reports suggest that the triggering factor that turns these juveniles into gangs is conflict with others, including conflict with other groups of youths, other gangs, and the police. Conflict with others is often an effective mechanism for uniting a group of people, and such conflict is often what turns the unorganized peer group into a gang. It has also been suggested that many of these juveniles may form gangs in response to media portrayals of gang life (more below).

How Can the Increase and Spread of Gangs Bo Explained?

There was a dramatic increase in the number of gangs and gang members in recent decades. Gangs are no longer confined to poor, urban communities. They are spreading to many suburban communities, small towns, and even rural areas. How can one explain these changes?

It is most commonly argued that these changes are due to a fundamental change in the U.S. economy over the past few decades—a change that has devastated lower-income urban communities and affected many working-class and lower-middle-class communities as well.

This change is the rapid decline in the number of manufacturing jobs in urban areas. Certain of these jobs have disappeared as a result of technological advancements; others have moved overseas because of the cheap cost of foreign labor; and still others have moved to suburban areas for financial and other reasons. The loss of manufacturing jobs has been more than matched by an increase in technology and service sector jobs. The technology jobs, however, have high educational requirements and are beyond the reach of most inner-city residents. Most of the service-sector jobs have low educational requirements, but they offer low pay and few benefits (e.g., serving hamburgers at a fast food restaurant). As a result of these changes, poor urban residents now have a more difficult time obtaining decent jobs (see Chapter 14 for a fuller discussion).

The loss of manufacturing jobs, in turn, has led to additional problems. Most notably, it has contributed to the high rate of family disruption in our society, particularly in low-income urban areas. Perhaps the major reason for this increase is the fact that there are now proportionately fewer males earning decent incomes in inner-city communities. Females are therefore less likely to marry, and males are less likely to become part of stable family units.

The increase in poverty and family disruption, especially in urban communities, affects mostly minority groups. Due to the effects of past and current discrimination, they are most heavily concentrated in urban areas and in blue-collar jobs so they have been hurt the most as manufacturing jobs have fled urban communities. Certain additional changes have made conditions still worse in urban communities. There have been cutbacks in social service programs over the past two decades, so government assistance has become harder to get at the very time that people have a greater need for it. Also, many middle- and working-class minority group members have been leaving inner-city areas over the past two decades. Such individuals used to live in urban communities along with the poor. Housing and economic discrimination prevented them from living elsewhere. The departure of such individuals is a major loss to the community, since these individuals were a major source of control and social support. Among other things, they functioned as role models, offered advice and assistance to others, and supported a range of community institutions.

The net result of the economic changes mentioned is an increase in the number of urban communities characterized by high rates of poverty, family disruption, and other problems. These communities are especially low in control and high in strain. And there is some evidence that the increase in the number of these communities helps explain the increase in the number of gangs in recent decades.

As noted above, however, gangs are also spreading to many working-class and even middle-class communities, including suburban areas and small towns. How might this be explained? The economic changes described above are also having some effect on these communities. Many working- and lower-middle-class adolescents, especially those doing poorly in school, now find themselves in a situation where their economic future is uncertain. They can no longer count on getting well-paying blue-collar jobs. Also, many suburban areas and small towns have been experiencing a large increase in population, particularly as many urban residents leave the city. Dramatic changes in population can reduce control and might also contribute to conflicts between youth groups. An excellent illustration of these arguments can be found in Blazak's (1999) discussion of the rise of Skinhead groups among working- and lower-middle-class white juveniles.

It has also been argued that the media and manufacturers have contributed to the spread of gangs by introducing juveniles to gang culture, including gang dress, talk, hand signals, graffiti, and behavior (see Klein, 1995). That is to say, the media and manufacturers have provided juveniles with gang models to imitate. As Klein et al. (1995:110) point out:

> baggy pants, Pendleton-style shirts, high-top shoes, ball caps worn backward or at angles, graffiti styles, words like 'homey' and 'hood' and other signs of affiliations have become part of the larger youth culture. In essence, commercial America has taught youthful America how to walk, talk, dress, and act 'gangster-style.'

Many juveniles, especially those experiencing the low control and strain described above, copy what they see.[23]

Summary

In sum, delinquent peer groups and gangs are major causes of delinquency. It is true that delinquent individuals are more likely to associate with other delinquents and join gangs. It is also true that both delinquency and membership in delinquent groups are caused by many of the same third variables. At the same time, the data suggest that an individual's association with delinquent others, especially gang members, causes a substantial increase in the individual's delinquency. This increase was explained in terms of strain, social learning, and control theories.

Our examination of the social environment has so far considered the family, school, and peer group/gang. These are perhaps the major social environments impinging on juveniles. I want to finish our discussion of these environments by applying the research we have just reviewed. As indicated in Chapter 4, gender is one of the best predictors of delinquency. We know that more males than females are delinquent, especially when it comes to serious delinquency. I earlier tried to explain this difference by arguing that males are more likely to possess the *individual traits* conducive to delinquency. Males may be more likely to possess such traits partly for biological reasons and partly because of differences in the way they are socialized. Several studies, however, *suggest* that gender differences in delinquency are not simply a function of individual traits; they also result from differences in the social environment of males and females. I next want to examine this argument by focusing on the family, school, and peer experiences of males and females.

Applying the family, school, and peer group research: Gender and delinquency. We have examined a range of family, school, and peer variables that may cause delinquency. Researchers argue that males and females differ on many of these variables, and such differences go a long way toward accounting for gender differences in delinquency. Among other things, it is said that females (1) are more closely supervised by family members; (2) are more strongly attached to family members; (3) like school more; (4) spend more time on schoolwork; (5) do better in school; and (6) are more likely to associate with conventional as opposed to delinquent peers. It is claimed that such differences explain much of the gender difference in delinquency.[24]

The data regarding these claims is mixed. Some studies, for example, show that females are more strongly bonded to family members; others show that males are more strongly bonded; and still others show that there are no gender differences in family bonding. Perhaps the most consistent findings deal with delinquent peer associations and, to a lesser extent, with parental supervision. Females are less likely to associate with delinquent peers and are more likely to be closely supervised by parents. Studies suggest that gender differences in supervision and especially peer association explain much but not all of the gender difference in delinquency. It is important to emphasize that these gender differences in supervision and peer association reflect differences in the views and expectations that most people have for males and females. Females, for example, are more likely to be seen as submissive and weak, and therefore in need of greater supervision and protection. And females are under greater pressure to maintain their "sexual virtue," which once again fosters greater supervision and control over their lives.

It should be noted that these data do not mean that individual traits are unimportant in explaining gender differences in delinquency. Factors like parental supervision and peer associations explain only part of the gender difference. Further, individual traits may influence peer associations and parental supervision (e.g., individuals high in sensation seeking may be more likely to associate with delinquent peers). Unfortunately, no study contains good measures of individual traits, supervision, peer associations, and other environmental variables; therefore, it is not possible to determine the relative importance of these variables. At present, the safest conclusion to draw is that gender differences in delinquency are a function of both gender differences in individual traits and environmental variables.

Are the causes of female delinquency the same as the causes of male delinquency? Most studies suggest that the same independent variables cause delinquency among both males and females. Further, these variables tend to have similar effects on males and females, although the data are somewhat mixed in this area. Both males and females are more likely to engage in delinquency if they experience certain family problems, have certain negative school experiences, and associate with delinquent peers. As a consequence, many researchers argue that the causes of male and female delinquency are similar. (The reason that males are more delinquent than females, as indicated above, is because they are more likely to be in environments that are conducive to delinquency, such as delinquent peer groups.)

At the same time, some researchers argue that certain variables have a special relevance to the explanation of male or female delinquency (see Heimer, 1995). Certain strain theorists argue that the inability to achieve masculine status through legitimate channels is a major cause of male delinquency. The inability to achieve masculine status, however, is not seen as an important cause of female delinquency. Also, some research suggests that delinquent peers may have a greater effect on males than on females, partly because females are more likely to condemn delinquency (Mears et al., 1998).

Meda Chesney-Lind (1989) has made another argument in this area.[25] She contends that abuse or neglect by family members, especially sexual abuse, plays a special role in the explanation of female delinquency. While abuse or neglect may lead to delinquency among males, females are much more likely to be the victims of sexual abuse than males, and such abuse is said to have an especially devastating effect on females. Females, in particular, often respond to such abuse by running away from home. And they often find that they must turn to crime in order to survive on the street. Their age and runaway status rule out legitimate work as an option, so they engage in income-generating crimes like prostitution, drug selling, and petty theft. Life on the street, including their involvement in activities like prostitution, leads to further abuse and exploitation. The police and juvenile court provide little assistance to these females. In fact, such females are frequently arrested and returned to their home environment, where they may suffer further abuse. Interviews with female offenders provide tentative support for this argument.[26]

In sum, the causes of male and female delinquency are similar, although there is reason to believe that certain variables may have a special relevance for the explanation of male *or* female delinquency. More research is clearly needed in this area.

Notes

1. For overviews and selected studies on peers and delinquency, see Agnew, 1991b; Elliott et al., 1985; Elliott and Menard, 1996; Gorman and White, 1995; Huizinga et al., 1998; Jang, 1999; Krohn et al., 1995; Matsueda and Anderson, 1998; Meier et al., 1984; Patterson and Dishion, 1985; Patterson et al., 1992; Reed and Rountree, 1997; Reiss, 1988; Rutter and Giller, 1983; Sampson and Laub, 1993a; Thornberry, 1996; Thornberry et al., 1994, 1998; Warr, 1993, 1996, 1998; Warr and Stafford, 1991; Wilson and Herrnstein, 1985.
2. Also see Akers, 1998; Matsueda and Anderson, 1998; Rutter et al., 1998; Thornberry, 1996; Thornberry et al., 1994, 1998; Warr, 1993, 1996.
3. *See* Agnew, 1990a, 1991b, 1993; Elliott et al., 1985; Warr and Stafford, 1991.
4. Also see Agnew, 1993; Elliott and Menard, 1996; Hagan, 1991.
5. *See* Briar and Piliavin, 1965; Johnson et al., 1987; Short and Strodtbeck, 1965; Tittle et al., 1986.
6. *See* Johnson, 1979; Patterson and Dishion, 1985; Thornberry et al., 1994; Thornberry, 1996.
7. *See* Elliott et al., 1985; Jensen, 1972; Patterson et al., 1992; Sampson and Laub, 1993a; Patterson and Dishion, 1985.
8. *See* Elliott et al., 1985; Hawkins and Lishner, 1987; Johnson, 1979; Thornberry, 1987, 1996.
9. There have been several excellent ethnographies or case studies of specific gangs in recent years. Curry and Decker (1998) and Shelden et al. (1997) list and provide

brief summaries of these studies. For recent overviews of the research on street gangs, see Curry and Decker, 1998; Howell, 1995, 1998a; Huff, 1996; Klein, 1995, 1998; Klein et al., 1995; Office of Juvenile Justice and Delinquency Prevention, 1999a; Shelden et al., 1997; Short, 1997; and Spergel, 1995; Thornberry et al., 1998.

10. *See* Klein, 1995; Howell, 1998a; Spergel, 1995.

11. *See* Bursik and Grasmick, 1993; Klein, 1995; Short, 1997; Spergel, 1995.

12. *See* Esbensen and Deschenes, 1998; Esbensen and Huizinga, 1993; Esbensen et al., 1993; Howell, 1995, 1997b; Office of Juvenile Justice and Delinquency Prevention, 1999a; Spergel, 1995:31–32; Thornberry and Burch, 1997.

13. *See* Bjerregaard and Lizotte, 1995; Curry and Decker, 1998; Howell, 1995, 1998a, 1999; Huff, 1996; Lizotte et al., 1994.

14. *See* Curry and Decker, 1998; Howell, 1995, 1998a; Huff, 1996; Klein, 1995; Klein et al., 1995; Maxson, 1995; Spergel, 1995.

15. *See* Bjerregaard and Smith, 1993; Curry and Decker, 1998; Howell, 1995, 1997b; Esbensen and Huizinga, 1993; Fagan, 1990; Huff, 1996, 1998; Thornberry, 1998; Thornberry et al., 1993; Thornberry et al., 1998.

16. *See* Battin et al., 1998; Huizinga, 1996; Howell, 1998a; Thornberry, 1998.

17. *See* Esbensen et al., 1993; Huff, 1998; Thornberry, 1998; Thornberry et al., 1993, 1998.

18. *See* Decker and Van Winkle, 1996; Howell, 1998a; Shelden et al., 1997; Short and Strodtbeck, 1965; Spergel, 1995.

19. *See* Bjerregaard and Smith, 1993; Chesney-Lind et al., 1996; Curry and Decker, 1998; Esbensen and Deschenes, 1998; Esbensen et al., 1999; Esbensen and Osgood, 1997; Esbensen et al., 1993; Shelden et al., 1997; Spergel, 1995.

20. *See* Moore and Cook, 1999; also see Curry and Decker, 1998; Howell, 1997b; Spergel, 1995.

21. For a fuller discussion of female gang involvement, see Bowker and Klein, 1983; Campbell, 1990; Chesney-Lind and Hagedorn, 2000; Chesney-Lind et al., 1996; Chesney-Lind and Shelden, 1998; Curry, 1998; Curry and Decker, 1998; Esbensen and Deschenes, 1998; Esbensen et al., 1999; Fishman, 1995; Klein, 1995; Moore and Hagedorn, 1996; Shelden et al., 1997.

22. For examples and discussions of the research in this area, see Bjerregaard and Smith, 1993; Bowker and Klein, 1983; Curry and Decker, 1998; Esbensen and Deschenes, 1998; Esbensen et al., 1993; Fagan, 1990; Hill et al., 1999; Howell, 1998a; Klein, 1995, 1998; Klein et al., 1995; Shelden et al., 1997; Short, 1997; Spergel, 1995; Thornberry, 1998; Vigil and Yun, 1996.

23. For fuller discussions of these arguments, see Bursik and Grasmick; 1993; Fagan, 1996; Hagedorn, 1988; Jackson, 1991; Klein, 1995; Klein et al., 1995; Shelden et al., 1997; and Spergel, 1995.

24. For overviews and selected studies in this area, see Bartusch and Matsueda, 1996; Berger, 1989; Canter, 1982; Cernkovich and Giordano, 1987; Chesney-Lind and Shelden, 1998; Cloward and Piven, 1979; Daly, 1998; Daly and Chesney-Lind, 1988; Giordano, 1978; Giordano et al., 1986; Hagan et al., 1979; Hagan et al., 1996; Heimer, 1995,1996; Jensen and Eve, 1976; Mears et al., 1998; Morash, 1986; Rowe et al., 1995; Simons et al., 1980; Smith and Paternoster, 1987; Steffensmeier and Allan, 1996, 2000; Thornberry et al., 1998; Wilson and Herrnstein, 1985.

25. Also see Acoca, 1998; Chesney-Lind and Shelden, 1998; Daly, 1998.

26. *See* Acoca, 1998; Daly, 1992; Gilfus, 1992. ✦

What Effects Do Religion, Work, Mass Media, and the Community Have on Delinquency?

❖ ❖ ❖ ❖   The family, school, and peer group constitute the major social environments for most adolescents. They spend most of their time at home, at school, and associating with friends; and they of course form close relationships with their family, friends, and perhaps teachers at school. So it is not surprising that family, friends, and sometimes people at school affect them so strongly. But these are not the only social influences on adolescents. They may also be influenced by their religion, their work experiences, the mass media, and the communities in which they live. This chapter examines these other social influences. I address several questions that have been receiving a great deal of attention in the media lately: Does religion reduce delinquency? Does work prevent delinquency among juveniles attending school? Does mass media violence contribute to violent behavior? And are adolescents in certain types of communities more likely to engage in delinquency?

Does Religion Reduce Delinquency?

A letter to the editor of my local newspaper claimed that there was little mystery regarding the causes of crime and delinquency: "The answer is so simple. The answer is this: A lack of religion in these persons' lives has caused them to fail in our society." The letter writer went on to speculate that few delinquents attend church on a regular basis. Like this letter writer, many people believe that a lack of religion is a major cause of delinquency. In fact, many politicians and other people have claimed that the lack of religion (or the absence of school prayer) is one of the major causes of crime and violence in our society—like the shooting deaths of 13 people at Columbine High School and other well-publicized incidents of school violence. Many politicians are now actively searching for ways to increase the role of religion in people's lives. One of the responses to the shootings at Columbine High School, for example, was the passage of legislation by the U.S. House of Representatives giving schools the right to post the Ten Commandments. The sponsor of this legislation stated that "I am proud to see that people are waking up to the real problem in our society, and that's the loss of morality."[1]

There are good reasons for believing that religion has an effect on delinquency. Most notably, religion may increase control. Religion may increase direct control, since religious juveniles may come under the watchful eye of those in their religious community. And religion may instill a fear of supernatural sanction in juveniles—punishment by God. Religion may also increase one's stake in conformity; religious juveniles may develop good reputations and strong emotional bonds to others in their religious community. They may be fearful of jeopardizing their reputations and bonds through delinquency. Further, religion may increase internal control, since religious juveniles may be more likely to learn beliefs that condemn delinquency and to be taught self-control. It is the effect of religion on internal control that is most commonly mentioned in discussions on the topic.

In terms of social learning theory, religion may increase the likelihood that juveniles are exposed to conventional models, are taught conventional beliefs, are punished for deviance, and are reinforced for conformity. Finally, it has been suggested that religious participation may reduce strain, since religious communities may provide the juvenile with social support, and religious beliefs may divert attention from current problems to the rewards of the afterlife. What do the data indicate; does religion reduce the likelihood of delinquency?

❖ ❖ ❖ ❖

There have been a moderate number of studies in this area. Religion is most commonly measured by asking respondents how frequently they attend religious services. Many studies also ask respondents what their religion or religious denomination is, how important religion is in their daily lives, and whether they hold certain religious beliefs (e.g., "Is there life after death?" "Will evil people suffer in hell?"). Most studies are cross-sectional, and many fail to control for potentially relevant third variables. Nevertheless, certain conclusions can be drawn from the data.

Most data indicate that religious juveniles are somewhat less delinquent than nonreligious juveniles, especially when it comes to "victimless crimes" like alcohol and marijuana use. Recent data, however, suggest that a good part of the association between religion and delinquency is caused by third variables, including variables like sensation seeking, impulsivity, parental attachment, and parental supervision. But even after one takes account of these third variables, the data tentatively suggest that religion has a small effect on delinquency, especially on "victimless crimes" like alcohol and marijuana use. This effect appears to be largely indirect. One longitudinal study suggests that religion affects the commission of victimless crimes primarily through its effect on the peers with whom the juvenile associates. Religious individuals are less likely to associate with deviant peers (Burkett and Warren, 1987; also see Evans et al., 1996).

Why is it that religion affects victimless crimes more than serious crimes? The most commonly offered explanation is that serious crimes are condemned by both religious and nonreligious individuals and groups. Therefore, both religious and nonreligious juveniles are equally likely to refrain from such crimes. Victimless crimes, however, are condemned more strongly by religious groups, so we find that religious individuals are less likely to engage in such crimes.

I have been talking about religion in general up to this point. You might be wondering whether different religions or religious denominations have different effects on delinquency. The data in this area are mixed, although studies tend to indicate that the members of more fundamentalist or conservative religious groups commit fewer victimless crimes. Such groups include Baptists and Mormons (as opposed to more liberal religious groups like Unitarians and Presbyterians).

Researchers continue to study the effect of religion on delinquency. One major line of research argues that religion is more likely to affect delinquency in some circumstances than others. For example, some researchers argue that the effect of religion on delinquency depends on the religious climate of the community. They claim that religion should have a stronger effect in communities where a high percentage of the population is religiously active (or where the person is part of an isolated and tightly integrated religious group). If you are surrounded by people who are religiously active, you are more likely to take account of religious considerations in your daily life. But if you are surrounded by people who are indifferent to religion, you may ignore or put aside religious considerations. Some studies support this argument, while others do not.[2]

In sum, religion appears to have a small effect on delinquency, especially victimless crimes. The effect of religion is overshadowed by that of other groups, such as the family, peer group, and school.

Does Work Reduce Delinquency Among Juveniles Attending School?

The percentage of juveniles who work has increased dramatically since World War II. It is estimated that 90 percent of all students now hold jobs at some point, and 80 percent of all students work during the school year at some point. One recent study of high school students found that during the academic year, employed juniors worked an average of 18.6 hours per week and employed seniors worked an average of 23.5 hours per week. The world of work now occupies a central place in the lives of many adolescents—alongside the family, school, and peer group. It is important therefore to ask whether work has an effect on delinquency among juveniles attending school.[3]

There are good reasons for expecting work to reduce delinquency, many of them derived from strain and control theories. Work provides adolescents with money for cars, clothing, socializing, and other things. (Data indicate that juveniles tend to spend most of their wages on personal items and activities rather than giving money to parents for family expenses or saving it for college.) Work should, then, reduce economic strain. Work may also function as an "investment in a conventional activity"; employed juveniles may be less delinquent because they fear that delinquency will cost them their jobs. Work may result in an increase in direct control; employed juveniles may spend less time in unsupervised activities with peers and more time under the supervision of their employers. And work may increase the juvenile's acceptance of conventional moral values by increasing interaction with and attachment to adults who transmit such values. Finally, limited data suggest that employment often reduces crime among adults.

It is not surprising that most people believe work is beneficial for juveniles and reduces the likelihood of delinquency. One often hears, for example, that "work builds character and responsibility" (Williams et al., 1996). Several prominent national commissions have also argued that work benefits juveniles, and they have recommended that society provide adolescents with more work experience. Many antidelinquency programs attempt to provide juveniles with work. What do the data show about the effect of work on delinquency?

The data suggest that adolescents who attend school and also work are *slightly more* likely to engage in delinquency. This relationship tends to hold even when certain third variables are controlled (although some of the factors that increase the likelihood of delinquency also appear to increase the likelihood of work). This relationship tends to hold in longitudinal analyses. The relationship is strongest for alcohol/drug use and minor delinquency. And it applies mainly to adolescents who work long hours (about 15 hours per week or more while in school) in menial jobs. Unfortunately, most working adolescents fall into this category (see Agnew, 1986, for a discussion of types of work and delinquency).

How can one explain the fact that work may cause a slight increase in delinquency among in-school juveniles? Limited data provide support for several explanations. Most adolescent jobs pay poorly and involve menial, unpleasant work. It is unlikely that adolescents are fearful of losing these jobs or that these jobs provide much positive interaction with adults. Rather than increasing control, there is some evidence that these jobs may reduce certain forms of control, such as attachment to parents, academic performance, and attachment to school. Employed adolescents have less time to spend with family members and to devote to schoolwork. Also, the money provided by these jobs may reduce the direct control to which adolescents are subject. Employed adolescents are less dependent on parents for money, so parental power over the adolescent is reduced. And juveniles may use their money to purchase a car, which further reduces their dependence on adults. Further, adolescents are not necessarily well supervised at work. They usually spend much time in the company of other peers at work, and they often engage in crime there (e.g., employee theft).

While adolescent work may reduce economic strain, it appears to contribute to other types of strain. The working conditions associated with most adolescent jobs are rather poor, and the long hours worked by many adolescents—in combination with school, family, and social demands—can be stressful. In addition, the money from work makes it easier for adolescents to purchase drugs or alcohol and to engage in certain other illegal activities. (Data suggest that adolescents with more spending money are somewhat more likely to be delinquent; see Agnew, 1990b; Cullen et. al., 1985.) Finally, some evidence suggests that employed adolescents are more likely to have delinquent friends and to spend time with these friends (Ploeger, 1997). Work may be a source of friends, they may interact with friends at work, and the money from work may allow them to finance more active social lives. Work, then, may also increase delinquency for reasons related to social learning theory.

In sum, common views regarding the benefits of work for in-school adolescents appear to be mistaken. Among other things, the evidence suggests that work may lead to a slight increase in delinquency.

Does Mass Media Violence Cause Violence Among Juveniles?

Most research on media violence has focused on television, although there is limited data suggesting that violent video games and certain types of music with violent themes may foster violent behavior (e.g., Griffiths, 1999; Singer et al., 1993). This discussion, however, focuses on TV violence because of the massive presence of TV in our society and the abundant research in the area.

About 98 percent of all households in the United States have TVs, and these TVs get watched a lot. They are on for an average of 28 hours a week in homes with children between 2 and 11, and 23 hours a week in homes with teenagers. Juveniles spend more time watching TV than they do in any other activity, except sleeping and attending school. Further, they see much violence on TV. If we focus on the three major television networks, there are about 5 to 6 acts of violence per hour on prime time TV and about 20 to 25 acts per hour on Saturday morning children's programs. Cable TV contains more violence than the three major networks, and the spread of VCRs has provided juveniles with the opportunity to watch unedited versions of violent movies. It is estimated that by the time children have finished elementary school, they have seen over 8,000 murders and 100,000 other acts of violence on TV. They have seen over 200,000 acts of violence by the time they leave high school.[4]

Does this extensive exposure to TV violence increase the likelihood that juveniles will engage in violent behavior? Most people believe that TV violence is a major cause of violent behavior, and the federal government has been actively involved in efforts to limit the amount and severity of TV violence or restrict access to violent programs. As a consequence of such efforts, there is now a ratings system that alerts viewers to the violence content of TV shows. Also, new TVs now contain "V chips," which allow parents to block violent shows. It is unclear if the government will take further action to restrict access to TV violence or to reduce the amount of TV violence, but the shooting deaths at Columbine High School and other incidents have sparked renewed interest in the effects of media violence. Media violence, in fact, is frequently mentioned as one of the leading causes of youth violence in our society.

What do the data show about the effect of TV violence on juvenile violence? There have been literally hundreds of studies in this area. We know that violent juveniles are more likely to watch violent TV shows. That does not, of course, mean that TV violence *causes* juvenile violence. It might be that juvenile violence and watching violent TV shows are both caused by the same third variables, such as the individual traits or family variables mentioned in earlier chapters. It might also be that engaging in violence causes one to watch violent TV shows. Violent juveniles may simply prefer violent TV shows. There is, in fact, some evidence for these arguments. At the same time, most studies—not all—suggest that TV violence does have a causal effect on violent behavior.

Hundreds of experiments have been conducted in this area. In most such experiments, one group of juveniles is exposed to media violence while a similar group of juveniles is not (these groups are similar on relevant third variables like individual traits and family variables). The experimenter then determines whether the juveniles exposed to the media violence engage in more subsequent violence than the unexposed group (so causal order is not a problem). The experimenter, for example, determines whether the juveniles exposed to media violence are more likely to hit a doll in a playroom or press a button that allegedly harms another person. Most experiments suggest that exposure to media violence does increase violent behavior. Some individuals, however, claim that the experiments set up an artificial situation in which it is easy for juveniles to engage in violence. The juveniles are often provided with a readily available opportunity to engage in violence, and their violence is rarely punished or condemned (e.g., hitting a doll). As such, the results of these experiments may not apply to the "real world."

In response to this criticism, researchers have conducted a number of studies in the real world that attempt to take account of relevant third variables and issues of causal order (see Chapter 5). One study, for example, determined whether childhood exposure to TV violence is related to violent behavior in adolescence and adulthood. This study controlled for several relevant third variables, such as social class, intelligence, and parenting practices. Another study examined the levels of juvenile violence in an isolated Canadian community before and after the introduction of TV. Still another study examined whether levels of violence increased after media coverage of violent events, like championship heavyweight prizefights. These studies are not perfect. Researchers often do not control for all potentially relevant third variables; sometimes it is impossible to do so (an excellent illustration of a flawed study in this area is provided by Jensen, 1998). Nevertheless, most—not all—studies in this area suggest that TV violence affects violent behavior.

Overall, the most reasonable conclusion to draw from the data is that TV violence has a small to modest effect on juvenile violence. It does not appear to be the major cause of violence that some claim, but it is not an unimportant cause either. TV violence is most likely to cause violent behavior when it is committed by attractive characters; when it is rewarded and not punished; when it is presented as justified; when the negative consequences of the violence are not shown; and when it is realistic. Unfortunately, much of the violence on TV is like this. For example, as the National Television Violence Study (1997:137) states: "Violence is typically sanitized on television. It is rarely punished in the immediate context in which it occurs and it rarely results in observable harm to the victims. In fact, violence is often funny on television." TV violence is also most likely to lead to violent behavior when the juvenile identifies with the aggressor and the juvenile is otherwise predisposed to engage in violence.

The effect of TV violence is usually explained in terms of the leading delinquency theories. TV violence exposes juveniles to violent models. These models are often attractive characters, and their violence is frequently rewarded. As a consequence, juveniles may come to feel that violence is an appropriate response in certain situations. TV violence may evoke aggressive thoughts or ideas in people and thus increase the likelihood of a violent response. Further, TV violence may desensitize watchers to violence. That is, heavy exposure to TV violence may make violence seem less bad and reduce concern for the victims of violence. In effect, TV violence may reduce our level of internal control. Finally, there is evidence that TV violence makes viewers see the world as a more dangerous, violent place. They become more fearful and suspicious of others as a result, potentially increasing the likelihood of a violent response.

Are Adolescents in Certain Types of Communities More Likely to Engage in Delinquency?

There is little doubt that some communities have much higher crime rates than others. In particular, some neighborhoods within a city have much higher crime rates than other neighborhoods. I am sure that many of you can think of neighborhoods in your home cities that have relatively high crime rates or at least have reputations for having high crime rates. Likewise, some cities have higher crime rates than other cities. Each year the FBI publishes data on the crime rates of cities throughout the United States, and newspapers and TV stations often carry stories about the city with the highest crime rate (the "crime capital" of the United States) or the highest murder rate (the "murder capital"). You might look up the crime rate in your city and compare it to that of other cities (see the latest edition of the FBI Uniform Crime Reports at *http://www.fbi.gov/ucr/ucreports.html*). You should be aware however, that the FBI data are not well suited for comparing crime rates in different cities. Among other things, cities differ in the extent to which victims report crimes to the police and in police record-keeping practices. Nevertheless, researchers do know that some neighborhoods and some cities have much higher crime rates than other neighborhoods and cities.

There has been much research on the characteristics of the neighborhoods and cities with high crime rates. Although the results of this research are sometimes contradictory, researchers now have a reasonably good idea what those characteristics are. Most of this research has focused on crimes committed by both adults and juveniles, but some data suggest that the conclusions which follow apply to juvenile delinquency alone.[5]

What Are the Characteristics of High-Crime Neighborhoods and Cities?

The major characteristics of high-crime communities are listed below.[6]

Economic deprivation. The most distinguishing characteristic of high-crime cities and neighborhoods is that they are economically deprived. Deprivation has been measured in a variety of ways, including the average or median family income level in an area, the percentage of families below the poverty line ($16,660 for a family of four in 1998), the percentage of unemployed adult males, the percentage of families that receive welfare, the average or median educational level, and the percentage of adults employed in professional or managerial occupations. These measures are highly correlated with one another and they are often combined into more general measures of economic deprivation. Virtually all studies indicate that deprived cities and neighborhoods are much higher in crime (see Land et al., 1990). For example, a recent study of neighborhoods in Columbus, Ohio, examined the relationship between the percentage of residents below the poverty line and neighborhood crime rates (based on crimes known to the police). Neighborhoods with extremely high levels of poverty (40 percent or more of residents below the poverty line) had violent crime rates that were approximately five times as high as neighborhoods with low levels of poverty (5 percent or fewer below the poverty line). The difference in property crime rates was less extreme but still substantial (Krivo and Peterson, 1996).

Large size, high density, overcrowded. High-crime communities also tend to be large in size, high in population density, high in multi-unit housing, and, according to some studies, overcrowded. Population density is usually measured by the number of people per square mile. Multi-unit housing is often measured by the percentage of housing units in structures of five or more units (usually apartment buildings). And overcrowding is typically measured by the average number of people per room in an area (see Gove et al., 1979). High-crime communities, then, tend to have a lot of people in close contact with one another. Such conditions are more common in deprived communities, but data suggest that these factors bear some independent relationship to crime rates.

Residential mobility. High-crime communities also tend to have high rates of residential mobility; that is, people frequently move into and out of the community. Residential mobility is often measured by the percentage of residents that lived in different houses five years ago. Residential mobility is more common in poor communities. New immigrants to the city often locate in poor communities because they cannot afford to live elsewhere, so people are frequently moving into the community. And the residents of poor communities often move elsewhere as soon as they are able, so people are frequently moving out of the community. Some data suggest that residential mobility is related to crime only in poor communities. That is, poor communities with high rates of mobility have higher crime rates than poor communities with low rates of mobility. Mobility may be unrelated to crime rates in wealthier communities.

Family disruption. High-crime communities tend to have higher rates of family disruption. Disruption is usually measured by the percentage of families headed by females and/or the percentage of residents who are divorced or separated. Economic deprivation is a major cause of family disruption, since, among other things, it leads to a decline in the proportion of males who are able to support a family.[7] Nevertheless, data indicate that family disruption has an independent effect on community crime rates. In fact, certain data suggest that family disruption partly explains the effect of economic deprivation on community crime rates. That is, economic deprivation affects community crime rates partly through its effect on family disruption (Sampson, 1985, 1987).

Is race related to community crime rates?. High-crime communities tend to have a higher percentage of black residents (race and ethnic groups other than whites and blacks have not been well studied). Data, however, suggest that the percentage of black residents does not have a causal effect on crime rates. Race is associated with variables like economic deprivation and family disruption. Blacks are more likely than whites to be poor and to live in high-poverty areas (where 40 percent or more of the residents are below the poverty line). Data from 1998 indicate that 10 percent of white, non-Hispanic children lived in poverty whereas 36 percent of black children did (Federal Interagency Forum on Child and Family Statistics, 2000). Further, about 10 percent of poor whites live in high-poverty areas versus over 40 percent of poor blacks (Hawkins et al., 1998:42). Blacks are also more likely to live in disrupted families and in areas with high levels of family disruption (Sampson, 1986a; Sampson and Wilson, 1995). Data from 1998 indicate that 77 percent of white, non-Hispanic children lived with two parents whereas 35 percent of black children did. Given these facts, one might ask whether the association between the percentage of black residents and community crime rates is due to third variables such as economic deprivation and family disruption.

The answer appears to be "yes." In particular, data suggest that advantaged communities have similar crime rates regardless of whether they are populated by whites or blacks. Likewise, economically deprived communities have similar crime rates regardless of whether they are populated by whites or blacks.[8] Similar findings are obtained for family disruption: that is, communities with similar levels of family disruption tend to have similar crime rates regardless of whether they are populated by whites or blacks (Sampson, 1985, 1987).

❖ ❖ ❖ ❖   In sum, high-crime communities tend to be very poor; large, dense and overcrowded; high in residential mobility; and populated by disrupted families.

The Increase in Communities With Characteristics Conducive to High Crime

The number of communities with characteristics conducive to high crime has *increased* over the past three decades. This may surprise you, since you have probably heard a lot about the economic prosperity that the United States is now enjoying. And it is true that most people in the United States are doing quite well. In fact, the percentage of children living in families with high incomes increased from 17 percent to 27 percent between 1980 and 1998 (high income is defined as at least four times the poverty level—or $66,640 for a family of four in 1998). At the same time, the percentage of children living in poverty has been relatively stable since 1980, and there has been a slight increase in the number of children living in extreme poverty (incomes less than half the poverty level—or less than $8,300 for a family of four in 1998). About 18 percent of all children live in families below the poverty line, and almost half of these children live in extreme poverty. So the gap between the rich and poor is becoming wider in the United States. Further, poor children—especially poor black children—are now much more likely to live in high-poverty communities (communities where a high percentage of the other people are poor). The number of census tracts in the United States with high rates of poverty grew by two-thirds from 1970 to 1980. The increase in the number of high-poverty communities is the result of certain social and economic changes, changes that have had a particularly devastating effect on black, inner-city communities.[9]

First, the increase in the number of high-poverty communities is due partly to the *migration of working- and middle-class blacks to more affluent communities*. As late as the 1960s, inner-city communities contained many working- and middle-class residents as well as poor residents. Working- and middle-class blacks were prevented from living elsewhere by discriminatory housing policies. Also, discriminatory employment practices made it difficult for them to earn a living outside of black communities. As these discriminatory practices declined, working and middle-class blacks started to move to more affluent communities—leaving the poor behind.

Second, the increase in the number of high-poverty communities is partly due to *government housing policies*. The government placed public housing projects in inner-city communities, which further increased the concentration of poor people there. (As you may have noticed, there are few public housing projects in suburban areas.) Consequently, there was a dramatic change in the class composition of inner-city communities over the space of just a few decades, with these communities changing from mixed-class to largely poor.

Further, the economic situation of the poor people in these communities deteriorated as a result of several major changes in the economy. Most notably, low-skill jobs paying a decent wage became scarcer. There was a decline in the number of manufacturing jobs, partly due to technological changes and partly due to the movement of manufacturing jobs from the central city to suburban areas and overseas. For example, Philadelphia, Chicago, New York, and Detroit have lost more than half their manufacturing jobs since the 1960s (Wilson, 1996). The wages in manufacturing jobs also became less competitive, owing to such factors as foreign competition, the increase in the size of the work force, and the decline of unions. There was an increase in low-skill jobs in the service sector (e.g., sales, food service, government work), but most of these jobs had low salaries and were located at a distance from inner-city communities. There was also an increase in high-skill jobs in the technology/information processing areas, but these jobs were beyond the reach of most inner-city residents. Changes in the job market, then, made it much more difficult for unskilled workers—particularly those in inner city communities—to earn an adequate living. Further, these changes occurred along with cuts in government services to the poor, which further compounded their problems.

These economic problems created additional problems for inner-city residents. Family disruption became more common as it became more difficult for males to earn an adequate income. While researchers do not have good data on the rates of family disruption in inner-city areas, they know that there has been a dramatic increase in rates of family disruption over the last three decades; the rates of family disruption are especially high among blacks. Approximately 25 percent of all black families were headed by a female in 1967, whereas 52 percent were female headed in 1997 (Federal Interagency Forum on Child and Family Statistics, 2000; Wilson, 987:21). Female-headed households are much more likely to be below the poverty line, and this partly explains why the percentage of black children living below the poverty line is so high. In addition, these economic problems lead to such problems in the inner city as the "rapid deterioration of housing, schools, businesses, recreational facilities, and other community organizations" (Wacquant and Wilson, 1989:10).

In sum, there has been an increase in the number of communities possessing the characteristics associated with high crime rates, and this increase has affected blacks much more than whites. There remains, however, the question of why communities with these characteristics are higher in crime.

Why Are Deprived Communities Higher in Crime?

High-crime communities may be high in crime for two fundamental reasons. First, crime-prone individuals may be attracted to these communities or they may be more likely to live in these communities because they (or their families) cannot afford to live elsewhere. Second, the characteristics of high-crime communities may *cause* individuals to engage in crime. High-crime communities, then, may both attract or select for crime-prone individuals and cause these individuals to engage in crime. The most recent data suggest that both explanations have some merit, although there is still some uncertainty about the size of the causal effect of communities on crime.[10] In this section, I examine the ways in which the characteristics of high-crime communities may cause crime.

Not surprisingly, researchers have argued that the characteristics of high-crime neighborhoods cause crime for reasons related to strain, social

❖ ❖ ❖ ❖   learning, and control theories. Explanations based on control theory now dominate the literature, so I will begin there.

Deprived Communities Are Lower in Control

According to control theorists, the characteristics of high-crime neighborhoods reduce the ability of community residents to exercise effective control (see Chapter 8 for a description of control theory). In particular, the residents of high-crime communities are less able or willing to exercise direct control over people in the community, provide young people with a stake in conformity, and socialize young people so that they condemn delinquency and develop self-control. Residents are less likely to engage in these forms of control for at least three reasons.[11]

First, they often lack the skills and resources to assist others in the community. As indicated, they often have low incomes, limited educations, and poor work histories. Many are single parents struggling with family responsibilities. And many are "demoralized by racism and the wall of social resistance facing them" (Anderson, 1990:66). As a consequence, they are less able to help juveniles do well in school, secure adequate jobs, or deal with other life challenges. Elijah Anderson (1990) provides an excellent illustration of this point in his description of the Northton community. The Northton community was once a mixed-income black community with a relatively low crime rate. Juveniles in the community often received assistance from many adults, including adults outside their family. These adults, referred to as "old heads," would often function as surrogate fathers, providing guidance, encouragement, financial aid, and help in finding jobs. More generally, they served as conventional role models. As Anderson states, they "served the black community well as visible, concrete symbols of success and moral value, living examples of the fruits of hard work, perseverance, decency, and propriety" (1990:58). In recent years, however, the working- and middle-class residents of the community have moved to more affluent areas, so there are fewer old heads to assist youth. And the old heads that remain have less influence, partly because decent-paying jobs have become scarcer, making it difficult for the old heads to assist youth and undermining their lessons about the rewards of hard work and a conventional lifestyle. Juveniles in the community are now much less likely to receive support from adults, and, perhaps partly as a consequence, crime rates have increased.

Second, community residents are *less likely to have close ties to their neighbors and to care about their community*. They do not own their own homes, which lowers their investment in the community. They may hope to move to a more desirable community as soon as they are able, which also lowers their investment in the community. They live in high-density neighborhoods, with many of the residents living in multi-unit apartment buildings. Further, people are constantly moving into and out of their neighborhood. This makes it difficult for them to form close ties with their neighbors. In fact, they may have trouble recognizing their neighbors. As you might imagine, these factors make residents reluctant to get involved in community affairs, including such risky activities as confronting delinquents in their neighborhood.

Third, residents are *less likely to support or form community organizations*, including educational, religious, and recreational organizations. This lack of participation is partly a consequence of their limited resources and their lower attachment to the community. Their failure to get involved in community organizations further limits their ability to assist others in the community. Organizations like church groups provide direct assistance to community residents, including child care, health care, recreational services, and educational and jobs programs. Also, organizations help ensure that outside agencies—like the police and schools—are more responsive to community needs. For example, organizations may lobby for better schools and more police protection.

Factors like economic deprivation, density, mobility, and family disruption, then, may affect control in a number of ways. Direct control, for example, includes monitoring the behavior of others and punishing deviance. At the community level, direct control occurs through activities like "taking note of and/or questioning strangers, watching over each other's property, assuming responsibility for supervision of general youth activities, and intervening in local disturbances" (Sampson, 1986a:27). Individuals with limited resources and little attachment to their neighbors and community are going to be less willing and less able to engage in such activities. Also, there are fewer organizations, such as church and recreational groups, in the community to engage in such supervisory activities. As a consequence, unsupervised teenage peer groups are more common in the community, and people feel freer to engage in crime without fear of external sanction. (You should test your understanding of this discussion by describing how the characteristics just discussed may affect the other two major forms of control: stake in conformity and internal control.)

Recent data provide some support for these arguments. Factors like economic deprivation, mobility, and family disruption influence the extent to which community residents know their neighbors, care about their community, intervene in neighborhood problems, and get involved in community organizations. These factors, in turn, lead directly to crime or lead to crime indirectly by allowing for the development of unsupervised teenage peer groups.[12]

Deprived Communities Foster the Social Learning of Crime

Social learning theorists argue that the characteristics discussed in the preceding pages increase the likelihood of delinquency because they increase the likelihood that juveniles will be reinforced for delinquency, exposed to criminal models, and taught beliefs favorable to delinquency (see Akers, 1998; Sutherland et al., 1992).

The reinforcement and modeling of delinquency. Juveniles in communities with the above characteristics are more likely to find themselves in situations where the costs of delinquency are relatively low and the potential benefits seem high. As indicated above, juveniles in such communities are less likely to be punished for delinquency. Direct control is low and juveniles often fail to develop a strong stake in conformity or high levels of internal control. At the same time, juveniles are more likely to have access to criminal opportunities and be exposed to the benefits of crime. Illicit markets, such as drug markets, are more common in such communities because control is low and conventional avenues to success are often blocked (Hagan, 1994). Related to this, juveniles are more likely to be exposed to criminal models, including "successful" criminals. Among other things, the juveniles in such communities are more likely to be part of unsupervised peer groups whose members often model and reinforce crime. As a consequence, the juveniles in such communities may be more likely to conclude that "crime pays."

Delinquent beliefs. The residents of high-crime communities may also be more likely to develop beliefs favorable to crime. It has been argued that they are more likely to approve of or hold neutral attitudes toward minor forms of crime, view crime as justified under certain conditions, and emphasize values like toughness (see Chapter 7). Young males in such communities are said to be particularly likely to hold such views. These beliefs have not been well studied with survey data but are frequently reported in observational or ethnographic studies of high-crime communities.[13]

The origin of such beliefs may be partly explained using strain theory. Individuals who cannot obtain money through legitimate channels may attempt to obtain it through delinquent channels, such as theft and drug selling. In the process, they may come to justify or rationalize their delinquency. For example, they may claim that while theft in general is bad, it is justified or excusable if decent jobs are unavailable. Also, individuals who cannot obtain the more general goal of social status through legitimate channels may attempt to obtain it through violence. That is, they may attempt to coerce or intimidate others into treating them with respect. Among other things, these attempts may take the form of maintaining a tough demeanor, responding to even minor shows of disrespect with violence, and occasionally "campaigning for respect" by assaulting others. In the process, the juveniles may come to value toughness and feel that violence is a justified response to a wide range of provocations.[14] As such individuals interact with one another in the community, they may form a subculture centered on such "beliefs favorable to delinquency" (see Cohen, 1955, for a fuller discussion of this process).

Deprived Communities Are Higher in Strain

Strain theorists argue that the residents of communities with the above characteristics described here are more likely to experience the types of strain described earlier: the failure to achieve positively valued goals and the loss of positive stimuli or the presentation of negative stimuli. Also, the residents of such communities may be less able to cope with their strain through legitimate channels.[15]

Goal blockage. It is clear that the residents of such communities are less able to achieve the goal of economic success. In particular, the residents have less access to jobs in general and to stable, well-paying jobs in particular. Manufacturing and service-sector jobs (e.g., retail sales, restaurant workers) are often located at a distance from deprived communities, so they are less accessible; relatively few individuals in the community have job contacts or job information; and there are fewer individuals in the community to teach and model the skills and attitudes necessary for successful job performance. As a consequence, residents may be more likely to engage in theft, drug selling, prostitution, or other illicit income-generating activities. Also, the frustration that results from goal blockage may result in violent behavior as well. Related to this, residents in these communities are also less able to achieve social status, including "masculine status," through conventional means. As a consequence, they may attempt to achieve such status through illegitimate means, or they may strike out at others in their frustration. These arguments have not received a good test, but certain data are compatible with them (Agnew, 1999; Messerschmidt, 1993).

Loss of positive stimuli/presentation of negative stimuli. The residents of high-crime communities are also subject to a range of additional types of strains, many of them having their origins in the economic deprivation of the community. Not only are the residents of deprived communities more likely to experience economic hardships of various types, but they are more likely to experience family disruption and the strains associated with such disruption, such as family conflict. They are more likely to live in dense, overcrowded, and substandard housing. They are more likely to get into conflicts with others, because they live in such close contact with these others; they are less able to establish close ties to these others, because they are often in competition with these others over scarce resources like money. Not surprisingly, they have higher rates of criminal victimization and child abuse. Also, blacks and certain other groups are more likely to experience racial discrimination.

Coping with strain. Finally, it has been argued that the residents of high-crime communities may be less able to cope with strain through legitimate channels. Among other things, they have fewer coping resources, like money and power. As noted earlier, they are less likely to receive assistance or support from others in their community, either from individuals or from organizations. Further, it has been argued that residents' continued experience with strain increases their underlying level of anger and their sensitivity to slights. That is, they develop what has been called a "short fuse," which increases their propensity to respond to strain with crime.[16] As indicated above, they are also subject to less control and are more likely to be predisposed to crime for reasons explained by social learning theory. These factors also increase the likelihood that the residents will respond to strain with crime.

Summary

In sum, religion, work, the mass media, and the community do have an effect on delinquency, although only a small to moderate effect in some cases. Religion reduces "victimless" crimes by a small to moderate amount. Work by in-school juveniles—especially long hours of work—increases delinquency by a small amount. Mass media violence has a small to moderate effect on violent behavior. And living in certain types of communities, particularly very poor communities, increases the likelihood of delinquency, although there is still some uncertainty over how much.

Notes

1. For overviews and recent examples of the research on religion and delinquency, see Burkett and Warren, 1987; Cochran et al., 1994; Elifson et al., 1983; Evans et

al., 1996; Evans et al., 1995; Jensen and Rojek, 1998; Stark and Bainbridge, 1996; Tittle and Welch, 1983.

2. *See* Evans et al., 1995; Stark and Bainbridge, 1996; Tittle and Welch, 1983.

3. For overviews and selected studies in this area, see Agnew, 1986; Cullen et al., 1997; Ploeger, 1997, Steinberg, 1996, Willlamis et al., 1996, Wright et al., 1997.

4. For overviews of the research on TV violence and violent behavior, see Binder et al., 1997; Donnerstein and Linz, 1995; Donnerstein al., 1994; Freedman, 1984; Levine, 1996; National Television Violence Study, 1997, 1998.

5. *See* Shaw and McKay, 1942; Kornhauser, 1978; Sampson, 1997.

6. For overviews of the research in this area, see Byrne and Sampson, 1986; Bursik and Grasmick, 1993, 1995; Kornhauser, 1978; Land et al., 1990; Office of Juvenile Justice and Delinquency Prevention, 1999a; Sampson, 1995, 1997; Sampson and Lauritsen, 1993; Sampson and Wilson, 1995; Thornberry et al., 1998; White, G. 1999.

7. *See* Sampson, 1987; Shihadeh and Steffensmeier, 1994; Wilson, W. 1987.

8. *See* Hawkins et al., 1998; Krivo and Peterson, 1996; Peeples and Loeber, 1994.

9. For overviews, see Hagan, 1994; Sampson and Wilson, 1995; Wilson, W. 1987, 1996.

10. *See* Bursik and Grasmick, 1996; Elliott et al., 1996; Farrington, 1993a; Peeples and Loeber, 1994; Sampson et al., 1997.

11. *See* Bursik, 1988; Bursik and Grasmick, 1993, 1995; Kornhauser, 1978; Sampson, 1995; Sampson and Groves, 1989; Sampson et al., 1997; Sampson and Wilson, 1995.

12. Elliott et al., 1996; Sampson and Groves, 1989; Sampson et al., 1997.

13. *See* Anderson, 1994, 1999; Fagan, 1998; also see Sampson and Bartusch, 1999.

14. *See* Anderson, 1994, 1999; Fagan, 1998; Majors and Billson, 1992.

15. *See* Agnew, 1999; Bernard, 1990; Hagan, 1994.

16. *See* Agnew, 1999; Balkwell, 1990; Bernard, 1990. ✦

Delinquent Situations, Drugs, and Guns: Is Delinquency More Likely in Certain Types of Situations—Including Situations Where Drugs and Guns Are Present?

Chapters 6 through 14 focus on factors that create a *general predisposition*, or willingness, to engage in delinquency. Such factors include individual traits and a range of family, school, peer group, and other experiences. Individuals who are predisposed to delinquency tend to commit more delinquent acts than those who are not predisposed. But even the most predisposed individuals do not commit delinquent acts *all the time*. In fact, they obey the law in most situations.

Research suggests that predisposed individuals are more likely to commit delinquent acts in certain types of situations. The first part of this chapter provides a general overview of the types of situations most conducive to delinquency. The second part discusses the factors that influence the likelihood that predisposed individuals will encounter situations conducive to delinquency. And the third and fourth parts discuss the role of drugs and guns in promoting delinquency. In particular, I ask whether delinquency is more likely in situations where drugs and guns are present.

What Types of Situations Are Most Conducive to Delinquency?

While the leading delinquency theories focus on the factors that *predispose* individuals to delinquency, we can draw on these theories and certain other research to describe the types of situations most likely to result in delinquency. In brief, juveniles are most likely to engage in delinquency when they are in situations where they are provoked by others, where the benefits of delinquency are high, and where the costs are low.[1]

Strain Theory

Strain theory argues that delinquency is most likely to occur in situations where individuals are subject to strain. Several types of situational strain have been described in the literature. The most common type is provocations by others, especially verbal and physical attacks that are perceived as deliberate. Such provocations involve the presentation of negative stimuli, and they may also be seen as threats to one's status, especially on the part of certain males who view them as threats to their "manhood."

Several studies suggest that such provocations typically precede violent crimes. Someone does or says something that the offender does not like. Perhaps a person calls the offender a name, criticizes the offender, or refuses to do what the offender says. The "provocation" that initiates the violence often seems trivial to outsiders (e.g., staring at someone too long). Using data from a national sample of adolescents, Agnew (1990) found that over 60 percent of the juveniles engaging in assault said they did so because they were intentionally provoked in some way. Among other things, they said that they were insulted, annoyed, threatened, molested, or had their property damaged or taken. Being provoked or mistreated by others was also the main reason given for vandalism and running away.

A recent study by Lockwood (1997) also highlights the central role of provocations in producing violence. Lockwood interviewed 110 middle and high school students from schools with high rates of violence. These students discussed 250 violent incidents in which they had been involved. About half these incidents occurred at school; others occurred in public areas (e.g., sidewalks or streets, parks) and homes. Most of these incidents involved acquaintances (58 percent); others occurred with friends (16 percent) and family members (15 percent). Only 11 percent involved strangers. The most common setting for a violent incident, then, was an encounter with an "acquaintance" at school. These violent incidents almost always began when one of the students did something that the other student did not like, that is, when one student provoked the other. The most common provocation was "offensive touching," such as pushing, grabbing, hitting, or throwing something. Other provocations included interfering with the other's possessions; refusing to do something when requested; saying something bad about someone to someone else; verbally teasing someone; and deliberately insulting someone. Such provocations typically led to an argument; the argument escalated and insults were exchanged; and violence was the result. Violence was performed to end the disliked behavior, seek revenge, and/or save face.

It is important to stress that many offenders are *not the innocent victims* of provocations by others. Data suggest that many offenders mistreat others and, in doing so, *elicit* negative reactions from them (see Felson, R. 1993; Jensen and Brownfield, 1986). They then respond to these negative reactions with delinquency. A school bully, for example, may regularly "pick on" or harass another juvenile. When the harassed juvenile complains or objects, the bully may respond with violence, claiming that he or she was "provoked." Many offenders behave in ways that call forth "provocations," or negative responses, from others.

When offenders are "provoked," they may immediately attack the victim. As suggested earlier, however, the offender and victim more commonly engage in a series of verbal exchanges. The offender, for example, may demand that the victim apologize. The victim may refuse. The offender may then insult the victim. The victim, in turn, may reply with an insult. Neither the victim nor the offender is willing to back down, and violence eventually results.

Other types of situational strain have received less attention, although certain researchers state that delinquency is sometimes prompted by such things as a desperate need for money (e.g., for drugs) and the loss of positive stimuli (e.g., the murder of a friend). Short and Strodtbeck (1965) found that gang leaders often initiate violence against other groups when they feel that their status as leader is in doubt or they are being challenged by others. Such violence enhances their status by allowing them to demonstrate their aggressive skills in a way that does not disrupt the group.

Strain theorists, of course, recognize that most instances of situational strain do not result in delinquency. A delinquent response is more likely when the situational strain is severe and is seen as intentionally inflicted. Several researchers note that severe physical and verbal attacks are especially likely to provoke a delinquent response, particularly when males are attacked by other males. A delinquent response is also more likely when the individual is in a situation where the delinquent response is likely to be reinforced rather than punished (discussed below). Finally, a delinquent response is, of course, more likely among individuals who are predisposed to delinquency. So two individuals may respond to the same situational strain differently. For example, an individual who is predisposed to delinquency may respond to a shove by throwing a punch, while another individual may do nothing in response to a shove.

Social Learning/Control Theories

I treat social learning and control theories together here, since the arguments they make overlap to some extent. According to these theories, crime is most likely in situations where the benefits of crime are seen as high and the costs as low. The *benefits of crime* may be tangible, like money or property. And they may be intangible, like social approval from others and the thrills or excitement associated with the crime (see Katz, 1988). Agnew (1990), for example, found that most of the juveniles who had stolen things said they did so because they needed to obtain a certain item or because it was fun or enjoyable. The *costs of crime* include the likelihood of being caught and punished, as well as the "moral costs" of committing the crime. That is, how bad or guilty would the juvenile feel if he or she committed a crime in that situation?

Few researchers argue that juveniles *carefully consider all* the benefits and costs of crime in a particular situation. Most juveniles (and adults) are not that rational or thoughtful. Researchers, however, argue that *most* juveniles give at least *some limited thought* to the rewards and costs of crime. For example, juveniles in a particular situation may not pause and carefully calculate the probability that they will be caught and punished if they commit a crime. At the same time, they usually do not commit crimes when their parents are present or the police are nearby. Thus, they give some rough consideration to the costs (and benefits) of crime.

The amount of consideration given to benefits and costs varies by the characteristics of the juvenile, the type of crime under consideration, and other factors, like alcohol and drug use. Some juveniles are very impulsive; they often commit crimes with little thought as to the consequences. Other juveniles are more thoughtful. Also, juveniles usually give more consideration to the costs and benefits of property crime than of violent crime. Violent crimes are often committed "in the heat of anger," although they too may involve some consideration of costs and benefits. For example, offenders are generally more likely to attack smaller or weaker targets than larger or stronger ones. This fact partly explains why males are more likely to engage in aggression than females (Felson, 1996).

Factors Influencing the Calculation of the Benefits and Costs of Crime

Several researchers have discussed the features of a situation that influence the individual's calculation of benefits and costs. In the language of social learning theory, we might describe these features as "discriminative stimuli" (see Chapter 7). They indicate the probability that a criminal act will be reinforced or punished in a given situation. For example, imagine a predisposed offender who encounters a luxury car parked on a deserted street with the key in the ignition. The features of this situation are such that the predisposed offender is likely to conclude that the benefits of auto theft are high and the costs are low. But if the same offender encounters an old, beat-up car in a well-lit parking lot with an attendant, he or she will likely conclude that the benefits of auto theft are low and the potential costs are high (see Miethe and McCorkle, 1998, for a full discussion).

At a general level, the benefits of crime are likely to be seen as high in situations where an *attractive target is present* (Cohen and Felson, 1979; Felson, M. 1998). With respect to property, attractive targets are *visible, accessible, valuable, and easy to move*. That is, before a potential offender concludes that the benefits of crime are high, the offender must be able to see the target and gain access to it. The target must also be valuable, like cash or jewelry. And it must be easy to move, like a CD player or automobile (which can be driven). Items like refrigerators and washing machines are valuable but are seldom stolen because they are difficult to move. The ideal targets have a high value proportionate to their weight. Marcus Felson (1998), for example, reports that washing machines cost about $5 per pound, while other electronic goods cost much more per pound and so are more likely to be stolen. With respect to human beings, attractive targets are (1) visible and accessible and (2) believed to possess valuable items like cash and jewelry (perhaps they "flash" their money or are wearing expensive clothes).

There have been efforts to reduce crime by reducing the value of targets and by employing certain "target hardening" techniques which make targets less visible, less accessible, or more difficult to move. The robbery of bus drivers, for example, was dramatically reduced when transit companies installed theft-proof change boxes on buses and required exact change (which reduced the amount of money drivers carry). Anti-theft devices on automobiles and burglar bars on windows are other examples of "target hardening" (see Clarke, 1992, 1995, for numerous case studies in this area).

The costs of crime are likely to be seen as low when there is *no one around who might interfere with the crime*. Individuals who might interfere with the crime are sometimes described as "capable guardians"(see Felson, 1994, 1998). The police often function as capable guardians, but it is more common for ordinary people to play this role. For example, the presence of people walking the street at night is often enough to prevent a robbery. The presence of neighbors during the day is often enough to prevent a burglary. And the presence of teachers in the school cafeteria is often enough to prevent fights. Offenders fear that guardians may directly intervene if they commit a crime or that they may indirectly intervene by calling the police.

The costs of crime are also likely to be seen as low when *potential crime victims are unable to offer effective resistance* (e.g., they are elderly, alone, small, or unlikely to call the police because of their involvement in the drug trade). Further, the offender is likely to see the costs as low when he or she sees potential crime victims as (1) *deserving of their victimization because of their behavior or status* (e.g., they provoked the offender or are rival gang members), or (2) *little affected by their victimization* (e.g., their insurance will cover the loss, they are rich and can easily replace the things stolen from them). The latter factors reduce the "moral costs" of crime; that is, they reduce the likelihood that offenders will feel guilty about their crimes.

There have been efforts to reduce crime by increasing the ability of potential victims to offer effective resistance and by increasing the likelihood that others will intervene. For example, convenience stores are frequently the target of robberies. Research suggests that the likelihood of robbery can be reduced by altering the staffing and layout of such stores. In particular, potential offenders are much less likely to rob stores where two clerks rather than one are on duty; when the cashier is visibly stationed in the middle of the store rather than off to the side; and when the store is surrounded by businesses open in the evening. Potential offenders avoid such stores because two clerks are able to offer more resistance and because the offenders do not want to risk encountering or being noticed by others who might intervene. Other examples can be given (see Felson, M. 1998; Sherman et al., 1989). For example, parking lots with attendants have lower rates of auto theft than those without. Also, large households have lower rates of victimization than small households.

Summary

Delinquency, then, is most likely in situations where predisposed offenders are provoked and where they perceive the benefits of crime to be high and the costs to be low. Provocation is most relevant to violent crimes, and benefits and costs are most relevant to property crimes. These statements may seem straightforward, but they have led to a number of important, not-so-obvious conclusions about delinquency. In particular, researchers have argued that the delinquency rate is dependent not only on the number of predisposed offenders but also on such things as the supply of attractive targets and the presence of capable guardians. The delinquency rate may increase if there is an increase in attractive targets or a decrease in the presence of capable guardians, *even if there is no change in the number of predisposed offenders*. Several examples are provided below.

What Factors Influence the Likelihood That Predisposed Offenders Will Encounter Situations Conducive to Delinquency?

Sometimes individuals who are predisposed to delinquency *deliberately seek out* situations that are conducive to delinquency. They are more likely to do so for property crimes than for violent crimes. Predisposed offenders might actively search for good homes to burglarize or individuals to rob. Several studies, however, suggest that such searching behavior is not as wide-ranging as some people believe. Individuals tend to search for targets in areas that are convenient and familiar to them, so they select targets near their homes, near the places they frequent—like school and recreational sites—and along the routes they frequently travel—like the routes to and from school and the mall. Selection of targets in these areas requires less effort on their part. And they feel less conspicuous and more secure in these areas, since they know them well. (Offenders, however, usually do not commit property crimes *too close* to home because they might be recognized. Violent crimes, on the other hand, are frequently committed close to home or in the juvenile's home, since they often involve family members, friends, and acquaintances.)

At other times, predisposed offenders *do not deliberately* seek out situations that are conducive to crime. Rather, they encounter such situations during the course of their everyday, routine activities—attending school, going to

work, and hanging out with friends. For example, a juvenile might spot a
tempting target for burglary while on the way to school or might encounter a
good opportunity for shoplifting while hanging out with friends at the mall.
Violent crimes are especially likely to emerge out of everyday activities. Such
crimes are usually not planned but rather stem from the frictions of everyday
life, such as disputes at school or work.

Although individuals may seek out situations conducive to crime or simply encounter them during the course of everyday activities, certain factors
influence the *likelihood* that individuals will find or encounter situations that
are conducive to crime. Most prominent among these factors is the nature of
the individual's routine, or everyday, activities.

Routine Activities

The likelihood that potential offenders will encounter situations conducive to crime depends partly on the nature of their routine, or everyday, activities. That is, it depends on what they do each day, with whom they do it, when
they do it, and where they do it.

What they do and with whom they do it. Delinquency is higher among
adolescents who spend a lot of time in *unstructured activities with peers in the
absence of authority figures*. Authority figures include parents, teachers,
coaches, and others who have some responsibility for intervening if deviance
occurs. Unstructured activities include hanging out, riding around in a car,
going to parties, and certain other recreational activities.[2]

Unstructured activities with peers are conducive to delinquency for several reasons. Individuals who spend a lot of time with peers are more likely to
get into conflicts with them, especially when the time is unstructured and
authority figures are absent, so provocations are more likely. Also, the presence of peers influences the benefits and costs of crime in a particular situation. Peers, especially delinquent peers, often reinforce crime by offering social approval and status. And they often reduce the costs of crime by helping
the juvenile commit delinquent acts and by convincing the juvenile that such
acts are justifiable or excusable (thereby reducing the moral costs of crime).

When they do it. Violent crimes involving juveniles are more frequent on
school days, and they peak in the few hours immediately following the end of
school. On nonschool days, juvenile violence peaks between 8 and 10 P.M.
(Snyder and Sickmund, 1999). This temporal pattern is easily explained since
it is at these times that peers are most likely to engage in unstructured activities with one another in the absence of authority figures.

Where they do it. Public settings are generally more conducive to delinquency than private settings. In fact, each hour spent in public space is about
ten times more risky than each hour spent at home (Felson, M. 1994:39).
Also, data suggest that certain locations are especially conducive to delinquency. Delinquency is most likely in settings that bring young people
together in the absence of authority figures. Such settings include the area
around schools and the routes to and from school. As indicated, much crime
occurs as juveniles are leaving school. When crime does occur in school, it is
more likely to occur in hallways and restrooms than in classrooms, where
teachers are typically present. Other locations, like bars, are also risky. Bars
often bring together large numbers of young, intoxicated males.

Factors Influencing Routine Activities

Age and sex have an especially strong effect on routine activities. Adolescents are much more likely than other age groups to engage in unstructured activities with peers in the absence of authority figures. This fact partly explains why crime rates peak in adolescence. Also, males are much more likely than females to engage in unstructured activities in the absence of authority figures. This fact partly explains the gender difference in delinquency (see Osgood et al., 1996).

Routine activities are also influenced by many of the factors discussed in Chapters 6 through 14, such as the level of parental supervision, the school the juvenile attends, the peers the juvenile associates with, and the community in which the juvenile lives. Most notably, individuals who are poorly supervised by parents are more likely to engage in unstructured activities with peers in the absence of authority figures. In this area, evidence suggests that there has been a sharp decline in parental supervision since the 1950s. Parents are less likely to be home after school; they are less likely to engage in shared activities with their children; and they grant their children more freedom than in the past. Children today, for example, have fewer chores or duties around the house, later curfews, and greater access to automobiles. These changes can be traced to a number of factors, including increases in female employment, in single-parent families, and in multi-car households. As a consequence of these changes, there has been a change in the routine activities of juveniles: Juveniles now spend more time with peers away from parents. This change may partly explain the large increase in juvenile crime rates during the 1960s and early 1970s (see Felson, M. 1998, for a fuller discussion).

The large increase in juvenile crime rates may also be the result of certain social changes that have increased the likelihood that juveniles will encounter attractive targets in the absence of capable guardians. Over the past few decades people have started spending less time at home and more time in public places. There are several reasons for this trend, including the rise in female employment and an increase in the number and length of vacations. As a consequence, potential offenders are more likely to encounter empty or unprotected homes and to come across "attractive targets" in public settings (e.g., people going to a movie or at a bar). Further, there has been a dramatic increase in the number of lightweight, valuable products—like CDs, VCRs, and computers. Offenders, then, are also more likely to encounter attractive *property* targets during the course of their routine activities. Related to this, there has been a change in merchandising. Products are now more likely to be displayed on open shelves in large, high-volume stores with a limited number of clerks. The potential cost of shoplifting in such stores is much lower than in small stores, where goods are kept behind the counter. (For an excellent discussion of these trends, see Felson, M. 1998. Felson also argues that the very recent *decrease* in crime reflects the fact that people are using cash less and credit/debit cards more, among other things.)

Summary

Individuals, then, may deliberately seek out situations conducive to delinquency, or they may encounter such situations during the course of their everyday, routine activities. Individuals who frequently engage in unstructured activities with peers in the absence of authority figures are especially likely to find themselves in situations conducive to delinquency. Adolescents, males, and those who are poorly supervised by their parents, among others, are more likely to fall into this category.

There are, however, two final features of the situation that deserve special consideration—the presence of drugs and guns. In the remaining two sections of this chapter, I ask whether delinquency is more likely in situations where drugs and guns are present. As you well see, some researchers argue that drugs and guns influence such things as the perceived benefits and costs of delinquency and the likelihood of encountering provocations to delinquency.

Do Drugs Increase the Likelihood of Delinquency?

Is delinquency more likely in situations where drugs are present? It is commonly argued that drug use and sales are a major cause of delinquency. And part of the motivation behind the current "war on drugs" is the belief that reducing drug use/sales will have a major impact on other types of delinquency. Drug use/sales are said to contribute to delinquency for at least four reasons.[3]

Reasons That Drugs May Affect Delinquency

The first reason has to do with the *pharmacological effect of certain drugs*. Drugs like alcohol, cocaine, amphetamines, and PCP are said to weaken self-control and/or increase irritability. Also, withdrawal from drugs like heroin and crack may increase irritability and frustration. Drug use, then, may contribute to crime by reducing control and increasing strain. In particular, individuals on drugs may be more likely to (1) engage in behaviors that upset or provoke others; (2) take offense at the behavior of others; and (3) respond to provocations with violence—partly because they are less concerned with or aware of the costs of crime (e.g., Fagan, 1998). Researchers, however, emphasize that not all drugs have this effect. Further, the impact of drugs is influenced by the individual and the social situation. For example, the effect of alcohol on aggression is strongest among individuals already predisposed to aggression.

Second, juveniles may engage in crime in order to *obtain money to purchase drugs*, especially individuals addicted to expensive drugs like heroin and cocaine. That is, drug use may lead to a particular type of strain—a desperate need for money. Individuals may then engage in a wide range of income-generating crimes, like larceny, burglary, robbery, prostitution, and drug sales. Some of these crimes, such as robbery, may result in violence. In one study of inner-city youth, about a quarter of the respondents who committed burglary said they did so in order to get money for drugs. About 36 percent of the youth who sold drugs and 19 percent who engaged in robbery said they committed these crimes to get money for drugs (Altschuler and Brounstein, 1991).

Third, the *drug trade contributes to crime*. Individuals who buy and sell drugs often carry large amounts of money and drugs, and they are generally reluctant to involve the police when disputes arise. As a consequence, crime is often the result (the benefits of crime are seen as high and the costs as low). Drug sellers may employ violence against one another as they compete for turf or customers. Both drug sellers and customers are often attractive targets for robbers. And drug sellers and their customers often employ violence against one another when they get into disputes. These problems have been especially severe in the crack trade, where there are many young, inexperienced dealers competing against one another.

Fourth, some researchers argue that drug use, especially chronic use, may *increase the juvenile's predisposition to engage in delinquency* by reducing the juvenile's bonds to family and school, lowering academic performance, and increasing the likelihood of association with delinquent peers. Juveniles are frequently brought into contact with such peers when they buy and use drugs.[4]

It is also argued that drug use not only increases the likelihood that individuals will commit crimes but also increases the likelihood that they will be victims of crime. Among other things, drug users may be more likely to be victimized because they are less able to offer effective resistance and because their lifestyles sometimes place them in close contact with offenders. The former argument has recently been made with respect to rohypnol, or "roofies," the "date rape drug."[5]

The arguments set out in the preceding paragraphs play a central role in a debate over whether drugs should be legalized. Individuals who want to legalize drugs claim that drugs are expensive largely because they are illegal. Legalization will lower their cost and thereby reduce much income-generating crime. Further, legalization will also reduce the crime associated with the illicit drug trade. Individuals opposed to legalization claim that drug use will increase if drugs are legalized. They point to several negative consequences of this increase, including increased crime arising from the pharmacological

effects of drug use and the effects of drug use on such things as family bonds
and school performance.[6]

❖ ❖ ❖ ❖

The Evidence

What does the evidence suggest? Do drugs contribute to delinquency?

The evidence clearly indicates that there is a strong association between
drugs and delinquency. Individuals who commit crimes are frequently under
the influence of drugs (including alcohol). Also, juveniles who use drugs and
especially those who sell drugs are much more likely to engage in crime.
Some categories of drug users, like heroin addicts and heavy users of crack,
engage in enormous amounts of crime. This does *not*, of course, mean that all
crimes are committed under the influence of drugs. Nor does it mean that all
drug users are delinquents or that all delinquents are drug users. Estimates of
the association between drug use and delinquency vary from study to study,
reflecting the different samples that are examined and the different measures
of drug use and delinquency that are employed.

Despite these different estimates, much data suggest that drugs often
play a part in situations where crimes occur. For example, a 1997 study of
arrested male juveniles in twelve sites around the country found that the percentage testing positive for drugs other than alcohol ranged from about 40
percent to 65 percent, with the percentage being around 60 percent in most
sites. Marijuana was by far the most common drug, followed by cocaine.[7]
Victimization data suggest that nearly four in ten violent crimes involve the
use of alcohol (Greenfeld, 1998).

Data also indicate that delinquents are more likely to use drugs than
nondelinquents (and drug users are more likely to engage in delinquency
than nonusers). For example, a self-report study found that a little more than
half the *serious* delinquents (those who admitted to three or more Part I
crimes in the past three years) were also serious drug/alcohol users. About a
third of the serious drug/alcohol users were serious delinquents.[8]

An association between drugs and delinquency, however, does not mean
that drugs *cause* delinquency. Some researchers argue that drugs and delinquency are associated because both are caused by the same third variables.
The data do indicate that drug use/sales and delinquency share many of the
same causes, such as individual traits, family problems, school problems,
and association with delinquent peers.[9] Also, some researchers argue that
drugs and delinquency are associated because delinquency causes drug use/
sales. Engaging in delinquency increases the likelihood that a person will be
exposed to others who possess and use drugs, who reinforce drug use, and
who hold values conducive to drug use. Data here indicate that delinquency
typically *precedes* drug use. Also, some studies have found that prior delinquency increases the likelihood of subsequent drug use.

At the same time, the evidence suggests that drug use, especially serious
drug use, does contribute to delinquency. For example, although drug addicts
typically engaged in crime before they became addicts, their level of crime
increases during periods of high drug use and decreases during periods of
low drug use. Also, longitudinal data suggest that serious drug use contributes to the maintenance of serious delinquency (Elliott et al., 1989; Huizinga
et al., 1989, 1998). The effect of drug use on delinquency, however, is not as

large as many imagine or as the associational data suggest. As indicated, much of the association between drugs and delinquency arises because both are caused by the same third variables and because delinquency has an effect on drug use.

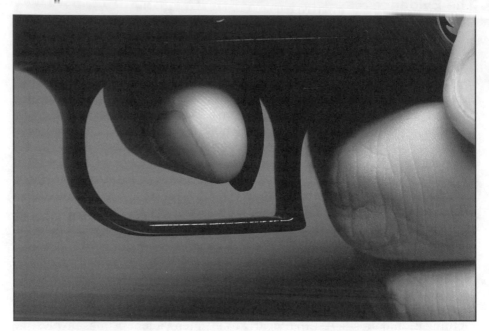

Do Guns Increase the Likelihood of Delinquency?

Most criminologists agree that many juveniles own and carry guns and that there is reason to believe that guns *contribute to* lethal violence and perhaps certain other types of delinquency. There is, however, a major debate over the extent to which guns contribute to crime/delinquency versus the extent to which they *prevent* crime/delinquency. Some researchers claim that guns prevent more crime/delinquency than they perpetuate. Let us examine the evidence in these areas.[10]

How Common Is Gun Ownership and Possession Among Juveniles?

There are now about 220 million guns in the United States; a third of these are handguns. (Handguns are much more likely to be used in crimes than long guns like rifles and shotguns. For example, 80 percent of all gun-related homicides are committed with handguns.) About 40 percent of all households in the United States have guns, with these gun-owning households each having an average of 4.5 guns. There is little doubt, then, that guns are common in the United States.

How common is it for juveniles to own or possess guns? It is illegal for juveniles to purchase guns, and, in most states, it is illegal for juveniles to possess handguns. Several studies have attempted to estimate the extent of gun ownership and possession among juveniles. These studies have focused on institutionalized delinquents, arrested delinquents, gang members, juveniles in high-crime inner-city areas, juveniles in urban areas, and juveniles throughout the country. A 1991 survey of male *institutionalized delinquents* in six correctional facilities throughout the country found that 83 percent owned a gun at the time they were incarcerated, and 55 percent said they carried a gun all or most of the time. Seventy-three percent had committed a crime with a gun (Sheley and Wright, 1995). A 1995 survey of *arrested male delinquents* in seven sites around the country found that 20 percent said they carried a gun all or most of the time—a percentage higher than that for arrested adults. For arrested gang members, the percentage was 31 percent. Five out of ten of the arrested juveniles said they had been shot at; the figure for gang members was eight out of ten (Decker et al., 1997; Sickmund et al., 1997). Other studies have found that anywhere from a quarter to more than half of all gang members own guns, and even more have ready access to guns. The gang, for example, often has a stash of guns that members can use. A 1991 study of males in ten *inner-city high schools* throughout the United States found that 22 percent owned guns, and 12 percent carried a gun all or most of the time (Sheley and Wright, 1995). Finally, a 1996 national survey of male tenth- and eleventh-graders from fifty-three high schools found that 29 percent possessed a gun and 6 percent had carried the gun outside their home at least once during the past year; 2 percent stated that they carried a gun all or most of the time (Sheley and Wright, 1998). These percentages clearly indicate that gun ownership and possession is fairly common among certain categories of juveniles.

Several studies have asked juveniles why they own or carry guns. The most common reason given is "for protection." Juveniles most likely to own guns are heavily involved in crime, belong to gangs or delinquent peer groups, and live in dangerous, inner-city communities. Most have witnessed violent crimes and have been the victims of violence themselves. Their criminal activity puts them in situations where violence is a very real possibility, and they are surrounded by others who own and carry guns. It is no surprise, then, that they feel they need a gun for "protection." Contrary to certain media accounts, juveniles are less likely to say that they own or carry a gun because it is a status symbol or because it makes you popular with peers— although some juveniles do say this. Some juveniles also say that they own guns for sport or recreational purposes, such as hunting and target shooting. Such juveniles differ from those who say that they own guns for protection. Among other things, they are much less likely to be involved in crime.

The large majority of juveniles with guns get them illegally, primarily from family members, friends, and street sources. In many communities, it is easy to purchase high-quality guns at prices well below retail. Also, the guns currently possessed by juveniles are more lethal than those owned in the past. Juveniles tend to own and carry high-quality, large-caliber, automatic or semi-automatic guns.

A few studies have examined the factors associated with gun ownership. Juveniles are more likely to own guns if they are male, their parents own guns, their peers own guns, they belong to gangs, they have been threatened or shot at with a gun, they sell drugs, or they engage in most other types of delinquency (although some data suggest that using drugs is not that strongly associated with owning or carrying a gun). The dramatic increase in gun-related juvenile homicide from the mid-1980s to the mid-1990s has been tied to the increased involvement of juveniles in drug selling and gangs during these years (see Chapter 3).

Do Guns Contribute to Delinquency?

It is commonly pointed out that the United States has the highest rates of gun ownership *and* lethal violence in the industrialized world. About 25 to 30 percent of United States households contain handguns. In most other industrialized nations, the rate of handgun ownership is 7 percent or lower (Messner and Rosenfeld, 1997). Further, the United States homicide rate is several times that of other industrialized countries. Differences in homicide rates are especially pronounced for gun-related homicides (about 70 percent of all homicides in the United States and 80 percent of all juvenile homicides are committed with guns). The gun-related juvenile homicide rate in the United States is from 4 to 73 times higher than the rate in other industrialized countries (Berkowitz, 1994). These data are reflected in the fact that teenage males in the United States are now more likely to die from gunshot wounds than from all natural causes combined (this is especially true for young black males, who are more likely to both commit and be the victims of homicide).

In short, the United States has a lot of guns and a lot of gun-related crime. Most studies find that there is a positive association between the rate of gun ownership and the rate of gun-related crime in a country or community. That is, there is more gun-related crime in countries and communities where guns are more prevalent. It is important to note, however, that this association is far from perfect. There are certain communities and countries with high rates of gun ownership but low rates of gun-related crime (e.g., Switzerland). The rate of gun-related crime is likely dependent on both the availability of guns and the willingness of people to use them.[11]

Data also indicate that juveniles who own or carry guns are much more likely to engage in most forms of delinquency. This is most true of juveniles who own guns for protection. It is less true of juveniles who own guns for sport (see Lizotte et al., 1994; Sheley and Wright, 1995). So guns and crime/delinquency are associated at the country, city, and individual levels.

As you know, however, the association between guns and delinquency does not demonstrate that guns increase the likelihood of delinquency. The association may be explained in other ways. It may be that gun possession and delinquency are both caused by the same third variables, such as association with delinquent peers. There is some evidence for this view. It may also be that crime/delinquency causes gun ownership. People who live in high-crime countries or communities may purchase guns to protect themselves. Juveniles who engage in delinquency may likewise purchase guns for protection, since their delinquency is often associated with a risky lifestyle.

At the same time, many criminologists argue that guns do *contribute to* delinquency, especially lethal violence. The most prominent argument in this area is that guns increase the likelihood that certain crimes, such as assault and robbery, will result in death. For example, it has been argued that the increased availability of guns played a key role in the dramatic increase in juvenile homicides from the mid-1980s to the mid-1990s. As guns became more widespread throughout the community, disputes that used to be settled with fists or knives were more likely to be settled with guns. And death was more likely to result.

Data indicate that gun attacks are more likely to be fatal than attacks with knives, fists, or other weapons. One study, for example, found that attacks with guns were five times more likely to be fatal than attacks with knives. One might argue that gun attacks are more fatal because people who attack with a gun are *more intent on killing their victims*. Limited data, however, suggest that differences in the intent to kill do not fully explain the higher fatality rate of guns. Data, for example, suggest that most offenders who fire guns do not intend to kill their victims.[12] Guns, then, appear to increase the likelihood that crimes like assault and robbery will result in death. (At the same time, it should be noted that assaults and robberies with guns are *less* likely to result in *nonfatal* injuries, partly because victims are less likely to resist.)

Some researchers argue that guns increase the likelihood of delinquency in still other ways. For example, it is said that the presence of guns increases the likelihood that *certain predisposed* adolescents will engage in crimes like assault and robbery. A gun may provide adolescents with the courage or the means to commit a crime they might otherwise avoid. That is, guns may reduce some of the costs of crime. And the presence of a gun may "trigger" an aggressive response in certain individuals. It is also said that as guns become more common, many adolescents arm themselves for "protection" and become more likely to respond to conflicts with gun use. The evidence regarding these arguments, however, is less certain.[13]

Nevertheless, there is reason to believe that guns contribute to at least certain types of delinquency. One might therefore conclude that there would be less delinquency, or at least less *fatal* delinquency, if guns were not so widespread. The situation, however, is not so simple.

Do Guns Prevent More Crime Than They Contribute To?

Some individuals acknowledge that guns may contribute to crime, but they claim that guns *prevent* more crime than they cause (you may have heard the expression that "a well-armed society is a polite society"). Many individuals buy guns for protection, and they may well use their guns to stop crimes from occurring or to subdue criminals. Likewise, many criminals may avoid victimizing people for fear they are armed. Many criminals, in fact, state that they have been scared off by armed victims or that they have avoided victimizing individuals because they thought these individuals were armed (Sheley and Wright, 1995). (It is unclear, however, whether these criminals then selected victims they thought were unarmed, thus *displacing* rather than *preventing* crime.)

Several studies have tried to determine whether guns prevent more crime than they cause. Research by Kellermann and associates suggests that family members in households with guns are much more likely to use their guns to kill and injure one another than they are to protect themselves from strangers. Further, family members in households with guns are much more likely to die from homicide, suicide, and gun accidents than family members in similar households without guns (Kellermann and Reay, 1986; Kellermann et al., 1993). Data from the National Crime Victimization Survey indicate that guns are only used for self-defense purposes about 100,000 times a year. The same survey, however, indicates that guns are used to commit about one million crimes each year. These studies, then, suggest that guns contribute to more crimes than they prevent. By contrast, other surveys indicate that guns are more likely to be used for self-defense purposes than they are to commit crimes. One recent survey, for example, estimates that guns are used for self-defense purposes at least 2.5 million times per year—far more than the one million gun-related crimes that occur each year (Kleck and Gertz, 1995). There is now a lively debate about the accuracy of these different studies.[14]

The outcome of this debate will allow society to better determine the *net* impact of guns on crime/delinquency. This debate also has important policy implications: If guns do prevent more crime than they cause, efforts to restrict or control gun ownership in the *general population* may not reduce crime. Even so, virtually everyone agrees that it is desirable to take guns away from criminals and delinquents and to at least restrict handgun possession by juveniles. I will return to this point in Chapter 22, when strategies for reducing delinquency are discussed.

Summary

Delinquency is most likely to occur when predisposed juveniles encounter situations conducive to delinquency. The juvenile's predisposition to delinquency is influenced by all the factors discussed in Chapters 6 through 14, including individual traits as well as family, school, and peer group experiences. The situations most conducive to delinquency are those where juveniles are provoked by others, the benefits of delinquency are high, and the costs are low. Individuals who engage in a lot of unstructured activities with peers in the absence of authority figures are especially likely to find themselves in such situations. In addition, there is some evidence that delinquency may be more likely in situations where drugs are present, and lethal delinquency may be more likely in situations where guns are present.

Notes

1. For overviews and examples of the research in this area, see Agnew, 1990a; Akers, 1990; Birkbeck and LaFree, 1993; Bottoms, 1994; Brantingham and Brantingham, 1984; Briar and Piliavin, 1965; Clarke and Cornish, 1985; Cohen and Felson, 1979; Cohen et al., 1981; Cornish and Clarke, 1986; Felson, M. 1987, 1994, 1998; Felson, R. 1993, 1997; Garofalo et al., 1987; Hindelang et al., 1978; Jensen and Brownfield, 1986; Kennedy and Baron, 1993; Kennedy and Forde, 1990, 1996; McCarthy, 1995; Massey et al., 1989; Miethe and McCorkle, 1998; Miethe and Meier, 1990, 1994; Mustaine and Tewksbury, 1998a; Osgood et al., 1996; Sampson and Wooldredge, 1987; Sherman et al., 1989.

2. *See* Agnew and Petersen, 1989; Felson, R. 1997; Hundleby, 1987; Jensen and Brownfield, 1986; Lotz and Lee, 1999; Office of Juvenile Justice and Delinquency Prevention, 1999a; Osgood et al., 1996; Riley, 1987.

3. For overviews and examples of the recent research on drugs and delinquency, see Akers, 1992; Altschuler and Brounstein, 1991; Boyum and Kleiman, 1995; Bureau of Justice Statistics, 1992; Chitwood et al., 1996; Crowe, 1998; Elliott et al., 1989; Gentry, 1995; Goldstein, 1985; Goode, 1993; Huizinga et al., 1989; Inciardi and McElrath, 1998; McBride and McCoy, 1993; Office of National Drug Control Pol-

icy, 1999; White et al., 1987; White and Hansell, 1996; White and Labouvie, 1994; Zhang et al., 1997.

4. *See* Crowe, 1998; Thornberry et al., 1998; Zhang et al., 1997.

5. *See* Saum, 1998; also see Crowe, 1998; Mustaine and Tewksbury, 1998b.

6. For a fuller discussion of these issues, see Boyum and Kleiman, 1995; Gentry, 1995; Goode, 1993; Inciardi and McElrath, 1998; Meier and Geis, 1997.

7. *See* National Institute of Justice, 1998b; also see Elliott et al., 1989; Altschuler and Brounstein, 1991.

8. *See* White et al., 1987; also see Akers, 1992; Elliott et al., 1989; Huizinga et al., 1998.

9. *See* Elliott et al., 1989; White et al., 1987; White and Labouvie,1994.

10. For overviews and examples of recent research on guns and delinquency/crime, see Berkowitz, 1994; Bjerregaard and Lizotte, 1995; Blumstein, 1995; Cook, 1991; Cook and Ludwig, 1997; Cook and Moore, 1995; Decker et al., 1997; Greenbaum, 1997; Kleck, 1997; Lizotte et al., 1994; Office of Juvenile Justice and Delinquency Prevention, 1996; Reiss and Roth, 1993; Sheley and Wright, 1995, 1998; Walker, 1998; Wright, J. et al., 1992; Wright J. and Vail, 2000; Zawitz, 1995; Zimring and Hawkins, 1997.

11. For overviews, see Cook, 1991; Cook and Moore, 1995; Kleck, 1997; Reiss and Roth, 1993; Zimring and Hawkins, 1997.

12. *See* Berkowitz, 1994; Cook and Moore, 1995; Kleck, 1997; Reiss and Roth, 1993; Zimring and Hawkins, 1997.

13. *See* Berkowitz, 1994; Blumstein, 1995; Kleck, 1997; Zimrig and Hawkins, 1997.

14. *See* Cook and Ludwig, 1997, 1998; Cook and Moore, 1995; Kleck, 1997; Kleck and Gertz, 1995; Lott, 1998; McDowell et al., 1991; McDowell and Wiersema, 1994; Reiss and Roth, 1993; Wright and Vail, 2000; Zimring and Hawkins, 1997. ✦

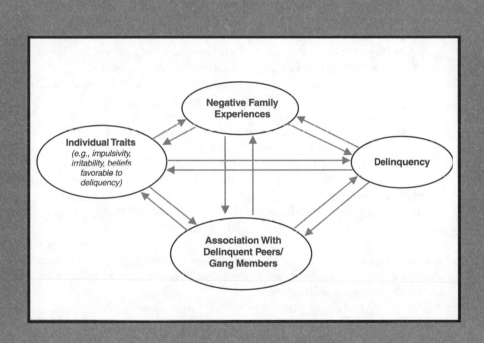

Pulling It All Together: Is It Possible to Construct an Integrated or General Theory of Delinquency?

We have now reviewed the three major theories of delinquency: strain, social learning, and control theories (Chapters 6 through 9). We have also reviewed a large body of research that is derived from, or at least compatible with, these theories. Some aspects of this research focus on the individual traits that may cause delinquency (Chapter 10), while others focus on the juvenile's social environment, and examine the family, school, peer group, and other factors that may cause delinquency (Chapters 11 through 14). Together, Chapters 10 through 14 focus on the factors that create a *general predisposition*, or willingness, to engage in delinquency. Whether predisposed individuals actually commit a delinquent act, however, is dependent on the particular situation they are in. And Chapter 15 focuses on the types of situations in which predisposed individuals are most likely to engage in delinquency.

You may be feeling somewhat overwhelmed by now. We have reviewed three theories and a lot of research based on these theories. You might be wondering how everything fits together. In particular, you might be wondering whether it is possible to pull all the theories and research together and construct an integrated or general theory of delinquency.

Several criminologists have tried to do this, and some of the integrated theories that they have produced are attracting a lot of attention right now.[1] Few criminologists, however, view these integrated theories as finished products. Rather, they are preliminary attempts to pull together the relevant theory and research on the causes of delinquency.

I am not going to present an integrated theory of delinquency in this chapter or describe all the integrated theories that have been constructed. That is far too ambitious a goal for this text. Rather, I will suggest the *general form* that an integrated theory of delinquency should take. In particular, I will present six general principles that researchers should keep in mind when constructing an integrated theory. These principles reflect the central ideas in many integrated theories. The principles should give you a general sense of how the theories and research discussed here might be integrated to form a general theory of delinquency.

Before presenting these principles, I first want to briefly review the major points from Chapters 6 through 15 dealing with the theories and research on the causes of delinquency.

Review of Theories and Research on the Causes of Delinquency

The three major delinquency theories describe the independent variables that cause delinquency and the reasons *why* these independent variables cause delinquency.

Strain theory argues that delinquency is caused by stressful events or conditions. The theory focuses on two major types of strain: the failure to achieve positively valued goals and the loss of positive stimuli/presentation of negative stimuli. The experience of strain leads to negative emotions like anger and frustration, and juveniles may turn to delinquency in an effort to cope with strain and these emotions. Delinquency may allow them to reduce or escape from their strain, seek revenge against those who have wronged them, or manage their negative emotions (through illicit drug use).

Social learning theory argues that delinquency is caused by associating with others who present beliefs favorable to delinquency, model delinquency, and reinforce delinquency. These activities lead individuals to conclude that delinquency is a desirable or at least justifiable response in certain situations.

Control theory argues that delinquency results from weak controls, including direct controls, stakes in conformity, and internal controls. Weak controls free juveniles to satisfy their needs and desires in the most expedient way possible, which is often delinquency.

The research derived from these theories focuses on a wide range of independent variables that may cause delinquency. Factors that appear to have at least a small to moderate effect on delinquency are:

Individual traits: Low verbal IQ, learning disabilities, hyperactivity/impulsivity/attention deficit, sensation-seeking, reduced ability to learn from punishment, irritability, insensitivity to others/low empathy, poor problem-solving/interpersonal skills, and beliefs favorable to delinquency. Evidence suggests that these traits are the product of biological factors and/or environmental influences, especially the family environment.

Family experiences: Broken homes, teenage motherhood, large families, criminal parents and siblings, parental rejection of child, low attachment to parents, family conflict, child abuse, poor parental supervision, poor family problem-solving techniques, and lack of "positive parenting."

School experiences: Low academic performance, low school involvement, low attachment to school, poor relations with teachers, low educational/occupational goals, and school misbehavior.

School characteristics: Large schools with poor resources, poor discipline, limited opportunities for student success, low expectations for students, unpleasant working conditions for students, and poor cooperation between administration and teachers.

Peer group/gang experiences: Delinquent peers, gang membership.

Religion, work, mass media, community: Nonreligious; extensive exposure to media violence; and long hours of work while attending school. Communities that are economically deprived, large, dense and overcrowded, high in residential mobility, and high in family disruption.

Situational variables: Provocations by others, especially insults, threats, and attacks by others. Exposure to "attractive targets," vulnerable and deserving victims, and the absence of "capable guardians." Unstructured activities with peers in the absence of authority figures. Serious drug use and especially drug selling. Availability of guns (for lethal violence).

Six Principles for Constructing an Integrated Theory of Delinquency

The preceding overview indicates that delinquency is caused by many factors and that these factors affect delinquency for several reasons. Most of these factors have small to moderate effects on delinquency. A few factors, however, appear to have stronger effects on delinquency than the others. They include certain individual traits such as hyperactivity/attention deficit/

impulsivity; family problems like parental rejection and poor supervision; and association with delinquent peers and gang members.

Although this overview is useful and advances our understanding of delinquency, it is not entirely satisfactory. In particular, it does not tell us how these variables are related to one another and how they might work together to produce delinquency. Integrated theories, however, attempt to do just that. I next want to present six principles that researchers should follow in constructing an integrated theory.

1. High Motivation for Delinquency, Low Constraints Against Delinquency, and Opportunity

Most criminologists agree that an integrated theory must take account of the motivation for delinquency, the constraints against delinquency, and the opportunities to engage in delinquency. Delinquency is said to be most likely when the motivation for delinquency is high, the constraints against delinquency are low, and opportunities to engage in delinquency are available.[2]

The theories and research described in this book deal with motivation, constraints, and opportunity to varying degrees. Strain and social learning theory deal with the motivation for delinquency. Social learning and control theory deal with the constraints against delinquency. And all three theories deal with the factors that influence the opportunities for delinquency, such as exposure to "attractive targets" and the "absence of capable guardians."

The research on these theories also deals with factors that directly index or influence the motivation for delinquency, the constraints against delinquency, and the opportunities for delinquency. The individual traits listed, for example, affect delinquency largely through their effect on motivation, constraint, and/or opportunity. Take the trait of hyperactivity/impulsivity/ attention deficit (HIA); as suggested in Chapter 10, someone high in this trait is likely to be high in the motivation for delinquency and low in constraint. HIA is associated with high strain, and people with HIA are more likely to be attracted to the immediate rewards of delinquency. At the same time, HIA reduces concern with the negative consequences of delinquency and, more generally, is associated with low control.

An integrated theory of delinquency, then, must incorporate the major theories and research considered in this book, since the theories and research point to factors that index or influence motivation, constraint, and opportunity. One problem with many of the current integrated theories is that they do not incorporate all of the theories discussed here or certain major independent variables considered (see the discussion in Tittle, 1995). Many integrated theories, for example, do not take account of individual traits.

2. The Causes of Delinquency Affect One Another

An integrated theory has to do more than incorporate the major causes of delinquency as described by delinquency theories and research. It must also describe how these causes are related to one another. The variables that cause delinquency do not stand in isolation from one another. They influence one another. And one of the central tasks of an integrated theory is to describe these influences. Two major arguments can be made in this area.

❖ ❖ ❖ ❖

Most of the causes of delinquency have reciprocal effects on one another. A reciprocal effect refers to a situation where two variables have causal effects on one another, so that variable X causes variable Y and variable Y causes variable X. For example, individual traits like HIA have an effect on family experiences. Juveniles with HIA are difficult to raise, and they often overwhelm and frustrate parents. Many parents respond by becoming overly coercive or by just giving up attempts to control the child's behavior. At the same time, family experiences affect HIA. Although juveniles may have a biological predisposition for HIA, a warm but firm family environment may reduce the likelihood that HIA develops. So HIA influences family experiences, and family experiences influence HIA.

Many other examples of reciprocal effects can be given. Thornberry (1987) has developed an integrated theory that stresses the reciprocal effects between the causes of delinquency. For example, he argues that family experiences and school experiences have reciprocal effects on one another. Juveniles with close ties to parents tend to do better at school, while school performance has an effect on how well juveniles get along with parents. To give another example, he argues that juveniles who associate with delinquent friends are more likely to develop beliefs favorable to delinquency, and those with such beliefs are more likely to select delinquents as friends.

I invite you to pick any two variables from the theories or the research that we have discussed (e.g., low academic performance and gang membership). With a little creativity, I am confident that you can list reasons why these two variables might be reciprocally related (e.g., why academic performance might influence gang membership, and why gang membership might influence academic performance).

There is reason to believe that most of the causes of delinquency may have reciprocal effects on one another. Not all of these reciprocal effects have been empirically examined, but the limited data available suggest that many of the causes of delinquency are reciprocally related to one another.[3]

Some effects are stronger than others. Although most of the causes of delinquency have reciprocal effects, it is not simply the case that "everything causes everything else." Some effects are stronger than others, and one of the things that an integrated theory must do is describe the effects that are relatively strong. In this area, delinquency theory and limited research suggest that the following causal effects may be especially important.

There are certain *background variables* that have small to moderate *direct* effects on delinquency but often have substantial effects on many of the variables that cause delinquency, such as individual traits; family, school, peer group, and other experiences; and situations conducive to delinquency. These background variables are of two types. The first set of background variables refers to one's *social position*—that is, one's gender, age, race/ethnicity, social class, and community. As previously discussed, these variables can affect such things as family upbringing, peer associations, and the types of situations one encounters. The second set of background variables refers to *biological influences*, including genetic inheritance and biological damage caused by such things as exposure to toxic substances and poor prenatal care. Biological influences affect many of the individual traits discussed here.

Certain family experiences have moderate to large direct effects on delinquency, as well as large effects on individual traits, school experiences, association with delinquent peers, and exposure to situations conducive to delinquency. Family experiences like parental rejection and poor supervision often have a large direct effect on delinquency. As discussed in Chapter 10, family experiences often have a large effect on individual traits. Family experiences also have a large impact on how well the juvenile does in school, whether the juvenile associates with delinquent peers, and whether the juvenile spends a lot of unstructured time with peers in the absence of authority figures. To illustrate, data indicate that juveniles who do not get along with their parents and who are poorly supervised by parents are much more likely to associate with delinquent peers.

Certain individual traits have a large direct effect on delinquency— and a large effect on the situations juveniles confront and on their family, school, and peer group experiences. Such traits influence how a juvenile behaves in a particular situation and how others react to the juvenile. For example, individuals with HIA may be more likely to antagonize others and elicit negative responses from them. They are therefore more likely to encounter situations where they are provoked (or at least believe they have been provoked). Such traits also influence the family, school, peer group, and other experiences of the juvenile. For example, individuals with HIA may overwhelm their parents. As a consequence, their parents may reject them or employ lax or overly punitive disciplinary techniques. Individuals with HIA may lack the interest and skills to do well in school, so they may have problems with teachers and get poor grades. And individuals with HIA may find that conventional peers are reluctant to associate with them, so they may come to associate with delinquent peers.

Association with delinquent peers and *gang membership* have a large direct effect on delinquency. These variables are typically the best predictors of delinquency, other than prior delinquency.

I should note that not all criminologists would agree with the preceding list; some would delete effects that I list or add effects that I do not list. Some criminologists, for example, would argue that school experiences have large direct or indirect effects on delinquency. Unfortunately, there have not been very many longitudinal studies of delinquency, and the studies that have been done often fail to include certain potentially important variables. As a consequence, there is still some uncertainty about which variables have the strongest direct and indirect effects on delinquency. Nevertheless, the foregoing list should give you an idea of the direction in which integrated theories are moving.

At this point in the discussion, you might find the following exercise useful. Drawing on this chapter and Chapters 10 through 15, make a list of variables that have a relatively strong effect on delinquency. These variables might have a large *direct* effect on delinquency or a large *indirect* effect (they affect delinquency primarily through their effect on other variables). Try to limit yourself to five to ten variables. You can list quite specific variables (e.g., parental rejection of child, family conflict) or more general variables (e.g., negative family experiences). Next, describe how these variables affect one another and delinquency, focusing on effects you feel are fairly strong. This description can be presented in the form of a "causal diagram," like the simple causal diagram in Figure 16.1. The arrows in this diagram indicate that one variable has a causal effect on another. Be prepared to explain *why* the variables in your model cause one another.

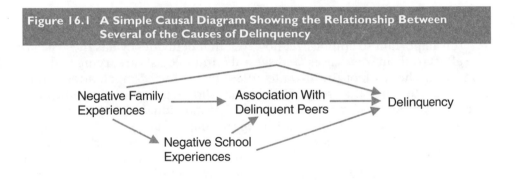

Figure 16.1 A Simple Causal Diagram Showing the Relationship Between Several of the Causes of Delinquency

3. Delinquency May Affect Its Causes

I have treated delinquency as a dependent variable throughout this book; my focus has been on the factors that cause delinquency, such as individual traits, family experiences, and association with delinquent peers. Many researchers, however, argue that delinquency may influence some of its causes. In particular, they argue that engaging in delinquency may influence family, school, peer group, and other experiences, and it may influence the juvenile's beliefs regarding delinquency. An integrated theory must take account of these possible effects.

To be more specific, engaging in delinquency may disrupt relations with family members. It may, for example, create conflict between parents and juveniles. It may affect school performance and relations with teachers. For example, it may lead teachers to form a negative opinion of juveniles and start treating them differently. It may increase the likelihood of association with delinquent peers, since conventional peers may be reluctant to associate with the juveniles who engage in delinquency. And it may lead juveniles to adopt beliefs favorable to delinquency as they seek to justify or rationalize their delinquent behavior. Engaging in delinquency, in short, may increase strain, reduce control, and foster the social learning of delinquency.

These effects are said to be most likely when a juvenile is officially "labeled" a delinquent by the police and court system. That is, a juvenile is arrested, found to be "delinquent" by the court, and officially punished. Official labeling is said to have a large effect on how others view and treat a juvenile. In particular, it increases the likelihood that others will view the juvenile primarily as a "delinquent" and treat him or her as delinquent. These effects, however, may also occur in the absence of official labeling. Even if juveniles are never caught by the police, their delinquency may become known to parents, peers, teachers, and others, and it may influence how these others view and treat the juveniles.

There is some evidence for these effects, although the effects are not always large.[4] These effects are nonetheless important because they suggest that engaging in delinquency may *sometimes* set a "vicious cycle" in process. Engaging in delinquency may have negative impacts on beliefs and on family, school, and peer experiences; these altered beliefs and experiences then increase the likelihood of further delinquency. Such effects also suggest that efforts to punish delinquency may sometimes backfire. Rather than reducing delinquency, the process of arresting and officially sanctioning delinquents

❖ ❖ ❖ ❖   may actually *increase* delinquency in *certain* cases. These effects are discussed in detail by Thornberry (1987, 1996) and by "labeling" theorists.[5]

It is important to emphasize, however, that delinquency has these negative effects only in *some* cases, and several criminologists are trying to determine why. The work of Braithwaite (1989) has attracted much attention in this area. He notes that some individuals who engage in delinquency are rejected by others, like family and friends. The individuals come to be viewed as "delinquents," and conventional people no longer want to have anything to do with them. As a consequence, the vicious cycle described earlier is set in motion. Other juveniles, however, are punished for their delinquent acts but are *not* rejected by others. In particular, they are made to feel a sense of shame or guilt for what they have done, but they are eventually forgiven and are reintegrated into conventional groups, such as family and peer groups. Braithwaite calls this process "reintegrative shaming" and argues that it reduces rather than increases the likelihood of subsequent delinquency.

To illustrate, imagine two juveniles who get caught burglarizing a house. In one case, the parents call the juvenile "a no-good thief" and say they no longer want to have anything to do with him or her. In the other case, the parents strongly condemn the act and punish the child but make it clear that they still love him or her (they condemn the *offense* but not the *offender*). The child eventually apologizes for the offense and is forgiven by the parents. According to Braithwaite, the first type of reaction will promote delinquency while the second will reduce it. Braithwaite discusses some of the factors that may influence this difference in reaction. One such factor is the degree of attachment between the parent and child. Reintegrative shaming is more likely when attachment is high. When the parent and child love one another, the child is more likely to feel shame when he or she violates parental expectations, and the parents are more likely to forgive and accept the child. Efforts to test Braithwaite's theory are now under way.

4. The Causes of Delinquency Have a Larger Effect on Delinquency Under Certain Conditions

A large number of factors that may cause delinquency have been discussed. None of these factors, however, comes close to fully explaining delinquency. Most simply increase the likelihood that delinquency will occur by a small to moderate amount. For example, individuals who have been abused are somewhat more likely to engage in delinquency, but this relationship is far from perfect. Many abused individuals *do not* engage in delinquency, and many *non*abused individuals *do* engage in delinquency. It may be the case, however, that abuse is more likely to lead to delinquency under certain conditions. For example, data described in Chapter 5 indicate that abuse is more likely to lead to delinquency when the child is doing poorly in school. Integrated theories should try to *specify the conditions under which the causes of delinquency are most likely to lead to delinquency*.

Let me provide another example. Data suggest that low attachment to parents has a small to moderate effect on delinquency. That is, juveniles who do not like and respect their parents are somewhat more likely to engage in delinquency. The effect of low parental attachment on delinquency, however, is strongly influenced by association with delinquent friends. Low parental attachment has a moderately strong effect on delinquency when the juvenile has delinquent friends, but it has a weak effect when the juvenile has conventional friends. Low parental attachment frees the juvenile to engage in delinquency, while delinquent friends provide the motivation to engage in delinquency. One would expect delinquency to be most likely when constraint is low and motivation is high.

Certain delinquency theories describe the conditions under which their independent variables are most likely to affect delinquency. For example, strain theory predicts that strain should be most likely to lead to delinquency when the juvenile associates with delinquent peers, is low in control, and has opportunities to engage in delinquency (among other things). And certain empirical research has investigated conditioning effects, as indicated above. Overall, however, not much attention has been paid to such effects.[6] Nevertheless, an integrated theory should indicate the conditions under which its independent variables are most likely to affect delinquency.

Several general arguments have been made in this area. Individual traits should be most likely to affect delinquency when juveniles are in social environments conducive to delinquency, such as problem families, delinquent peer groups, and communities of the type described in Chapter 14. Likewise, environmental variables should be most likely to affect delinquency when juveniles have individual traits conducive to delinquency. More generally, one would expect the factors that increase the motivation for delinquency to have the greatest effect on delinquency when constraints are low and opportunities are high. Likewise, factors that reduce constraints should have the greatest effect when the motivation and opportunities for delinquency are high.

5. Most Causes Lead to Delinquency for Several Reasons

An integrated theory does several things. It lists the causes of delinquency, describes how they are related to one another, and describes the conditions under which the causes are most likely to affect delinquency. An integrated theory also describes *why* variables cause delinquency.

You probably have already noticed that most variables may cause delinquency for several reasons. For example, a variable like child abuse may cause delinquency for reasons related to strain, control, and social learning theories. Child abuse is a form of strain, and abused juveniles may turn to delinquency in an effort to escape from or alleviate their abuse, seek revenge against those who abused them, or deal with the negative emotions they are experiencing. Child abuse may also affect the juvenile's level of control. For example, it may reduce the juvenile's attachment to parents, thereby weakening the restraints against delinquency. Finally, child abuse may teach the juvenile that violence is an appropriate way to deal with one's problems.

Similar arguments can be made for most of the other variables considered. Unfortunately, only a few researchers have tried to determine *why* the independent variables in their studies cause delinquency (e.g., does child abuse increase anger, weaken parental attachment, or lead to the belief that violence is sometimes acceptable?). The few studies in this area tend to confirm that variables usually do affect delinquency for several reasons.[7]

6. An Integrated Theory May Have to Be Modified Depending on the Group and Type of Delinquency Under Consideration

It is doubtful that criminologists will be able to construct a single theory of delinquency that applies equally well to all groups and all types of delinquency. Let me provide a few examples. A theory that works well for males may not work as well for females (see Chesney-Lind and Shelden, 1998). A theory that works well for young adolescents may not work as well for older adolescents. A theory that works well for high-rate, chronic offenders may not work as well for low-rate offenders who limit their offending to adolescence. A theory that works well for violent offending may not work well for drug use.

These sorts of issues are now beginning to receive serious attention in criminology. And several theories, including certain integrated theories, describe modifications that must be made when the theory is applied to different groups and types of delinquency. For example, Thornberry's (1987, 1996) integrated theory argues that certain causes are more important for younger adolescents than for older adolescents (also see Jang, 1999). In particular, family experiences are said to be more important for younger adolescents. Delinquent beliefs and school and peer group experiences are said to be more important for older adolescents. Moffitt's (1993, 1997) integrated theory argues that there are two types of delinquents: those who offend at a high rate over much of their lives ("life-course persistent offenders") and those who limit their offending to the adolescent years ("adolescent-limited offenders"). She states that the causes of delinquency differ between these groups. Individual traits like HIA, for example, are said to be an important cause of "life-course persistent" offending but not of "adolescent-limited" offending.

There is not enough research to draw any definitive conclusions in these areas. However, it is beginning to appear as if criminologists will be able to develop a general model of delinquency that works reasonably well for most groups and types of delinquency but that it will have to be modified somewhat when applied to specific groups or types of delinquency.

Conclusion

It should be evident by now that any integrated or general theory of delinquency will be fairly complex. It will consider a sizable number of variables and will have much to say about how these variables are related to one another, the conditions under which they are most likely to cause delinquency, why they cause delinquency, and whether they are more or less relevant to different groups and types of delinquency.

You may be feeling a little confused and overwhelmed. If that is the case, do not worry. Many criminologists feel the same. Keep in mind that while many issues remain to be resolved, you now know quite a bit about the causes of delinquency. You can now list most of the major causes of delinquency. And you have a rough sense of how these causes are related to one another and why they might affect delinquency. As you will see in the final chapters of this book, that knowledge can go a long way toward reducing delinquency.

Notes

❖ ❖ ❖ ❖

1. For overviews and examples, see Akers, 1997; Bernard and Snipes, 1996; Catalano and Hawkins, 1996; Cullen and Agnew, 1999; Elliott et al., 1985; Johnson, 1979; Messner et al., 1989; Miethe and Meier, 1994; Pearson and Weiner, 1985; Shoemaker, 1996; Thornberry, 1987; Tittle, 1995; Vila, 1994; Vold et al., 1998.

2. *See* Miethe and Meier, 1994; Pearson and Weiner, 1985; Sheley, 1983; Tittle, 1995; Vila, 1994.

3. *See* Elliott and Menard, 1996; Thornberry, 1987, 1996; Thornberry et al., 1991, 1994, 1998.

4. *See* Elliott and Menard, 1996; Thornberry, 1996; Thornberry et al., 1998.

5. *See* Akers, 1997; Matsueda, 1992; Paternoster and Iovanni, 1989.

6. *See* Cullen, 1984; although see Loeber, Farrington, Stouthamer-Loeber, and Van Kammen, 1998.

7. *See* Agnew, 1993, 1995a; Brezina, 1998; Farrington, 1993b. ✦

Part III

The Control and Prevention of Delinquency

Controlling Delinquency: How Is It Determined If Some Policy or Program Is Effective in Controlling/Preventing Delinquency?

❖ ❖ ❖ ❖ Now that the causes of delinquency have been examined (Chapters 6 through 16), it is appropriate to ask how to control or reduce delinquency. At one level, the answer to this question is rather simple. Society can control delinquency by alleviating or eliminating the causes of delinquency. For example, it is known that several family factors cause delinquency like parental rejection, family conflict, and poor parental supervision. Therefore, society can reduce delinquency by increasing parents' acceptance of their children; reducing family conflict; and improving parental supervision. We can also reduce delinquency by doing such things as reducing certain types of biological trauma (e.g., drug use during pregnancy, lead exposure); preventing juveniles from associating with delinquent peers or gangs; and improving schools. More generally, we can reduce delinquency by reducing strain, reducing the social learning of delinquency, and increasing control. The key question, however, is how do we accomplish these goals?

Chapters 17 through 23 examine the efforts of public and private agencies to control delinquency. The focus is on the juvenile justice system: the police, juvenile courts, and juvenile correctional agencies that run juvenile institutions and community-based programs. These government agencies have primary responsibility for controlling delinquency in our society.

Chapter 18 focuses on the police and Chapter 19 focuses on the juvenile court and juvenile correctional agencies. I ask what these agencies are doing to control delinquency, how effective they are, and what is being done to increase their effectiveness. Chapter 20 then examines whether these agencies discriminate against certain groups in their efforts to control delinquency. Although we want these agencies to do all they can to control delinquency, we also want them to do so in a way that is fair to everyone in our society.

Chapters 21 and 22 examine four general strategies for controlling delinquency that are employed by these agencies and other groups. These strategies are deterrence, incapacitation, rehabilitation, and prevention. Deterrence tries to scare potential offenders from committing crimes by increasing the certainty and severity of punishment. Incapacitation tries to control delinquency by locking up serious offenders so they cannot commit crimes on the street. The "get tough" strategies of deterrence and incapacitation now dominate the juvenile justice system. I describe these strategies and examine the evidence on their effectiveness in Chapter 21. Rehabilitation tries to reform offenders, while prevention tries to stop individuals from becoming offenders by attacking the root causes of crime. I describe these strategies and the evidence on their effectiveness in Chapter 22. I then present a general discussion of what I think society should do to control delinquency in Chapter 23, the final chapter of the book.

You will find that most efforts to control delinquency attempt to eliminate or alleviate the causes of delinquency. Most commonly, they attempt to increase social control, especially *direct control* (see Chapter 8). In particular, one of the major functions of the juvenile justice system today is to catch and punish juvenile offenders for their delinquent acts. The police focus on catching suspected juvenile offenders; the juvenile court determines whether these suspected offenders have committed delinquent acts and, if so, what sanctions they will receive; and juvenile correctional agencies administer many of the sanctions, such as incarceration.

The juvenile justice system and other agencies also attempt to deal with many of the other causes of delinquency. For example, they sometimes attempt to increase other forms of social control, such as a stake in conformity and internal control. And they sometimes attempt to reduce strain and the social learning of crime. In these areas, they often focus on many of the specific causes of delinquency examined in this text, such as those involving individual traits, the family, school, peer group, community, and situation. The juvenile justice system, however, has come to place an increased emphasis on direct control in recent years, although there are some signs that this is beginning to change.

The central theme in Chapters 18 through 23 is that this focus on direct control is a mistake; data suggest that efforts to exercise direct control over juveniles have only a moderate effect on delinquency. Efforts to deal with the other causes of delinquency will not eliminate delinquency, but data suggest that properly implemented efforts may result in a substantial reduction in delinquency. It is suggested that the best approach to delinquency is one that combines the careful use of direct controls with a serious effort to deal with the other causes of delinquency.

But before we begin our examination of efforts to control delinquency, I must first address the question of how criminologists determine whether a given program or policy is effective in controlling delinquency.

How Is It Determined if Some Policy or Program Is Effective in Controlling Delinquency?

I will be examining many programs and policies designed to control delinquency, and the central question I will be asking about these programs and policies is whether they are effective. But how does one go about determining whether a program is effective in controlling delinquency?

Judging effectiveness is an important issue. Politicians and others often claim that some program is or is not effective. They claim, for example, that trying juveniles as adults or placing them in boot camps is an effective way to reduce delinquency. Or they claim that many rehabilitation and prevention programs are ineffective and a waste of taxpayers' money. Much of what you hear, however, is wrong or has little basis in fact. You will be in a much better position to judge the accuracy of the claims you hear if you know the proper way to evaluate the effectiveness of a program. You will also have a more solid foundation on which to construct your own views about what society should and should not do to control delinquency.

The Experimental Model for Determining Program Effectiveness

What is the best way to determine if a program is effective in reducing delinquency? The answer is a *randomized experiment*. As you may recall from Chapter 5, experiments involve doing something to a group of people and then observing the consequences. In evaluating program effectiveness, we place juveniles in a delinquency control or prevention program and observe the consequences. In particular, we observe whether participation in the program leads to a reduction in delinquency. But the experiment must have certain special features if it is to provide accurate information about the program's effectiveness. Let me describe these features and their importance with an example.

A criminologist develops a program designed to increase the social skills of juveniles. A group of serious juvenile offenders then participate in the program. The criminologist measures the delinquency of these juveniles in the year before they enter the program and in the year after they complete the program. The criminologist discovers that these juveniles commit 50 percent fewer delinquent acts, including serious delinquent acts, in the year after they complete the program. Can we conclude that the program is effective?

I should note that many program evaluations are like this. Researchers do a "before and after" study, examining levels of delinquency before and after juveniles participate in a program. If the juveniles experience a large drop in delinquency, the program is declared a success.

In fact, we *cannot* safely claim that the social skills program is effective. While the juvenile offenders *may* have reduced their delinquent behavior *because of the program*, they may have reduced their delinquency for other reasons as well. For example, perhaps most of the juveniles in the program were 16 and 17 years old. One of the things criminologists know about delinquency is that it peaks at around 16 and 17 and then declines as juveniles enter adulthood. So the reduction in delinquency detected by the criminologist may not have been due to the program. It may simply have reflected the fact that these juveniles, like most juveniles their age, were entering adulthood and maturing out of delinquency. These juveniles would have reduced their level of delinquency even if they had not participated in the program. To give another example, it may be that the police in the city where the program was run instituted a crackdown against local gangs at about the time the program ended, so the reduction in delinquency may be due to this police crackdown rather than the program. Thus, simply comparing levels of delinquency before and after a program begins is not a good way to determine if a program is effective.

What should researchers and policy makers do? How can they determine whether the reduction in delinquency is due to the social skills program or to some other factor? They can *compare the delinquency levels of program participants to the delinquency levels of a roughly identical group of juveniles who did not participate in the program*. The juveniles who participate in the program are called the *treatment group*, while the juveniles who do not participate in the program are called the comparison group or *control group*. The two groups of juveniles are roughly identical to one another, except that those in the treatment group participate in the program. If the juveniles in the treatment group experience a greater reduction in delinquency than those in the control group, *it can only be because they participated in the program*. It cannot be because they are older and more likely to mature out of delinquency, since the juveniles in both the treatment and control groups are roughly identical in terms of age. Nor can it be because the juveniles in the treatment group were subject to a police crackdown while those in the control group were not. Both groups of juveniles were subject to the police crackdown. The juveniles in the treatment and control groups differ in only one way: The juveniles in the treatment group participated in the social skills program. So if these juveniles experience a greater reduction in delinquency, it can only be because they participated in the program. One can then say that the program is effective: It caused a reduction in delinquency.

A key question, however, is how do researchers ensure that the juveniles in the treatment and control groups are roughly identical? The best way to do this is through a procedure known as *random assignment*. Researchers start out with a single group of juveniles, and they randomly assign each juvenile to either the treatment group or the control group. For example, they flip a coin. If it comes up "heads," the juvenile is in the treatment group. If it comes up "tails," the juvenile is in the control group. If they are dealing with a fairly large group of juveniles, they can be reasonably confident that the juveniles in the two groups are roughly identical in terms of age, sex, class, race/ethnicity, prior levels of delinquency, and all other variables.

I should note that the juveniles *randomly assigned* to the control and treatment groups may or may not be a *random sample* of juveniles (see Chapter 5). In most cases, they are not a random sample. For example, they may be a group of juveniles who were referred to a particular juvenile court for serious offenses. The court may then randomly assign certain of these juveniles to participate in a new treatment program and others to go through normal court processing. But these juveniles do not constitute a random sample of all juveniles or even of juveniles in that particular locale. I'll return to this point shortly, because it points to a weakness in many experiments.

You now know the proper way to determine whether a program is effective in reducing delinquency. Let me summarize the essential elements of a randomized experiment. You begin with a single group of juveniles. You randomly assign each juvenile to either the treatment group or the control group. The juveniles in the treatment group participate in the delinquency control program, while those in the control group do not. You may not do anything to the juveniles in the control group, which would allow you to compare the effectiveness of your program to "doing nothing." Or you may treat the juveniles in the control group the way that such juveniles are normally treated; for example you might place minor offenders on regular probation. This would allow you to compare the effectiveness of your program to probation. You measure the delinquency of the juveniles in both the treatment group and the control group before and after the program has begun. You then determine if those in the treatment group experienced a larger reduction in delinquency. If they have, you can conclude that the treatment or program was effective. (Since juveniles are randomly assigned to the treatment and control groups, you can assume that they are roughly identical in prior levels of delinquency. Many researchers therefore argue that it is only necessary to compare the delinquency levels of those in the treatment and control groups after the program has ended. If those in the treatment group have lower levels of delinquency than those in the control group, you can conclude that they experienced a larger reduction in delinquency—and that the treatment was effective.)

This model, then, allows criminologists to determine whether the program *caused* a reduction in delinquency. If you would like a challenging exercise, I invite you to stop reading and describe how this experimental model meets the four conditions for making causal statements described in Chapter 5: association; association not due to chance; association not due to third variables; and correct causal order (now is a good time to review the discussion in Chapter 5).

Let me begin with association. If those in the treatment group are lower in delinquency than those in the control group, it has been demonstrated that the treatment is associated with lower delinquency. This association may be due to chance, but a chance association is unlikely if the treatment and control groups are large and the difference between them in delinquency is large. As was the case with survey research, researchers can estimate the probability that the association is due to chance. The association may be due to a third variable, but that is quite unlikely if individuals are randomly assigned to the treatment and control groups. For example, suppose those in the treatment group are found to be lower in delinquency. Someone might claim that this difference is due to the third variable of age: Those in the treatment group are older and so are more likely to have matured out of delinquency. But if the researchers have used random assignment, they know that those in the treatment and control groups are roughly identical in terms of age and all other third variables. Any association they find, therefore, cannot have arisen because those in the treatment and control groups differ in terms of some third variable that causes delinquency. Finally, the experimental model is set up in such a way that researchers administer the treatment or program and then examine *subsequent* levels of delinquency, so causal order is not a problem: the treatment precedes any change in delinquency that might occur.

Problems in Doing Randomized Experiments in the 'Real World'

Criminologists often encounter difficulties when they attempt to employ the model described in the preceding section in the real world. Some of the more common difficulties are described in the paragraphs that follow.

The people responsible for randomly assigning juveniles to the treatment and control groups are often workers in the juvenile justice system, such as police, probation officers, and judges. Sometimes these individuals violate the random assignment procedure. A judge, for example, may refuse to assign someone to the control group because she feels that the juvenile is in desperate need of the treatment. As a consequence, criminologists cannot be sure that the juveniles in the treatment and control groups are roughly identical.

Many of the juveniles randomly assigned to the treatment and control groups may not complete the experiment. Some of the juveniles may drop out of or fail to successfully complete the treatment program. Or the researchers may not be able to locate many of the juveniles who participated in the experiment when they are collecting follow-up data on delinquency. As a result, they cannot be sure that the juveniles who remain in the treatment and control groups are roughly identical. For example, many treatment programs are very demanding, and individuals with little motivation to change their behavior often drop out of them. The individuals who successfully complete such programs, then, may be those most motivated to change. If these individuals experience a greater reduction in delinquency than those in the control group, we do not know if it is because of the treatment or because they were more motivated to change to begin with.

Another problem involves the measurement of delinquency. Delinquency is often measured in terms of arrest rates. Program evaluations, for example, often report that those in the treatment group were less likely to be arrested during the follow-up period after the treatment ended. Arrest data, however, are not a very accurate measure of delinquency. It may be that those in the treatment group are less likely to be arrested, even though there is no difference in the true rates of delinquency between the treatment and control groups. For example, the police may be more likely to give juveniles in the treatment group a "break" because they run the program and have a vested interest in its success. On the other hand, those in the treatment group are sometimes more likely to be arrested, even though they are not more delinquent. For example, many delinquency control programs call for the close supervision of juveniles and include features like frequent home visits and random drug tests. Such features increase the likelihood that delinquent acts will be detected and juveniles will be arrested.

Yet another problem with randomized experiments was briefly mentioned above and involves the issue of *generalizability*. Researchers who evaluate a program almost never begin with a *random sample* of juveniles or juvenile offenders. Rather, they typically begin with a nonrepresentative group of juveniles in a single location. They might, for example, examine all minor offenders who are referred to a particular juvenile court. They might then find that the program they are evaluating is effective in reducing delinquency *among these juveniles*, but that is no guarantee that this program will be effective for other juveniles. It may not be effective for more serious offenders or for minor offenders in other locations. One cannot, then, necessarily generalize the results of a program evaluation to other juveniles or to other settings.

Other problems in running randomized experiments can be listed, but this short list is enough to let you know that evaluating a program is not as straightforward as it might seem. Researchers sometimes take steps to deal with these problems. For example, they try to ensure that random assignment proceeds as planned; they go to great lengths to prevent juveniles from leaving the experiment; they measure delinquency using self-report data and other methods such as drug testing; and they evaluate the same program with different groups of juveniles in different locations. Many researchers, however, do not take these sorts of steps; also, these steps are not always effective. For example, the juveniles in the treatment program may not be truthful when they are providing self-reports on their delinquency. As a result of these problems, it is often difficult to state with a high degree of certainty that a program is generally effective at reducing delinquency. Rather, researchers must state that a program is "promising" or that it shows "signs of success." Some programs, however, have been the subject of a number of fairly rigorous evaluations, and criminologists are more confident about their effectiveness (or lack of effectiveness).

What If One Is Not Able to Do a Randomized Experiment?

Randomized experiments are often difficult to carry out, but they are the best way to determine whether a program is effective. However, it is not always possible to do a randomized experiment. Sometimes ethical problems present themselves. To illustrate, researchers have developed a number of programs that are designed to provide alternatives to imprisonment or incarceration. Intensive probation programs, which provide close supervision of juveniles in the community, are an example. Juvenile court judges, however, may feel that it is unethical to randomly send some juveniles to institutions and place others on intensive probation. Sometimes the problems are more practical in nature. To illustrate, lawmakers may implement a particular policy that affects everyone in the community, such as a new law that increases the penalties for certain crimes. Random assignment is obviously not possible in this case. One cannot use random assignment procedures to decide that some people in the community are subject to the law and others are not.

Researchers usually deal with these situations by employing nonrandomized experiments of various types. For example, researchers may employ *nonequivalent control-group designs*. Since they cannot randomly assign individuals to the treatment and control groups, they may attempt to deliberately create a control group that is similar to the treatment group. To illustrate, imagine a situation where a judge is unwilling to randomly assign people to prison or intensive probation. The researcher can examine the characteristics of the juveniles sent to prison and then attempt to find a similar group of juveniles who were placed on intensive probation. The researcher ideally attempts to match the two groups on all relevant variables that may affect subsequent delinquency, such as age and prior delinquency. The researcher can then compare the subsequent delinquency of the two groups. To give another illustration, imagine that a state passes a law increasing the penalties for certain crimes. The researcher may attempt to find a similar state that does not have such a law. The researcher can then compare trends in subsequent delinquency in the two states. This strategy, however, is often difficult to carry out in practice, and one can never be sure that the treatment and control groups are roughly identical. Perhaps they differ on some crucial variable that the researcher did not consider.

Another type of nonrandomized experiment is the *time-series design*. The researcher periodically measures delinquency before the program or policy takes effect and then after the program or policy takes effect. For example, monthly levels of delinquency in a community are measured before a new law takes effect and then after the new law takes effect. If there is a noticeable decrease in delinquency after the new law takes effect, that suggests the new law may be effective. However, it is possible that the decrease in delinquency was due to factors that coincided with the introduction of the new law. For example, perhaps the economy started to improve around the time the new law was introduced.

There are still other types of nonrandomized experiments. None of them are as good as randomized experiments, but they do provide us with some information about program effectiveness.

Summary

You now know the proper way to determine whether a program or policy is effective in reducing delinquency. In actual practice, few program evaluations live up to the ideal model I have presented. Researchers conducting randomized experiments often encounter one or more of the problems I've mentioned. And many researchers find that it is not possible for them to do randomized experiments. Good program evaluations are nevertheless occasionally done, and there has been increased pressure in recent years to do such evaluations. A few programs have been the subject of several evaluations. These evaluations involve different types of juveniles in different locations, and they often complement one another in terms of their strengths and weaknesses. For example, some of the evaluations measure delinquency using arrest data, but others use self-report data or teacher and parental reports. If these evaluations are in general agreement with one another, one can safely conclude that the program is generally effective (or ineffective).

I should note that there are two general reasons why researchers find some programs ineffective. The first is that the program does not work. (In the chapters that follow, I will mention several programs for controlling delinquency that do not appear to work, including some programs that are popular right now.) The second reason is that the program was not properly implemented. It is often the case that programs are not carried out as planned. The program may not be delivered to the appropriate group of juveniles. It may be intended for serious offenders but instead focus on minor offenders. The services that should be provided by the program may not be provided. The juveniles in the program, for example, may receive less counseling or less supervision than they were supposed to receive. The staff may not be properly trained or committed to the program, so they do not render services in an appropriate manner. As a result of such possibilities, many researchers now do what are known as "implementation" or "process" evaluations. These evaluations are not designed to determine whether a program is effective in reducing delinquency. Rather, they are designed to determine whether the program was properly implemented. It is sometimes found that programs are not properly implemented, which may help explain why they are not effective in reducing delinquency.[1]

Note

1. For a fuller discussion of evaluation research in the delinquency field, see the excellent overview article by Sechrest and Rosenblatt, 1987; also see Babbie, 1995; Gartin, 1995; Kempf, 1990. ✦

Chapter 18

The Police: What Do the Police Do to Control Delinquency?

I begin this chapter with a discussion of how the police operate; that is, how they attempt to control crime and delinquency. I then ask how effective the police are in controlling delinquency. Finally, I examine three strategies for improving police effectiveness. The first is hiring more police. The second two strategies call for changing what the police do to control delinquency. One strategy calls for an increased use of "police crackdowns," and the other calls for a greater emphasis on "community policing."[1]

How Do the Police Operate?

What image comes to mind when you think of the police? If you are like most people, your image of the police has been heavily influenced by the mass media and you think of the police as *crime fighters*. They spend most of their time dealing with crime, often serious crime. They cruise around in a patrol car, responding to calls for service and discovering crime on their own. They usually end up catching and arresting most offenders.

This image of the police as crime fighters, however, is partly mistaken. Criminologists have spent much time studying the police. They have ridden with the police, interviewed police officers, and analyzed such police records as logbooks and dispatch records. Some criminologists were police officers before they became criminologists. And a few criminologists have served as police officers for periods of time in order to better understand the police. Based on such data sources, the following facts about how the police operate are now known to criminologists.

Preventive Patrol Is the Major Type of Policing

In preventive patrol, a uniformed police officer cruises an assigned beat in a marked patrol car. When the officer is not answering calls or engaged in other activities, he or she usually patrols the beat. It is felt that this patrol *prevents* crime, since potential offenders never know when a police car might appear. (Most police departments assign just one officer per car. This practice

allows them to put more cars on the street, and studies suggest that one-person cars are as safe and productive as two-person cars.)

Most juveniles who encounter the police deal with officers on preventive patrol. Most police departments, however, also have juvenile officers or divisions. They conduct follow-up investigations on cases referred by patrol officers. They handle special youth problems—like gangs and school crime—and they may run prevention programs.

The Police Spend Only a Small Amount of Their Time Dealing With Crime

❖ ❖ ❖ ❖

The police spend most of their shift cruising their beat, performing administrative tasks like filling out paperwork, and taking breaks. Less than half their time is spent answering calls or on officer-initiated encounters with the public. This pattern varies by police department, police beat, day, and shift, however (officers working the Saturday night shift in a high-crime beat in a major city may spend most of their time answering calls). Further, most calls to the police involve noncriminal matters, such as traffic accidents, medical emergencies, barking dogs, and disputes between neighbors. Finally, most of the calls they do get about criminal matters involve minor crimes. Several studies have found that, on average, the police spend less than 20 percent of their time on crime-related matters. Police often complain about this; many enter the job expecting to be crime fighters but find that most of their time is taken up with noncriminal matters. They often feel as if they function more as social workers than as "crime fighters."

The Police Are Primarily Reactive in Nature

The police usually do not discover crimes on their own. In fact, it is quite rare for a police officer to encounter a serious crime in progress. Rather, someone else calls the police and lets them know that a crime has occurred. Usually it is the victim who calls. The police, however, sometimes make special efforts to discover crime on their own, especially for certain "victimless" crimes such as drug crimes and prostitution. The police, for example, may put certain areas under surveillance or employ undercover agents to catch drug offenders or prostitutes. For the most part, however, the police are largely reactive in nature.

When the Police Do Discover or Hear About a Crime, They Usually Do Not Catch the Offender

As you may recall, only about 21 percent of all crimes known to the police result in arrest. This percentage varies by type of crime. The police are more likely to make an arrest for violent crimes than for property crimes. For example, 56 percent of all aggravated assaults and 53 percent of all rapes known to the police are cleared by arrest, while only 13 percent of all burglaries and 20 percent of all larcenies are cleared by arrest.

When the police do make an arrest, it is usually because they catch the offender at the scene or there is someone who can identify or help identify the offender. Violent crimes are more likely to result in arrest because the victims of violence almost always see the offender and often can identify him or her (most violence is committed by relatives, friends, and acquaintances). The victims of property crimes like burglary and larceny, however, rarely see the offender. Contrary to mass media accounts and popular views, diligent detective work plays no role or only a minor role in solving the large majority of crimes (Chaiken et al., 1977). If the police do not catch the offender at the scene or there is no one who can identify the offender, the crime will probably go unsolved.

The police recognize this problem, and they have tried to increase their speed in responding to crimes—particularly crimes in progress—with the hope of catching the offender at the scene. Unfortunately, such efforts have had only a small effect on arrest rates. The large majority of crime victims do not call the police until after the crime is over, so response time makes little difference. The victim often does not discover the crime until after it has occurred (e.g., you arrive home and discover your house has been burglarized). And in almost half the cases where the victim confronts the offender, the victim waits five minutes or longer after the crime is over before calling the police.

If the Police Do Catch the Offender, They Usually Do Not Arrest the Person

The police do not arrest all suspected offenders they encounter. In fact, only a minority of police encounters with suspected juvenile offenders result in arrest—even if the police have adequate legal grounds for making an arrest. Most suspected offenders are handled informally. The police, for example, may lecture the juvenile, call the juvenile's parents, and/or ask the juvenile to make restitution to the victim. But an arrest is not made. In some cases, the police may refer the juvenile to a social service agency or a diversion program (see Chapter 19). When the police do make an arrest, the juvenile is referred to juvenile court about two-thirds of the time.

The police exercise much discretion in deciding whether to arrest suspected offenders. The decision to arrest depends on several factors, including the seriousness of the offense; whether the offender has a prior record; whether the complainant presses for arrest; the offender's demeanor or attitude; whether the offender's parents seem willing and able to help solve the problem; and the norms of the police department and community. Some police departments are more likely to handle matters informally than others (see Wilson, 1976), and communities differ in their views about how the police should respond to juvenile offenders. There is also some evidence that the age, race, class, and gender of suspected offenders influence the likelihood of arrest (see Chapter 20).

There are several reasons why the police do *not* arrest all suspected offenders (see Anderson and Newman, 1998, for a fuller discussion). The police and courts would soon be overwhelmed if all suspected offenders were arrested. The police often have a low opinion of the juvenile court, feeling that most offenders only get a "slap on the wrist"; they may therefore feel that arrest and referral would be useless and perhaps even waste their time with paperwork. Further, the police often feel that many offenders are best dealt with in an informal manner. They might encounter a juvenile who has committed a minor offense but otherwise seems like a "good kid." Rather than stigmatizing this juvenile with an arrest record, they handle the matter informally.

How Effective Is Preventive Patrol?

Most criminologists acknowledge that the police are somewhat effective in controlling crime and delinquency. In particular, they agree that the crime rate would increase if there were no police. Limited data support this conclusion. For example, when the police went on strike in Montreal in 1969, the hourly burglary rate rose by 13,000 percent and the hourly bank robbery rate rose by 50,000 percent (Sherman, 1995:331). At the same time, most criminologists feel that the police can be more effective than they now are in controlling delinquency. Among other things, they point to the low arrest rate. Only a small percentage of the crimes known to the police are cleared by arrest. Also, the rapid rise in crime and disorder during the 1960s and early 1970s raised doubts about the effectiveness of preventive patrol, although many factors contributed to this rise.

How Can the Police Increase Their Effectiveness?

Several suggestions for increasing the effectiveness of the police have been offered. Some of these suggestions are designed to increase the ability of the police to catch offenders, thereby increasing direct control. Other suggestions are designed to increase the ability of the police to deal with other causes of crime.

Will Hiring More Police Reduce Delinquency?

One obvious suggestion for increasing police effectiveness is to hire more police. And a key provision of the 1994 Violent Crime Control and Law Enforcement Act provides funds to hire 100,000 additional police, which would increase the number of state and local police by almost 20 percent. Studies on the relationship between the number of police and crime rates have produced mixed results. Most studies suggest that putting more police on the streets has little or no effect on crime rates (e.g., Greenberg et al., 1983; Kelling et al., 1974). Such studies, however, suffer from a number of problems. They include many of the problems described in Chapter 5, such as the failure to take account of potentially relevant third variables that might affect the number of police, on the one hand, and crime rates, on the other. A recent study that attempted to correct for these problems found some evidence that increasing the number of police does reduce crime. In particular, Marvell and Moody (1996) found that each additional police officer added to the force in a major city prevented twenty-four Part I crimes per year on average (also see Sherman et al., 1998). Additional police did not prevent as many crimes outside major cities. It may be that the police have a greater impact on crime in high-density, high-crime areas like major cities.

One may tentatively conclude, then, that hiring more police will reduce crime, especially in major cities. Hiring more police, however, is not the only way to increase police effectiveness. Departments may also change *what the police do when they are on the street*. Two proposals have been made in this area.

Will Police Crackdowns Reduce Delinquency?

Police resources are usually spread thin, even in the best of circumstances. As a consequence, many offenders may feel that they can commit crimes with little fear of police detection. Some police departments, however, have tried to increase the likelihood they will detect crime by focusing their resources on certain areas, or "hot spots," where crime is common and on certain types of crime. That is, they "crack down" on the hot spots of crime or on selected types of crime.

Cracking down on the hot spots of crime. Many police departments try to put the most police where there is the most crime. They may assign more patrol cars to beats with the highest crime rates, or they may have more police working on Friday and Saturday nights, when crime is most likely. Such efforts at focused patrol, however, are somewhat crude because there is much variation in crime even within a high-crime area. Some sections of a high-crime area have little or no crime, while other sections—called hot spots—have much crime. Less than 3 percent of the addresses in a city produce more than half of all calls to the police (Sherman, 1995; Sherman and Weisburd, 1995). Some of these addresses may produce several hundred calls to the police each year. Further, crime is more likely to occur on certain days and certain times of the day at these addresses.

There have been several recent efforts to aggressively target these hot spots of criminal activity.[2] In particular, the police *dramatically* increase their presence in these areas. In some cases, they saturate a particular area, doing such things as establishing mini-precincts, increasing patrols, setting up roadblocks, and mounting undercover operations. These police crackdowns attempt to increase the certainty and sometimes the severity of punishment. Crackdowns, then, attempt to deter criminals from committing crime by increasing direct control.

Recent data suggest that such crackdowns are often effective at reducing crime, although their effect is sometimes modest and short-lived. After the crackdown has ended, crime *gradually* returns to its former level. One solution to this problem is for the police to crack down on all hot spots on a *permanent* basis, but they do not have the resources to do this. Sherman and his associates (Sherman, 1995; Sherman and Weisburd, 1995), however, have proposed another, more realistic solution to this problem. The police should *rotate* their crackdowns in an unpredictable manner: The police might crack down on one hot spot of crime for a period of time and then move on to another. But they return to the first hot spot before crime has returned to its former level. This rotating series of crackdowns may allow the police to reduce crime in a large number of hot spots.

The Minneapolis Hot Spots Patrol Experiment tested this idea (Sherman and Weisburd, 1995). Researchers randomly selected 55 of 110 hot spots for this rotating series of crackdowns. Each hot spot was a small area that had generated a large number of police calls. The typical hot spot consisted of a group of attached buildings clustered around a street corner, with a few businesses like bars, restaurants, and convenience stores. On average, each hot spot generated 355 calls for service in the year before the experiment began, with most calls coming between 7 P.M. and 3 A.M. The hot spots that were part of the rotating crackdown were supposed to receive three hours of police presence per day, while the other hot spots were to be patrolled in the usual manner. This allocation did not always happen, but the police presence in the "crackdown" hot spots was generally much greater than in the other hot spots, usually by a factor of two or more. The police would visit the hot spots that were part of the crackdown several times each day, remaining for a few minutes to an hour or more each time. Sometimes they would just sit in the car; at other times they would get out and walk around. The increased police presence was associated with a modest reduction in crime, as measured by calls to the police and observer ratings of disorders like fights, drug sales, solicitation for prostitution, and playing loud music. Further, the reduction occurred not only when the police were present, but also when they were absent. This finding suggests that the police do not have to have a permanent presence in an area to reduce crime. Periodic visits or crackdowns by the police may be an effective strategy for reducing crime.

Cracking down on selected crimes. In addition to focusing on hot spots of crime, the police will sometimes target particular crimes. For example, they may focus on drug crimes, drunk driving, prostitution, or juvenile gun violence. The police will intensify patrols and other police activities in the areas where these crimes are most likely to occur, and they will make a special effort to sanction or control individuals who commit these crimes, often but not always through arrest. Such crackdowns are often accompanied by media coverage, to help convey the message that the certainty and perhaps severity of punishment have increased.

One example of this strategy is the crackdown on gun violence by youth gangs in Boston (Kennedy, 1997, 1998; Kleiman, 1999). Research indicated that a substantial number of the youth homicides in Boston were the result of gang members killing one another. Most of these gangs and gang members were well known to the police and community organizations. The police delivered a clear message to these gangs and gang members: Stop the violence or face intensive police scrutiny. The police said they would saturate the areas in which the gangs congregated and did business, which would disrupt drug markets, among other things. Severe restrictions would be placed on gang members on probation and parole, including bed checks and room searches. Also, gang members engaged in illegal activities, including disorderly acts like drinking in public, would be severely punished. The police backed up this promise on several occasions; a number of gang members were sentenced to long prison terms. The police did not have the resources to crack down on all gangs at once, but "like an old-West sheriff facing down a band of desperadoes with one bullet in his gun, direct communication with gangs allowed the [police] to say, 'We're ready, we're watching, we're waiting: Who wants to be next?' " (Kennedy, 1998:6). The program has not yet been formally evaluated, but youth homicides in Boston were *substantially reduced* after the program went into effect.

Another example of a police crackdown on selected types of crime has attracted much attention throughout the country. Kelling and his associates have argued that the police should crack down on visible signs of "disorder" in a neighborhood, such as aggressive panhandling, public drinking, rowdy teenagers hanging out on the street corner, and prostitution (see Wilson and Kelling, 1982; Kelling, 1988; Kelling and Coles, 1996). This disorderly behavior, although not serious in nature, inspires much fear in community residents. If the behavior goes unchecked, community residents become less likely to use public spaces like streets and parks. They interact less with one another and they play a less active role in their community. Among other things, they become less likely to sanction deviance. Such signs of disorder, then, may lead to a breakdown in direct control at the community level. Further, these signs of disorder may encourage more serious crime by criminals.

Criminals may assume that it is easier to get away with serious crime in communities that cannot keep minor crimes under control.

The police, then, are encouraged to crack down on minor signs of disorder. Kelling suggests several strategies for doing so. Among other things, he says that it is easier to crack down on minor crimes when the police are on foot patrol, which puts them in closer contact with minor offenders and allows them to develop a closer relationship with the noncriminal segment of the community. Several cities have followed Kelling's approach, most notably New York. Police were assigned to foot patrol in *high-crime areas* and told to crack down on all offenses, however minor. And the large reduction in crime that New York has experienced has been attributed by police officials to this crackdown, although others have offered alternative explanations (see Kelling and Coles, 1996; Sherman et al., 1998; Walker, 1998:82). It is important to note, however, that such crackdowns may lead to increases in abusive police behavior unless carefully managed (see Sherman, 1998; Sherman et al., 1998).

There is some evidence, then, that police crackdowns focusing on hot spots or on particular types of crime may be effective in reducing crime, although the effect is sometimes modest in size. However, not all crackdowns are effective (see Sherman et al., 1998). Limited data suggest that crackdowns are most likely to be effective when the police are able to do the following: (1) identify the individuals or high-crime areas to be targeted; (2) clearly communicate to these individuals or the people in these areas that some or all illegal acts will be not be tolerated; (3) adequately monitor the behavior of these individuals or the people in these areas; and (4) consistently punish illegal acts, with punishments being reasonably swift and meaningful (see Kennedy, 1998; Kleiman, 1999). The police, in short, need to do what effective parents do: State clear rules for behavior, adequately monitor behavior, and consistently sanction rule violations in an appropriate manner. These actions are certainly possible in many cases. Most cities have hot spots of crime and neighborhoods plagued by disorder. Further, the police in some cities can identify and monitor the individuals most likely to commit certain types of crime, such as homicide. But delinquency is less concentrated in some communities than others, making it more difficult to adequately monitor and sanction behavior. And certain types of delinquency—like drug use—are spread widely throughout the community, making crackdowns especially difficult. Nevertheless, properly implemented police crackdowns are a promising strategy for reducing at least some delinquency.

Will Community Policing Reduce Delinquency?

There is another major effort underway to transform the nature of policing, and this effort promises to fundamentally alter the nature of police work in the United States. Many researchers and policy makers are arguing that the police should move away from preventive patrol and employ a strategy known as "community policing." As an example, the 1994 Violent Crime Control and Law Enforcement Act mandates that all of the 100,000 new police hired be used for community policing. A recent survey found that over 80 percent of a national sample of police departments claim that they are now using community policing, although many are only making minimal efforts in this area (McEwen, 1994). As you will see, community policing is different from police crackdowns, although police crackdowns may sometimes emerge from community policing efforts.

What is community policing? The best way to answer this question is to review some of the problems of preventive patrol, because community policing was developed in response to these problems.[3]

Problems of preventive patrol. Preventive patrol has been criticized for several reasons, including the following. First, preventive patrol *isolates the police from the communities they patrol*. Police officers spend much time in a patrol car cruising a large area. In some areas, they are rotated between beats on a regular basis. Rotation is done to prevent corruption; some departments feel that you can reduce corruption by preventing officers from developing close ties to the people they police. As a result, the officers do not get to know community residents. In some cases, particularly in minority communities, there may be tension or outright hostility between the police and many community residents. This tension is unfortunate, since residents are more likely to call the police if they know and trust them. As discussed in Chapter 2, only about a third of all crimes are reported to the police. The police cannot do anything to solve crimes they do not know about. Residents can also function as good information sources, helping the police solve crimes and better understand the community problems that contribute to crime. Further, some evidence suggests that community residents are more likely to obey the law if they respect and are well treated by the police (Sherman, 1998; Sherman et al., 1998).

Second, preventive patrol *does not deal with the underlying causes of crime*. Officers on preventive patrol respond to one crime incident after another, but they rarely examine the underlying causes of those incidents and ask how such causes might be addressed. That is to say, they deal with the symptoms of the problem but not the underlying problem. For example, over the course of a few months an officer might get several calls regarding burglaries at an apartment complex. The officer responds to each call in turn, and then resumes patrol. The officer never steps back and asks why this apartment complex has so many burglaries and what can be done about it.

Finally, preventive patrol *does not fully involve community residents in crime-control efforts*. Community residents might be asked for information about specific crimes, but police stress that the fight against crime should be left to the police. The police, however, have limited resources, and criminologists argue that any successful crime-control program needs to involve community residents.

What is community policing? Preventive patrol has been heavily criticized. Community policing was designed to deal with these criticisms. Community policing does not refer to one specific strategy or approach, such as the use of foot patrols. Rather, it encompasses a number of related approaches. At the most general level, community policing tries to do three things.

First, it tries to *foster closer ties between the police and community residents*. As indicated earlier, there are a number of advantages to such ties (although efforts must also be made to control police corruption). The police have tried to foster such ties in several ways. Most efforts involve: (1) assigning officers to the same community for long periods, so they identify with and become an integral part of the community; and (2) getting officers to spend

less time in patrol cars and more time interacting with community residents. The officers may walk a beat, especially in downtown areas or other densely packed areas. They may spend time on bicycles or motor scooters, where interaction with the public is easier. They may open storefront police stations in the community, where they are more accessible. They may visit community residents in their homes, going door-to-door. They may serve as substitute teachers in the school system. They may attend community meetings and get involved in community organizations, like the YMCA and Boys and Girls Clubs. They may set up their own community programs, like PAL, or the Police Athletic League.

Second, community policing attempts to *solve the underlying problems that led to crime*. In some cases, special police officers or police units are charged with the task of dealing with the underlying causes of crime. The advocates of community policing, however, argue that regular officers should also be involved in this process. The officer who is assigned to a community on a day-to-day basis has a special advantage when it comes to understanding that community's problems and developing solutions to them. Most police officers usually have some time when they are not responding to calls or engaged in other tasks. They are encouraged to use this time to deal with the underlying causes of crime on their beat. In particular, they are often urged to engage in what is known as "problem-oriented policing"—discussed below— which provides a model for how one goes about dealing with the underlying causes of crime. The solutions they develop to these problems often involve efforts to increase direct control, but they sometimes involve efforts to increase other forms of social control, reduce the social learning of crime, or reduce strain.

Third, community policing attempts to *actively involve community residents in the fight against crime*. Such involvement might take the form of neighborhood watch programs, where community residents watch out for one another's homes and report suspicious activity to the police. It might also include such things as volunteering with the police and participating in a wide range of crime prevention and control programs, such as recreational and mentoring programs.

The proper implementation of community policing is not easy. Community policing generally requires more police, since the police are asked to do more. They not only respond to crime incidents, they also try to foster ties with community residents and attempt to deal with the underlying causes of crime. Some police have the time for such extra activities, but others do not. Community policing also represents a major change in the police role, and many police are resistant to this change. Community police officers are sometimes referred to as the "grin and wave" squad, and they are often viewed more as social workers than as police. Further, many police administrators are resistant to community policing since it means giving more responsibility to regular officers and community residents. Officers and residents play a central role in identifying and responding to community problems.

Nevertheless, community policing is becoming increasingly popular. Let me provide a few brief examples.

Problem-Oriented Policing (POP). The city of Newport News has been a pioneer in the use of Problem-Oriented Policing (POP), which can be classified as a type of community policing. POP is designed to deal with the underlying causes of crime, and it encourages police officers to work with community residents and organizations in doing so. POP proceeds in four steps:

1. Scanning: The police are encouraged to identify problems in their community or across the entire city. These problems are groups of related crime incidents, and they might include such things as car thefts in a certain neighborhood, drug sales in an apartment complex, the robbery of tourists, or juveniles who run away from home on a repeated basis.

2. Analysis: The police analyze the problem, in the hope of understanding its causes and developing possible solutions. They collect information from a wide range of sources, including community residents, arrested offenders, and organizations that deal with the problem (e.g., social welfare agencies, the local housing authority, religious institutions).

3. Response: The police decide on a solution to the problem and then implement it. The solution may or may not involve a police response. For example, they may decide to launch a police crackdown on drug sales in a particular community or they may decide to set up a drug education program in the schools. The police often work with community residents, community organizations, and other government agencies in implementing the solution.

4. Assessment: The police evaluate the effectiveness of the solution. If it is not effective, they try other solutions. (For additional information, see Eck and Spelman, 1987; Trojanowicz et al., 1998.)

As an illustration of POP, the residents of a quiet neighborhood in Newport News began to complain about groups of rowdy teenagers in their community on Friday and Saturday nights. While the teenagers were not violent, they played loud music and occasionally engaged in acts of vandalism. The police responded to a number of incidents involving these teenagers, but the problem persisted. Relations between the police, the teenagers, and community residents were deteriorating. The beat officer was asked to examine the underlying causes of this problem and propose a solution. He discovered that a roller-skating rink in the area was trying to increase business by offering lower rates and free bus service to the rink on Friday and Saturday nights. This offer attracted many teenagers to the rink from outside the community. Conversations with these teenagers revealed that there were not enough buses to take them home after the rink closed. As a consequence, the teenagers would walk home through the neighborhood, creating problems. The rink owner was informed of the problem, and he agreed to lease more buses to take the teenagers home. This action effectively ended the problem (see Trojanowicz et al., 1998:174). Other examples of the successful use of POP are provided in Braga et al. (1999) and Spelman and Eck (1987).

Drug Abuse Resistance Education (D.A.R.E.) program. Another example of community policing is the Drug Abuse Resistance Education program (D.A.R.E.). D.A.R.E. did not emerge out of problem-oriented policing, but it does represent another effort of the police to work with the community in dealing with the underlying causes of crime (see Carter, 1995). The program was developed by the Los Angeles Police Department but has been adopted by police departments all over the country. In fact, police officers run this program in over half the school districts in the United States. The D.A.R.E. program is presented to schoolchildren by a uniformed police officer and focuses on preventing drug abuse, violence, and gang affiliation. The full D.A.R.E. program begins in kindergarten and continues through high school. The program tries to prevent delinquency in a number of ways. Among other things, it tries to build positive relations with the police, foster anti-drug values, and teach kids to resist negative peer pressure. The police also gain valuable information about the problems faced by youths in their communities, and they sometimes develop special programs to deal with these problems.

Youth organizations. As a final example of community policing, the police in many communities have become actively involved in youth organizations that try to prevent delinquency, such as the YMCA, Boys and Girls Clubs, and the Boy and Girl Scouts. Such organizations provide youths with supervised recreational opportunities and other services, like tutoring and mentoring. The police serve as advisers to these organizations; they participate in a variety of program activities; they help provide security in and around the youth centers; and they help recruit high-risk youth to participate in these organizations. In many cases, the police have started and run their own youth programs; the Police Athletic League is an example (see Chaiken, 1998). I encourage you to find out what your home police department is doing to implement community policing.

Effectiveness of community policing. Does community policing work? Is it effective in reducing crime and delinquency? Many claims for its success have been made. Unfortunately, most community policing efforts have not yet been subject to rigorous evaluation. The limited data that now exist suggest that most community policing efforts are effective in reducing the *fear of crime* and in *improving police-community relations*, but not all efforts reduce crime and delinquency rates. Some do and some do not. There is evidence, for example, that the D.A.R.E. program does not reduce drug use (see Chapter 22). Likewise, neighborhood watch-type programs are generally not effective in reducing crime. Problem-oriented policing, however, appears to reduce crime in at least some circumstances. Certain efforts to establish closer ties to community residents—like door-to-door visits by the police—show some success at reducing crime. And certain of the youth organizations with which the police are affiliated show some success at reducing crime. (Sherman et al., 1998, provide an excellent overview of the research in these areas.) Many community policing efforts, however, have not been well evaluated. Criminologists are still in the process of learning which community policing efforts work and which do not. Certain community policing pro-grams, however, do appear to hold some promise for reducing crime and delinquency rates.

Summary

Data suggest that society might lower crime rates somewhat by hiring more police and changing what the police do when they are on the street. In particular, police crackdowns focusing on hot spots and selected types of crime are sometimes effective. Such crackdowns reduce crime by improving the ability of the police to monitor situations and individuals prone to crime and to sanction crime when it occurs. That is, these crackdowns increase direct control by the police. Likewise, community policing efforts are some-times effective at reducing crime. At the most general level, community polic-ing involves efforts to establish closer ties between the police and the commu-nity; to deal with the underlying causes of crime; and to better involve the community in crime control efforts. Community policing sometimes involves efforts to increase direct control (e.g., neighborhood watch–type programs) and sometimes involves efforts to address the other causes of crime (e.g., D.A.R.E.). Criminologists are still in the process of determining which of the many specific types of community policing are most effective, although data are beginning to point to those community policing programs that do and do not work.

Notes

1. For overviews and selected studies on the police, see Anderson and Newman, 1998; Brandl and Barlow, 1996; Chaiken, 1998; Cox and Conrad, 1996; Eck and Spelman, 1987; Gaines and Cordner, 1999; Kappeler et al., 1996; Kelling, no date, 1988; Kelling and Coles, 1996; Mastrofski, 2000; Moore et al., 1988; Muraskin, 1998; Petersilia, 1989; Sherman, 1995, 1998; Sherman et al., 1998; Trojanowicz et al., 1998; Walker, 1998.
2. Braga et al., 1999; Erez, 1995; Sherman, 1990, 1995; Sherman et al., 1998; Sherman and Weisburd, 1995.
3. For overviews and selected studies on community policing, see Braga et al., 1999; Brown, 1989; Cordner, 1999; Eck and Spelman, 1987; Kelling and Coles, 1996; McEwen, 1994; Moore et al., 1988; National Institute of Justice, 1992; Sherman et al., 1998; Spelman and Eck, 1987; Trojanowicz et al., 1998. ✦

Juvenile Court and Corrections: What Do the Juvenile Court and Juvenile Correctional Agencies Do to Control Delinquency?

In this chapter, I first examine what happens when juveniles are sent to juvenile court. Next, I examine the ways in which the juvenile correctional system sanctions and attempts to reform juvenile offenders. Finally, I examine the effectiveness of the juvenile court and correctional system. In this connection, I consider two major criticisms of the court and correctional system: that they are not "tough enough" with juvenile offenders and that they do not place enough emphasis on rehabilitation and prevention.[1]

What Happens When Juveniles Are Sent to Juvenile Court?

This section examines the goals of the juvenile court; the number and types of cases handled by the juvenile court; and the major stages in the juvenile court process, beginning with the referral to juvenile court and finishing with the "disposition" or sentence that is given out by the juvenile court. Not all juvenile courts operate in the same manner, but this discussion should give you a general sense of what happens in juvenile court.

What Are the Major Goals of Juvenile Court?

As indicated in Chapter 1, the juvenile court was originally set up to *rehabilitate* juveniles rather than to punish them. It was felt that juveniles were not fully responsible for their behavior, including their delinquent behavior, so the court was set up to provide them with the guidance and assistance they needed to lead conventional lives. The court often failed to live up to this lofty goal in actual practice, but the major goal of the juvenile court was nevertheless rehabilitation rather than punishment. And rehabilitation was to be achieved by addressing many of the causes of delinquency examined earlier, such as family and school problems.

Rehabilitation is still an important goal of the juvenile court, but juvenile courts have also come to place an increased emphasis on *holding juveniles accountable* for their offenses and *punishing them*. Juvenile offenders, particularly serious offenders, are now more likely to be severely sanctioned for their offenses. The juvenile court, then, has started to place more emphasis on direct control, at least for serious offenders.

There are several reasons for this shift in focus from rehabilitation to accountability/punishment. First, a series of studies in the 1970s raised serious doubts about society's ability to rehabilitate delinquents (see Chapter 22 for more information). Second, doubts about the effectiveness of rehabilitation were also raised by the rapid increase in delinquency rates during the 1960s and early 1970s—as well as by the more recent increase in violent delinquency. Third, conservative politicians began to aggressively attack rehabilitation and prevention programs in the late 1960s. They claimed that crime and serious delinquency were not caused by social problems like poverty but rather were the result of deliberate choices by bad people. It was said that such people deserved punishment and that punishment was the most effective way to stop their crime. The criminal and juvenile justice systems were portrayed as "too lenient," and there were calls to "crack down" or "get tough" on crime. The conservative call to crack down on crime was aided by the extensive and often biased coverage of crime in the news media and entertainment industry (see Beckett and Sasson, 2000, for an excellent discussion).

How Many and What Types of Cases Are Handled by Juvenile Court?

There were about 1.8 million *delinquency* cases handled by juvenile courts in 1997—or 6.1 cases for every 100 juveniles age 10 and older who were eligible for juvenile court referral. This does not mean that 1.8 million *different* juveniles were handled by juvenile court. Many juveniles pass through the juvenile court more than once in a given year, and each visit is counted as a separate case. The *number* of cases handled by juvenile court increased 48 percent over 1988, while the *rate* increased 30 percent (the number of cases handled per 1,000 juveniles). The rate of increase has been greatest for violent offenses and drug crimes (see Puzzanchera et. al., 2000, for statistics on juvenile court).

About half the court cases were for property crimes like larceny-theft, burglary, vandalism, and motor vehicle theft. Larceny-theft, in fact, accounted for more cases than any other offense—with about a quarter of all cases being for larceny. Violent crimes like homicide, rape, and assault accounted for 22 percent of all cases (more than half of these violent crimes involved simple assaults). Public order offenses like disorderly conduct, weapons offenses, and obstruction of justice accounted for 19 percent of the cases. And drug offenses, including sales and use, accounted for 10 percent of the cases.

About 77 percent of the delinquency cases were males. I should note, however, that the number of females handled by the juvenile court has increased 83 percent since 1988, compared to an increase of 39 percent for males. Older juveniles were much more likely to be processed by the court than younger juveniles, with 16- and 17-year-old juveniles having the highest rates of court processing. For example, 16- and 17-year-old juveniles had rates of court processing about twenty times higher than 10-year-olds. Blacks had rates of court processing about 2.4 times higher than that of whites (3.4 times higher for violent crimes). The number of blacks handled by the court has increased 57 percent since 1988, as compared to an increase of 43 percent for whites.

Juvenile courts *formally processed* about 159,000 *status offense* cases in 1997. It is estimated that only about one out of five status offense referrals are formally processed, so the number of status offense cases handled by the court is much higher. Most of these cases are handled informally or dismissed. Good data exist only for the status offense cases that were formally processed, however. Most of these formally processed cases were for liquor law violations (40,700), truancy (40,500), running away (24,000), and ungovernability or incorrigibility (21,300). The *number* of formally processed status offense cases increased 101 percent from 1988 to 1997, while the *rate* of formally processed status offense cases increased 78 percent. Males were involved in 59 percent of the status offense cases (versus 77 percent of the delinquency cases). Males were more than twice as likely as females to be involved in liquor law violations. Males were only slightly more likely to be involved in truancy and ungovernability. And six out of ten runaway cases involved females.

What Are the Major Stages in the Juvenile Court Process?

Referral to juvenile court. The first step in the juvenile court process is referral to the juvenile court. Most youths are referred to the juvenile court by the police. In 1997, about 85 percent of all *delinquency* cases handled by the court came from the police. (By contrast, only 47 percent of the formally processed *status offense* cases were referred to the court by the police.) Usually the arresting officer physically takes the juvenile to juvenile court or a juvenile detention center. The officer provides the court staff with a "complaint," which describes the offense(s) the juvenile has committed.

The remaining 15 percent of the delinquency cases handled by the court were referred by parents, victims, school officials, probation officers, and others. For example, it is not uncommon for parents to go to juvenile court, claim that they cannot do anything to control their child, and fill out a complaint describing the offense(s) the child has committed. Also, probation officers will often file complaints against juveniles under their supervision, claiming that these juveniles have committed new offenses or have otherwise violated the conditions of their probation.

Intake screening. Juveniles referred to juvenile court are screened by an intake officer, who is usually a probation officer associated with the court. The intake screening typically includes an interview with the juvenile and his or her parent(s) or guardians, although the police, victims, and others are sometimes interviewed as well. The main purpose of the intake screening is to gather information about the case and decide what to do with the juvenile. Should the case be dismissed, handled informally, or formally processed by the juvenile court? And if the case is to be formally processed, should the juvenile be released or held by the court while awaiting trial? The decision of the intake officer is often reviewed by a prosecuting attorney in the court.

The intake officer considers a number of factors about the case. How strong is the evidence against the juvenile; specifically, is there "probable cause" to believe that the juvenile committed the offense? How serious is the offense? Does the juvenile admit to the offense? Does the juvenile have a prior record? How old is the juvenile? Does the juvenile have a good or bad attitude? How is the juvenile doing in school? How strongly is the complainant pressing for action? How concerned are the parents and what action have they taken or do they plan to take? In reaching a decision about what to do with the juvenile, the intake officer considers not only what the juvenile may have done (the offense) but also what the juvenile is like (the offender).

About 43 percent of all delinquency cases referred to the juvenile court are dismissed or handled informally, although this percentage varies greatly from court to court. Cases involving minor offenses are especially likely to be dismissed or handled informally, particularly if the juvenile does not have a prior record. (As indicated, the large majority of status offense cases are dismissed or handled informally.) Cases are *dismissed* for a variety reasons. For example, the evidence against the juvenile may be poor; the offense may be trivial; or the intake officer may feel that the situation is best dealt with by another agency, such as a social service agency. Usually, before a case is *informally pro-*

cessed, the juvenile must admit to the offense. There is strong pressure to do so, since a failure to admit to the offense may result in formal processing, with the possibility of an official record and more severe sanctions.

Informally processed cases are dealt with in a number of ways. Most commonly, the juvenile is placed on informal probation for a brief period of time, say, ninety days. The juvenile is supervised in the community by a probation officer. The officer may provide some counseling to the juvenile, and the officer may require the juvenile to do such things as attend school on a regular basis, attend a drug treatment program, participate in family counseling, or make restitution to the victim. Some informally processed offenders are not placed on informal probation but are nevertheless required to do things like apologize and make monetary restitution to the victim of their crime. If the juvenile successfully completes informal probation or meets the requirements of the court, the case is usually dismissed.

Many juvenile courts have set up "diversion" programs that offer services like individual and family counseling, mentoring, drug treatment, tutoring, and employment counseling (Lundman, 1993). These services are sometimes grouped in a central location. The purpose of these programs is to divert youth away from formal processing by the court so that they will not be stigmatized with a delinquent label. Such programs often save money, since it is cheaper to divert youth from the court than it is to formally process them. Many of the diverted youth, however, would have been released by the court in the past rather than formally processed, so the amount of money saved is less than expected. Evidence suggests that *certain* of these diversion programs are more effective in reducing delinquency than doing nothing or formally processing the juvenile (the characteristics of successful programs are discussed in Chapter 22).

Petition. If the case is going to be formally processed, the intake officer or prosecutor will prepare a formal petition. The petition describes the offense or offenses that brought the youth to juvenile court. The juvenile is often brought into court, read the charges in the formal petition, and told of his or her rights, such as the right to have an attorney.

Detention hearing. If the case is to be formally processed, the intake officer must also decide whether to release the juvenile to his or her parents/guardians or detain the juvenile while he or she is awaiting trial. If the intake officer decides to detain the juvenile, there must be a detention hearing within a short period of time (twenty-four hours in most states). This hearing is held before a juvenile court judge and is designed to determine whether the juvenile should continue to be held in detention.

The judge considers whether there is probable cause to believe that the juvenile committed the offense and whether there is good reason to detain him or her. In particular, the judge asks whether the juvenile poses a threat to the community, whether the juvenile might flee if released, and whether the juvenile would be in any danger if released.

If the judge decides that detention is warranted, the juvenile may be detained in a secure facility or detention center, which is like an adult jail. For example, juveniles are typically held in locked cells with bars on the windows. The conditions in these detention centers are often quite bad: many centers are overcrowded, many have inadequate living space, educational programs, health services, and/or treatment services; and many are plagued by violence (see Abt Associates, 1994; Acoca, 1998). Some towns or cities lack juvenile detention centers, so juveniles may be detained in adult jails. Federal regulations require that such juveniles have no sight or sound contact with the adults in these jails.

Some juveniles may be detained in less secure facilities, such as group homes and foster homes, and some juveniles may be placed on home detention. They are required to remain at home, except for school, work, or emergencies. They are regularly visited by court staff, and they may be subject to electronic monitoring. That is, they may be fitted with an electronic wrist or ankle bracelet, which alerts authorities if they leave home.

Juveniles are detained in about one out of five delinquency cases, but detention rates differ by race. About 15 percent of whites and 27 percent of blacks are detained. (I will shortly discuss possible reasons for this difference.) About 326,800 juveniles were detained in 1997. There were about 28,000 juveniles in detention on October 29, 1997—the date that the Office of Juvenile Justice and Delinquency Prevention conducted their last Census of Juveniles in Residential Placement (Snyder and Sickmund, 1999). The average length of time these juveniles had been in detention was about forty days.

About 9,400 of the youths detained in 1996 were charged with status offenses. Federal regulations strongly discourage the detention of status offenders, and there has been a dramatic decrease since the 1970s in the number of status offenders who are detained (although see the discussion of status offenders and out-of-home placements below).

Waiver. Some juvenile offenders have their cases waived or sent to adult court. This can occur in three major ways.

First, the prosecuting attorney in some juvenile courts can decide whether to try a case in juvenile court or adult court. This decision is often made at intake or shortly thereafter. Second, the juvenile court judge can often decide to waive a case to adult court. When the judge decides, a waiver hearing must be held. This hearing usually occurs after intake and petition. Prosecutors and judges cannot send all cases to adult court. Guidelines usually limit waivers to juveniles above a certain age who are accused of certain offenses—like felonies or serious crimes. When deciding to waive a case, prosecutors and judges usually ask whether there is probable cause to believe that the juvenile has committed the offense and whether the juvenile is "amenable to treatment" by the juvenile court. That is, can the juvenile court help the juvenile. Among other things, they consider the juvenile's offense, prior record, prior dispositions or sentences, age, and the resources available to the juvenile court. They may conclude that the juvenile is not amenable to treatment if he or she has committed a number of previous offenses and has not responded to the previous treatment efforts of the court.

Third, many states have recently passed laws stating that certain juvenile offenders will automatically be sent to adult court. Typically, such laws state that the juveniles be above a certain age and be accused of certain serious offenses, usually violent offenses. In my home state of Georgia, for example, juveniles age 13 and above who commit one of the "seven deadly sins" are automatically sent to adult court. The seven deadly sins are murder, voluntary manslaughter, rape, aggravated sodomy, aggravated child molestation, aggravated sexual battery, and armed robbery committed with a firearm. Juveniles who commit one of these offenses are taken directly to the adult system by the police.

The number of *serious* cases being waived to adult court has increased dramatically in recent years. For example, the number of violent crime cases waived to adult court *by judges* increased 74 percent from 1988 to 1997. The number of drug cases waived to adult court by judges has also increased. (The number of property crime and public order cases waived to adult court by judges has stayed about the same.) However, it is still the case that only a small fraction of all juvenile court cases are waived. For example, in 1997 only about 1 percent of all formally processed cases were waived to adult court by judges. There are no good data on the number of cases waived by prosecutors or automatically sent to adult court, although the number is not believed to be large. A 1996 survey of prosecutors estimated that about 27,000 juveniles were handled in adult criminal courts (Snyder and Sickmund, 1999:176).

There is, however, another way in which juveniles can be tried in adult court. Most juvenile courts have jurisdiction over juveniles until they turn 18, but ten states end jurisdiction when juveniles turn seventeen, and three states end jurisdiction when juveniles turn sixteen. So juveniles ages 17 or 16 in these states are tried as adults. (For the jurisdictions in question, this amounts to upwards of 200,000 juveniles.)

Adjudication. Adjudication is the juvenile equivalent of an adult trial. It is a hearing before the juvenile court judge to determine whether the juvenile committed the offense(s) described in the petition. Most juveniles admit to the offense(s), so a full hearing is not necessary. If it is determined that the juvenile committed the offense, the juvenile is "adjudicated delinquent." The juvenile is not found "guilty" of a specific offense. For example, juveniles are not found guilty of robbery or assault. Guilt implies that one is responsible for the offense and deserves punishment. Rather, they are adjudicated delinquent. (States use the term "delinquent" for juveniles who have committed offenses that would be crimes if committed by adults. Juveniles who commit status offenses are usually referred to by such other terms as "Persons in Need of Supervision" or "Children in Need of Supervision.")

As discussed in Chapter 1, juvenile court hearings used to be relatively informal—very different from those held in adult court. In particular, juveniles had few due process rights, such as the right to an attorney, to present and cross-examine witnesses, and to protection against self-incrimination (that is, being forced to testify against oneself). Also, the standard of proof was lower in juvenile court than in adult court. Rather than "proof beyond a reasonable doubt," the juvenile court required only a "preponderance of evidence." The rationale behind these differences was that the juvenile court was set up to assist rather than to punish the juvenile. Therefore, the legal protections available in adult court were not necessary.

These informal practices changed during the 1960s and 1970s, when a series of Supreme Court decisions extended several due process rights to juveniles, particularly at the adjudicatory hearing. The Supreme Court essentially said that the juvenile court often does punish juveniles; for example, it often confines them in institutions that offer little in the way of treatment. Juveniles therefore should receive many of the same due process protections as adults. (Research suggests, however, that these rights are still not extended to juveniles in some courts and that juveniles often elect not to exercise their rights, such as the right to be represented by an attorney.)

Juvenile court hearings have become more formal—more like those in adult court—as a result of the Supreme Court decisions. Juveniles, however, still do not have all the due process rights available to adults, most notably the right to a trial by jury. The Supreme Court recognized that there is still some difference between the goals of juvenile court and those of adult court, with the juvenile court focusing more on the rehabilitation of the child. It was felt that "juries would be highly disruptive of the informal, cooperative atmosphere in which everyone tried to find the child's best interests, and would tend to create an adversarial atmosphere in which each side attempted to win the case" (Bernard, 1992:125).

About 58 percent of the cases that are formally processed result in an adjudication of delinquency. The remaining cases are dismissed or dealt with informally. For example, the judge will sometimes withhold adjudication and place a juvenile on informal probation or require that the juvenile make restitution to the victim. If the juvenile successfully completes probation or makes restitution, the judge does not adjudicate the juvenile a delinquent.

Social history or predisposition report. Once a juvenile is adjudicated delinquent, a probation officer will complete a social history or predisposition report on the juvenile. The report is designed to provide a detailed picture of the juvenile and his or her problems, and to suggest a treatment plan. The judge uses the report to decide what sentence or "disposition" to give the juvenile. The disposition is not simply designed to punish the juvenile for the offense that was committed. Rather, the disposition is also designed to deal with the problems that caused the juvenile to get in to trouble with the law. The probation officer writing the social history will explore such things as the juvenile's family environment, school environment, peer relations, neighborhood, and prior history with the court. The juvenile may also undergo a psychological examination.

A consideration of the different dispositions or sentences that are available brings us to the juvenile correctional system.

Juvenile Corrections: What Happens to Juveniles Who Receive a Disposition or Sentence From the Court?

The judge has a number of sentencing or disposition options, ranging from a verbal reprimand of the juvenile to incarceration. In 1997, 55 percent of adjudicated delinquents were placed on probation, 28 percent were placed in out-of-home facilities, and 13 percent were subject to other sanctions, such as fines, community service, or treatment/counseling of various types (but no probation). About 4 percent of the adjudicated delinquents were not subject to formal sanctions.

Regular Probation

The most commonly used option is formal probation, which involves the supervision and treatment of the juvenile in the community by a probation officer. Slightly more than half of all adjudicated delinquents were placed on formal probation in 1997. As indicated above, a large number of juveniles were also placed on informal probation. In 1997, approximately 650,000 juveniles were placed on probation, about half on formal probation and half on informal probation.

Juveniles on probation visit with their probation officer anywhere from several times a week to once a month or less. The probation officer provides counseling and assistance to the juvenile and determines whether the juvenile is meeting the conditions of probation. Such conditions may include reporting to the probation officer at regular intervals, attending school regularly, being home at a certain hour every day, and not associating with certain people. The juvenile may also be required to participate in certain treatment programs, such as counseling programs, drug treatment, and after-school programs that provide a range of services. The conditions of probation must be reasonable and relevant to the juvenile's offense. Juveniles are typically placed on probation for a period of six months to a year. If the juvenile does not meet the conditions of probation or commits a new offense, probation may be revoked and the juvenile may face more severe sanctions, such as being sent to an institution.

Although probation is supposed to provide supervision and treatment in the community, probation officers often have heavy caseloads, and they frequently provide little supervision of or treatment to the juveniles under their control. In many juvenile courts, regular probation often involves little more than doing nothing to the juvenile. It is therefore not surprising that regular probation does little to lower recidivism rates or rates of reoffending (Lipsey, 1992; also see Kurlychek et al., 1999).

Intermediate Sanctions

Most juvenile courts have developed a range of "intermediate sanctions." These sanctions are designed to provide more control and punishment than juveniles receive on regular probation, but they are less extreme and costly than confinement in an institution. These sanctions include restitution and fines, "Scared Straight"–type programs, intensive supervision programs—often combined with home confinement, day treatment centers, and boot camps. Sometimes these sanctions are used along with probation, so juveniles will be placed on probation *and* will be subject to certain of the sanctions described in the following paragraphs. Sometimes these sanctions are used in place of probation; juveniles might be required to make restitution to their victims but would not be placed on probation.

- *Restitution* may be made directly to the crime victim, in the form of a monetary payment or—less commonly—work. Also, restitution may be made to the community, usually in the form of community service; for example, juveniles may clean up a public park or work in a nursing home. Restitution holds juveniles accountable for their offense(s) and allows them to pay back the victim or community for the harm they have caused.

- *"Scared Straight"*–type programs typically involve a tour of an adult prison and a meeting with prison inmates. The inmates describe the horrors of prison life, including such things as homosexual rape and suicide. The students are told they will eventually end up in prison if they continue on their current path, and they are urged to "go straight."

- *Intensive Supervision Programs (ISP)* are run by probation officers with small caseloads. Juveniles in ISPs are subject to frequent home visits and, in many programs, random drug tests. In some cases, juveniles may be confined to their homes except for school, emergencies, and possibly work. This confinement may be enforced through electronic monitoring. A tamper-proof strap with a transmitting device may be attached to the juvenile's wrist or ankle. The device signals a receiver if the juvenile leaves his or her home.

- *Day Treatment Centers* are after-school facilities that provide educational, recreational, and treatment services. Juveniles report to the center after school and may receive tutoring, counseling, drug treatment, and other services.

- *Boot camp* is perhaps the most extreme of the intermediate sanctions. Juveniles are usually sent to military-style boot camps for three to six months. The guards at such camps are like drill sergeants. They demand strict obedience from the juveniles under them. They secure such obedience by screaming at and otherwise intimidating these juveniles and by frequently imposing punishments like push-ups on them. The juveniles have their heads shaved, are given military-style fatigues, and are treated like military recruits. In particular, there is much emphasis on discipline, close-order drill, physical exercise, and hard labor.

Although certain of these intermediate sanctions provide treatment to juveniles, most focus on control and punishment. These sanctions have proved reasonably popular. On the one hand, they satisfy the demand for the control and punishment of juvenile offenders, especially serious offenders. On the other, they are much cheaper than incarceration. It now costs about $40,000 a year, on average, to confine a juvenile offender. Intermediate sanctions cost only a fraction of that. Certain of these sanctions, in fact, were explicitly developed as alternatives to institutions, with the idea that they would save money and reduce overcrowding in institutions. So rather than sending an offender to an institution, a judge might place the offender in an intensive supervision program or in a boot camp. These sanctions, however, have not saved as much money as anticipated because they are frequently used for juveniles who otherwise would have been placed on regular probation.

Out-of-Home Placements

In 1997, about 28 percent of adjudicated delinquents were placed out of their homes in residential facilities (see Stahl, 1999); that amounts to 163,200 delinquents. About 14 percent of adjudicated status offenders were placed out of home. That amounts to about 11,600 status offenders. These juveniles were placed in a range of public and private residential facilities, including group homes, wilderness programs, and training schools. There has been an increase in the *number* of juveniles being placed out of home and the *rate* of out of home placements (see MacKenzie, 1999; Smith, 1998). For example, the number of adjudicated delinquents placed in residential facilities increased 56 percent from 1988 to 1997.

A census of juveniles in correctional facilities found that 76,503 delinquents and status offenders were serving sentences in juvenile correctional facilities on October 29, 1997. The census surveyed 1,121 public and 2,310 private facilities. Although there are more private than public facilities, about 66 percent of the confined juveniles were in public facilities (which are larger, on average, than private facilities). The average length of confinement was just over six months.

As indicated earlier, about 28,000 juveniles were being *detained* in juvenile facilities on October 29, 1997. So about 105,000 juveniles were serving sentences or being detained in juvenile correctional facilities on October 29, 1997. That amounts to about 3.7 juveniles for every 1,000 juveniles in the population (about half the confinement rate for adults).

What offenses are juveniles confined for? According to the 1997 census, about 94 percent of juveniles serving sentences in correctional facilities were there for *delinquent* offenses. The remaining 6 percent were there for status offenses. About 28 percent of the sentenced juveniles were confined for serious violent crimes (homicide, sexual assault, robbery, aggravated assault). The rest were confined for simple assault (6 percent), property crimes (32 percent), drug offenses (9 percent), public order offenses such as weapons and alcohol violations (9 percent), and violations of probation, parole, and court orders (8 percent). Contrary to the impression that many people hold, most confined juveniles are *not* being held for violent crimes.

The confinement of status offenders. Federal guidelines strongly discourage the confinement of status offenders. While these guidelines have been reasonably successful, some status offenders are nevertheless still confined. Further, juvenile courts will sometimes charge status offenders with minor criminal offenses, which allow confinement. For example, ungovernable children might be charged with simple assault if they threatened their parents at some point. Also, status offenders who violate the conditions of their probation can be charged with violation of probation, which allows confinement. For example, a truant may be placed on probation, with the requirement that he or she attend school on a regular basis. If the truant fails to attend school, he or she can then be charged with violation of probation and sent to an institution (see Bernard, 1992). In addition, many *nonadjudicated* delinquents and status offenders are placed out of home. The juveniles' parents, for example, may agree to voluntarily place them out of home. In exchange, the court does not formally process the case, or it withholds adjudication. Many criminologists feel that such "voluntary" placements are becoming increasingly common.

What are the demographic characteristics of confined juveniles? About 86 percent of all confined juveniles are male (this number includes all confined offenders, both those serving sentences and those being held in detention centers). The rate of confinement, however, has been increasing faster for females than for males. About 40 percent of confined juveniles are black, even though black juveniles make up just 15 percent of the juvenile population. About 18 percent of confined juveniles are Hispanic, even though Hispanic juveniles make up about 15 percent of the juvenile population. About 37 percent of confined juveniles are white (whites make up about 66 percent of the juvenile population.) A recent study of thirty-six states examined the percentage of juveniles in different race/ethnic groups who were confined at some point prior to their eighteenth birthday. The study found that black juveniles were about five times more likely to be confined than whites and three times more likely to be confined than Hispanics (DeComo, 1998; also see Snyder and Sickmund, 1999). I should note that the rate of confinement has been increasing much faster for blacks and Hispanics than for whites. Also, blacks and Hispanics are more likely than whites to be confined in public facilities. Public facilities tend to be larger, more secure, more crowded, and less oriented to treatment than private facilities.

What are juvenile facilities like? Juvenile facilities differ from one another along a number of dimensions. Some are small, housing as few as ten to twenty juveniles; others house several hundred juveniles. Some provide a moderate amount of freedom, with juveniles attending school in the community and having much freedom to move around the facility. Others are like adult prisons: they are surrounded by a fence; juveniles are held in secure cells, and the juvenile's movement about the institution is closely controlled. Some institutions place much emphasis on treatment, while others focus on the control and punishment of juveniles. Some are well run, while others suffer from a host of problems, such as overcrowding, violence, and inadequate educational, health, recreational, and treatment services. Most offenders are confined in overcrowded institutions that suffer from a range of problems.[2]

One type of juvenile facility is the *group home* or *halfway house*. These are usually nonsecure facilities that house a small number of juveniles. Group homes and halfway houses are quite similar to one another, except that juveniles are typically sent to a group home *instead of* being sent to a more secure institution, and they are sent to a halfway house *after* serving time in an institution. Their stay in the halfway house is designed to ease their transition back into the community. They live in the group home or halfway house, receiving counseling and other services. But they usually attend school in the community. The small size of the house often allows juveniles to build a close relationship with the staff.

Wilderness or *outdoor programs* provide juveniles with physically challenging activities, such as rock climbing and ocean sailing. The juveniles are usually part of a small group; they learn to work together, follow directions, and overcome challenges that are designed to increase their coping skills and self-esteem (see Roberts, 1998, for an overview). Some wilderness programs last only a week or so, while others last more than year, often involving outdoor work like maintaining and restoring wilderness areas.

Training schools are most like adult prisons. (Training schools are called by different names in different states; in your state they may be called youth development centers, youth centers, or the like.) Many are large, focus on security, do not offer sufficient treatment, and suffer from a host of other problems. The juveniles in such institutions often develop a subculture that discourages cooperation with the staff, encourages the exploitation of weaker inmates, and rewards toughness. Further, as indicated above, such institutions are expensive.

A number of individuals and groups have recommended that the justice system reduce or eliminate the use of training schools for juveniles. They point to the problems and expenses associated with such schools; and they argue that the juveniles in these schools can be better handled in other types of facilities or in the community. One study of 14 states found that 31 percent of the juveniles confined in secure facilities scored low on a risk assessment scale, a scale designed to assess the test takers' likelihood of committing more delinquent acts (Krisberg and Howell, 1998). As a consequence, several states are moving away from the use of large, secure training schools. They are placing juvenile offenders in smaller, more treatment-oriented facilities in the community. Massachusetts adopted such an approach in the 1970s, and states such as Pennsylvania, Vermont, Utah, Maryland, and Florida are following suit. The *general* trend, however, is toward the increased confinement of juvenile offenders in secure public facilities and the increased transfer of juveniles to the adult system.

Aftercare services. Once juveniles are released from an institution, they sometimes receive "aftercare" services to ease their transition back into the community. Aftercare is similar to probation: The juvenile is supervised by someone associated with the juvenile justice system. The juvenile may also receive counseling and participate in special treatment programs. Aftercare services, however, are generally viewed as poor, and several commentators have called for an increased focus on the provision of good aftercare (e.g., Armstrong and Altschuler, 1998). Several innovative programs in this area are under way (e.g., Altschuler, 1998; Altschuler et al., 1999).

An Overview of the Juvenile Justice Process

An overview of the juvenile court process is provided in Figure 19.1. Looking at the process as a whole, one finds that 57 percent of the *delinquency* cases referred to juvenile court are formally processed (have a petition filed). Of these, 58 percent are adjudicated delinquent. And of these, 55 percent are placed on probation. About 28 percent are placed out of home, and about 13

Figure 19.1 An Overview of the Juvenile Court Process (for Delinquency Cases Processed in 1996)

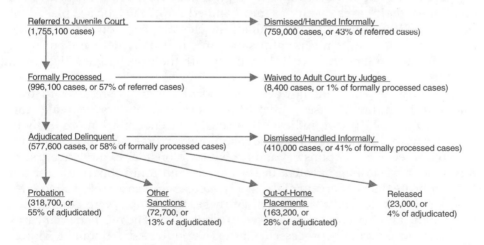

Source: Puzzanchera et al. (2000).

percent receive other sanctions (but no probation). Some of the juveniles on probation and some who receive "other sanctions" are subject to the intermediate sanctions listed earlier. If you do the appropriate math, you will discover that about 9 percent of the delinquency cases referred to juvenile court are placed out of home. About 32 percent receive a *formal* sanction/treatment of some type, including probation, fines, and/or restitution. Many others are informally sanctioned/treated.

How Effective Is the Juvenile Justice System at Controlling Delinquency?

Now that I have described how the court and juvenile correctional system operate, I next ask whether the court and correctional system are effective at controlling delinquency. Many people claim that the court and correctional system are not "tough" enough, particularly with serious offenders. This claim is driving the current trend to get tougher with juvenile offenders. In addition, some people claim that the court and correctional system do not do enough to prevent delinquency and rehabilitate delinquents.

The Juvenile Court and Correctional System Are Not Tough Enough, Especially With Serious Offenders

Perhaps the most common criticism of the juvenile court is that it is not tough enough, especially in dealing with serious offenders. This charge is often voiced by politicians and the media, and it is shared by many in the juvenile justice system. Many police, for example, complain that the offenders they send to juvenile court usually receive little more than a "slap on the wrist." Court workers often note that unless juveniles commit a very serious offense, they must appear in court several times before they receive a meaningful sanction (see Stone, 1998). Does this charge have any merit?

As pointed out, the large majority of juveniles who are referred to juvenile court have their cases dismissed, are handled informally, or are placed on probation. While probation may call for the close supervision of the juvenile and the imposition of meaningful sanctions, it usually does not. In most cases, juvenile offenders have little contact with their probation officers and are subject to only minimal sanctions.

We must keep in mind, however, that most juveniles are referred to juvenile court for minor offenses. It may be that serious offenders are treated differently. Data do, in fact, indicate that serious offenders are more likely to receive severe sanctions. It is still the case, however, that most serious offenders do not receive sanctions beyond probation. Consider two relatively serious violent crimes: aggravated, or serious, assault and robbery. Data from 1997 indicate that 72 percent of the aggravated assault cases referred to juvenile court were formally processed. Of these, 57 percent were adjudicated delinquent, and 2 percent were waived to adult court. The rest had their cases dismissed or informally processed. Of those adjudicated delinquent, 31 percent were placed out of home. The rest were placed on probation or, in a small number of cases, sanctioned in some other way, handled informally, or dismissed. If we do the appropriate math, we find that 13 percent of the aggravated assault cases referred to juvenile court were placed out of home, and 1 percent were waived to adult court. The numbers for robbery are as follows: 88 percent of the robbery cases referred to juvenile court were formally processed. Of these, 60 percent were adjudicated delinquent, and 4 percent were waived to adult court. Of those adjudicated delinquent, 44 percent were placed out of home. Overall, 23 percent of the robbery cases referred to juvenile court were placed out of home, and 4 percent were waived to adult court (see Puzzanchera et al., 2000). Most serious offenders referred to juvenile court, then, do not receive severe sanctions (It should be noted, however, that aggravated assault and robbery cases, vary in their level of seriousness; some aggravated assaults involve threats to injure someone with a weapon like a bat, and some robberies involve taking someone's lunch money under threat of violence). Further data suggest that adult court is more likely to incarcerate serious juvenile offenders than juvenile court and to incarcerate them for longer periods of time (Jensen and Rojek, 1998; Strom and Smith, 1998); Data such as this have led many people to conclude that juvenile court is not tough enough.

There are several reasons for this state of affairs, some of which are difficult to address. For example, juvenile courts cannot be expected to sanction a juvenile when they lack good evidence that the juvenile committed an offense, but other reasons can be addressed. The court staff are limited, which makes it impossible to formally process and impose meaningful sanctions on most juvenile court cases. Although politicians have devoted enormous sums of money to the control of adult crime, they have been reluctant to make substantial investments in the juvenile justice system. Also, most juvenile courts are still guided by a philosophy that emphasizes rehabilitation over punishment. This philosophy influences the sanctions that are imposed. As indicated earlier, this focus on rehabilitation is based on the view that juveniles are not fully responsible for their behavior and are more in need of assistance and direction than punishment.

The fact that juvenile courts do not impose more severe sanctions is seen as a serious problem by many people. They view the juvenile court as the last line of defense against delinquency. They claim that juveniles must be held accountable for their actions and punished for their offenses if society is to effectively control delinquency. This viewpoint has led many to recommend that the juvenile court get tougher with offenders, especially serious offenders.

The federal government has been a leading advocate in this area. In particular, federal experts have recently developed a comprehensive strategy for responding to delinquency, particularly serious delinquency. One of the cornerstones of this strategy is the proposition that juvenile offenders need to be held accountable for their behavior. One of the major recommendations made by the federal government is that juvenile courts institute a system of "graduated sanctions," which include "immediate sanctions in the community for first-time, nonviolent offenders; intermediate sanctions in the community for more serious offenders; and secure care programs for the most violent offenders. Youths should move between different levels of the continuum through a well-structured system of phases. At each level of the continuum, offenders should understand that they will be subject to more severe sanctions if they reoffend" (Krisberg et al., 1995).

Most juvenile courts have attempted to get tough with juvenile offenders, especially serious offenders, in recent years. In fact, this "get-tough" movement constitutes the major trend in juvenile justice in recent years (see Feld, 1993; Howell, 1997a; Torbet and Szymanski, 1998).

Efforts to Get Tough With Serious Offenders

Juvenile courts have initiated several efforts to get tough with offenders, especially serious offenders.

Many juvenile courts are attempting to make more efficient use of their limited court staff so they can better concentrate on serious offenders. One of the reasons that diversion programs were developed is that they allow court staff to divert less serious cases out of the court system and focus on more serious cases. Also, many juvenile courts are now employing "risk assessment" instruments that attempt to predict which juveniles are most likely to commit offenses in the future. These instruments are usually developed by examining the associations between various characteristics of juvenile offenders—prior record, school performance, and family characteristics, for example—and subsequent offending. The instruments are then used to classify adjudicated delinquents as being at low risk, medium risk, or high risk for future offending. The high-risk offenders are subject to greater supervision. Although the predictions made with these instruments are far from perfect, they are more accurate than the predictions made by probation officers.[3] Unfortunately, many juvenile courts are so understaffed that they cannot devote much attention to even high-risk juveniles.

Juvenile courts are also imposing more severe sanctions on offenders, especially serious offenders. The desire for more severe sanctions is one of the reasons for the development of the *intermediate* sanctions described above, such as restitution, intensive supervision, home confinement, and boot camps. Further, juvenile courts are confining more juveniles in institutions. In this connection, many states have passed laws that mandate or strongly encourage judges to confine certain serious offenders. Many states have also passed laws that increase the length of time juveniles can be confined. Georgia, for example, passed a law that increased the length of time that juveniles committing certain serious crimes could be confined from two years to five years. In some states, juvenile courts can now sentence certain offenders to serve time in the adult correctional system after their juvenile sentence is completed (see Snyder and Sickmund, 1999:108).

Many individuals, however, argue that the juvenile court is limited in the punishments it can inflict. Most juvenile courts, for example, can sentence juveniles only to short periods of confinement. Juvenile courts in Georgia cannot sentence juveniles to periods of confinement that extend beyond their twenty-first birthday. And no juvenile court can impose the death penalty (although a number of states permit 16- and 17-year-olds who are tried as adults to receive the death penalty). As a consequence, over forty states have recently passed laws making it easier to try juveniles as adults. Studies reveal that juveniles tried in adult court do not always receive more severe sanctions than they would have in juvenile court. The court may perceive such juveniles as mild compared to the hardened offenders it usually deals with. Overall, however, most data suggest that juveniles tried in adult court are more likely to be incarcerated and to be incarcerated for longer periods of time (see Howell, 1997a). The most recent data suggest that about six in ten of the juveniles transferred to adult criminal court were convicted of felonies or serious crimes, and about half of those convicted of felonies were sent to prison, the average sentence being nine years (Snyder and Sickmund, 1999). The other juveniles convicted of felonies were sent to jail (19 percent), placed on probation (31 percent), or fined (1 percent). Data also indicate that the number of offenders under age 18 admitted to state prison has more than doubled from 3,400 in 1988 to 7,400 in 1997 (Strom, 2000). Clearly there has been a major movement to get tough with juvenile offenders, especially serious offenders.

How Effective Are These Get-Tough Measures?

Has this get-tough movement worked? Is it effective? It is difficult to give a definitive answer since not all strategies have been carefully evaluated, and the evaluations do not always produce consistent results. There are, however, enough evaluation data to draw some *tentative* conclusions about the effectiveness of these get-tough efforts. In most evaluation studies, the get-tough effort is compared to "traditional" programs. For example, intensive supervision programs may be compared to regular probation. Or juveniles tried in adult court may be compared to similar juveniles tried in juvenile court. The evaluations usually try to determine whether the get-tough approach reduces the likelihood of future delinquency, with future delinquency most often measured in terms of arrests or court referrals.

One general conclusion that is emerging from the evaluations is that the get-tough approaches have no effect or only a small effect on future offending. In certain cases, they may actually increase future offending. The two major get-tough initiatives have been sending more juveniles to institutions and trying juveniles as adults. Evaluations suggest that sending juveniles to institutions is no more effective at reducing offending than many community-based alternatives. Some data, in fact, suggest that it may be easier to reduce reoffending in community-based programs than in institutions. Likewise, data suggest that trying juveniles as adults does not reduce reoffending. In fact, trying juveniles as adults may increase their rate of future offending.

Many of the *intermediate* sanctions discussed likewise have little effect on rates of future offending. Some data suggest that fines and restitution do lower future offending, but only by a small amount. "Scared Straight"–type programs do not reduce future offending, and some data suggest that they may even increase offending. Most data suggest that intensive supervision programs have little effect on rates of reoffending. The data on halfway houses are mixed: they reduce offending in some studies but not in others. There are no good data on the effectiveness of day treatment programs. And data indicate that boot camps do not reduce future offending.

Overall, the data suggest that programs which focus on punishing juveniles, scaring them, or controlling them are not effective at reducing offending. When these programs are combined with efforts to treat or rehabilitate juveniles, they do sometimes work. But simply getting tough is not more effective than traditional methods at reducing future rates of offending.[4]

How have people reacted to such research? These findings are still tentative and they are not well known by people outside of criminology, so they have not had a major impact on the get-tough movement. Also, many people favor get-tough approaches even if they do not reduce the offending rate of those who are punished. Some argue that these get-tough approaches reduce the offending of juveniles in the general population who are not punished. This argument is evaluated in Chapter 21, in the discussion of "general deterrence." Also, many people argue that while incarcerating juveniles may not reduce their future offending, the incarcerated juveniles cannot commit any offenses while they are locked up. This is referred to as an "incapacitation effect," and we will also evaluate this argument in Chapter 21. Finally, many citizens favor getting tough with juveniles because they believe that it is the *just* thing to do. Juveniles who commit serious crimes deserve serious punishments as a matter of justice, even if such punishments do not reduce delinquency. Other individuals make a rather different argument, as discussed below.

The Juvenile Court and Correctional System Need to Focus More on Rehabilitation and Prevention

Some argue that society is placing too much emphasis on get-tough approaches. Such approaches are usually no more effective than the alternatives; they are expensive, especially when they involve institutionalizing juveniles; and they expose many juveniles to the often inhumane conditions of juvenile institutions.

According to these individuals, it is no surprise that these approaches do not reduce the offending rate of those who are punished. These approaches attempt to reduce delinquency by increasing direct control by the juvenile justice system. In particular, they attempt to impose *more severe* sanctions on juveniles who violate the law. There are several reasons why these approaches are ineffective. First, data described in Chapter 21 suggest that the certainty, or probability, of punishment is much more important than the severity of punishment. In particular, severe punishments have little effect when the certainty of punishment is low. We know that the vast majority of juvenile offenses are not detected and punished. For example, Elliott (1995) calculated that the probability of arrest for a self-reported violent offense is about 2 in 100. Thus, many juvenile offenders—even those who have been caught and punished—may feel they can still get away with future crime. Rather than simply increasing the severity of punishment, it would be better to focus more resources on increasing the certainty of punishment (perhaps by employing those strategies described in Chapter 18).

Second, many serious juvenile offenders are difficult to control through punishment. They possess traits like impulsivity and a failure to learn from punishment, so the threat or administration of punishment has little meaning for them. Or they commit their offenses under the influence of drugs/alcohol or in response to peer/gang influences, which also reduce concern for punishment. Third, efforts at direct control usually fail to address all the other causes of delinquency, such as direct control by family members and community residents; other forms of social control; strain; and the social learning of crime. These other causes have a powerful influence on the individual, and it is doubtful that one can substantially reduce delinquency unless one attends to them. Fourth, efforts at direct control may sometimes backfire and increase the likelihood of delinquency. In particular, severe punishments may increase delinquency by reducing other forms of social control, as when the punishments disrupt a juvenile's education and reduce ties to conventional others. Severe punishments may increase delinquency by creating strain (see Sherman, 1993), and they may contribute to the social learning of crime. Incarceration, for example, isolates a juvenile from conventional others; fosters close contact with fellow delinquents in the juvenile institution; labels one a serious delinquent; and is sometimes viewed as a source of status among delinquents in certain neighborhoods.

Rather than simply getting tough, many argue, the justice system should place more emphasis on rehabilitating juvenile offenders and preventing juveniles from becoming delinquent in the first place. Although the juvenile court places much emphasis on rehabilitation *in theory*, juvenile offenders often do not receive effective rehabilitation programs *in practice*, and, with certain exceptions, little is done to prevent delinquency. The strategies of rehabilitation and prevention are evaluated in Chapter 22, but for now I will note that the most recent data suggest that properly designed and implemented rehabilitation/prevention programs appear to be more effective at reducing delinquency than programs that simply try to punish or control juveniles.

Notes

1. For overviews of the juvenile court and correctional system, see Altschuler, 1998; Bernard, 1992; Champion, 1998; Clement, 1997; Cox and Conrad, 1996; Feld, 1998, 1999; Future of Children, 1996; Howell, 1997a; Kurlychek et al., 1999; Lundman, 1993; Petersilia, 1997; Puzzanchera et al., 2000; Roberts, 1998; Rubin, 1998; Sherman et al., 1998; Snyder and Sickmund, 1999; Stahl, 2000.
2. *See* Abt Associates, 1994; Acoca, 1998; Smith, 1998; Snyder and Sickmund, 1999.
3. For overviews, see Clear, 1988; Funk, 1999; Le Blanc, 1998; Wiebush et al., 1995.
4. For overviews of the evaluation research, see Altschuler, 1998; Andrews et al., 1990; Bishop et al., 1996; Cullen and Applegate, 1997; Cullen, Wright, and Applegate, 1996; Fagan, 1995; Greenwood et al., 1996; Howell, 1997a; Howell et al., 1995; Krisberg et al., 1995; Krisberg and Howell, 1998; Lipsey, 1992; Lipsey and Wilson, 1998; Lundman, 1993; Schneider, 1990; Sherman et al., 1998. ✦

Does the Juvenile Justice System Discriminate Against Certain Groups in Its Efforts to Control Delinquency?

The juvenile justice system is not simply supposed to control delinquency; it is supposed to control delinquency in a *fair or just manner*. Among other things, that means that the system is supposed to treat similar offenders in similar ways. It is commonly charged, however, that the system discriminates against certain groups of people. This charge is perhaps most often made with respect to minority groups, but discrimination based on class and gender are also alleged. This section examines whether the juvenile justice system discriminates against minorities and, to a lesser extent, class and gender groups.[1]

Does the Juvenile Justice System Discriminate Against Blacks?

Most of the research on discrimination has focused on racial discrimination, particularly discrimination against blacks. There has been much less research on discrimination against other racial and ethnic groups (but that is starting to change). As a consequence, the discussion that follows focuses on blacks—but limited data indicate that groups such as Hispanics and Native Americans face discrimination as well.

As discussed in previous chapters, blacks are over represented in all aspects of the juvenile justice system. While blacks make up 15 percent of the juvenile population, they make up 26 percent of all juvenile arrests, 31 percent of all cases handled by the juvenile court, 44 percent of all delinquency cases involving detention, 40 percent of all confined juveniles, and 46 percent of all cases waived to adult court by judges (see Building Blocks For Youth, 2000; Snyder and Sickmund, 1999).

These data, however, do not prove that discrimination exists. That is, they do not prove that blacks are treated more severely than whites who commit similar offenses and have similar records. Perhaps the reason that blacks are over represented in the juvenile justice system is that they commit more delinquent acts and more serious delinquent acts than other groups. As indicated in Chapter 4, evidence suggests that blacks may be involved in more serious delinquency than whites, especially serious violence.

Most data, however, indicate that the overrepresentation of blacks in the juvenile justice system cannot be fully explained in terms of race differences in the extent and seriousness of delinquency. Rather, the data suggest that this overrepresentation is partly due to discrimination against blacks. A large number of studies have been done in this area, and *most* find evidence of racial discrimination.

The typical study focuses on a state or one or more counties within a state; it examines one or more decision points in the juvenile justice process, such as the decision to arrest a juvenile; to refer the juvenile to juvenile court; to formally process the juvenile; to detain the juvenile; or to place the juvenile in an institution. It is important to note that *discrimination can occur at any one of these points in the process*. The criminologist conducting the study will attempt to determine whether the race of the juvenile influences the decision that is made *after other relevant factors have been taken into account*. Virtually all studies, for example, take account of the seriousness of the juvenile's offense and the juvenile's prior record. So the criminologist will ask whether blacks are likely to be treated more severely than whites who have committed similar offenses and have similar records. For example, are blacks more likely to be arrested or detained or sent to an institution than similar whites?

Again, most studies—not all—find some evidence for discrimination against blacks. It is important to emphasize, however, that while most studies find evidence of racial discrimination, they also tend to find that the *most important* determinants of how someone is treated in the justice system are the seriousness of the offense and the person's prior record (although see the discussion of indirect discrimination below). If one looks at the data as a whole, there are several general conclusions that can be drawn with some confidence.

The Extent of Discrimination Varies Across Police Departments and Juvenile Courts

Some police departments and juvenile courts often discriminate against blacks while others do not seem to engage in direct or overt discrimination. This conclusion should not be too surprising. Police departments and juvenile courts differ from one another in many ways and exist in different community environments. It is reasonable to expect some differences in the extent of discrimination. This conclusion helps explain why studies examining discrimination sometimes produce contradictory results. While most studies find evidence of racial discrimination, some studies do not. The studies on discrimination usually examine different police departments and juvenile courts, so we would expect some difference in results.

Criminologists are starting to gain some idea of the factors that influence the extent of discrimination, although not much research has been done in this area. Some data, however, suggest that discrimination is *less* likely in highly professionalized police departments, where officers are well trained and supervised and are taught to "go by the book." Such departments tend to make a lot of arrests, but there is less discrimination in terms of who gets arrested (Wilson, 1976). Several studies have examined the factors that influence the extent of discrimination by juvenile courts (e.g., Bridges et al., 1995; Leiber and Stairs, 1999; Sampson and Laub, 1993b). For example, there is some evidence that discrimination may be more likely in rural areas, where the juvenile justice process is more informal and court workers often have more discretion.

The Extent of Discrimination May Vary by Type of Crime

There is also some evidence that discrimination may be greater for less serious crimes, where the police and court officials have more discretion over how to handle the cases. There is little question about whether to make an arrest when someone has committed homicide or armed robbery (although there may be race differences in the punishments imposed by the courts), but much discretion can be exercised when someone is caught using drugs or shoplifting. There is much evidence, in fact, for the existence of discrimination in the enforcement of drug laws. Blacks, in particular, have been especially hard hit by the "war on drugs" during the 1980s and 1990s. Blacks and whites use drugs at about the same rate overall, but black juveniles are several times more likely to be arrested for drug abuse violations than white juveniles (see Donziger, 1996; Tonry, 1995). This dramatic difference has occurred partly because the war on drugs has a special focus on crack cocaine. Crack is used more by blacks than whites. Powdered cocaine, however, is used more by whites.

Most Studies Find Some Evidence of Discrimination

While the extent of discrimination varies, most studies find evidence of discrimination. In some cases, studies find evidence *for small amounts of discrimination at several points in the juvenile justice process*. For example, it may be that blacks are slightly more likely to be arrested than whites, slightly more likely to be referred to juvenile court when arrested, slightly more likely to be detained, slightly more likely to have their cases formally processed, and slightly more likely to be sent to institutions. *These small amounts of discrimination add up*, however, *so that in the end we find that a much larger proportion of blacks than whites are confined in institutions*.

The fact that there may be small amounts of discrimination at several points in the justice process means that it is important for researchers to examine *all major decision points in the process*. Some researchers fail to do this. They focus on just one decision point, such as the decision to send adjudicated juveniles to institutions. They may find little or no evidence of discrimination at this point and conclude that discrimination is not a problem. But discrimination may have occurred at several other points in the process.

In other cases, researchers find evidence *for moderate and in a few cases large amounts of discrimination at certain points in the juvenile justice process*. A few studies, in particular, have found evidence of substantial discrimination by the police.[2] The police have much discretion over whether to make an arrest, and most suspected offenders are released. Likewise, they have much discretion over whether to refer arrested juveniles to court. Further, they must often make their decisions quickly and without much information. There is typically little review of the decisions they make, since their decisions are made in private and there is often no written record of their actions. The potential for discrimination is therefore high. One of the best studies in this area found that blacks were two to three times more likely to be arrested for Part I offenses than whites with similar levels of self-reported delinquency (Huizinga and Elliott, 1987).

Racial Discrimination May Be Direct or Indirect

Researchers examining discrimination usually try to determine whether blacks are treated more severely than *similar whites*. So a researcher may compare blacks and whites who are similar in terms of such variables as the seriousness of their offense, their prior record, their social class, their family status, and so on. The researcher usually includes a range of variables that influence arrest and treatment by the court. If blacks are treated more severely than *similar whites*, that is evidence for direct, or overt, discrimination. It suggests that the police or court officials may be racist, treating blacks more harshly solely because of their race. But what if the researcher finds that there is no difference in the way blacks and whites are treated. Does that mean that discrimination does not exist?

The answer is no. The researcher is comparing blacks and whites who are *similar to one another* on a range of variables that influence arrest and court processing. But in the real world, blacks and whites are *not similar* on many of these variables. Take family status as an example. Black juveniles are more likely to reside in single-parent homes than white juveniles, and some evidence suggests that juveniles from single-parent homes are more likely to be arrested and treated severely by the court. As a consequence, blacks are treated more severely than whites. This more severe treatment may not stem from direct or overt racial discrimination; blacks and whites who are similar in terms of family status may be treated the same. Rather, the discrimination occurs because race is associated with a variable that influences treatment by the police and courts—family status in this case. This is *indirect* discrimination. Blacks are treated more severely than whites not because of direct discrimination based on race but because *race is associated with other variables that influence treatment by the police and court*.

Let me give another example of indirect discrimination. While most blacks are *not* poor, blacks are *more likely* to be poor and to live in poor communities than whites. Some evidence suggests that individuals are more likely to be arrested and treated severely by the court if they are poor or live in poor communities. Among other things, the police may be more likely to patrol poor communities and to stop and question the people there, and the police and court officials may be more likely to discriminate against the poor juveniles they encounter. As a consequence of this association between race and poverty, blacks are more likely to be arrested and treated severely by the court. The more severe treatment in this case is not due directly to race but rather is due to the indirect effect of race. Race affects social class, which in turn affects treatment by the police and courts. Discrimination, then, may be direct or indirect. But the effect is the same in both cases: the overrepresentation of blacks in the juvenile justice system.

What Can Be Done to Address the Overrepresentation of Minorities in the Juvenile Justice System?

There has been some discussion about how to respond to the overrepresentation of minorities in the juvenile justice system. The federal government recently asked each state to determine whether minorities were over represented in its secure institutions—both detention centers and long-term institutions. Every state except one reported that minorities were over represented in their detention centers and every state reported that minorities were over represented in their long-term institutions (Building Blocks For Youth, 2000). The states must now determine the reasons for such overrepresentation and develop a plan to reduce it. States that fail to do this may lose some of their federal funding for delinquency control, so most states are complying with the federal government. Some evidence suggests that minority overrepresentation is partly due to the fact that minorities are more involved in delinquency, especially serious delinquency. Programs are currently being developed to reduce crime by minorities; many of these programs are similar to the prevention and rehabilitation programs discussed in Chapter 22 (see Welsh, Jenkins, and Harris, 1999, for an example of one promising program). And some evidence suggests that minority overrepresentation is due to direct and indirect discrimination against minorities. Programs are being developed to reduce such discrimination. Such programs include sensitivity training for police and court workers; closer monitoring of police and court decisions for fairness; developing more explicit guidelines for making decisions; and increasing the representation of minorities in the police and court systems. For further information, see Feyerherm (1995), Hsia and Hamparian (1998), and Leonard et al. (1995).

Does the Juvenile Justice System Discriminate Against the Poor and Against Males or Females?

There has been less research on class- and gender-based discrimination, and the research that has been done in these areas has produced somewhat contradictory results. Nevertheless, there are a few *tentative* conclusions one can draw.

Although the evidence is somewhat mixed, the data suggest that there is discrimination against lower-class juveniles in at least certain communities (e.g., Sampson, 1986b; Sealock and Simpson, 1998). Data suggest that both the *individual's* social class and the economic status of the *community* in which the individual lives may be important. In particular, the economic status of the community may have an important effect on the likelihood of arrest. The police may be more likely to patrol low-income communities, stop and question people in such communities, and arrest people from such communities. Also, juveniles in many lower-class communities are more likely to congregate on the street, where they are more visible to the police. The *individual's* social class, however, may have a larger effect on how juveniles are treated once they have been referred to juvenile court.

Data on gender suggest that males may be somewhat more likely to be arrested and treated severely for *serious* crimes than similar females who engage in such crimes. Among other things, it is argued that females are seen by the juvenile justice system as less of a threat than males. Some data, however, suggest that this attitude may be changing: serious female offenders have been treated more like serious male offenders in recent years. This new equality of treatment is especially true for females who do not conform to gender stereotypes (e.g., do not act submissive when confronted by the police). This change may partly account for the fact that female arrests for violence are increasing faster than male arrests. Females, however, are more likely to be arrested and treated severely for *many status offenses* than similar males who commit such offenses. This is especially true for offenses like running away from home and being incorrigible. It is argued that the police and court officials often associate these status offenses with sexual behavior or the possibility of sexual behavior on the part of females, and that they feel that it is necessary to more closely regulate the sexual behavior and "moral life" of females than males (see Chesney-Lind and Shelden, 1998, for an excellent discussion).

Summary

❖ ❖ ❖ ❖

This chapter's discussion has focused on race, class, and gender discrimination by the police and juvenile court and has concluded that there is some evidence for such discrimination. The variables of race, class, and gender, however, were examined in isolation from one another. A few recent studies indicate that researchers must consider these variables in combination with one another if we are to fully understand discrimination. For example, some data suggest that black females are treated more severely than white females by the court system (see Chesney-Lind and Shelden, 1998). Also, a recent study offers good reason to believe that the group most likely to experience discrimination is older juveniles who are male and black (Steffensmeier et al., 1998). Future research will likely focus on the joint effects of race, class, sex, and age, as well as attempts to reduce discrimination in the juvenile justice system.

Notes

1. For overviews and selected studies in this area, see Austin, 1995; Bridges and Steen, 1998; Building Blocks For Youth, 2000; Chesney-Lind and Shelden, 1998; Dannefer and Schutt, 1982; DeJong and Jackson, 1998; Donziger, 1996; Feld, 1995; Frazier and Bishop, 1995; Hsia and Hamparian, 1998; Huizinga and Elliott, 1987; Lauritsen and Sampson, 1998; Leiber and Stairs, 1999; Leonard and Sontheimer, 1995; Leonard et al., 1995; Miller, 1996; Piliavin and Briar, 1964; Pope and Feyerherm, 1993; Reiman, 1995; Sampson, 1986b; Sealock and Simpson, 1998; Snyder and Sickmund, 1999; Steffensmeier et al., 1998; Tonry, 1995; Walker et al., 1996; Zatz, 1987.
2. Dannefer and Schutt, 1982; Huizinga and Elliott, 1987; Sampson, 1986b; Wordes and Bynum, 1995. ✦

Deterrence and Incapacitation: Is It Possible to Control Delinquency by Punishing More Offenders and Punishing Them More Severely?

This chapter and the next examine four general strategies for controlling delinquency, strategies that involve the police, juvenile court, juvenile correctional agencies, and sometimes other organizations like schools and social service agencies. These strategies are deterrence, incapacitation, rehabilitation, and prevention. I focus on the "get-tough" strategies of deterrence and incapacitation in this chapter. These strategies now dominate the justice system's efforts to control delinquency. They are quite popular with politicians and most people in the general public. In particular, when politicians and people are asked what society should do to control delinquency, they often respond by saying that we need to "get tough" with juvenile offenders. We need to start punishing more offenders and start punishing them more severely, especially serious offenders. They claim that this strategy will deter many juveniles from engaging in delinquency. Juveniles who are not deterred can simply be locked up, or incapacitated, for a long time, so they cannot commit crimes on the street. The strategies of deterrence and incapacitation obviously involve efforts to increase *direct control by the juvenile justice system*. These strategies make much common sense and they appeal to our desire to punish individuals who commit serious crimes. But are these strategies effective in controlling delinquency? I consider the strategy of deterrence first, and then turn to incapacitation.

Is It Possible to Deter Delinquency by Increasing the Certainty and Severity of Punishment?

One major strategy for controlling delinquency is deterrence. The basic idea behind deterrence is simple: Society should punish more offenders and punish them more severely. This practice will deter *those who are punished* from committing delinquent acts, and it will deter *others* from committing delinquent acts, since they will come to realize that there is a good chance that they will also be caught and punished if they engage in delinquency.

The strategy of deterrence, then, involves increasing the *certainty* and/or the *severity* of punishment, that is, increasing the likelihood that offenders will be punished and increasing the severity of their punishment. Deterrence is based on the *fear of punishment*. If society increases the certainty and severity of punishment, it increases the fear of punishment, among both those who are punished and those who are *not* punished. It is this fear that deters juveniles from committing delinquent acts.[1]

The strategy of deterrence assumes that juveniles are rational to some extent. In particular, it assumes that they pay some attention to the costs of crime and that they are less likely to engage in crime when the costs are high. Increasing the certainty and severity of punishment raises the costs of crime and so should reduce the likelihood of crime among rational individuals.

This argument is compatible with control and social learning theories. If you recall, one of the major types of control is *direct control*. Direct control refers to the probability that your criminal acts will be detected and punished by others. The strategy of deterrence tries to increase one type of direct control—direct control by the juvenile justice system. People who advocate deterrence want to increase the likelihood that juvenile offenders will be caught by the police and will receive meaningful sanctions by the juvenile

❖ ❖ ❖ ❖

court. Advocates of deterrence usually pay less attention to direct control exercised by family members, friends, school officials, and others. They also pay less attention to other forms of social control, such as one's stake in conformity and internal control.

Social learning theorists argue that delinquency is less likely if it is punished. Again, advocates of deterrence focus on one type of punishment—punishment by the juvenile justice system. They pay less attention to the punishments administered by family members, friends, and others. Also, they do not focus on the other causes of crime in social learning theory, such as the reinforcements for crime, beliefs conducive to crime, and exposure to delinquent models.

Many of the efforts to control delinquency described in Chapters 18 and 19 are designed to *deter* delinquency. The police, for example, have developed several strategies designed to increase the likelihood that they will catch offenders (i.e., increase the certainty of punishment). And every state has made efforts to increase the severity of punishment for juvenile offenders, especially serious offenders. For example, most states have made it easier to try juvenile offenders as adults. In my home state of Georgia, officials made a video describing the more severe punishments that juvenile offenders might receive. This video was then shown to students throughout the state in a deliberate attempt to deter them from committing delinquent acts (more severe penalties cannot deter unless people are *aware* of these penalties).

The key question I want to address is whether efforts to increase the certainty and/or severity of punishment are an effective way to control delinquency. Some of the studies on deterrence focus on what is known as "specific deterrence," while others focus on "general deterrence."

Specific Deterrence

One of the central ideas of deterrence is that punishing juveniles or punishing them more severely reduces the delinquency of *those who are punished;* this is known as "specific deterrence." For example, if five students are caught cheating and are punished, these students should be less likely to cheat in the future.

Is there any evidence for specific deterrence? Do punishments by the juvenile justice system decrease the likelihood of delinquency among those who are punished? A number of studies have tried to determine whether increasing the *severity* of punishment reduces delinquency. These studies compare the subsequent delinquency of juveniles who receive *more severe* and *less severe* punishments. Also, a few studies have tried to determine whether juveniles *punished* by the juvenile justice system are less likely to engage in delinquency than similar juveniles who have *not been punished*.

As indicated in Chapter 19, most data suggest that *more severe* punishments are no more effective at reducing delinquency than *less severe* punishments. In fact, some studies suggest that more severe punishments may increase the likelihood of subsequent delinquency. Administering severe punishments to juveniles, then, does not appear to reduce their subsequent delinquency.

Are punished juveniles less likely to commit delinquent acts than juveniles who have not been punished by the juvenile justice system? Only a few studies have addressed this issue, and these studies are problematic. The ideal way to address this issue is to do a randomized experiment. For example, we might ask the police to flip a coin whenever they catch a juvenile offender. If the coin comes up "heads," they should release the offender. If it comes up "tails," they should arrest the offender and refer that person to juvenile court for punishment. We could then determine whether punished offenders have lower rates of subsequent delinquency than released offenders. If the punished offenders do have lower rates, that suggests that punishment does deter those who are punished. But as you might imagine, a study of this type has never been done.

A few studies, however, have compared arrested or convicted juveniles to comparable juveniles who have not been arrested or convicted. The two groups are usually comparable in terms of the offenses they have committed and sociodemographic characteristics like age, sex, race, and class. Since random assignment is not used, however, it may be that the two groups differ in important ways that researchers are not aware of. The results of these studies are mixed, but they tend to suggest that the arrested/convicted juveniles do *not* have lower rates of subsequent delinquency. Some studies, in fact, find that the arrested juveniles have *higher* rates of subsequent delinquency.[2] Overall, then, one may *tentatively* conclude that *formally* punishing offenders does not reduce their subsequent delinquency.

Why doesn't punishing offenders deter them from delinquency? There are at least four possible reasons why punishing offenders may not deter them from committing delinquent acts.

First, the juvenile justice system does not punish in an effective way. In order to be effective, punishments must be reasonably certain, swift, and meaningful—although not excessive (see Chapter 8 for a fuller discussion). But the certainty or likelihood of punishment is usually very low. As a consequence, punished offenders may feel that they can get away with crime in the future. In fact, some data suggest that punished offenders do *not* increase their estimates of the certainty of future punishment.[3] In addition, punishments are often delayed by several weeks or more, and the punishments that juveniles receive often involve little more than a "slap on the wrist." As indicated earlier, juveniles must often commit several offenses before they receive punishments beyond simple probation. While excessive punishments may be counterproductive (discussed later), juveniles must receive meaningful punishments if they are to be deterred from delinquency.

Second, many juveniles are not very responsive to punishment. Some have a low "stake in conformity," or little to lose by engaging in delinquency, so they are not very threatened by the prospect of punishment. Some are not very rational; that is, they do not give much thought to the possible costs of their delinquent acts. Rather, they are impulsive and often act without thinking about the consequences of their behavior (see Chapter 10). Further, many juveniles commit their offenses under the influence of drugs or alcohol or delinquent peers, which also reduces their concern for the costs of crime (see Chapter 15).

Third, there are several major causes for an individual's delinquency. Punishing a person for his or her delinquency does little to address these causes. For example, it usually does not reduce the strain that the offender may be experiencing or reduce the extent to which he or she learns crime from others. While punishment does increase one form of direct control, it usually does not increase all the other forms of control.

Fourth, punishments may sometimes backfire and *increase* the likelihood of subsequent crime. In particular, punishments may increase strain. Punishments that are excessive, overly harsh, or applied in a discriminatory manner may themselves create strain. Institutionalized offenders sometimes state that their imprisonment turned them into angry, vengeful individuals. Further, punishment may make it more difficult for individuals to achieve their goals and may increase the likelihood of negative treatment by others. As indicated in Chapter 16, individuals who are labeled delinquent through punishment often face negative treatment from others. Punishment may also reduce many types of social control and increase the social learning of crime. If you are confined in an institution, you are physically isolated from conventional others and forced to associate with other delinquents—who teach you to be a better delinquent. It is for this reason that institutions are sometimes referred to as "schools for crime." In addition, individuals who have been labeled delinquent through punishment often find that conventional others are reluctant to associate with them. Such individuals are isolated from conventional society, and they often find it easiest to associate with other delinquents. (For fuller discussions, see Chapters 16 and 19; Braithwaite, 1989; Sherman, 1993.)

Can we punish in an effective way? A number of criminologists argue that the effect of punishment on delinquency depends on the nature of the punishment and on who is punished. So while punished offenders *as a whole* may not reduce their subsequent delinquency, it may be that some punished offenders reduce their delinquency, while other punished offenders increase their delinquency. A few studies, conducted mostly with adults, provide some support for this argument.

Limited data suggest that punishment is likely to deter offenders from committing additional crimes under the following circumstances: (1) The likelihood of meaningful punishment is reasonably high (certain studies on police crackdowns, for example, demonstrate that it is possible to deter offenders from further crime when the probability of meaningful punishments is high); (2) the individuals who are punished have some concern for the costs of crimes (for example, they have a "stake in conformity," such as a decent job or close ties to their family members); (3) punishment is combined with treatment, so that some of the other causes of delinquency are addressed, and (4) steps are taken to minimize or counteract the negative effects of punishment (for example, efforts are made to punish in a fair, respectful manner and to reintegrate punished offenders back into conventional society.)[4]

Restorative justice. Some criminologists and policy makers have drawn on these and other arguments to advocate an alternative style of "punishment" known as "restorative justice." Restorative justice is a broad approach with a range of objectives, but one of its central objectives is to sanction offenders in a more effective manner. Advocates of restorative justice argue that it is important to hold delinquents accountable for their offenses and to impose meaningful sanctions on them. At the same time, they argue that such sanctions should not be excessive and should not isolate offenders from conventional society. Rather, such sanctions should allow offenders to repair the harm they have done, restore their ties with conventional others, and address at least certain of the causes of their delinquency.

The first step in the restorative justice process is to make offenders aware of the harm they have caused. In this connection, offenders often meet with the victims of their crime and hear first-hand accounts of how such victims have suffered. They may also meet with others in the community to discuss the harm they have caused. Offenders are then required to take action to repair the harm they have caused. The action that is taken is often determined in a mediation session involving the offender, the direct victim(s) of the crime, and sometimes others in the community. Among other things, the offender may issue an apology to the victim and other affected people, make financial restitution to the victim, perform personal services for the victim, and engage in community service. The offender is also obligated to take steps to make sure that no further crimes are committed. The steps may involve treatment, but advocates of restorative justice place great stress on involving offenders in positive community activities that increase their skills and ties to conventional others. The offender, for example, may perform community service, become a mentor to a younger child, and get involved in work activities. The offenders, then, repair the damage they have caused and rebuild their ties with the larger community. Many communities are now implementing aspects of the restorative justice approach, and the effectiveness of these efforts is being evaluated.[5]

Summary

For now, we can draw the following tentative conclusion: *Overall*, when the juvenile justice system punishes someone or punishes them more severely, that does not reduce their subsequent delinquency. It is probably the case, however, that *some* juveniles reduce their delinquency in response to punishment, and *some* juveniles increase their delinquency in response to punishment. Future research will better identify the factors that influence the effect of punishment. Such research is, of course, very important, since it may help the juvenile justice system to design punishments that are effective in controlling delinquency.

General Deterrence

Studies on *specific* deterrence ask whether punishment deters delinquency among *those who are punished*. Studies on *general* deterrence ask whether punishment deters delinquency among juveniles *in the general population*. In particular, it has been argued that punishment may deter delinquency among those *who are not punished*. For example, suppose five students are caught cheating and are punished. Their punishment may deter *other* students in the class from cheating, even though these other students were not punished. The nonoffending students may come to fear that they might be caught and punished if they cheat.

Numerous studies have tried to determine whether there is a general deterrent effect, that is, whether increasing the certainty and severity of punishment reduces crime in the general population. Some studies compare geographic areas that differ in terms of the certainty and/or severity of

❖ ❖ ❖ ❖

punishment. Usually states are compared, but sometimes cities or counties are compared. Certainty of punishment is usually measured in terms of the arrest rate; that is, the number of offenses known to the police that result in arrest. Severity is often measured in terms of the average length of prison sentence served for various crimes. These studies try to determine whether areas with a higher certainty and/or severity of punishment have lower crime rates.

Such studies, however, are only able to determine whether there is an *association* between the certainty and severity of punishment and crime rates. They cannot determine whether the certainty and severity of punishment have a *causal effect* on crime rates. For example, many of these studies find that areas with a high certainty of punishment have lower crime rates. But the association between certainty and crime rates may be due to third variables, like poverty. High levels of poverty may cause crime, on the one hand, and may lead to a low certainty of punishment, on the other. Areas high in poverty, for example, may have less money to spend on their police and so may have less efficient police forces. Also, the association between the certainty of punishment and crime rates may be due to the fact that crime rates affect the level of certainty. High rates of crime may overwhelm the police, reducing their ability to catch offenders and thereby lowering the certainty of punishment.

Researchers have tried to overcome these problems by taking account of third variables and doing longitudinal studies. In particular, researchers try to take account of third variables that may influence both the certainty/severity of punishment and crime rates. For example, they may examine the relationship between the certainty of punishment and crime rates in areas that have similar levels of poverty. Also, researchers do longitudinal studies that examine whether the certainty and severity of punishment at one point in time affect crime rates at a *subsequent* point in time. For example, they may examine whether areas that increase their certainty or severity of punishment are more likely to experience subsequent reductions in crime. In this area, several studies have examined the effectiveness of policies designed to crack down on drunk driving and drug sales.

These studies, however, have also been criticized. Criminologists argue that the studies assume that people are aware of the certainty and severity of punishment in the area where they live. Data, however, suggest that this assumption is often wrong. Many people have little idea of the true certainty and severity of punishment. (Do you know the certainty and severity of punishment for marijuana use in your hometown or state?) In particular, people who are law-abiding often greatly overestimate the certainty and severity of punishment.

Some criminologists argue, therefore, that the best way to determine whether people are deterred by the threat of punishment is to ask them to estimate the certainty and severity of punishment. In particular, ask them to estimate the likelihood that they will be punished if they commit a particular offense and ask them what their punishment will be. If people are deterred by the threat of punishment, their estimate of the certainty and severity of punishment should have an effect on their level of crime. So people who state that they will be caught and severely punished if they engage in crime should be less likely to engage in crime.

A number of studies have been done in this area. For example, students are asked to estimate the likelihood that they will be caught by the police if they use marijuana, and they are asked what punishment they would probably receive if caught. The responses to these questions allow researchers to measure the students' perceptions about the certainty and severity of punishment. The researchers then determine whether these perceptions are related to delinquency. The more recent and better studies are longitudinal in nature and they take account of third variables. So researchers compare the subsequent offending of similar juveniles who differ in terms of their perceived certainty and severity of punishment. If deterrence works, the juveniles who believe they will definitely receive severe punishments should have lower levels of subsequent delinquency.

Thus, a range of studies has tried to determine whether the certainty and severity of punishment are related to crime in the general population. These studies do not always agree with one another, but the more recent and best research offers a few *tentative* conclusions.[6]

Most notably, increasing the *certainty* of punishment may reduce crime by a moderate amount in some circumstances. The certainty of punishment, however, is only one of many factors influencing the level of crime. And the certainty of punishment is less important than other factors, such as the individual's beliefs regarding delinquency and the threat of informal punishment from family members and others. The severity of punishment is less important than the certainty of punishment. Most studies suggest that changes in the severity of punishment have little or no effect on delinquency, although certain studies suggest that increasing the severity of punishment may reduce delinquency *if the certainty of punishment is high*.

As indicated, the certainty of punishment reduces delinquency in *some* circumstances. Limited research suggests that the effect of punishment is short-lived and is confined to the specific geographic area in which the punishment is administered. Punishments administered a year earlier therefore have little or no effect on current levels of delinquency. (Likewise, individuals' perception of the certainty of punishment a year earlier often has little effect on their current delinquency.) Also, punishments administered outside one's community appear to have little deterrent effect. This makes sense: People are most responsive to recent punishments administered in their communities. Finally, some data suggest that punishments must be reasonably certain if potential offenders are to be deterred. A few studies estimate that the probability of punishment needs to be above 30 to 40 percent if potential offenders are to be deterred, although more research is needed in this area.

Increasing the certainty of punishment, then, may cause a moderate reduction in delinquency in the general population, although this effect tends to be short-lived and confined to the immediate area where the certainty is increased. And it may be that society has to substantially increase the certainty of punishment before one can observe an effect on crime. This is something that is not easily done. Among other things, it typically involves hiring more police and changing the way that they function (see Chapter 18). Increasing the severity of punishment appears to have little or no impact on delinquency, unless, perhaps, the certainty of punishment is high.

Unfortunately, many politicians simply increase the severity of punishment. That is, they pass legislation that increases the penalties for various crimes. This is easy to do and may win them votes, but it is doubtful whether it has much of an effect on rates of delinquency. It is possible, however, to increase the certainty of punishment and perhaps have something of an effect on delinquency rates. The discussion of police crackdowns in Chapter 18 describes how this may be done. As you may recall, the evidence suggests that police crackdowns do result in a moderate reduction in crime in the immediate area where they are instituted. The effect of the crackdowns is typically short-lived, with crime returning to its former level soon after the crackdowns end. But a strategy of "rotating crackdowns" (discussed earlier) has the potential for reducing crime over the long term (also see the excellent discussion in Kleiman, 1999).

Summary

Increasing the certainty of punishment may reduce delinquency by a moderate amount in the general population, but increasing the certainty of punishment should not be society's only or even major delinquency control strategy. It is not easy to increase the certainty of punishment, and the effect on delinquency is often not large. This result is not surprising, since increasing the certainty of punishment only addresses one of the many causes of crime: direct control. We should also employ strategies that address the other causes of crime.

Will Locking Up Delinquents Reduce Delinquency?

Deterrence is based on the fear of punishment. Increasing the certainty and severity of punishment is supposed to increase the fear of punishment and thereby deter people from committing crime. As indicated above, however, it is often difficult to deter juveniles from committing crimes—both juveniles who have been punished and those in the general population. Partly as a consequence, many people have come to recommend another "get-tough" approach to controlling delinquency. They argue that we should lock up serious and high-rate juvenile offenders for long periods. This strategy, they claim, will substantially reduce crime. The reason is simple: If you lock up juveniles, they cannot commit crimes on the street. Crime is therefore reduced—*even if no one is deterred from committing crime*. This delinquency-control strategy is known as incapacitation.[7]

Incapacitation has become the major strategy in the United States for controlling *adult* crime. The number of adults held in prisons in the United States increased from 200,000 in 1971 to over 1,200,000 in 1998, and the *rate* of incarceration has more than quadrupled during this time. Society is sending many more adults to prison and confining them for longer periods. The average length of confinement for a violent crime, for example, has more than tripled since 1975. The primary reason for this dramatic increase in incarceration rates is the belief that it will reduce crime. Again, locking up criminals prevents them from committing crimes on the streets.

Incapacitation is not the major strategy for controlling *juvenile delinquency*, but it is an important strategy and there is reason to believe that it will become more important in the years ahead. As discussed in Chapter 19, there has been a movement to increase the number of juveniles sent to institutions and to increase the length of time they serve in such institutions. Many states have passed laws that make it easier for juvenile court judges to confine juveniles, that increase the length of time juveniles can be confined, and that mandate confinement for certain crimes. Although these laws are partly designed to *deter* delinquency, they are also partly motivated by a desire to protect society by getting serious offenders off the street. Also, most states have passed laws making it easier to try juvenile offenders as adults. Juveniles tried in adult court are subject to long prison sentences.

How Can One Determine How Much Crime Incapacitation Prevents?

The strategy of incapacitation makes much common sense: If you lock people up, you prevent crime on the streets. But how do criminologists go about determining just how much crime is prevented? On the face of it, it seems as if it should be easy to calculate the amount of crime prevented through incapacitation. One simply estimates how many crimes incarcerated offenders commit each year when they are free. This estimation can be done by surveying such offenders or examining their arrest records, although there are, of course, concerns about the accuracy of such estimates (see Zimring and Hawkins, 1997). Such estimates, then, can be used to determine how many crimes are prevented by locking up criminals.

For example, suppose researchers find that the average juvenile in a training school commits ten crimes per year when free. And suppose that 50,000 juveniles are in training schools. Incarceration, then, prevents 500,000 offenses per year (10 multiplied by 50,000). If society incarcerates an additional 50,000 offenders, it might prevent another 500,000 crimes. Estimates of this sort were offered during the 1970s, when incapacitation was becoming a popular crime-control strategy. Several researchers claimed that incapacitating offenders prevents a large amount of crime and that incapacitating additional offenders will prevent much more crime.

It turns out that such claims were exaggerated. Assume that researchers obtain accurate estimates of the number of crimes incarcerated offenders commit each year when free. For example, suppose they determine that the average incarcerated offender commits ten crimes per year when free. One might then conclude that locking an offender up prevents ten crimes per year. But this conclusion is not necessarily correct.

First, it may be that when society locks up one offender, another criminal takes that offender's place. So if we lock up someone for selling drugs on a street corner, someone else may start selling drugs on the same corner the next day. As a result, no crime is prevented. This phenomenon is known as a substitution effect. It is difficult to estimate how much substitution occurs; it may be high for certain crimes like drug selling but low for other crimes like robbery.

Second, we know that most juvenile offenses are committed in groups. Locking up one juvenile in the group may have little or no effect on the amount of crime committed by the group. Once again, there is no reduction in crime. This is known as a group effect. Again, it is difficult to estimate the size of this effect.

Third, many juvenile offenders substantially reduce their level of offending toward the end of adolescence. This phenomenon, sometimes referred to as "maturing" out of delinquency, occurs as juveniles leave their delinquent peers, get jobs or enter college, and form families of their own. Imprisoning such juveniles for long periods would not prevent a large amount of crime since these juveniles would have stopped committing crimes on their own.

Fourth, estimates about the effect of locking up *additional* offenders may be exaggerated because these additional offenders may not commit as much crime as the offenders who are already locked up. That is, the offenders who are *already locked up* may commit more crimes per year when free than *those who are not locked up;* high-rate offenders are probably more likely to be in prison than low-rate offenders. As a result, locking up *additional* offenders may not prevent as many crimes as one would estimate, since these additional offenders commit crimes at a lower rate.

It is therefore difficult to estimate the amount of crime that is prevented through incapacitation and the amount of crime that *will be prevented* by incapacitating *additional* juveniles. Nevertheless, there have been several efforts to estimate the effectiveness of incapacitation as a crime-control strategy. Some of these estimates are based on studies that attempt to determine the number of crimes offenders commit each year when free. Such estimates are then used to calculate the amount of crime prevented by incapacitation. As indicated, however, there are serious problems with this strategy: it likely exaggerates the size of the incapacitation effect. As a consequence, some researchers have employed alternative strategies.

In particular, some researchers compare states or other areas that have different rates of incarceration. The objective is to determine whether areas with high rates of incarceration have lower crime rates. However, one must take account of all the other factors that affect crime rates—something that is not easy to do. Also, it is possible that any association between incarceration rates and crime rates is due to the effect of crime rates on incarceration rates. For example, high rates of crime may overwhelm the criminal justice system and lead to low rates of incarceration.

Other researchers examine incarceration rates and crime rates *in the same area over time*. The objective is to determine whether changes in the incarceration rate are associated with changes in the crime rate. For example, what impact has the massive increase in incarceration rates in recent decades had on crime rates? Such studies, however, must also take account of the other factors that might affect the crime rate.

What Is the Impact of Incapacitation on Crime Rates?

None of the types of studies just discussed is problem free. Taken together, however, they give us a rough sense of the effectiveness of incapacitation as a crime-control strategy. Most studies have focused on adults and they have examined the massive increase in incarceration since the 1970s. The best studies suggest that this increase in incarceration has had a *modest effect* on crime rates, particularly on rates of property crime like burglary and larceny. Offenders often engage in these crimes at a high rate, so locking up offenders has a larger effect on the number of these crimes than on the number of violent crimes.

To illustrate, one recent study examined the effect of California's massive increase in imprisonment during the 1980s. California's prison population quadrupled during this time. The researchers estimate that this increase in imprisonment reduced the total number of offenses that would otherwise have occurred by 15 percent—with most of the reduction in the area of burglaries and larcenies (Zimring and Hawkins, 1995). Further, there are reasons to believe that this estimate may be on the high side.

These studies, as indicated, are based largely on adults. It is not clear to what extent their findings apply to juveniles. On the one hand, juveniles are more likely to offend in groups, so incapacitation may have a smaller effect on juvenile crime rates. Also, juveniles who are incarcerated will eventually be released. If incarceration increases their level of subsequent offending, the benefits of incarceration may be lost. Some data suggest that this is the case with trying juveniles as adults. We prevent some crime by confining these juveniles, but these juveniles offend at higher rates when released, which more than wipes out the benefits of confinement. On the other hand, a larger portion of juveniles than adults offend at high rates. Further, the juvenile incarceration rate is now lower than the adult rate. So there are proportionately more high-rate juvenile offenders on the street than high-rate adult offenders. As a consequence, incapacitation may hold more potential for crime reduction among juveniles. This area is clearly in need of more research. But for now, we may cautiously conclude that the effect of incapacitation on juvenile crime rates is likely to be modest.

Is It Possible to Better Identify the High-Rate Offenders and Just Confine Them?

Juveniles who commit serious offenses or have long records are the most likely to be confined. At the same time, no one would deny that many high-rate offenders escape confinement and that many low-rate offenders are confined. Some individuals argue that we should try to *better distinguish* between juveniles who are likely to offend at high rates in the future and those likely to offend at low rates. Once such a distinction is made, we should confine only the high-rate offenders or we should confine them for longer periods. This strategy of *selective incapacitation* will allow the system to achieve a larger incapacitation effect.

It is difficult, however, for juvenile justice officials to accurately distinguish high-rate from low-rate offenders. You might think that the high-rate offenders are simply the juveniles with the longest arrest records. But many juveniles with extensive arrest records are not high-rate offenders—they are simply inept offenders. They do not commit that many crimes; they just get caught a lot. Further, most high-rate offenders do not have extensive arrest records. Dunford and Elliott (1984), for example, found that only 19 percent of the juveniles who self-reported over 200 offenses during a two-year period were arrested.

Several efforts have been made to develop techniques for distinguishing high-rate from low-rate offenders. These techniques do improve our ability to distinguish between offenders by a modest amount, but they are still very inaccurate (see Auerhahn, 1999; Gottfredson and Gottfredson, 1994). Many of the individuals predicted to be high-rate offenders turn out to be low-rate offenders. And some of the individuals predicted to be low-rate offenders turn out to be high-rate offenders.

Also, there are ethical issues to consider. For example, an individual predicted to be a high-rate offender might be confined for a much longer period than another individual predicted to be a low-rate offender, even though both committed the same offense. Do you think it is appropriate to base a juvenile's punishment on the number of crimes he or she *might* commit in the future— rather than simply on the crimes they have already committed?

Summary

Overall, one can tentatively conclude that the strategy of incapacitating serious and high-rate juvenile offenders prevents a modest amount of crime. Confining additional offenders will prevent more crime, but the reductions in crime are likely to be modest as well. The reasons for this are twofold. We are able to incapacitate only a small portion of all juvenile offenders, even high-rate offenders. And the crime reduction that does result from such incapacitation is not as large as was originally thought, for reasons indicated (e.g., substitution effect, group effect).

In addition, incapacitation carries a heavy price tag. It is expensive to maintain the juvenile institutions that we now have, and it will be expensive to build and maintain additional institutions. Some argue that incapacitation more than pays for itself in terms of the crime it prevents, although there is much debate here. Also, some data suggest that alternatives to incapacitation, such as prevention and rehabilitation programs, may be more cost-effective than incapacitation. Further, many commentators have pointed to the devastating effect that incapacitation has on both the people who are locked up and the larger community—with special note being made of the negative effect of incapacitation on the black community (see Tonry, 1995). Finally, incapacitation does not address the causes of crime. It isolates offenders from society but does not attempt to reform those offenders or deal with the conditions that prompt offending in the first place.

This is not to discount incapacitation. No one would deny that there are dangerous offenders who need confinement. And no one would deny that such confinement protects society by preventing such individuals from committing crimes on the street. But incapacitation should not be our sole or even major strategy for responding to delinquency. While certain offenders should be confined, more effort can be made to rehabilitate them during their confinement. And much more can be done to rehabilitate offenders in the community and to prevent delinquency from occurring in the first place. The strategies of rehabilitation and prevention are addressed next.

Notes

1. For overviews of the deterrence literature, see Akers, 1997; Krohn, 2000; Nagin, 1998a, 1998b; Paternoster, 1987; Rutter et al., 1998; Schneider, 1990; Sherman et al., 1998; Williams and Hawkins, 1986; Wright, R., 1994.
2. *See* Browning and Huizinga, 1999; Farrington, 1977; Farrington et al., 1978; Gold and Williams, 1969; Huizinga et al., 1998; Paternoster and Piquero, 1995; Schneider, 1990; Sherman, 1993; Sherman et al., 1998; Wolfgang et al., 1972.
3. *See* Bridges and Stone, 1986; Paternoster and Piquero, 1995; Piquero and Paternoster, 1998; Schneider, 1990.
4. For fuller discussions, see Braithwaite, 1989; Nagin and Paternoster, 1994; Sherman, 1993; Sherman et al., 1992, 1998.
5. For fuller discussions of the philosophy and practice of restorative justice, see Bazemore and Umbreit, 1994; Office of Juvenile Justice and Delinquency Prevention, 1998a; also see Levrant et al., 1999.
6. *See* Chamlin, 1991; Chamlin et al., 1992; Foglia, 1997; Grasmick and Bursik, 1990; Klepper and Nagin, 1989; Nagin and Paternoster, 1991, 1994; Paternoster and Piquero, 1995; Sherman et al., 1992; Yu and Liska, 1993.
7. For overviews, see Auerhahn, 1999; Blumstein, 1998; Currie, 1998; Nagin, 1998b; Sherman et al., 1998; Visher, 2000; Walker, 1998; Wright, R., 1994; Zimring and Hawkins, 1995. ✦

Prevention and Rehabilitation: Is It Possible to Prevent Delinquency and to Rehabilitate Delinquents?

❖ ❖ ❖ ❖   The strategy of deterrence tries to reduce delinquency by threatening juveniles with punishment by the juvenile justice system. The strategy of incapacitation tries to reduce delinquency by locking delinquents up, so they cannot commit crimes on the street. In both cases, the focus is on one type of *direct control:* direct control by the juvenile justice system. These two strategies have come to dominate the juvenile justice system in recent years. As indicated above, however, these strategies are likely to have only a moderate effect on the amount of delinquency. This result is not surprising, since they neglect all the other causes of delinquency. Many criminologists and others are now arguing that society should place an increased emphasis on two additional strategies for reducing delinquency: prevention and rehabilitation.

Prevention and rehabilitation do *not* try to reduce delinquency by increasing direct control by the juvenile justice system. Rather, they try to stop or reduce delinquency by focusing on the other causes of delinquency. At the most general level, the more effective prevention and rehabilitation programs attempt to increase the other types of control, reduce strain or the tendency to respond to strain with crime, and/or reduce the social learning of crime. At a more specific level, they try to do such things as alter the individual traits that contribute to crime, increase family bonding, improve parental supervision and discipline, reduce family conflict and abuse, increase school attachment and performance, and reduce association with delinquent peers and gangs.

Prevention programs are distinguished from rehabilitation programs in the following way. Prevention programs try to prevent juveniles from becoming delinquent in the first place; rehabilitation programs try to reduce the delinquency of juveniles who already are delinquent. Some prevention programs focus on *all or most* juveniles. For example, the federal government is now sponsoring a major advertising campaign that is partly designed to convince juveniles that drug use is both wrong and harmful. You may have seen or heard some of these ads or ads from earlier campaigns ("just say no," "this is your brain on drugs"). Other prevention programs target juveniles believed to be *at risk* for engaging in delinquency. For example, they may target low-birthweight infants, juveniles in high-crime communities, or juveniles whose teachers or parents say they are at risk for delinquency. Prevention and rehabilitation programs are sometimes discussed separately, but I discuss them together because many of the same programs are used for both prevention and rehabilitation purposes.

This chapter is in three parts. I begin with a brief history of prevention and rehabilitation programs. I then discuss the effectiveness of prevention/rehabilitation programs and describe the *general* features of the most successful programs. Finally, I describe the characteristics of successful prevention and rehabilitation programs that focus on the early family environment, parent training, the school, individual traits, and delinquent peer groups and gangs. Most prevention and rehabilitation programs focus on these areas. I also briefly discuss programs in other areas. As you will see, the most successful prevention and rehabilitation programs address many of the causes of delinquency discussed in Chapters 6 through 16.[1]

A Brief History of Prevention and Rehabilitation

Prevention programs have never played a major role in delinquency control efforts, except for a brief period in the 1960s and early 1970s during the heyday of the "War on Poverty" (see Sherman et al., 1998). The War on Poverty was initiated by President Kennedy in the early 1960s and largely implemented by his successor, President Johnson. One of the purposes of the War on Poverty was to reduce crime and delinquency by increasing the opportunities for people to achieve success through legitimate channels. Some of the programs that made up the War on Poverty provided educational assistance and job training to juveniles in disadvantaged communities. The War on Poverty, then, was partly based on strain theory, which views the failure to achieve monetary success as a major cause of crime. Most of the programs that were part of the War on Poverty have since been dismantled, but a few remain, like Project Headstart and Job Corps.

You might wonder why prevention does not play a greater role in society's efforts to control delinquency. Prevention seems to make a lot of sense; it seems better to prevent delinquency from developing in the first place than to react to delinquency after it occurs. But several objections have been raised to prevention programs: They are said to interfere in the private affairs of individuals and families (e.g., "It is none of the government's business how parents raise their children"—unless the parents or children engage in illegal behavior). They are said to be costly and ineffective. Conservatives often point to the fact that crime and delinquency rates increased dramatically during the 1960s and early 1970s, at the very time that the War on Poverty was being mounted (data on the effectiveness of the War on Poverty are mixed; see Empey et al., 1999). Finally, prevention programs are at odds with the current "get tough" approach to controlling delinquency, which claims that offenders are responsible for their behavior and deserve punishment. Politicians who advocate prevention programs expose themselves to charges of being "soft on crime."

Although prevention has played only a small role in delinquency control in the United States, rehabilitation was the guiding philosophy of the juvenile justice system from its inception in the 1800s until the 1970s. That does not mean that the juvenile justice system made a serious effort at rehabilitation; there was often a large gap between philosophy and practice. But the major *goal* of the juvenile justice system was said to be the rehabilitation of delinquents. And rehabilitation is still part of the guiding philosophy of the juvenile justice system, although "get-tough" approaches have become increasingly popular.

Rehabilitation fell out of favor during the 1970s for several reasons. Rising crime rates during the 1960s and early 1970s caused many to question its effectiveness. These doubts about rehabilitation were reinforced by several studies in the 1970s and 1980s that claimed rehabilitation was largely ineffective. The best known of these studies, the "Martinson Report," examined a wide range of rehabilitation programs employed from 1945 to 1967. The report came to the conclusion that "with few and isolated exceptions the rehabilitative efforts that have been reported so far have had no appreciable effect on recidivism" (Martinson, 1974:25). Finally, the political climate of the country became more conservative. Criminals, including older delinquents, were said to be responsible for their behavior. And politicians and others argued that such individuals deserved punishment and that punishment was the best way to reduce crime and delinquency. In particular, punishment would reduce crime through deterrence and incapacitation.

❖ ❖ ❖ ❖   The past few years, however, have seen a renewed interest in prevention and rehabilitation, especially on the part of many criminologists and, increasingly, on the part of the federal government and certain states. The federal strategy for controlling delinquency now emphasizes both punishment (as described above) and an increased emphasis on prevention and rehabilitation. The federal government has done much to publicize the prevention and rehabilitation programs that show promise. The web site for the Office of Juvenile Justice and Delinquency Prevention (OJJDP) contains much information on prevention and rehabilitation programs, including a number of publications that you can download (*http://ojjdp.ncjrs.org*). One federal publication is titled simply *Delinquency Prevention Works* (Office of Juvenile Justice and Delinquency Prevention, 1995). Also, the OJJDP has formed a partnership with several groups to publicize the programs—including prevention and rehabilitation programs—that are effective (Ingersoll, 1999).

This renewed interest in prevention and rehabilitation stems partly from recent research suggesting that *some* prevention and rehabilitation programs are effective at reducing delinquency; this research is discussed in the next section. This renewed interest also stems from recent research suggesting that deterrence and incapacitation have only a moderate effect on crime. The massive increase in imprisonment in recent decades has not had the large impact on crime rates that many people anticipated. The United States has more than quadrupled its rate of imprisonment in the last twenty-five years, but crime rates are about the same as they were twenty-five years ago—although they have fluctuated somewhat over this period (Blumstein, 1998). Further, the rapid increase in imprisonment has come with high financial and social costs (see Currie, 1998; Tonry, 1995). As a result, many individuals are starting to look at additional strategies for controlling delinquency, including prevention and rehabilitation.

How Effective Are Prevention and Rehabilitation Programs?

Several researchers have recently reviewed the evaluations of prevention and rehabilitation programs. In one case, 443 evaluations were reviewed (Lipsey, 1992). All of these reviewers faced a major problem; most prevention and rehabilitation programs were not properly evaluated. That is, researchers did not employ the procedures for evaluation research described in Chapter 17. Most commonly, they did not *randomly* assign juveniles to the treatment and control groups. The evaluations also frequently suffer from other problems, such as high dropout rates from the treatment group, a failure to conduct long-term follow-ups, and a failure to examine how well the program was implemented. Further, many of the decent evaluations that have been done are in need of replication. As noted in Chapter 17, programs should be evaluated across different settings and populations. A program that works well in one setting or with one group of juveniles may not work well in another setting or with another group. As a result of these problems, criminologists know much less about the effectiveness of prevention and rehabilitation programs than they would like. Virtually every review of prevention and rehabilitation programs stresses the need for more and better evaluation research.

At the same time, there have been enough moderately well-done evaluations to allow us to draw some tentative conclusions about the effectiveness of prevention and rehabilitation programs. The reviews suggest that *well-designed and well-implemented* prevention and rehabilitation programs can reduce rates of delinquency anywhere from 20 percent to 50 percent.[2] These estimates vary because different reviews look at different programs and employ different definitions of "well-designed" programs. But the evidence is sufficient to suggest that prevention and rehabilitation programs have an important role to play in efforts to control delinquency. As criminologists learn more about the characteristics of effective programs and how to best implement them, the role of prevention and rehabilitation will likely increase. This is not to say that prevention and rehabilitation programs will solve the delinquency problem in the immediate future. But it is to say that society should make greater use of such programs—along with well-designed efforts to deter delinquency and incapacitate serious offenders. This strategy is precisely the one that the federal government is now advocating.

General Characteristics of Effective Prevention and Rehabilitation Programs

It is important to emphasize that the reviews cited in the preceding section find that only *some* prevention and rehabilitation programs are effective at reducing delinquency; other programs have little effect on delinquency or actually increase delinquency. For example, some evaluations suggest that group discussions involving delinquent and conventional juveniles are counterproductive. The conventional juveniles are supposed to influence the delinquents in positive ways, but often the reverse occurs.

Criminologists now have a rough idea of what characteristics distinguish effective from ineffective programs. Such information, of course, is vital if society is to effectively control delinquency. Many individuals and groups are unaware of this information, and they continue to invest resources in programs that are likely to have little effect on delinquency. Drawing on several reviews, we can *tentatively* state that the most effective prevention and rehabilitation programs have the following characteristics:

1. *Focus on the major causes of delinquency in the group being treated.* This may sound obvious, but many prevention and rehabilitation programs focus on factors that are not causes, or at least not important causes, of delinquency. For example, they try to increase the juvenile's level of self-esteem. Other programs have no clear focus. Many programs, for example, employ unstructured counseling sessions. Counselors frequently hold "rap sessions" with juveniles where they discuss a wide range of issues. These types of programs have little effect on delinquency. In order for a program to be effective, it must address the causes of delinquency described in earlier chapters, such as individual traits, family and school characteristics, and association with delinquent peers.

Further, programs should attempt to target the causes of delinquency that are most relevant to the group being treated. For example, it makes little sense to target hyperactivity in a group where the rate of hyperactivity is low. Programs should also attempt to target all or most of the major causes of delinquency in a group. Delinquency is usually caused by several factors. Programs that focus only on one factor, even if it is an important cause of delinquency, will be less effective.

2. *Are intensive.* The most effective programs usually last a long time and employ several techniques to influence the juvenile or group. One cannot change a juvenile's traits or alter a juvenile's social environment in a short period of time with minimal effort. For example, you cannot change the juvenile's level of irritability in a single counseling session. Likewise, you cannot change the way that family members relate to one another by simply giving parents a pamphlet to read over the weekend. Individual traits and interactional patterns have developed over many years, and they can be resistant to change. The most effective programs, then, tend to be the most intensive.

Many programs that try to change the behavior of individuals employ the following strategy, sometimes referred to as the *cognitive-behavioral approach*. First, instructors *describe* what they want the juvenile (or parent, etc.) to do. For example, they might tell the juvenile that he or she should employ a particular anger-management technique when mad at others. The technique and its use are described in detail. The juvenile may also be given reading material on the technique. Second, the instructors display or *model* what it is that they want the juvenile to do; they may stage several situations in which someone gets angry and then uses the technique. Third, they get the juvenile to *practice* the technique, so juveniles may participate in a number of role-playing situations: someone pretends to anger the juvenile and the juvenile then employs the anger-management technique. The instructors provide the juvenile with feedback, taking special care to reinforce successful performances. Fourth, the juvenile begins to *apply* the technique to situations in the "real world." The juvenile might be asked to use the anger management technique the next time someone makes him or her angry. After reporting the "real world" outcome and receiving feedback, the juvenile applies the technique to additional "real world" situations. Still more feedback and reinforcement are provided. Fifth, the juvenile reaches a point where regular instruction is no longer necessary. But the instructors are available for consultation if necessary, and the juvenile may periodically participate in *refresher or booster courses*. Influencing individuals and groups, then, is not an easy process. You should be suspicious if you hear someone claim that a program can reduce delinquency in a short period of time with minimal effort.

The fact that the most successful programs are intensive poses some problems for policy makers. It raises the cost of such programs, although most good programs are cost-effective, saving more money than they cost over the long run. Also, the intensive nature of many prevention and rehabilitation programs makes it difficult to implement them on a large scale. Most programs have been implemented in small groups, where it is easier to ensure that they are properly run. It is more difficult to ensure that programs are properly run if they are implemented at many sites with many thousands of juveniles. The large-scale implementation of good prevention and rehabilitation programs, in fact, is perhaps the major challenge facing policy makers (beyond securing support for such programs).

3. *Focus on juveniles at high risk for subsequent delinquency.* Juveniles at high risk for delinquency are the ones who can benefit the most from prevention and rehabilitation programs, and programs focusing on such juveniles achieve the greatest reductions in subsequent delinquency. It makes little sense to provide programs to juveniles at low risk for delinquency; such juveniles will likely refrain from delinquency whether they participate in prevention/rehabilitation programs or not.

4. *Begin early.* Some data suggest that it is easier to reduce subsequent delinquency if intervention begins at an early age, before the traits and interactional patterns that contribute to delinquency have become firmly established. Also, problems that develop early in life often have a "snowball effect"; that is, they lead to additional problems as the juvenile ages. For example, juveniles who are hyperactive often encounter problems with their family and at school. As a result, they may become alienated from both family and school. They may eventually come to associate with delinquent peers as a result. They may then start engaging in delinquency, which leads to further problems with family and school and to an increased association with delinquent peers (see Thornberry et al., 1995). It is easier to intervene at an early age before problems like hyperactivity lead to these additional problems. The juvenile justice system can still help older juveniles, but some evidence suggests that it is easier to influence younger juveniles.

5. *When they are run in the community.* Some data suggest that programs may be slightly more effective when they are run in the community rather than in juvenile institutions. It is easy to think of reasons why this might be the case. Juveniles confined in institutions are cut off from the larger community, including family, school, peer group, and neighborhood. As a result, it is more difficult for rehabilitation programs to address the family, school, and other problems that cause delinquency. Further, juveniles confined in institutions are exposed to other delinquents on a regular and intimate basis. These other delinquents often encourage delinquency and discourage cooperation with the staff. The staff, in fact, are often defined as the "enemy." Rehabilitation is obviously difficult under such circumstances. Finally, juveniles in institutions are often preoccupied with the stresses of confinement, including the threat of physical and sexual assault from others. These circumstances also make rehabilitation difficult. It is possible to help juveniles in institutions, but it may be somewhat more difficult to do so.

6. *Have a warm but firm relationship between counselors and juveniles.* Some evidence suggests that programs are more effective

when counselors establish a warm or close relationship with the juveniles, and when they strongly discourage deviant behavior while encouraging conventional behavior. A close bond between counselors and juveniles reduces strain. Also, the juveniles are more likely to model the counselors' behavior, accept their beliefs, and respond to their sanctions. At the same time, it is important that the counselors clearly promote conventional behavior and condemn deviance. The counselors cannot be lax or let the juveniles take advantage of them. I should note that the importance of being "warm but firm" was also emphasized in the context of the family and school.

What Are the Characteristics of Successful Prevention/Rehabilitation Programs in Different Areas?

Many programs have shown some success at preventing delinquency and rehabilitating delinquents. It is impossible to describe all these programs in this short book, but this section describes the key features of programs in several areas: programs focusing on the early family environment, parent training, the school, individual traits, and delinquent peers and gangs. In addition, I provide a brief overview of programs in other areas. These programs all address one or more of the causes of delinquency described in earlier chapters.

A few words of caution are in order, however, before I present the program descriptions. First, many different programs have been employed in each of the areas cited. Rather than describing these individual programs, I describe what I believe are the key features of successful programs in an area. Many of the individual programs contain only some of these key features. Second, while the evaluation research provides reason to believe that these programs can reduce delinquency, more and better research is needed. In certain cases, my conclusions are based on a small number of less-than-ideal evaluations. Third, while I describe the programs in each area separately from one another, these programs are sometimes combined in the real world. As indicated above, the most effective way to prevent delinquency or rehabilitate delinquents is to combine several programs so as to address the multiple causes of delinquency. Fourth, these programs—alone or in combination with one another—should not be viewed as the definitive solution to the delinquency problem. These programs can reduce delinquency in at least some circumstances, but it is unlikely that they will eliminate delinquency.

There are several reasons why these programs are unlikely to eliminate delinquency. They are often difficult to properly implement, especially on a large scale. It is often difficult to ensure that everyone who needs these programs participates in them. In fact, the people who need these programs the most are often the least likely to participate in them—especially prevention programs, where participation is often voluntary. Further, even if these programs are properly administered to the people who need them the most, they are still able to help only *some* of the program participants.

Programs Focusing on the Early Family Environment   ❖ ❖ ❖ ❖

As you know, the family has a major impact on delinquency. The family affects the juvenile's level of social control, strain, and the social learning of crime. Some parents, for example, fail to develop a strong emotional bond with their children, fail to properly supervise their children, and abuse and neglect their children. These (in)actions directly increase the likelihood of delinquency. Also, they indirectly increase the likelihood of delinquency through their effect on such things as individual traits, school experiences, and association with delinquent peers and gangs (see Chapter 11 and the other chapters on the causes of delinquency for a full discussion). Juveniles in certain types of families, for example, more often experience harm from biological mishaps like drug use during pregnancy, birth complications, head injuries, and exposure to toxic substances. They are therefore more likely to develop traits conducive to delinquency.

Several early family intervention programs have been developed in an effort to reduce the likelihood that families produce delinquent children. These programs typically target disadvantaged families or families at risk for certain problems, such as child abuse. For example, these programs might target single parents, adolescent mothers, the parents of premature or low-birth-weight babies, and/or families where there is a history of drug abuse or family violence. Some programs begin before the birth of the child, while others begin at or shortly after birth. In the most effective programs, the parents are visited weekly by a nurse, social worker, or trained paraprofessional. When necessary, these home visitors can turn to physicians, psychologists, or teachers for further assistance. These programs last anywhere from a few months to several years, with the longer programs being more successful.[3] Programs focusing on the early family environment address the causes of delinquency in three major ways.

First, they attempt to reduce the child's exposure to biological harm by providing medical care to the child and mother and by providing health and safety training to the parents. Expectant mothers may be given prenatal care and advice. Among other things, they are encouraged to avoid smoking, alcohol use, and drug use during pregnancy. If necessary, the mother will be provided with counseling and drug treatment. Such activities help prevent problems like low birth weight and birth complications. After birth, the child receives regular medical care and the parents receive assistance in caring for the child. The child in particular receives regular pediatric exams, and steps are taken to address any developmental or other problems that arise. The parents are also given information on child development and how to best care for their child. Such information and assistance can prevent a range of harmful biological events, such as head injuries and exposure to toxic substances like lead.

Second, these programs also attempt to foster good parenting practices by reducing parental stress and providing information on good parenting. As you may recall from Chapter 11, two of the major determinants of poor parenting are stress and lack of knowledge. It is difficult to be a good parent if you do not have decent housing or a job, you struggle to put food on the table, you are involved in an abusive relationship, and the like. One of the first things these programs attempt to do is help parents address some of the basic problems they face. In particular, they may do such things as help the parents find decent housing, get a job, obtain food, secure medical care, arrange transportation, and end spouse abuse. Sometimes the home visitor provides this assistance. Home visitors often function as counselors to the family, discussing problems, offering advice and assistance, and providing emotional support. The home visitors also refer family members to various social service and treatment programs when necessary. The assistance of the home visitor not only makes it easier for the parents to engage in good parenting, but it also helps foster a bond between the home visitor and the parents.

It is also difficult to be a good parent if you were never exposed to good parenting, so the home visitors attempt to teach good parenting skills. They provide information on child development, offer advice on parenting, model parenting skills, and assist parents when necessary. They also monitor the progress of the child and intervene when necessary. For example, they may provide special assistance if it appears that the parents are not forming an emotional bond with their baby. In some cases, the parents may take special parent training classes or participate in parent support groups. Also, male home visitors may make a special effort to work with the father if the father is present.

It is important to emphasize that these home visitors do not attempt to coerce or "talk down" to the parents. Rather, they try to function as friends and allies to the parents. For example, the home visitor in the Hawaii Healthy Start program introduces herself to the parents by saying something like:

> I work with the Healthy Start program. I have new information about babies that I didn't know when I was raising my kids. It can make being a mother easier, but not easy! Also, you can look at me as your information center about this community. I live here, too, and I didn't know about WIC [Special Supplemental Food Program for Women, Infants, and Children] or the well baby clinic before I started this job. I hope you learn to think of me as your "special" friend, someone here completely for you and the baby. I am here to talk when you need to share something that concerns you. I know that it is hard to start with a new baby and to have so much on your mind. (Earle, 1995:6)

Third, these programs often provide educational child care. Such care better prepares the child for school. Also, it reduces the stress on the parents by providing them with a break from constant child care and by making it easier for them to obtain employment. In addition, the parents are taught how to provide a stimulating environment to their child so as to foster the child's cognitive development. Related to this, a toy- and book-lending library is often made available to the parents. See the web site *www.parentingresources.ncjs.org* for more information on parenting.

Programs focusing on the early family environment, then, address several of the most important causes of delinquency. They reduce the likelihood of biological harm, which in turn reduces the likelihood that juveniles will develop traits conducive to crime. They address several family factors that are related to delinquency, including the emotional bond between the parents and child, the level of parental supervision, and child abuse and neglect. (For a discussion of programs focusing specifically on child abuse, see Earls and Barnes, 1997; Feindler and Becker, 1994). They also supplement the socialization efforts of parents by placing the child in a well-designed preschool program. These effects, in turn, have an impact on other causes of delinquency, such as poor school performance and association with delinquent peers. It is not surprising, then, that early intervention programs have shown some success at preventing delinquency. Such programs are becoming more common, with a few states implementing them on a large scale.

Parent Training Programs

One of the most widely used programs to deal with delinquency is parent training. Parent training programs are sometimes used alone, and they are sometimes used in combination with other programs—such as programs focusing on the early family environment, school-based programs, and programs focusing on individual traits.[4]

Given the central role that the family plays in delinquency, it is not surprising that parent training is so widely used. As indicated, a variety of family factors affect delinquency, including weak emotional bonds between the parent(s) and child, poor supervision, abuse and neglect, and family conflict. These factors are important in and of themselves, and they are important because they affect certain of the other causes of delinquency, such as individual traits, school performance and attachment, and association with delinquent peers. Programs that can change the way parents relate to their children have much potential for controlling delinquency.

Parent training programs usually target the families of delinquents or juveniles "at risk" for delinquency. They also target *families* that are "at risk" for poor parenting, such as adolescent mothers or families where there is evidence of family violence. These programs are offered in the home, in clinics, or in other settings like schools. Sometimes they are provided to individual families and sometimes they are provided to several families at once.

Parent training programs typically have several components. Most notably, they teach parents how to more effectively discipline their children. Poor discipline is not only a major cause of delinquency, but it also undermines the emotional bond between the parent and child and contributes to family conflict. Parents are taught how to set clear rules, better monitor their child's behavior, recognize both deviant and prosocial behavior, and properly sanction deviant behavior and reinforce prosocial behavior. Parents are encouraged to make more use of positive reinforcers, such as praise, rewards, privileges, and attention and to make less use of punishers, such as criticism, yelling, and hitting. The preferred strategies of punishment involve time out (for children), loss of privileges, imposition of chores, clear expressions of disapproval, and reasoning. (If you would like to get a better sense of the disciplinary skills that parent-training programs try to teach, see the book *Living With Children* by Patterson and Gullion, 1977, which is used as a manual in one major parent training program. Also see the web site *www.parentingresources.ncjs.org*.)

Parent training programs also frequently teach family members how to better resolve conflicts with one another. While proper disciplinary techniques reduce family conflict, they do not eliminate it. The parents and juvenile, for example, may still disagree over the rules that parents try to enforce or the punishments that parents administer. A common strategy for resolving such conflicts involves the negotiation of a behavioral contract between the parents and the juvenile, particularly adolescents. The contract clearly specifies the rules that juveniles must follow and the consequences for following and breaking rules. For example, adolescents may agree to go to school every day during the week in exchange for the privilege of staying out until midnight on Friday and Saturday nights. The adolescent typically plays a major role in developing such contracts. Parents and juveniles are taught how to negotiate such contracts, and they may also call on a therapist for assistance. By reducing conflict, such negotiation also helps strengthen family bonds.

Parent training programs may also do such things as teach family members better communication skills; alter the expectations that parents have for their children (the unrealistic expectations of parents sometimes contribute to abuse and other problems); and encourage family members to spend more time together in pleasurable activities. Parents are taught such skills and practices through a variety of strategies: they receive reading materials and/or direct instruction; they are exposed to models who display these practices; they rehearse these practices themselves and receive feedback; and they receive continued guidance when they apply these practices in their homes.

Parent training programs have shown much promise in reducing delinquency, although they are not effective with all families. There are difficulties in inducing families to participate, especially the families that need it most (Kazdin, 1994). Also, parent training is often difficult to successfully implement when families face multiple stressors—poverty, poor housing, work problems, and family violence. Efforts, however, are being made to deal with these problems, including efforts to reduce family stressors and improve the ability of parents to cope with stressors. Also, there are efforts to provide financial and other incentives to participate in these programs.

The effectiveness of these programs is undoubtedly the result of a number of factors. As indicated, they strengthen the bond between parent and child, improve parental discipline, and reduce family conflict and abuse. At a more general level, they reduce strain. Adolescents are treated more fairly by parents: They have some say in the rules that govern their lives, and they are more consistently rewarded for prosocial behavior and punished for negative behavior. They are also subject to less negative treatment and receive more positive stimuli. In particular, family conflict and abuse are reduced. These programs also promote the social learning of conventional behavior. Parents clearly state rules that condemn deviance; parents function as conventional role models, avoiding the use of violent disciplinary techniques, among other things; conventional behavior is consistently reinforced; and deviant behavior is consistently punished. Finally, such programs clearly result in an increase in social control. Direct control is obviously increased; also, the adolescent's emotional bond to parents is increased, and the adolescent is more likely to internalize beliefs condemning deviance and develop a high level of self-control.

Several researchers have suggested that society make parent-training programs generally available, incorporating them into the high school curriculum or offering them to the parents of all newborn children. This would reduce the stigma of participating in such programs and might make it easier to secure funding for such programs (since they would no longer be seen as special programs for the poor or disadvantaged). Many European countries have moved in this direction, but only a few schools and areas in the United States have done so (see Sherman et al., 1998, for more information).

Programs Focusing on School Factors

As you know, delinquency is also related to a range of negative school experiences, including poor school performance, low attachment to school, low school involvement, low educational goals, and poor relations with teachers. Delinquency is also more common in certain types of schools, including schools that are large, have poor discipline, provide few opportunities for student success, have low expectations for students, have unpleasant working conditions for students, and have poor cooperation between teachers and administrators (see Chapter 12 for more information).

Several programs try to address these factors. Some programs focus on the individual, with most such programs attempting to boost school performance. It is felt that individuals who perform well in school will come to like school, get involved in school activities, develop high educational goals, and get along well with teachers. Other programs focus on the larger school environment—including the classroom and entire school—and attempt to change this environment in ways that will reduce delinquency.[5]

Preschool programs. Evidence suggests that good preschool programs can both improve school performance and reduce delinquency. Most such programs focus on preschool children in disadvantaged areas, and they attempt to promote the social and intellectual development of these children as well as increase their parents' involvement in the educational process. The best preschool programs begin early in life; last two years or more; have low student-to-teacher ratios; and employ carefully designed curriculums. In addition, the teachers meet regularly with the parents to discuss ways that the parents can foster their child's social and intellectual development. The success of preschool programs is further enhanced if the children continue to receive assistance once they have begun school.

In-school programs. A range of in-school programs attempt to improve the school performance of individual students and address other school experiences related to delinquency. These programs tend to focus on students doing poorly in school or on students rated as disruptive by teachers and others. The most straightforward of these programs provide tutoring to students, with the tutoring being done by other students, community volunteers, trained paraprofessionals, and teachers. Such programs are effective at boosting school performance, but it is not yet known whether they reduce delinquency.

Other programs are more elaborate, and several have been found to affect both school experiences and delinquency. In certain programs, for example, juveniles sign a contract with school officials. The juveniles agree to do such things as attend school on a regular basis, do their schoolwork, and behave properly in class. Program staff members provide needed services to the juveniles, such as tutoring and counseling. The program staff also train teachers and sometimes parents to monitor the juveniles' performance and provide assistance when necessary. The juveniles receive regular feedback about their performance from program staff. Staff members discuss ways in which the juveniles might improve when they receive negative reports, and they reinforce the juveniles when the juveniles meet the terms of their contracts. For example, they praise the juveniles and provide them with points that can be traded in for things like CDs and school trips.

Altering the classroom environment. Other programs attempt to alter the classroom environment in ways that improve classroom performance, increase school attachment and involvement, improve relations with teachers and classmates, and improve discipline.

For example, researchers have attempted to reduce delinquency through the strategies of interactive teaching, proactive classroom management, and cooperative learning groups. Interactive teaching provides students with specific objectives they must master; provides frequent feedback; provides help when necessary; employs objective grading; and bases grades on mastery of material and improvement over past performance—not on comparisons with other students. Such teaching increases the opportunities for the students to succeed, and the grading methods increase perceptions of fairness and decrease competition with other students. Teachers using proactive classroom management are taught to clearly state rules for classroom behavior, recognize and reward attempts to cooperate, make frequent use of encouragement and praise, and minimize the impact of disruptions. Cooperative learning groups consist of small, heterogeneous groups of students who help one another master classroom materials and who receive recognition as a team for their accomplishments. These groups serve to reduce alienation, reinforce cooperation, and promote attachment among students.

Another example of a successful program focusing primarily on the classroom environment is an anti-bullying program developed in Norway (Olweus, 1991; also see Arnette and Walsleben, 1998). Bullying is an important form of delinquency in itself, and it may contribute to further delinquency, partly for reasons related to strain theory. According to Olweus (1991:413), "a person is being bullied when he or she is exposed, repeatedly and over time, to negative actions on the part of one or more other persons." Negative actions are defined as intentional actions that inflict or attempt to inflict injury or discomfort upon another. Olweus found that teachers in Norway did relatively little to stop bullying at school and that parents were largely unaware of the problem. A national campaign provided teachers and parents with information on the extent of bullying and advice on how to stop it. Teachers were encouraged to establish clear rules against bullying; to regularly remind students of these rules; to closely monitor student activities; to use nonhostile, nonphysical sanctions against bullies; and to support and protect victims. Surveys of students suggest that the program was quite successful, and similar programs are being implemented in the United States.

Changing the school environment. A number of programs have tried to change the school environment as a whole. These programs usually employ several strategies, and it is often difficult to determine which of these strategies has the greatest impact on delinquency. Most programs try to change schools in ways that improve student performance, increase school attachment and involvement, improve school discipline, and generally make the school environment more satisfying.

These programs often begin by creating teams that include school administrators, teachers, parents, students, and others. These teams evaluate the school and then help plan and implement school improvements. Such improvements often include the following: Teachers are taught innovative teaching and classroom management techniques. Students help develop school disciplinary rules. Steps are taken to make sure that these rules are clearly stated; widely publicized through devices like newsletters, posters, and ceremonies; and enforced in a consistent and fair manner. There is an effort to make greater use of positive reinforcers, like praise and privileges, for conventional behavior. There is better communication with parents about the positive and negative behaviors of their children. An effort is made to involve parents more actively in the school. For example, volunteer opportunities are created for parents, and parental input is solicited on important issues. An effort is made to reduce student "down time," so that students have less unsupervised and unstructured time. There is increased monitoring of the lunchroom, restrooms, and school grounds. An effort is made to increase the involvement and success experiences of high-risk students, usually through an expansion of extracurricular activities and through such special academic and counseling programs as career exploration programs and job-seeking skills programs. A variety of programs addressing individual traits conducive to delinquency are developed. These include social skills training, anger management, and programs designed to instill conventional beliefs. Students, teachers and others launch school-pride campaigns, which include things like pep rallies and school clean-up programs. The problems associated with large schools are addressed by creating "schools within schools." That is, small groups of students are assigned to the same homeroom and many of the same classes.

Taken together, such programs can have a substantial impact on those school factors associated with delinquency. They reduce strain. Students are better able to achieve their educational goals, they are treated more fairly by school officials, they find school more interesting and pleasant, and they get along better with teachers and fellow students. These programs also increase social control. Students are better supervised at school; they develop a stronger bond to teachers and fellow students. They develop a greater investment in conventional activities—through their higher school performance and educational goals—and they are exposed to conventional beliefs and taught to exercise self-control. Finally, these programs foster the social learning of conventional behavior. Students are more likely to form close associations with conventional role models, be exposed to conventional beliefs, and be consistently reinforced for conventional behavior and punished for deviance.

Programs Focusing on Individual Traits

As indicated in Chapter 10, several individual traits contribute to delinquency, including hyperactivity/impulsivity/attention deficit, low intelligence, sensation seeking, irritability, low empathy, poor social and problem-solving skills, and beliefs favorable to delinquency. Many of the programs described in this chapter have an impact on these traits. As you may recall, the traits are often a function of biological factors and the early family environment. Many of the family programs I described attempt to reduce biological harm and improve the family environment, so they should affect a broad range of individual traits. Many school-based programs also affect individual traits, including traits like IQ and beliefs regarding delinquency.

The programs described in this section, however, focus directly on individual traits. These programs are offered in both preschool and regular school. They may be offered to all juveniles or to juveniles at risk for delinquency. Also, these programs are frequently used to rehabilitate juvenile delinquents who are in community treatment programs or institutions. There are several common programs, each focusing on a somewhat different set of traits. These programs go under a variety of names, including social and interpersonal skills training, problem solving training, anger management, conflict resolution, and violence prevention curriculums. [6]

Officials sometimes employ several programs or elements from several programs. They target a range of individual traits and often do the following: They teach juveniles the skills necessary for effective interaction with others. These include such basic social skills as maintaining eye contact when talking with someone. They also include more advanced skills, such as recognizing and showing sensitivity to the feelings of others. The programs teach juveniles how to respond to problems without engaging in delinquency. In particular, they teach juveniles how to be assertive (rather than aggressive), how to negotiate with others, how to manage their anger, and how to respond to a range of problems, including teasing from peers and criticism from teachers. Related to this, they teach basic problem-solving skills. In particular, juveniles are taught to stop and think before they act rather than responding in an impulsive manner. The programs teach juveniles how to recognize and resist negative peer pressure, and they attempt to promote beliefs that favor conventional behavior and condemn delinquency. This is done by providing information about the negative consequences of delinquency, letting students know that various forms of delinquency are less common among their peers than they might think, and getting students and classes to take public stands against various types of delinquency, such as drug use and violence. Peer leaders often assist in this process, since students may be more likely to trust and identify with them.

These programs, then, target a range of individual traits conducive to delinquency, including impulsivity, sensation seeking, irritability, lack of empathy, lack of social and problem-solving skills, and beliefs favorable to delinquency. In some cases, officials may also treat certain traits with medication. Most notably, hyperactivity/impulsivity/attention deficit is often treated with drugs like Ritalin. Such drugs have shown some effect at reducing delinquency, although certain evidence suggests that drugs are most effective when combined with programs of the type described here (see Wasserman and Miller, 1998).

Targeting individual traits may reduce strain, increase social control, and foster the social learning of conventional behavior. In particular, juveniles will be in a better position to achieve their goals, will be treated in a more positive manner by others, and will be less likely to respond to strain with delinquency. Likewise, they will be higher in social control—particularly the two major categories of internal control: self-control and beliefs condemning delinquency. And they will be better able to resist the influence of delinquent peers and act in conventional ways that result in reinforcement.

In order to give you a better sense of what these programs are like, let me describe the basic components of problem-solving training and anger management programs.

Problem-solving training. Dodge (1986) lists the following five steps in effective problem-solving: (1) search for cues in the environment; (2) interpret these cues; (3) generate possible responses to the situation; (4) consider the possible consequences of the responses; and (5) enact the chosen response. Data suggest that delinquents have problems at each of these steps. They attend to fewer environmental cues; they tend to focus on aggressive cues; they often attribute hostile intent when there is none; they generate fewer alternate solutions; they generate more aggressive responses; they fail to recognize the negative consequences of delinquent behavior; and they often lack the social skills to enact prosocial responses (see Kazdin,1994). Problem-solving training teaches juveniles to carefully perform each of the steps necessary for effective problem solving and to avoid the mistakes just listed. The instructor describes and models the steps in effective problem solving. The child is then asked to apply these steps to an imaginary problem, often making statements to himself or herself which call attention to the mental tasks that are to be performed. In the "Think Aloud" program, for example, children are taught to ask themselves a series of four questions: "What is my problem?" "What is my plan?" "Am I using my plan?" and "How did I do?" (Hollin, 1990a:66). The WISER way teaches youth to Wait, Identify the problem, generate Solutions, Evaluate the consequences, and self-Reinforce (Hollin, 1990b:485). The instructor prompts the youth when necessary and provides feedback and reinforcement. Eventually, the youths apply the steps to real-life problems.

Anger management. Anger management programs teach juveniles how to limit or control their anger, with the goal of promoting more adaptive behavior. Most programs have several features in common. First, juveniles explore the causes and consequences of their anger. They may do this by keeping a diary or log of events that made them angry and their reaction to these events. The causes of anger include not only external events but also the internal statements made about those events. Aggressive individuals, for example, are more likely to interpret the ambiguous acts of others as hostile in intent, so the stare of a stranger may be interpreted as a deliberate challenge. The diary may help identify such self-statements. It may also help identify the early warning signs of anger, such as tensed muscles or flushing. Second, the juveniles learn techniques for more effectively controlling their anger—counting backward, imagining a peaceful scene, deep breathing, muscle relaxation, and self-statements like "calm down" and "cool off." Some programs also attempt to increase the juvenile's level of self-efficacy, in an attempt to further increase self-control. In addition to teaching juveniles to reduce or more effectively control their anger, these programs often teach social and problem-solving skills that allow for a more adaptive response to situations. Finally, juveniles receive much practice applying the above techniques, first in response to imaginary provocations and eventually in real-life settings. And they receive much feedback and reinforcement as they apply these techniques (see Blackburn, 1993; Hollin, 1990a).

The most effective programs focusing on individual traits employ similar training techniques. These techniques include direct instruction; modeling of the desired behaviors by the trainer or others; role-playing by the youth, with feedback from the trainer and others; reinforcement for appropriate behavior; and homework assignments that require using the newly acquired traits or skills in real-life settings. Certain programs make special efforts to ensure that these skills will be used in the outside world, such as making the training as similar to real life as possible and attempting to ensure that the new skills are reinforced in real-life settings. Many of the parent training and other programs described earlier use similar training techniques. Such techniques are part of the "cognitive-behavioral" approach described earlier.

Programs Focusing on Peers/Gangs

As you know, peer relations have a major effect on delinquency. Peers are a major source of strain among adolescents; peers frequently victimize, antagonize, and otherwise get into disputes with one another. Peers may reduce social control. Delinquent peers and gangs, among other things, may reduce the influence of parents, the school, and other conventional groups on the juvenile. And peers are a major source for the social learning of crime. Delinquent peers and gang members provide models for delinquency, transmit beliefs favorable to delinquency, and reinforce delinquency.

The family, school, and individual-trait programs described in the preceding sections all have an impact on peer relations. They reduce the likelihood that juveniles will get involved with delinquent peers and gangs; they reduce the negative influence of peers on the juvenile; and they reduce the likelihood that peers will treat one another badly. For example, parent training programs teach parents how to better supervise their children. Well-supervised juveniles are less likely to join delinquent peer groups; are less likely to succumb to negative peer pressures; and are less likely to get into serious disputes with peers. In fact, one might argue that the best way to counter the effect of peers on delinquency is to strengthen individual traits and the family, school, and community. Delinquent peers often flourish when these agencies are weak.

This section, however, focuses on programs that directly target delinquent peer groups and gangs. Such programs usually focus on adolescents, since peer influence is greatest at this time. Some programs focus on adolescents in general; others on at-risk adolescents, such as adolescents in schools with gang problems; and still others focus on adolescents who belong to delinquent peer groups or gangs. These programs try to break up, transform, or reduce the influence of delinquent peer groups and gangs. Unfortunately, many of these programs have been ineffective, particularly for adolescents who are already involved with delinquent peers or gangs. Peers have a powerful influence on adolescents and it is often difficult to counter that influence.[7]

Breaking up delinquent peer groups/gangs. Some programs attempt to break up the delinquent peer group or gang. The most promising programs in this area combine police suppression with efforts to address the problems that contribute to gang formation.

The police typically attempt to suppress gang activity by targeting gangs in certain areas. They gather information on these gangs, increase patrols in areas where the gangs hang out (gang "hot spots"), and closely monitor gang members. They may also do such things as aggressively enforce curfew and truancy laws and conduct "street sweeps," rounding up and searching suspected gang members. And they attempt to severely sanction gang members for their crimes. The police are often supported by prosecutors and probation officers who focus on gang cases. These prosecutors seek serious penalties for gang-related crimes. In this connection, many states have passed laws increasing the penalties for gang-related crimes. Probation officers closely supervise gang members, strictly enforcing the conditions of their probation.

Police suppression alone, however, is often not sufficient to have a substantial impact on gang activities. Many communities have therefore combined police suppression with an effort to address the problems that contribute to gang formation. For example, they make a variety of social service and counseling programs available to gang members and communities with gang problems. The Boston Gun Project, described earlier, and the "Gang Violence Reduction Program" in Chicago are examples of programs combining police suppression with the provision of services (see Spergel, 1995; Decker and Curry, 2000; Howell, 1997b). Such combined programs are in need of proper evaluation, but they show some evidence of effectiveness.

Transforming the delinquent peer group/gang. Other programs attempt to change the delinquent peer group or gang and direct it toward more conventional activities. Some programs have assigned "street" or "detached workers" to gangs. These workers try to move the gang in the direction of conventional behavior. They provide a range of services to gangs, such as tutoring and job assistance. They act as advocates for the gang with the police, courts, and others. They provide recreational opportunities for the gang, like field trips and sports programs. And they hold regular meetings with the gang. Evidence on the effectiveness of these programs is somewhat mixed, but most data suggest that they do not work and may even contribute to an increase in gang delinquency. The detached workers are usually unable to effectively address the problems that contribute to gang membership. And the workers may sometimes increase the cohesiveness of the gang. In particular, the numerous activities they arrange may sometimes turn a loosely organized group of gang members into a more organized unit with a stronger gang identity.

Mediation programs are also sometimes run in communities with gang problems. Such programs try to reduce the propensity of gang members for violence. Much gang crime involves disputes between gangs or gang members. In some communities, mediators make an active effort to learn about disputes or conflicts that might erupt into violence. They patrol the streets in gang areas and encourage gang members and community residents to call them when problems arise. They attempt to reduce gang conflict in several ways: They challenge the rumors that sometimes fuel conflict. They attempt to discourage gang members from resorting to violence, sometimes enlisting the aid of the families of gang members and others close to the gang. And they mediate disputes between gangs and between gang members. In some cases, they may hold "gang summits" and try to negotiate truces between different gangs. Evidence on the effectiveness of such programs is somewhat encouraging, although these programs are in need of further evaluation.

Reducing the influence of delinquent peers/gangs. Some programs attempt to discourage juveniles from joining gangs and to teach juveniles the skills to resist gang/peer influence. For example, programs may provide information about gang violence and drug use, the negative consequences of gang membership, how gangs recruit individuals, and methods of resisting recruitment. Or programs may attempt to counter peer pressure to use drugs by providing juveniles with information about the negative consequences of drug use, letting them know that drug use is less common than they think, teaching them to recognize and resist peer pressure to use drugs, and getting them to make a public commitment against drug use.

Not all education programs in this area are effective. In fact, studies found that the most popular drug education program in the country—D.A.R.E. (Drug Abuse Resistance Education)—was not effective (see Sherman et al., 1998). The most effective programs tend to have certain traits in common. They make use of the cognitive-behavioral strategies described earlier—as opposed to simply lecturing juveniles or holding discussions with them. They employ individuals with whom the juveniles can identify, often making use of peer instructors. They not only focus on the negative consequences of gang membership or delinquency, but they also teach juveniles the skills they need to recognize and resist influence attempts. And they often try to establish a norm against gang membership or delinquency. For example, they may let juveniles know that most kids their age do not use drugs, or they may try to get class members to take a public stand against drug use.

Still other programs try to remove individuals from gangs or delinquent peer groups and place them in more conventional groups. The House of Umoja in Philadelphia, for example, provides a sanctuary for gang members and offers such members educational assistance, counseling, and job training and placement. Other programs attempt to place delinquents in conventional peer groups, where they are exposed to conventional role models, taught conventional beliefs, reinforced for conventional behavior, and punished for delinquency. Such programs, however, have shown mixed results. Putting delinquent and conventional juveniles together in the same group can often increase the delinquency of the conventional juveniles (see Farrington, 1996a,b; Gorman and White, 1995). Finally, some programs provide adult mentors to juveniles involved in delinquent peer groups or gangs.

As you can see, there have been a number of efforts to deal with delinquent peer groups and gangs. Many have failed, although some show promise.

Other Prevention and Rehabilitation Programs

A variety of other prevention and rehabilitation programs have shown promise. Many of these are run in the community, with some attempting to change the nature of the community in ways that reduce delinquency. Brief overviews of selected programs are provided below.[8]

Mentoring. Mentoring programs match at-risk or delinquent juveniles with nonprofessional volunteers, such as college students, community residents, and business people. Ideally, the mentors form a close relationship with the juveniles. They function as conventional role models, offer guidance, and help the juveniles deal with a range of problems, including family, school, and peer problems. Mentors, then, have the potential to reduce strain, increase social control, and foster the social learning of conventional behavior. Evidence on the effectiveness of mentoring programs is somewhat mixed, but data suggest that intensive mentoring programs may be effective in reducing delinquency.[9]

Supervised recreational opportunities. A number of programs provide supervised recreational activities for juveniles, especially after school, when rates of delinquency peak. Such programs attempt to monitor youth who might otherwise be unsupervised (and so increase direct control). They may also attempt to establish a relationship between the conventional adults who

run the program and the youths. Evidence on the effectiveness of these programs is also mixed, but data suggest that carefully constructed recreational
programs may reduce delinquency. Such programs provide structured activities, are well supervised, and make an effort to aggressively recruit and retain
youth in the community.

Vocational training and employment programs. These programs teach
job skills and help juveniles find employment. In doing so, they most obviously reduce strain and create a stake in conformity. Vocational programs
typically focus on delinquents and at-risk juveniles, like high school dropouts or juveniles doing poorly in school. Some vocational programs are based
in the community and some are incorporated into the school system. Once
again, evidence on the effectiveness of these programs is mixed. Many vocational programs do not appear to reduce delinquency, but certain well-
designed programs show much promise for reducing delinquency. Such programs are intensive and long-term; they help juveniles deal with other problems they may be facing; and they provide incentives for participation. The
Jobs Corps program of the federal government is an example.[10]

Situational crime prevention. As indicated in Chapter 15, crime is a
function of both the juvenile's predisposition for delinquency and the situations that the juvenile encounters. Predisposed juveniles are more likely to
engage in delinquency when they are in situations where they are provoked
by others, where the benefits of delinquency are high, and where the costs of
delinquency are low. A variety of strategies have been developed to reduce the
likelihood that individuals will encounter such situations. Certain of these
strategies were briefly described in Chapter 15, such as placing theft-proof
change boxes on buses and placing attendants in parking lots. Clarke (1992,
1995) describes twelve general techniques of situational crime prevention,
including "deflecting [potential] offenders" (e.g., separating rival fans at
sporting events); "target hardening" (e.g., putting steering locks on cars);
"target removal" (e.g., removable car radios); and "formal surveillance" (e.g.,
cameras to detect speeding). Clarke (1995) and Sherman et al. (1998) also
provide numerous examples of situational prevention approaches that
appear to be quite successful. These approaches reduce the likelihood that
individuals will encounter others who provoke them, reduce the potential
benefits of crime, or increase the potential costs of crime.

Drug and gun programs. Most of the family, school, individual, peer, and
other types of programs described in the previous sections have been
employed to reduce drug use as well as delinquency, and they have shown
some effect on levels of drug use. Hawkins, Arthur, and Catalano (1995) provide an excellent overview of drug control strategies and programs (also see
MacCoun and Reuter, 1998; Office of National Drug Control Policy, 1999).

A number of programs have also tried to reduce the prevalence of guns
among youths, or at least reduce the likelihood that youths will use guns.
Some programs, like gun buybacks, do not work. Evidence on other programs is mixed, including laws that restrict the purchase and sale of firearms
and laws that prohibit people from carrying firearms in public. These mixed
results may stem from the fact that jurisdictions differ in the extent to which
they enforce these laws. Some programs, however, show promise for reducing gun violence. Laws that impose severe penalties for the use of firearms in
a crime may reduce some types of gun violence. Likewise, police patrols that

target individuals who might be illegally carrying guns may reduce gun violence.[11]

Community crime prevention. Some programs attempt to reduce delinquency by attacking community problems that contribute to delinquency. As indicated in Chapter 14, economic deprivation and other factors increase community crime rates through their effect on strain, control, and the social learning of crime. (See Sherman et al., 1998, and Hope, 1995, for excellent overviews of community crime prevention programs.)

The most common community crime-prevention program is Neighborhood Watch. As you may recall, one reason that some communities have higher crime rates is that neighborhood residents fail to effectively monitor their communities and sanction deviance. That is, some communities are low in direct control. Neighborhood Watch programs try to address this problem by gathering neighborhood residents together, encouraging them to more closely monitor their community, and encouraging them to report suspicious activity to the police. Such programs, however, are difficult to implement in the high-crime communities that need them the most. Further, evidence suggests that they have little or no effect on crime rates in the communities where they are implemented. There are a number of possible reasons for this lack of effectiveness, one of which is the low involvement of many program participants (see Hope, 1995).

Other community crime prevention programs are more ambitious and attempt to address a range of community problems that contribute to crime—including economic deprivation. Although these programs are often initiated by people outside the community, an attempt is usually made to actively involve community residents in the program. Community programs may attempt to provide social services to juveniles and others in the community; such services include mentoring, tutoring and other educational programs, vocational programs, counseling, health programs, and recreational programs. Community programs may try to clean up the community and improve the condition of housing. They may attempt to increase the extent to which residents monitor their neighborhood and sanction deviance; for example, marches and rallies may be held in an effort to unite community residents. They may attempt to stimulate economic development in the community through such devices as tax breaks and other financial incentives to businesses. Most such programs have not been well evaluated. Limited data, however, suggest that these programs usually have only a minimal impact on crime, although some of the newer programs designed to create jobs in inner-city communities show promise and are in need of further evaluation (see Sherman et al., 199*8).

The fundamental problem with community crime prevention programs is that high-crime communities usually lack the resources to effectively address the causes of their crime problem. In particular, their crime stems primarily from the severe economic deprivation they face. This deprivation contributes to a range of problems and is ultimately responsible for high levels of strain, a breakdown in control, and an environment that fosters the social learning of crime. The economic deprivation in these communities, however, is a function of larger social forces, such as the decline in manufacturing jobs, the movement of manufacturing jobs to the suburbs, and a decline in certain social services. Local communities cannot adequately address these

problems without substantial outside assistance. And up to this point, the
outside assistance provided to such communities has not been sufficient to
have a meaningful impact on crime rates (see Hope, 1995, for a fuller discussion). This leads me to my final point regarding rehabilitation and prevention
programs.

A Note on the Larger Social Environment

Most of the prevention and rehabilitation programs described in the foregoing pages focus on the individual and the individual's immediate social
environment—family, school, peer group, and local community. The nature
of one's immediate environment, however, is strongly influenced by larger social forces. These forces play a major role in generating such problems as dys-
functional families, school failure, gangs, and neighborhoods plagued by
crime and other problems. Further, these forces influence the success or failure of prevention and rehabilitation programs, since they shape the context
in which these programs operate. It is difficult for parent training programs
to be successful, for example, when parents are unemployed and struggling
to survive.

Of all the social forces that I might discuss, economic forces are the most
important. A range of economic forces in the United States have contributed
to a high *overall* level of prosperity, but this prosperity has not been shared by
all. In fact, the United States has a much higher percentage of poor people
than other developed countries (see Currie, 1998; Messner and Rosenfeld,
1997). About 18 percent of children lived in families below the poverty line in
1998 (Federal Interagency Forum on Child and Family Statistics, 2000). The
percentage of children living in poverty has been relatively stable since 1980,
with a slight increase in the percentage of children in extreme poverty families (incomes less than half the poverty level). These poor people are increasingly concentrated in communities with other poor individuals. There are a
variety of reasons for these changes, including the loss of manufacturing
jobs, the movement of manufacturing jobs to the suburbs, the growth of service sector jobs that pay poorly and carry few benefits, an increase in single-
parent families, and a decline in some social services. As discussed in Chapters 4 and 14, black children are more likely to be poor and live in high poverty communities than white children (for fuller discussions, see Currie,
1998; Hagan, 1994; Lewit et al., 1997; Sampson and Wilson, 1995; Wilson,
1987, 1996).

This poverty, particularly the concentration of poverty, contributes to a
range of problems conducive to crime and delinquency, including poor
health care; family problems like broken homes, poor parenting, and abuse;
school problems; and a range of neighborhood problems.[12] The prevention
and rehabilitation programs described earlier have shown some success in
reducing the negative effects of this poverty and, in some cases, helping individuals escape from poverty. But any serious approach to reducing delinquency must devote greater attention to these larger economic forces.

A range of programs have been suggested in this area. Some argue that
society should do more to attract jobs to inner-city areas plagued by crime
and to induce employers to hire people from such areas. Several programs
are now trying to do this by offering tax breaks and other financial incentives

to businesses. Some argue that we should increase the pay and benefits associated with jobs so that all work pays a "living wage." Many full-time workers now earn less than the poverty level. And many workers do not receive and cannot afford health care. Some argue that we should make jobs located in suburban areas more accessible to inner-city residents through improved transportation and new housing policies. Some argue that we should create new jobs in the public sector, particularly in inner-city communities. Such jobs might be in areas like child care, health care, public safety, and child protection. Some argue that we should provide increased tax benefits and other financial assistance to families with children, and we should do more to help families collect child support. Some argue that we should increase social services, including job training, educational programs, health care, child care, food programs, housing assistance, and a range of pro-family policies like flexible work schedules and stronger family-leave policies. As you may know, the government is now in the midst of a major overhaul of the welfare system. Welfare benefits are now generally limited to a lifetime maximum of five years and welfare recipients are required to work after two years (these limits may vary by state). While these measures have dramatically reduced the number of people on welfare, there is some fear that they will increase the number of children living in poverty.[13]

Summary

A number of rehabilitation and prevention programs have been reviewed. Not all programs work. But criminologists now have a reasonably good idea of the characteristics that distinguish the most successful programs from the least successful ones. As indicated, the key feature of the most successful programs is that they address the causes of delinquency identified in earlier chapters. Further, these programs are cost-effective. Data indicate that they more than pay for themselves in terms of the crime and other problems they prevent, such as dropping out of school and going on welfare. One recent analysis suggests that society saves between 1.7 and 2.3 million dollars for each juvenile who is prevented from becoming a high-rate, chronic offender (Cohen, M., 1998). This saving far exceeds the per-person cost of prevention and rehabilitation programs. Further, data suggest that many prevention and rehabilitation programs are more cost-effective than get-tough strategies like incapacitation. On average, it now costs more than $32,000 per year to keep a juvenile in a public correctional facility and more than $45,000 per year to keep him or her in a private facility (Smith, 1998). While confining juveniles does stop some crime, many prevention and rehabilitation programs can stop crime at a much lower cost (Greenwood, 1998, 1999; Greenwood et al., 1996). Finally, these programs have wide popular support. Even though the public wants to get tough with offenders, they *also* support an increased emphasis on rehabilitation and prevention. In a 1996 Ohio survey, for example, 96.1 percent of the respondents agreed that "it is important to try to rehabilitate juveniles who have committed crimes and are now in the correctional system" (Applegate et al., 1997). In a 1996 California survey, 70 percent of voters said that they favored prevention over building more prisons as the best strategy for dealing with future violence.[14]

Prevention and rehabilitation programs probably will not solve the delinquency problem. As indicated, they reduce but do not eliminate delinquency. And as indicated, we are likely to encounter problems if we try to implement these programs on a large scale. It will be difficult to ensure that these programs are run as designed. And it will be difficult to ensure that the people who need these programs the most participate in them. But it is nevertheless clear that prevention and rehabilitation should be a central part of any serious effort to control delinquency.

❖ ❖ ❖ ❖

Notes

1. For overviews of rehabilitation and prevention, see Barlow, 1995; Catalano et al., 1998; Coordinating Council on Juvenile Justice and Delinquency Prevention, 1996; Cullen and Applegate, 1997; Currie, 1998; Farrington, 1996a,b; Greenwood, 1995; Guerra et al., 1994; Hawkins et al., 1995b; Howell and Hawkins, 1998; Kazdin, 1994; Kellermann et al., 1998; Kumpfer and Alvarado, 1998; Lipsey and Wilson, 1998; McGuire, 1995; Muller and Mihalic, 1999; Office of Juvenile Justice and Delinquency Prevention, 1995; Rutter et al., 1998; Sherman et al., 1998; Tremblay and Craig, 1995; Wasserman and Miller, 1998; Weissbourd, 1996.

2. *See* Andrews and Bonta, 1998; Andrews et al., 1990; Brewer et al., 1995; Catalano et al., 1998; Currie, 1998; Farrington, 1996a,b; Guerra, 1997; Guerra et al. 1994; Hawkins et al., 1995; Kazdin, 1994; Krisberg et al., 1995; Lipsey, 1992; Lipsey and Wilson, 1998; Losel, 1995; McGuire, 1995; Sherman et al., 1998; Tremblay and Craig, 1995; Wasserman and Miller, 1998; Yoshikawa, 1994.

3. *See* Currie, 1998; Earle, 1995; Farrington, 1996a,b; Guerra, 1997; Olds et al., 1998; Hawkins et al., 1995; Howell and Hawkins, 1998; Kazdin, 1994; Kumpfer and Alvarado, 1998; Sherman et al., 1998; Tremblay and Craig, 1995; Wasserman and Miller, 1998; Yoshikawa, 1994; Zigler et al., 1992.

4. For overviews of parent training programs, see Andrews and Bonta, 1998; Brewer et al., 1995; Farrington, 1996a,b; Guerra, 1997; Hollin, 1992; Kazdin, 1994; Kumpter and Tait 2000; McDonald and Frey, 1999; Patterson, 1982; Rankin and Wells, 1987; Sherman et al., 1998; Tremblay and Craig, 1995; Wasserman and Miller, 1998.

5. For overviews of school programs, see Arnette and Walsleben, 1998; Brewer et al., 1995; Catalano et al., 1998; Elliott et al., 1998; Hawkins and Lishner, 1987; Hawkins et al., 1995; Hawkins et al., 1998; Maguin and Loeber, 1996; Samples and Aber, 1998; Sherman et al., 1998; Tremblay and Craig, 1995; Wasserman and Miller, 1998.

6. For overviews of programs focusing on individual traits, see Blackburn, 1993; Brewer et al., 1995; Farrington, 1996a,b; Guerra, 1997; Guerra et al., 1994; Hawkins, Catalano, and Brewer, 1995; Hawkins et al., 1995b; Hawkins et al., 1998; Kazdin, 1994; Kellermann et al., 1998; Samples and Aber, 1998; Sherman et al., 1998; Wasserman and Miller, 1998.

7. For overviews and selected examples of peer programs, see Brewer et al., 1995; Burch and Kane, 1999; Catalano et al., 1998; Decker and Curry, 2000; Esbensen and Osgood, 1999; Farrington, 1996a,b; Fritsch et al., 1999; Gorman and White, 1995; Guerra, 1997; Hawkins et al., 1995; Howell, 1997b; 1998b, 1999; Klein, 1998; Sherman et al., 1998; Spergel, 1995.

8. Also see Brewer et al., 1995; Catalano et al., 1998; Kellermann et al., 1998; Sherman et al., 1998.

9. *See* Catalano et al., 1998; Grossman and Garry, 1997; Office of Juvenile Justice and Delinquency Prevention, 1998b; Sherman et al., 1998.

10. *See* Brewer et al., 1995; Currie, 1998; Lipsey, 1992; Sherman et al., 1998; also see Hamilton and McKinney, 1999.

11. *See* Brewer et al., 1995; Catalano et al., 1998; Kellermann et al., 1998; Kleck, 1997; Office of Juvenile Justice and Delinquency Prevention, 1996; Sherman et al., 1998.
12. *See* Brooks-Gunn and Duncan, 1997; Currie, 1998; Hagan, 1994; Sampson, 1997; Sampson and Wilson, 1995; Wilson, W., 1987, 1996.
13. For fuller discussions of these issues see Currie, 1998, Lewit et al., 1997, Messner and Rosenfeld, 1997; Plotnick 1997, and Wilson 1987, 1996.
14. Martin and Glantz as cited in Greenwood, 1998; also see Beckett and Sasson, 2000; Cullen and Applegate, 1997; Cullen et al., 1998; Flanagan and Longmire, 1996; Roberts and Stalans, 1998. ✦

Chapter 23

What Should We Do to Reduce Delinquency?

❖ ❖ ❖ ❖   If you tell someone that you have just read a book on delinquency or taken a course in the area, they may well ask you a question like: "So what should we do to reduce delinquency?" How would you respond?

If you are like many of the students in my classes, your initial response will be one of silence. You have been exposed to a great deal of material. Some of this material may have challenged your beliefs about the causes of delinquency and the best ways to control it. There is a lot to reflect on and pull together.

I want to help you in this process by presenting what I think is a reasonable strategy for reducing delinquency, a strategy that I think takes account of the research on the causes and control of delinquency; that is just or fair; that is within our means; and that is acceptable to most people in this country. This strategy reflects, in large measure, the strategy that is now being advocated by the federal government.[1] First, I believe that society should place much more emphasis on prevention and rehabilitation. And second, I believe that we should hold juveniles accountable for their behavior and protect the community from dangerous juveniles—but we should do so in a more effective and just manner than is now the case.

We Should Place More Emphasis on Prevention and Rehabilitation

I think we need to place much more emphasis on prevention and rehabilitation programs of the type described above. It makes more sense to prevent individuals from becoming delinquent in the first place rather than responding to their delinquency after the fact. And it makes more sense to attempt to reform or rehabilitate individuals who do become delinquent. The vast majority of these individuals are returned to the community after being processed by the juvenile justice system, sometimes immediately and sometimes after an out-of-home placement. We want to do all that we can to ensure that they cease or at least reduce their offending.

Most of the prevention and rehabilitation programs described above work or at least show much promise for success. The best of these programs are able to reduce offending rates 50 percent, and there is reason to believe that criminologists will be able to design even more effective programs as additional program evaluations are completed and our knowledge of the causes of delinquency increases. Such programs also represent a fair or just response to delinquency. Data suggest that delinquency is partly due to forces beyond the individual's control, forces like genetic inheritance, biological harms, the early family environment, the school one attends, the peers one is exposed to, and the community in which one lives. That is not to say that juveniles have no responsibility for their behavior. But it is to say that delinquency is not simply a matter of free choice. Delinquents are to some extent victims of their environment, and they both need and deserve our assistance. Further, most prevention and rehabilitation programs are cost-effective, as indicated earlier. Finally, there is strong public support for prevention and rehabilitation programs, as well as for "get tough" approaches to controlling delinquency.

But how should we go about putting such prevention and rehabilitation programs into place? The federal government and many states have come to place an increased emphasis on prevention and rehabilitation in recent years (although get-tough approaches still dominate). One model for implementing prevention/rehabilitation programs has shown some promise, although formal evaluations of this model are not yet available. This model is reflected to varying degrees in several programs sponsored by the National Institute of Justice and other agencies, programs like Weed and Seed; The Comprehensive Strategy for Serious, Violent, and Chronic Juvenile Offenders; SafeFutures; the Communities that Care model; the Strategic Approaches to Community Safety Initiative; Project PACT (Pulling America's Communities Together); and Empowerment Zones/Enterprise Communities.[2] Some of these programs focus specifically on crime and delinquency, while others focus on a broad range of social problems including crime. These programs are typically run in high-crime communities, sometimes in neighborhoods and sometimes in larger units, including entire cities.

The programs employ a similar strategy. First, community leaders are told about the program and an effort is made to enlist their support. These community leaders include the mayor; police chief; judges; school superintendent; leaders from the business, civic, and religious communities; and sometimes representatives from state and federal agencies. Second, if these community leaders are supportive, they put together a team of people responsible for implementing and running the program. This broad-based team includes representatives from the police and courts, social welfare agencies, school system, health system, business and religious communities, and community organizations. Third, after receiving some training this team proceeds to identify community problems that contribute to delinquency and community resources that might be used to deal with these problems. Among other things, the team collects information from community residents—including juveniles—and from experts in the area. Fourth, the team takes responsibility for designing and implementing a comprehensive approach for addressing the community problems they have identified. The team may be provided with a menu of promising programs from which they can choose. And they may appoint task forces in different areas. One task force, for example, may focus on the development of programs to address family problems. Finally, the team assumes responsibility for evaluating the approach they have developed and revising it if necessary.

The federal government and other organizations assist communities in this effort. The federal government, for example, provides technical assistance on a range of topics, such as promising programs, program implementation, and program evaluation. The government provides information on funding sources and often provides some funding itself. And the government facilitates communication with other teams across the country. (See the following web sites for examples of federally supported programs designed to spread information about promising programs, funding opportunities, and issues like program implementation and evaluation: *www.colorado.edu/cspv/ blueprints/* and *http://www.pavnet.org/*). Many communities, in addition, may develop a group of local experts to assist in the process.

The comprehensive approach that is mounted will likely differ somewhat from community to community, since different communities have different problems and different resources. For example, one community may have a serious gang problem and so may mount a variety of gang intervention programs. Another community may have little or no problem with gangs. At the same time, there are certain common features in the comprehensive approaches that are developed. Prevention programs are typically developed in a range of different areas, since delinquency is caused by a range of problems. These programs involve broad segments of the community, including the juvenile justice system, the schools, social service agencies, community organizations, the business community, and religious organizations. These programs usually target juveniles at high risk for delinquency. Efforts are sometimes made to encourage family members and school officials to identify such juveniles (e.g., family members are encouraged to seek help if they are having problems with their children). Likewise, a number of rehabilitation programs are usually developed. The local juvenile court develops a procedure to carefully screen all referred youths, so that they can be provided with the rehabilitation services they need. A special effort is made to target serious, high-rate, and chronic offenders for treatment, since they account for such a large share of the delinquency problem. Finally, a procedure is developed to carefully monitor the progress of delinquent youths and adjust their treatment if necessary.

We Should Hold Juveniles Accountable for Their Behavior and Protect the Community

I also believe that juveniles should be sanctioned for their delinquent acts and that the community should be protected from dangerous offenders. Data indicate that *one* of the reasons that juveniles engage in delinquency is low direct control. That is, they are not consistently sanctioned for their delinquent acts. Further, most people believe that juveniles, especially older juveniles, have at least some responsibility for their behavior. This issue is the subject of much debate in the social/behavioral sciences and philosophy (see Agnew, 1995c; Zimring, 1998). It is commonly argued that human behavior is not *fully determined* by outside forces, so holding juveniles accountable for their behavior may prevent *some* delinquency and may be viewed as a just approach in some cases. Further, this strategy has much political and public support.

The juvenile justice system, of course, is concerned right now with holding juveniles accountable for their behavior. But the system has not done so in an efficient manner. We pass laws that increase the *severity* of punishment, especially for serious offenders. Passage of such laws is easily done and is politically popular. Data, however, indicate that the *certainty* of punishment is much more important than the *severity*. Unfortunately, it is not so easy to increase the certainty of punishment. But among other things, those concerned with juvenile justice might do the following: We should teach parents, teachers and others how to better exercise direct control, for they are in the best position to detect and sanction delinquent acts. The juvenile justice system should also make a better effort to detect and sanction delinquency. As indicated in Chapter 18, communities can hire more police and improve strategies of policing in ways that increase the ability of the police to catch offenders. In particular, data suggest that focused police crackdowns and certain types of community policing are effective in this area. And society can

❖ ❖ ❖ ❖

provide more resources to the juvenile court and juvenile corrections system so that they can better sanction offenders. In particular, the juvenile justice system should employ a system of "graduated sanctions" such that all offenders receive meaningful sanctions and these sanctions increase in severity if offending continues.

We not only need to increase the certainty of punishment, but also need to change how we punish. The punishments now employed often have a number of negative effects: They increase strain, isolate juveniles from conventional society, and foster the social learning of crime. The system should punish in ways that minimize these negative effects. Community-based sanctions should be employed to the extent possible, since these sanctions avoid the sometimes negative effects of institutions. As indicated in Chapter 19, a range of new community-based sanctions have been developed, and these sanctions are more cost-effective than institutionalization. We should punish in a way that rebuilds the ties between offenders and the larger community, perhaps employing some of the initiatives associated with the restorative justice movement (e.g., offenders repair the damage they have caused to their victims and the larger community; efforts are made to involve offenders in positive community activities). We should work to eliminate discrimination in the justice system. Finally, sanctions should be combined with treatment of the types described previously. Data indicate that sanctions are most effective when combined with efforts that address the other causes of delinquency.

It is also important, of course, to protect the community from dangerous offenders. This protection is now often accomplished by institutionalizing juveniles in large facilities that place little emphasis on rehabilitation. Data, however, suggest that the system institutionalizes more juveniles than is necessary. And data suggest that it is better to confine juveniles in small-scale institutions that place a strong emphasis on treatment. Such juveniles are less likely to be harmed by their institutional confinement and are more likely to be rehabilitated, which, of course, contributes to the protection of the community. Adjudicated delinquents can be screened for their risk of future offending, particularly serious offending. Juveniles who pose some risk to the community can be placed under close supervision or confined in institutions, if warranted. Close supervision and institutional confinement may prevent some delinquency through their "incapacitation effect," as discussed in Chapter 21.

These strategies are described in detail in the publications listed in Notes 1 and 2. I also encourage you to examine the web sites of the National Institute of Justice and many of the agencies that are part of NIJ, like the Office of Juvenile Justice and Delinquency Prevention (*www.ojp.usdoj.gov/nij*). Also, call 800-WE-PREVENT to receive a booklet that describes what you can do to reduce delinquency (or visit *www.weprevent.org*). I hope that your examination of delinquency does not end with this book. Rather, I hope that this book represents the beginning of a serious commitment to work toward the reduction of delinquency in our society.

Notes

1. *See* Bilchik, 1998; Coordinating Council on Juvenile Justice and Delinquency Prevention, 1996; Howell, 1997a; Kurlychek et al., 1999.
2. *See* Coleman et al., 1999; Coolbough and Hansel 2000; Coordinating Council on Juvenile Justice and Delinquency Prevention, 1996; Dunworth and Mills, 1999;

Howell, 1997a; Howell and Hawkins, 1998; National Institute of Justice, 1996; Office of Juvenile Justice and Delinquency Prevention, 1999b; Office of Justice Programs, 1999; Robinson, 1996; Sherman et al., 1998. ✦

References

❖ ❖ ❖ ❖   **Abt Associates**
1994 Conditions of Confinement: Juvenile Detention and Corrections Facilities. Washington, DC: Office of Juvenile Justice and Delinquency Prevention.

Acoca, Leslie
1998 "Outside/inside: The violation of American girls at home, on the streets, and in the juvenile justice system." Crime and Delinquency 44:561–589.

Agnew, Robert
1983 "Physical punishment and delinquency." Youth and Society 15:225–236.

1984 "Autonomy and delinquency." Sociological Perspectives 27:219–240.

1985a "A revised strain theory of delinquency." Social Forces 64:151–167.

1985b "Social control theory and delinquency: A longitudinal test." Criminology 23:47–62.

1986 "Work and delinquency among juveniles attending school." Journal of Crime and Justice 9:19–41.

1990a "The origins of delinquent events: An examination of offender accounts." Journal of Research in Crime and Delinquency 27:267–294.

1990b "Adolescent resources and delinquency." Criminology 28:535–566.

1991a "A longitudinal test of social control theory and delinquency." Journal of Research on Crime and Delinquency 28:126–156.

1991b "The interactive effect of peer variables on delinquency." Criminology 29:47–72.

1992 "Foundation for a general strain theory of crime and delinquency." Criminology 30:47–87.

1993 "Why do they do it? An examination of the intervening mechanisms between 'social control' variables and delinquency." Journal of Research in Crime and Delinquency 30:245–266.

1994a "Delinquency and the desire for money." Justice Quarterly 11:411–427.

1994b "The techniques of neutralization and violence." Criminology 32:555–580.

1995a "Testing the leading crime theories: An alternative strategy focusing on motivational processes." Journal of Research in Crime and Delinquency 32:363–398.

1995b "Strain and subcultural theories of criminality." Pp. 305–327 in Joseph F. Sheley, ed., Criminology: A Contemporary Handbook. Belmont, CA: Wadsworth.

1995c "Determinism, indeterminism, and crime: An empirical exploration." Criminology 33:83–109.

1997 "Stability and change in crime over the life course: A strain theory explanation." Pp. 101–132 in Terence P. Thornberry, ed., Developmental Theories of Crime and Delinquency: Advances in Criminological Theory, Volume 7. New Brunswick, NJ: Transaction.

1999 "A general strain theory of community differences in crime rates." Journal of Research in Crime and Delinquency 36:123–155.

Forthcoming "An overview of general strain theory." In Ray Paternoster, ed., Essays in Criminological Theories. Los Angeles: Roxbury.

Agnew, Robert, and Timothy Brezina
1997 "Relational problems with peers, gender and delinquency." Youth and Society 29:84–111.

Agnew, Robert, Francis T. Cullen, Velmer S. Burton Jr., T. David Evans, and R. Gregory Dunaway
1996 "A new test of classic strain theory." Justice Quarterly 13:681–704.

Agnew, Robert, and Ardith A. R. Peters
1985 "The techniques of neutralization: An analysis of predisposing and situational factors." Criminal Justice and Behavior 13:81–97.

Agnew, Robert, and David M. Petersen   ❖ ❖ ❖ ❖
1989 "Leisure and delinquency." Social Problems 36:332–350.

Agnew, Robert, and Helene Raskin White
1992 "An empirical test of general strain theory." Criminology 30:475–499.

Akers, Ronald L.
1985 Deviant Behavior: A Social Learning Approach. Belmont, CA: Wadsworth.

1990 "Rational choice, deterrence, and social learning theory in criminology: The path not taken." Journal of Criminal Law and Criminology 81:653–676.

1992 Drugs, Alcohol, and Society. Belmont, CA: Wadsworth.

1997 Criminological Theories. Los Angeles: Roxbury.

1998 Social Learning and Social Structure: A General Theory of Crime and Deviance. Boston: Northeastern University Press.

Akers, Ronald L., Marvin D. Krohn, Lonn Lanza-Kaduce, and Marcia Radosevich
1979 "Social learning and deviant behavior: A specific test of a general theory." American Sociological Review 44: 635–655.

Akers, Ronald L., James Massey, William Clarke, and Ronald M. Lauer
1983 "Are self-reports of adolescent deviance valid? Biochemical measures, randomized response, and the bogus pipeline in smoking behavior." Social Forces 62:234–251.

Alexander, Karl L.
1997 "Public schools and the public good." Social Forces 76:1–30.

Altschuler, David M.
1998 "Intermediate sanctions and community treatment for serious and violent juvenile offenders." Pp. 367–388 in Rolf Loeber and David P. Farrington, eds., Serious and Violent Juvenile Offenders. Thousand Oaks, CA: Sage.

Altschuler, David M., Troy L. Armstrong, and Doris Layton MacKenzie
1999 Reintegration, Supervised Release, and Intensive Aftercare. Washington, DC: Office of Juvenile Justice and Delinquency Prevention.

Altschuler, David M., and Paul J. Brounstein
1991 "Patterns of drug use, drug trafficking, and other delinquency among inner-city adolescent males in Washington, D.C." Criminology 29:589–622.

Anderson, David C.
1998 "Curriculum, culture, and community: The challenge of school violence." Pp. 317–363 in Michael Tonry and Mark H. Moore, eds., Crime and Justice: A Review of Research, Volume 24. Chicago: University of Chicago Press.

Anderson, Elijah
1990 Streetwise: Race, Class and Change in an Urban Community. Chicago: University of Chicago Press.

1994 "The code of the streets." Atlantic Monthly 273(May):81–94.

1997 "Violence and the inner-city street code." Pp. 1–30 in Joan McCord, ed., Violence and Childhood in the Inner City. Cambridge, England: Cambridge University Press.

1999 Code of the Street. New York: W. W. Norton.

Anderson, Patrick R., and Donald J. Newman
1998 Introduction to Criminal Justice. Boston: McGraw-Hill.

Andrews, D. A., and James Bonta
1998 The Psychology of Criminal Conduct. Cinncinnati, OH: Anderson.

Andrews, D. A., Ivan Zinger, Robert D. Hoge, James Bonta, Paul Gendreau, and Francis T. Cullen
1990 "Does correctional treatment work? A clinically relevant and psychologically informed meta-analysis." Criminology 28:369–404.

Applegate, Brandon K., Francis T. Cullen, and Bonnie S. Fisher
1997 "Public support for correctional treatment: The continuing appeal of the rehabilitative ideal." The Prison Journal 77:237–258.

Archer, Dane, and Patricia McDaniel
1995 "Violence and gender: Differences and similarities across societies." Pp. 63–88 in R. Barry Ruback and Neil Alan Weiner, eds., Interpersonal Violent Behaviors. New York: Springer.

Aries, Philippe
1962 Centuries of Childhood. New York: Vintage Books.

Armstrong, Troy L., and David M. Altschuler
1998 "Recent developments in juvenile aftercare: Assessment, findings, and promising programs." Pp. 448–472 in Albert K. Roberts, ed., Juvenile Justice. Chicago: Nelson-Hall.

Arnette, June L., and Marjorie C. Walsleben
1998 "Combating Fear and Restoring Safety in Schools." Washington, DC: Office of Juvenile Justice and Delinquency Prevention.

Auerhahn, Kathleen
1999 "Selective incapacitation and the problem of prediction." Criminology 37:703–734.

Austin, James
1995 "The overrepresentation of minority youths in the California juvenile justice system." Pp. 153–178 in Kimberly Kempf Leonard, Carl E. Pope, and William H. Feyerherm, eds., Minorities in Juvenile Justice. Thousand Oaks, CA: Sage.

Babbie, Earl
1995 The Practice of Social Research. Belmont, CA: Wadsworth.

Baldwin, John D., and Janice I. Baldwin
1981 Behavior Principles in Everyday Life. Englewood Cliffs, NJ: Prentice Hall.

Balkwell, James W.
1990 "Ethnic inequality and the rate of homicide." Social Forces 69:53–70.

Bandura, Albert
1973 Aggression: A Social Learning Approach. Englewood Cliffs, NJ: Prentice Hall.
1986 Social Foundations of Thought and Action: A Social Cognitive Theory. Englewood Cliffs, NJ: Prentice Hall.
1990 "Selective activation and disengagement of moral control." Journal of Social Issues 46:27–46.

Barlow, Hugh D.
1995 Crime and Public Policy. Boulder, CO: Westview.

Baron, Robert A., and Deborah R. Richardson
1994 Human Aggression. New York: Plenum.

Baron, Stephen W., and Timothy F. Hartnagel
1997 "Attributions, affect, and crime: Street youth's reactions to unemployment." Criminology 35:409–434.

Bartol, Curt R., and Anne M. Bartol
1986 Criminal Behavior: A Psychosocial Approach. Englewood Cliffs, NJ: Prentice Hall.

Bartusch, Dawn R. Jeglum, Donald R. Lynam, Terrie E. Moffitt, and Phil A. Silva
1997 "Is age important? Testing a general versus a developmental theory of antisocial behavior." Criminology 35:13–48.

Bartusch, Dawn Jeglum, and Ross L. Matsueda
1996 "Gender, reflected appraisals, and labeling: A cross-group test of an interactionist theory of delinquency." Social Forces 75:145–177.

Battin, Sara R., Karl G. Hill, Robert D. Abbott, Richard F. Catalano, and J. David Hawkins
1998 "The contribution of gang membership to delinquency beyond delinquent friends." Criminology 36:93–115.

Bazemore, Gordon, and Mark S. Umbreit
1994 Balanced and Restorative Justice: Program Summary. Washington, DC: Office of Juvenile Justice and Delinquency Prevention.

Beckett, Katherine, and Theodore Sasson
2000 The Politics of Injustice. Thousand Oaks, CA: Pine Forge.

Berger, Ronald J.
1989 "Female delinquency in the emancipation era: A review of the literature." Sex Roles 21:375–399.

Berkowitz, Leonard
1993 Aggression: Its Causes, Consequences, and Control. New York: McGraw-Hill.
1994 "Guns and youth." Pp. 251–279 in Leonard D. Eron, Jacquelyn H. Gentry, and Peggy Schlegel, eds., Reason to Hope. Washington, DC: American Psychological Association.

Berman, Mitchell E., Richard J. Kavoussi, and Emil F. Coccaro
1997 "Neurotransmitter correlates of human aggression." Pp. 305–313 in David M. Stoff, James Breiling, and Jack D. Maser, eds., Handbook of Antisocial Behavior. New York: Wiley.

Bernard, Thomas J.
1984 "Control criticisms of strain theories: An assessment of theoretical and empirical adequacy." Journal of Research in Crime and Delinquency 21:353–372.
1990 "Angry aggression among the 'truly disadvantaged.' " Criminology 28:73–96.
1992 The Cycle of Juvenile Justice. New York: Oxford.
1999 "Juvenile crime and the transformation of juvenile justice: Is there a juvenile crime wave?" Justice Quarterly 16:337–356.

Bernard, Thomas J., and Jeffrey B. Snipes
1996 "Theoretical integration in criminology." Pp. 301–348 in Michael Tonry, ed., Crime and Justice, Volume 20. Chicago: University of Chicago Press.

Bilchik, Shay
1998 A Juvenile Justice System for the 21st Century. Washington, DC: Office of Juvenile Justice and Delinquency Prevention.

Binder, Arnold, Gilbert Geis, and Dickson D. Bruce, Jr.
1997 Juvenile Delinquency. Cincinnati: Anderson.

Birkbeck, Christopher, and Gary LaFree
1993 "The situational analysis of crime and deviance." Annual Review of Sociology 19:113–137.

Bishop, Donna M., Charles E. Frazier, Lonn Lanza-Kaduce, and Lawrence Winner
1996 "The transfer of juveniles to criminal court: Does it make a difference?" Crime and Delinquency 42:171–191.

❖ ❖ ❖ ❖   **Bjerregaard, Beth, and Alan J. Lizotte**
1995 "Gun ownership and gang membership." Journal of Criminal Law and Criminology 86:37–58.

Bjerregaard, Beth, and Carolyn Smith
1993 "Gender differences in gang participation, delinquency, and substance use." Journal of Quantitative Criminology 4:329–355.

Blackburn, Ronald
1993 The Psychology of Criminal Conduct. Chichester, England: John Wiley and Sons.

Blazak, Randy
1999 "Hate in the suburbs: The rise of the skinhead counterculture." Pp. 49–56 in Lisa J. McIntyre, ed., The Practical Skeptic: Readings in Sociology. Mountain View, CA: Mayfield.

Blumstein, Alfred
1995 "Youth violence, guns, and the illicit-drug industry." Journal of Criminal Law and Criminology 86:10–36.

1998 "U.S. criminal justice conundrum: Rising prison populations and stable crime rates." Crime and Delinquency 44:127–135.

Bottoms, Anthony E.
1994 "Environmental criminology." Pp. 585–655 in Mike Maguire, Rod Morgan, and Robert Reiner, eds., The Oxford Handbook of Criminology. Oxford, England: Clarendon Press.

Bowker, Lee H., and Malcolm W. Klein
1983 "The etiology of female juvenile delinquency and gang membership: A test of psychological and social structural explanations." Adolescence 18:739–751.

Boyum, David, and Mark A. R. Kleiman
1995 "Alcohol and other drugs." Pp. 295–326 in James Q. Wilson and Joan Petersilia, eds., Crime. San Francisco: ICS Press.

Braga, Anthony A., David L. Weisburd, Elin J. Waring, Lorraine Green Mazerolle, William Spelman, and Francis Gajewski
1999 "Problem-oriented policing in violent crime places: A randomized controlled experiment." Criminology 37:541–580.

Braithwaite, John
1981 "The myth of social class and criminality reconsidered." American Sociological Review 46:36–57.

1989 Crime, Shame and Reintegration. Cambridge, England: Cambridge University Press.

Brandl, Steven G., and David E. Barlow
1996 Classics in Policing. Cincinnati, OH: Anderson.

Brantingham, Paul, and Patricia Brantingham
1984 Patterns in Crime. New York: Macmillan.

Brennan, Patricia A., Sarnoff A. Mednick, and Jan Volavka
1995 "Biomedical factors in crime." Pp. 65–90 in James Q. Wilson and Joan Petersilia, eds., Crime. San Francisco: ICS Press.

Brennan, Patricia A., and Adrian Raine
Forthcoming "Biosocial bases of antisocial behavior: Psychophysiological, neurological and cognitive factors." Clinical Psychology Review.

Brewer, Devon D., J. David Hawkins, Richard F. Catalano, and Holly J. Neckerman
1995 "Preventing serious, violent, and chronic juvenile offending: A review of evaluations of selected strategies in childhood, adolescence, and the community." Pp.

61–141 in James C. Howell, Barry Krisberg, J. David Hawkins, and John J. Wilson, eds., A Sourcebook: Serious, Violent, and Chronic Juvenile Offenders. Thousand Oaks, CA: Sage.

Brezina, Timothy
1998 "Adolescent maltreatment and delinquency: The question of intervening processes." Journal of Research in Crime and Delinquency 35:71–99.

Briar, Scott, and Irving Piliavin
1965 "Delinquency, situational inducements, and commitment to conformity." Social Problems 13:35–45.

Bridges, George S., Darlene J. Conley, Rodney L. Engen, and Townsand Price-Spratlen
1995 "Racial disparities in the confinement of juveniles: Effects of crime and community structure on punishment." Pp. 128–152 in Kimberly Kempf Leonard, Carl E. Pope, and William H. Feyerherm, eds., Minorities in Juvenile Justice. Thousand Oaks, CA: Sage.

Bridges, George S., and Sara Steen
1998 "Racial disparities in official assessments of juvenile offenders: Attributional stereotypes as mediating mechanisms." American Sociological Review 63:554–570.

Bridges, George S., and James A. Stone
1986 "Effects of criminal punishment on perceived threat of punishment: Toward an understanding of specific deterrence." Journal of Research on Crime and Delinquency 23:207–239.

Broidy, Lisa, and Robert Agnew
1997 "Gender and crime: A general strain theory perspective." Journal of Research in Crime and Delinquency 34:275–306.

Brooks-Gunn, Jeanne, and Greg J. Duncan
1997 "The effects of poverty on children." The Future of Children 7:55–71.

Brown, Lee P.
1989 "Community policing: A practical guide for police officials." Washington, DC: National Institute of Justice.

Brownfield, David
1986 "Social class and violent behavior." Criminology 24:421–438.

Browning, Katharine, and David Huizinga
1999 Highlights of Findings From the Denver Youth Survey. Washington, DC: Office of Juvenile Justice and Delinquency Prevention.

Buikhuisen, W.
1988 "Chronic juvenile delinquency: A theory." Pp. 27–47 in W. Buikhuisen and Sarnoff A. Mednick, eds., Explaining Criminal Behavior. New York: E. J. Brill.

Building Blocks for Youth
2000 And Justice for Some. Available at *http://www.buildingblocksforyouth.org*

Burch, Jim, and Candice Kane
1999 Implementing the OJJDP Comprehensive Gang Model. Washington, DC: Office of Juvenile Justice and Delinquency Prevention.

Bureau of Justice Statistics
1992 Drugs, Crime, and the Justice System. Washington, DC: Bureau of Justice Statistics.

Burkett, Steven R., and Bruce O. Warren
1987 "Religiosity, peer associations, and adolescent marijuana use: A panel study of underlying causal structures." Criminology 25:109–131.

❖ ❖ ❖ ❖   **Bursik, Robert J., Jr .**
1986 "Delinquency rates as sources of ecological change." Pp. 63–74 in James M. Byrne and Robert J. Sampson, eds., The Social Ecology of Crime. New York: Springer-Verlag.
1988 "Social disorganization and theories of crime and delinquency: Problems and prospects." Criminology 26:519 551.

Bursik, Robert J., Jr., and Harold G. Grasmick
1993 Neighborhoods and Crime. New York: Lexington.
1995 "Neighborhood-based networks and the control of crime and delinquency." Pp. 107–130 in Hugh Barlow, ed., Crime and Public Policy . Boulder, CO: Westview.
1996 "The use of contextual analysis in models of criminal behavior." Pp. 236–267 in J. David Hawkins, ed., Delinquency and Crime. Cambridge, England: Cambridge University Press.

Burton, Velmer S., Jr., and Francis T. Cullen
1992 "The empirical status of strain theory." Journal of Crime and Justice 15:1–30.

Burton, Velmer S., Jr., Francis T. Cullen, T. David Evans, Leanne Fiftal Alarid, and R. Gregory Dunaway
1998 "Gender, self-control, and crime." Journal of Research in Crime and Delinquency 35:123–147.

Burton, Velmer S., Jr., Francis T. Cullen, T. David Evans, R. Gregory Dunaway, Sesha R. Kethineni, and Gary L. Payne
1995 "The impact of parental controls on delinquency." Journal of Criminal Justice 23:111–126.

Burton, Velmer S., Jr., and R. Gregory Dunaway
1994 "Strain, relative deprivation, and middle-class delinquency." Pp. 79–95 in Greg Barak, ed., Varieties of Criminology: Readings from a Dynamic Discipline. New York: Praeger.

Byrne, James M., and Robert J. Sampson
1986 "Key issues in the social ecology of crime." Pp. 1–22 in James M. Byrne and Robert J. Sampson, eds., The Social Ecology of Crime. New York: Springer-Verlag.

Campbell, Anne
1984 The Girls in the Gang. New York: Basil Blackwell.
1990 "Female participation in gangs." Pp. 163–182 in C. Ronald Huff, ed., Gangs in America. Newbury Park, CA: Sage.

Canter, Rachelle J.
1982 "Family correlates of male and female delinquency." Criminology 20:149–167.

Cao, Ligun, Anthony Adams, and Vickie J. Jenson
1997 "A test of the block subculture of violence thesis: A research note." Criminology 35:367–379.

Carey, Gregory, and David Goldman
1997 "The genetics of antisocial behavior." Pp. 243–254 in David M. Stoff, James Breiling, and Jack D. Maser, eds., Handbook of Antisocial Behavior. New York: Wiley.

Carter, David L.
1995 "Community policing and D.A.R.E.: A Practitioner's Perspective." Washington, DC: Bureau of Justice Statistics Bulletin.

Caspi, Avshalom, Daryl J. Bem, and Glen H. Elder, Jr.
1989 "Continuities and consequences of interactional styles across the life course." Journal of Personality 57:375–406.

Caspi, Avshalom, Terrie E. Moffitt, Phil A. Silva, Magda Stouthamer-Loeber, Robert F. Krueger, and Pamela S. Schmutte
1994 "Are some people crime-prone? Replications of the personality-crime relationship across countries, genders, races, and methods." Criminology 32:163–195.

Catalano, Richard F., Michael W. Arthur, J. David Hawkins, Lisa Berglund, and Jeffrey J. Olson
1998 "Comprehensive community- and school-based interventions to prevent antisocial behavior." Pp. 248–283 in Rolf Loeber and David P. Farrington, eds., Serious and Violent Juvenile Offenders. Thousand Oaks, CA: Sage.

Catalano, Richard F., and J. David Hawkins
1996 "The social development model: A theory of antisocial behavior." Pp. 149–197 in J. David Hawkins, ed., Delinquency and Crime. Cambridge, England: Cambridge University Press.

Cernkovich, Stephen A., and Peggy C. Giordano
1987 "Family relationships and delinquency." Criminology 25:295–321.
1992 "School bonding, race, and delinquency." Criminology 30:261–291.

Cernkovich, Stephen A., Peggy C. Giordano, and Meredith D. Pugh
1985 "Chronic offenders: The missing cases in self-report delinquency research." Journal of Criminal Law and Criminology 76:705–732.

Chaiken, Jan M., Peter W. Greenwood, and Joan Petersilia
1977 "The criminal investigation process: A summary report." Policy Analysis 3:187–217.

Chaiken, Marcia R.
1998 Kids, COPS, and Communities. Washington, DC: National Institute of Justice.

Chambliss, William J.
1973 "The saints and the roughnecks." Society 11(1):24–31.

Chamlin, Mitchell B.
1991 "A longitudinal analysis of the arrest-crime relationship: A further examination of the tipping effect." Justice Quarterly 8:187–199.

Chamlin, Mitchell B., Harold G. Grasmick, Robert J. Bursik, Jr., and John K. Cochran
1992 "Time aggregation and time lag in macro-level deterrence research." Criminology 30:377–395.

Champion, Dean J.
1998 The Juvenile Justice System. Upper Saddle River, NJ: Prentice Hall.
2000 Research Methods for Criminal Justice and Criminology. Upper Saddle River, NJ: Prentice Hall.

Chesney-Lind, Meda
1989 "Girls' crime and woman's place: Toward a feminist model of female delinquency." Crime and Delinquency 35:5–29.

Chesney-Lind, Meda, and Randall G. Shelden
1998 Girls, Delinquency, and Juvenile Justice. Pacific Grove, CA: Brooks/Cole.

Chesney-Lind, Meda, Randall G. Shelden, and Karen A. Joe
1996 "Girls, delinquency, and gang membership." Pp. 185–204 in C. Ronald Huff, ed., Gangs in America. Thousand Oaks, CA: Sage.

Chitwood, Dale E., James E. Rivers, and James A. Inciardi
1996 The American Pipe Dream: Crack Cocaine and the Inner City. Fort Worth: Harcourt Brace.

❖ ❖ ❖ ❖   **Clark, John, and Larry Tift**
1966 "Polygraph and interview validation of self-reported deviant behavior." American Sociological Review 31:516–523.

Clarke, Ronald V.
1992 Situational Crime Prevention. New York: Harrow and Heston.
1995 "Situational crime prevention." Pp. 91–150 in Michael Tonry and David F. Farrington, eds., Crime and Justice: A Review of Research, Volume 19. Chicago: University of Chicago Press.

Clarke, Ronald V., and Derek B. Cornish
1985 "Modeling offenders' decisions: A framework for research and policy." Pp. 147–183 in Michael Tonry and Norval Morris, eds., Crime and Justice: An Annual Review of Research, Volume 6. Chicago: University of Chicago Press.

Clear, Todd
1988 "Statistical prediction in correction." Research in Correction 1:1–39.

Clement, Mary
1997 The Juvenile Justice System. Boston: Butterworth-Heinemann.

Cloninger, C. Robert
1987 "A systematic method for clinical description and classification of personality variants." The Archives of General Psychiatry 44:573–588.

Cloward, Richard A., and Lloyd E. Ohlin
1960 Delinquency and Opportunity. New York: Free Press.

Cloward, Richard A., and Frances Fox Piven
1979 "Hidden protest: The channeling of female innovation and resistance." Signs 4:651–669.

Cochran, John K., Peter B. Wood, and Bruce J. Arneklev
1994 "Is the religiosity-delinquency relationship spurious? A test of arousal and social control theories." Journal of Research in Crime and Delinquency 31:92–123.

Cohen, Albert K.
1955 Delinquent Boys. New York: Free Press.

Cohen, Lawrence E., and Marcus Felson
1979 "Social change and crime rate trends: A routine activity approach." American Sociological Review 44:588–608.

Cohen, Lawrence E., James R. Kluegel, and Kenneth C. Land
1981 "Social inequality and predatory criminal victimization: An exposition and test of a formal theory." American Sociological Review 46:505–524.

Cohen, Lawrence E., and Bryan J. Villa
1996 "Self-control and social control: An exposition of the Gottfredson-Hirschi/Sampson-Laub debate." Studies on Crime and Crime Prevention 5:125–150.

Cohen, Mark
1998 "The monetary value of saving a high-risk youth." Journal of Quantitative Criminology 14:5–31.

Coleman, James S., Thomas Hoffer, and Sally Kilgore
1982 High School Achievement. New York: Basic Books.

Coleman, Veronica, Walter C. Holton, Jr., Kristine Olson, Stephen C. Robinson, and Judith Stewart
1999 "Using knowledge and teamwork to reduce crime." National Institute of Justice Journal: October 1999:17–23.

Compas, Bruce E.
1987 "Stress and life events during childhood and adolescence." Clinical Psychology Review 7:275–302.

Conger, Rand D.
1976 "Social control and social learning models of delinquent behavior." Criminology 14:17–54.

Conger, Rand D., Katherine J. Conger, Glen H. Elder, Jr., Frederick O. Lorenz, Ronald L. Simons, and Les B. Whitbeck
1992 "A family process model of economic hardship and adjustment of early adolescent boys." Child Development 63:526–541.

Conger, Rand D., Xiaojia Ge, Glen H. Elder, Jr., Frederick O. Lorenz, and Ronald L. Simons
1994 "Economic stress, coercive family process, and developmental problems of adolescents." Child Development 65:541–561.

Conger, Rand D., Gerald R. Patterson, and Xiaojia Ge
1995 "It takes two to replicate: A mediational model for the impact of parents' stress on adolescent adjustment." Child Development 66:80–97.

Conklin, John E.
1992 Criminology. New York: MacMillan.

Cook, Philip J.
1991 "The technology of personal violence." Pp. 1–71 in Michael Tonry, ed., Crime and Justice: A Review of Research, Volume 14. Chicago: University of Chicago Press.

Cook, Philip J., and John H. Laub
1998 "The unprecedented epidemic in youth violence." Pp. 27–64 in Michael Tonry and Mark H. Moore, eds., Crime and Justice: A Review of Research, Volume 24. Chicago: University of Chicago Press.

Cook, Philip J., and Jens Ludwig
1997 "Guns in America: National Survey on Private Ownership and Use of Firearms." Washington, DC: National Institute of Justice.
1998 "Defensive gun uses: New evidence from a national survey." Journal of Quantitative Criminology 14:111–130.

Cook, Philip J., and Mark H. Moore
1995 "Gun control." Pp. 267–294 in James Q. Wilson and Joan Petersilia, eds., Crime. San Francisco: ICS Press.

Coolbough, Kathleen and Cynthis J. Monsel
2000 The Comprehensive Strategy: Lessons Learned From the Pilot Sites. Washington, DC: Office of Juvenile Justice and Delinquency Prevention.

Coordinating Council on Juvenile Justice and Delinquency Prevention
1996 Combating Violence and Delinquency: The National Juvenile Justice Action Plan. Washington, DC: US Department of Justice.

Cordner, Gary W.
1999 "Elements of community policing." Pp. 137–149 in Larry K. Gaines and Gary W. Cordner, eds., Policing Perspectives. Los Angeles: Roxbury.

Cornish, Derek B., and Ronald V. Clarke
1986 The Reasoning Criminal. New York: Springer-Verlag.

Costello, Barbara J. and Paul R. Vowell
1999 "Testing control theory and differential association: A reanalysis of the Richmond youth project." Criminology 37:815–842.

Cox, Steven M., and John J. Conrad
1996 Juvenile Justice. Madison, WI: Brown and Benchmark.

Crowe, Ann H.
1998 Drug Identification and Testing in the Juvenile Justice System. Washington, DC: Office of Juvenile Justice and Delinquency Prevention.

Cullen, Francis T.
1984 Rethinking Crime and Deviance Theory. Totowa, NJ: Rowman and Allanheld.
1994 "Social support as an organizing concept for criminology." Justice Quarterly 11:527–559.

Cullen, Francis T., and Robert Agnew
1999 Criminological Theory: Past to Present. Los Angeles: Roxbury.

Cullen, Francis T., and Brandon K. Applegate
1997 Offender Rehabilitation. Dartmouth, England: Ashgate.

Cullen, Frances T., Martha Todd Larson, and Richard A. Mothers
1985 "Having money and delinquent involvement: The neglect of power in delinquent theory." Criminal Justice and Behavior 12:171–192.

Cullen, Francis T., Nicolas Williams, and John Paul Wright
1997 "Work conditions and juvenile delinquency: Is youth employment criminogenic?" Criminal Justice Policy and Research 8:119–143.

Cullen, Francis T., and John Paul Wright
1996 "Social support as the basis of social control." Paper presented at the annual meeting of the American Society of Criminology, Chicago.

Cullen, Francis T., John Paul Wright, and Brandon K. Applegate
1996 "Control in the community: The limits of reform?" Pp. 69–116 in Alan T. Harland, ed., Choosing Correctional Options That Work. Thousand Oaks, CA: Sage.

Cullen, Francis T., John Paul Wright, Shayna Brown, Melissa M. Moon, Michael B. Blankenship, and Brandon K. Applegate
1998 "Public support for early intervention programs: Implications for a progressive policy agenda." Crime and Delinquency 44:187–204.

Currie, Elliott
1998 Crime and Punishment in America. New York: Owl Books.

Curry, G. David
1998 "Female gang involvement." Journal of Research in Crime and Delinquency 35:100–118.

Curry, G. David, Richard A. Ball, and Scott H. Decker
1996 Update on Gang Crime and Law Enforcement Record Keeping. Washington DC: U.S. Department of Justice.

Curry, G. David, and Scott H. Decker
1998 Confronting Gangs. Los Angeles: Roxbury.

Curtis, Lynn A.
1974 Criminal Violence: National Patterns and Behavior. Lexington, MA: Lexington Books.

Daly, Kathleen
1992 "Women's pathways to felony court: Feminist theories of lawbreaking and problems of representation." Review of Law and Women's Studies 2:11–52.
1998 "Gender, crime, and criminology." Pp. 85–108 in Michael Tonry, ed., The Handbook of Crime and Punishment. New York: Oxford.

Daly, Kathleen, and Meda Chesney-Lind
1988 "Feminism and criminology." Justice Quarterly 5:497–538.

Dannefer, Dale, and Russell K. Schutt
1982 "Race and juvenile justice processing in court and police agencies." American Journal of Sociology 87:1113–1132.

Decker, Scott H., and G. David Curry
2000 "Responding to gangs: Does the dose match the problem?" Pp. 561–575 in Joseph F. Sheley, ed., Criminology: A Contemporary Handbook. Belmont, CA: Wadsworth.

Decker, Scott H., and Janet L. Lauritsen
1996 "Breaking the bonds of membership: Leaving the gang." Pp. 103–136 in C. Ronald Huff, ed., Gangs in America. Thousand Oaks, CA: Sage.

Decker, Scott H., Susan Pennell, and Ami Caldwell
1997 "Illegal firearms: Access and use by arrestees." Washington, DC: National Institute of Justice.

Decker, Scott H., and Barrik Van Winkle
1996 Life in the Gang. Cambridge, England: Cambridge University Press,

DeComo, Robert E.
1998 "Estimating the prevalence of juvenile custody by race and gender." Crime and Delinquency 44:489–506.

DeJong, Christina, and Kenneth C. Jackson
1998 "Putting race into context: Race, juvenile justice processing, and urbanization." Justice Quarterly 15:487–504.

DeMause, Lloyd
1974 The History of Childhood. New York: Harper Books.

Denno, Deborah W.
1990 Biology and Violence. Cambridge, England: Cambridge University Press.

Dodge, Kenneth
1986 Social Competence in Children. Chicago: University of Chicago Press.

Dodge, Kenneth A., and D. Schwartz
1997 "Social information processing mechanisms in aggressive behavior." Pp. 171–180 in David M. Stoff, James Breiling, and Jack D. Maser, eds., Handbook of Antisocial Behavior. New York: Wiley.

Donnerstein, Edward, and Daniel Linz
1995 "The media." Pp. 237–264 in James Q. Wilson and Joan Petersilia, eds., Crime. San Francisco: ICS Press.

Donnerstein, Edward, Ronald G. Sloby, and Leonard D. Eron
1994 "The mass media and youth agression." Pp. 219–250 in Leonard D. Eron, Jacquelyn H. Gentry, and Peggy Schlegel, eds., Reason to Hope. Washington, DC: American Psychological Association.

Donziger, Steven R.
1996 The Real War on Crime. New York: HarperCollins.

Dubow, Eric F., and Graham J. Reid
1994 "Risk and resource variables in children's aggressive behavior." Pp. 187–211 in L. Rowell Huesmann, ed., Aggressive Behavior: Current Perspectives. New York: Plenum.

Dunford, Franklyn W., and Delbert S. Elliott
1984 "Identifying career offenders using self-report data." Journal of Research in Crime and Delinquency 21:57–86.

D'Unger, Amy V., Kenneth C. Land, Patricia L. McCall, and Daniel S. Nagin
1998 "How many latent classes of delinquent/criminal careers? Results from mixed poison regression analysis." American Journal of Sociology 103:1593–1630.

❖ ❖ ❖ ❖   **Dunworth, Terence, and Gregory Mills**
1999 National Evaluation of Weed and Seed. Washington, DC: National Institute of Justice.

Earle, Ralph B.
1995 "Helping to prevent child abuse—and future criminal consequences." Washington, DC: National Institute of Justice.

Earls, Felton, and Jacqueline Barnes
1997 "Understanding and preventing child abuse in urban settings." Pp. 207–255 in Joan McCord, ed., Violence and Childhood in the Inner City. Cambridge, England: Cambridge University Press.

Eck, John E., and William Spelman
1987 Problem Solving. Washington, DC: National Institute of Justice.

Elifson, Kirk W., David M. Petersen, and C. Kirk Hadaway
1983 "Religiosity and delinquency." Criminology 21:505–527.

Elliott, Delbert S.
1982 "Measuring delinquency (a review essay)." Criminology 20:527–538.
1994 "Serious violent offenders: Onset, developmental course, and termination." Criminology 32:1–21.
1995 "Lies, damn lies and arrest statistics." Paper presented at the annual meeting of the American Society of Criminology, Boston.

Elliott, Delbert S., and Suzanne S. Ageton
1980 "Reconciling race and class differences in self-reported and official estimates of delinquency." American Sociological Review 45:95–110.

Elliott, Delbert S., Suzanne Ageton, and Rachel Canter
1979 "An integrated theoretical perspective on delinquent behavior." Journal of Research in Crime and Delinquency 16:3–27.

Elliott, Delbert S., Beatrix A. Hamburg, and Kirk R. Williams
1998 Violence in American Schools. Cambridge, England: Cambridge University Press.

Elliott, Delbert S., and David Huizinga
1983 "Social class and delinquent behavior in a national youth panel: 1976–1980." Criminology 21:149–177.

Elliott, Delbert S., David Huizinga, and Suzanne S. Ageton
1985 Explaining Delinquency and Drug Use. Beverly Hills, CA: Sage.

Elliott, Delbert S., David Huizinga, and Scott Menard
1989 Multiple Problem Youth. New York: Springer-Verlag.

Elliott, Delbert S., and Scott Menard
1996 "Delinquent friends and delinquent behavior: Temporal and developmental patterns." Pp. 28–67 in J. David Hawkins, ed., Delinquency and Crime: Current Theories. Cambridge, England: Cambridge University Press.

Elliott, Delbert S., William Julius Wilson, David Huizinga, Robert J. Sampson, Amanda Elliott, and Bruce Rankin
1996 "The effects of neighborhood disadvantage on adolescent development." Journal of Research in Crime and Delinquency 33:389–426.

Ellis, Lee, and Anthony Walsh
1999 "Criminologists' opinions about causes and theories of crime and delinquency." The Criminologist 24:1, 4–5.

Empey, LaMar T., Mark C. Stafford, and Carter H. Hay
1999 American Delinquency. Belmont, CA: Wadsworth.

England, Ralph W.
1960 "A theory of middle class juvenile delinquency." Journal of Criminal Law, Criminology, and Police Science 50:535–540.

English, Diana J.
1998 "The extent and consequences of child maltreatment." The Future of Children 8:39–53.

Erez, Edna, editor
1995 Justice Quarterly 12(4).

Esbensen, Finn-Aage, and Elizabeth Piper Deschenes
1998 "A multisite examination of youth gang membership: Does gender matter?" Criminology 36:799–828.

Esbensen, Finn-Aage, Elizabeth Piper Deschenes, and L. Thomas Winfree, Jr.
1999 "Differences between gang girls and gang boys." Youth and Society 31:27–53.

Esbensen, Finn-Aage, and David Huizinga
1993 "Gangs, drugs, and delinquency in a survey of urban youth." Criminology 31:565–589.

Esbensen, Finn-Aage, David Huizinga, and Anne W. Weiher
1993 "Gang and non-gang youth: Differences in explanatory factors." Journal of Contemporary Criminal Justice 9:94–116.

Esbensen, Finn-Aage, and D. Wayne Osgood
1997 Research in Brief: National Evaluation of G.R.E.A.T. Washington, DC: Office of Juvenile Justice and Delinquency Prevention.
1999 "Gang resistance education and training (GREAT): Results from the national evaluation." Journal of Research in Crime and Delinquency 36:194–225.

Evans, T. David, Francis T. Cullen, Velmer S. Burton, Jr., and Michael L. Benson
1997 "The social consequences of self-control: Testing the general theory of crime." Criminology 35:475–504.

Evans, T. David, Francis T. Cullen, Velmer S. Burton, Jr., R. Gregory Dunaway, Gary L. Payne, and Sesha R. Kethineni
1996 "Religion, social bonds, and delinquency." Deviant Behavior 17:43–70.

Evans, T. David, Francis T. Cullen, R. Gregory Dunaway, and Velmer S. Burton, Jr.
1995 "Religion and crime reexamined: The impact of religion, secular controls, and social ecology on adult criminality." Criminology 33:195–224.

Eysenck, Hans J.
1977 Crime and Personality. London; Routledge and Kegan Paul.

Fagan, Jeffrey
1989 "The social organization of drug use and drug dealing among urban gangs." Criminology 27:633–669.
1990 "Social processes of delinquency and drug use among urban gangs." Pp. 183–219 in C. Ronald Huff, ed., Gangs in America. Thousand Oaks, CA: Sage.
1995 "Separating the men from the boys: The comparative advantage of juvenile versus criminal court sanctions on recidivism among adolescent felony offenders." Pp. 238–260 in James C. Howell, Barry Krisberg, J. David Hawkins, and John J. Wilson, eds., A Sourcebook: Serious, Violent, & Chronic Juvenile Offenders. Thousand Oaks, CA: Sage.
1996 "Gangs, drugs, and neighborhood change." Pp. 39–74 in C. Ronald Huff, ed., Gangs in America. Thousand Oaks, CA: Sage.

1998 Adolescent Violence: A View From the Street. Washington, DC: National Institute of Justice.

Farber, Henry, and Leon Stafford
1999 "Parents mystified as to what set off son." Atlanta Constitution, August 11, E1, 3.

Farnworth, Margaret, Terence P. Thornberry, Marvin D. Krohn, and Alan J. Lizotte
1994 "Measurement in the study of class and delinquency: Integrating theory and research." Journal of Research in Crime and Delinquency 31:32–61.

Farrington, David P.
1977 "The effects of public labeling." British Journal of Criminology 17:112–125.

1986 "Age and crime." Crime and Justice 7:189–250.

1993a "Have any individual, family or neighborhood influences on offending been demonstrated conclusively?" Pp. 7–37 in David P. Farrington, Robert J. Sampson, and Per-Olof Wikstrom, eds., Integrating Individual and Ecological Aspects of Crime. Stockholm: National Council for Crime Prevention, Sweden.

1993b "Motivations for conduct disorder and delinquency." Development and Psychopathology 5:225–241.

1994 "Human development and criminal careers." Pp. 511–584 in Mike Maguire, Rod Morgan, and Robert Reiner, eds., The Oxford Handbook of Criminology. New York: Oxford University Press.

1995 "The development of offending and antisocial behaviour from childhood: Key findings from the Cambridge study in delinquent development." Journal of Child Psychology and Psychiatry 360:929–964.

1996a "The explanation and prevention of youthful offending." Pp. 68–148 in J. David Hawkins, ed., Delinquency and Crime: Current Theories. Cambridge, England: Cambridge University Press.

1996b "Criminological psychology: Individual and family factors in the explanation and prevention of offending." Pp. 3–39 in Clive R. Hollin, ed., Working With Offenders. Chichester, England: John Wiley and Sons.

1998 "Individual differences and offending." Pp. 241–268 in Michael Tonry, ed., The Handbook of Crime and Punishment. New York: Oxford.

Farrington, David P., Rolf Loeber, Magda Stouthamer-Loeber, Welmoet B. Van Kammen, and Laura Schmidt
1996 "Self-reported delinquency and a combined delinquency seriousness scale based on boys, mothers, and teachers: Concurrent and predictive validity for African-Americans and Caucasians." Criminology 34:493–517.

Farrington, David, Howard Snyder, and Terence Finnegan
1988 "Specialization in juvenile court careers." Criminology 26:461–485.

Farrington, David P., S. G. Soborn, and D. J. West
1978 "The persistence of labeling effects." British Journal of Criminology 18:277–284.

Federal Bureau of Investigation
1998 Crime in the United States, 1997. Washington, DC: US Government Printing Office.

Federal Interagency Forum on Child and Family Statistics
2000 America's Children: Key National Indicators of Well-Being. Washington, DC: US Government Printing Office.

Feindler, Eva L., and Judith V. Becker
1994 "Interventions in family violence involving children and adolescents." Pp. 405–430 in Leonard D. Eron, Jacquelyn H. Gentry, and Peggy Schlegel, eds., Reason to Hope. Washington, DC: American Psychological Association.

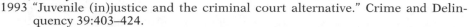

Feld, Barry C.
1993 "Juvenile (in)justice and the criminal court alternative." Crime and Delinquency 39:403–424.

1995 "The social construction of juvenile justice administration: Racial disparities in an urban juvenile court." Pp. 66–97 in Kimberly Kempf Leonard, Carl E. Pope, and William H. Feyerherm, eds., Minorities in Juvenile Justice. Thousand Oaks, CA: Sage

1998 "The juvenile court." Pp. 509–541 in Michael Tonry, ed., The Handbook of Crime and Punishment. New York: Oxford.

1999 Bad Kids. New York: Oxford University Press.

Felson, Marcus
1987 "Routine activities and crime prevention in the developing metropolis." Criminology 25:911–931.

1994 Crime and Everyday Life. Thousand Oaks, CA: Pine Forge.

1998 Crime and Everyday Life, 2nd edition. Thousand Oaks, CA: Pine Forge.

Felson, Richard B.
1993 "Predatory and dispute-related violence: A social interactionist approach." Pp. 103–125 in Ronald V. Clarke and Marcus Felson, eds., Routine Activity and Rational Choice; Advances in Criminological Theory, Volume 5. New Brunswick, NJ: Transaction.

1996 "Big people hit little people: Sex differences in physical power and interpersonal violence." Criminology 34:433–452.

1997 "Routine activities and involvement in violence as actor, witness, or target." Violence and Victims 12:209–221.

Felson, Richard B., and Henry J. Steadman
1983 "Situations and processes leading to criminal violence." Criminology 21:59–74.

Feyerherm, William H.
1995 "The DMC initiative." Pp. 1–15 in Kimberly Kempf Leonard, Carl E. Pope, and William H. Feyerherm, eds., Minorities in Juvenile Justice. Thousand Oaks, CA: Sage.

Finestone, Harold
1976 Victims of Change: Juvenile Delinquents in American Society. Westport, CT: Greenwood.

Finkelhor, David, and Richard Ormond
1999 Reporting Crimes Against Juveniles. Washington, DC: Office of Juvenile Justice and Delinquency Prevention.

Fischer, Donald G.
1984 "Family size and delinquency." Perceptual and Motor Skills 58:527–534.

Fishbein, Diana H.
1996 "The biology of antisocial behavior." Pp. 26–38 in John E. Conklin, ed., New Perspectives in Criminology. Boston: Allyn and Bacon.

Fishman, Laura T.
1995 "The vice queens: An ethnographic study of black female gang behavior." Pp. 83–92 in Malcolm Klein, Cheryl L. Maxson, and Jody Miller, eds., The Modern Gang Reader. Los Angeles: Roxbury.

Flanagan, Timothy, and Dennis Longmire
1996 Americans View Crime and Justice. Thousand Oaks, CA: Sage.

Foglia, Wanda D.
1997 "Perceptual deterrence and the mediating effect of internalized norms among inner-city teenagers." Journal of Research in Crime and Delinquency 34:414–442.

Fonseca, A. C., and W. Yule
1995 "Personality and antisocial behavior in children and adolescents: An enquiry into Eysenck's and Gray's theories." Journal of Abnormal Child Psychology 23:767–781.

Foshee, V., and K. E. Bauman
1992 "Parental and peer characteristics as modifiers of the bond-behavior relationship: An elaboration of control theory." Journal of Health and Social Behavior 33:66–76.

Fox, James Alan, and Marianne W. Zawitz
1999 Homicide Trends in the United States. Washington, DC: Bureau of Justice Statistics.

Frazier, Charles E., and Donna M. Bishop
1995 "Reflections on race effects in juvenile justice." Pp. 16–46 in Kimberly Kempf Leonard, Carl E. Pope, and William H. Feyerherm, eds., Minorities in Juvenile Justice. Thousand Oaks, CA: Sage.

Freedman, John L.
1984 "Effect of television violence on aggressiveness." Psychological Bulletin 96:227–246.

Fritsch, Eric J., Tory J. Caeti, and Robert W. Taylor
1999 "Gang suppression through saturation patrol, aggressive curfew and truancy enforcement: A quasi-experimental test of the Dallas anti-gang initiative." Crime and Delinquency 45:122–139.

Funk, Stephanie J.
1999 "Risk assessment for juveniles on probation: A focus on gender." Criminal Justice and Behavior 26:44–68.

Furstenberg, Frank F., Jr., J. Brooks-Gunn, and S. P. Morgan
1987 Adolescent Mothers in Later Life. Cambridge, England: Cambridge University Press.

Future of Children, The
1996 The Juvenile Court, Volume 6, Number 3. Los Altos, CA: Center for the Future of Children.

Gaines, Larry K., and Gary W. Cordner
1999 Policing Perspectives. Los Angeles: Roxbury.

Gallagher, Catherine A.
1999 Juvenile Offenders in Residential Placement, 1997. Washington, DC: Office of Juvenile Justice and Delinquency Prevention.

Garofalo, James, Leslie Siegel, and John Laub
1987 "School-related victimizations among adolescents: An analysis of national crime survey (NCS) narratives." Journal of Quantitative Criminology 3:321–338.

Gartin, Patrick R.
1995 "Dealing with design failures in randomized field experiments: Analytic issues regarding the evaluation of treatment effects." Journal of Research in Crime and Delinquency 32:425–445.

Gentry, Cynthia
1995 "Crime control through drug control." Pp. 477–493 in Joseph F. Sheley, ed., Criminology. Belmont, CA: Wadsworth.

Gerber, J., and S. Engelhardt-Greer
1996 "Just and painful: Attitudes toward sentencing criminals." Pp. 62–74 in T. Flanagan and D. Longmire, eds., Americans View Crime and Justice. Thousand Oaks, CA: Sage.

Gilfus, Mary E.
1992 "From victims to survivors to offenders: Women's routes of entry and immersion into street crime." Women and Criminal Justice 4:63–89.

Gilligan, Carol, and Jane Attanucci
1988 "Two moral orientations: Gender differences and similarities." Merrill-Palmer Quarterly 34:223–237.

Giordano, Peggy C.
1978 "Girls, guys and gangs: The changing social context of female delinquency." Journal of Criminal Law and Criminology 69:126–132.

Giordano, Peggy C., Stephen A. Cernkovich, and M. D. Pugh
1986 "Friendships and delinquency." American Journal of Sociology 91:1170–1202.

Glueck, Sheldon, and Eleanor Glueck
1950 Unraveling Juvenile Delinquency. New York: The Commonwealth Fund.

Gold, Martin
1966 "Undetected delinquent behavior." Journal of Research in Crime and Delinquency 3:27–46.

Gold, Martin, and Jay R. Williams
1969 "The effect of getting caught: Apprehension of a juvenile offender as a cause of subsequent delinquencies." Prospectus 3:1–12.

Goldsmid, Charles A., and Everett K. Wilson
1980 Passing on Sociology. Washington, DC: American Sociological Association.

Goldstein, Paul J.
1985 "The drugs/violence nexus: A tripartite conceptual framework." Journal of Drug Issues 15:493–506.

Goode, Erich
1993 Drugs in American Society. New York: McGraw-Hill.

Gorman, D. M., and Helene Raskin White
1995 "You can choose your friends, but do they chose your crime? Implications of differential association theories for crime prevention policy." Pp. 131–155 in Hugh Barlow, ed., Crime and Public Policy. Boulder, CO: Westview.

Gottfredson, Gary D., and Denise C. Gottfredson
1985 Victimization in Schools. New York: Plenum.

Gottfredson, Michael R., and Travis Hirschi
1990 A General Theory of Crime. Stanford, CA: Stanford University Press.

Gottfredson, Stephen D., and Don M. Gottfredson
1994 "Behavioral prediction and the problem of incapacitation." Criminology 32:441–474.

Gove, Walter R., and Robert D. Crutchfield
1982 "The family and juvenile delinquency." Sociological Quarterly 23:301–319.

Gove, Walter R., Michael Hughes, and Omer R. Galle
1979 "Overcrowding in the home: An empirical investigation of its possible pathological consequences." American Sociological Review 44:59–80.

Gove, Walter R., Michael Hughes, and Michael Geerken
1985 "Are uniform crime reports a valid indicator of the index crimes? An affirmative answer with minor qualifications." Criminology 23:451–502.

Grasmick, Harold G., and Robert J. Bursik, Jr.
1990 "Conscience, significant others, and rational choice: Extending the deterrence model." Law and Society Review 24:837–861.

Grasmick, Harold G., Charles R. Tittle, Robert J. Bursik, and Bruce J. Arneklev
1993 "Testing the core empirical implications of Gottfredson and Hirschi's general theory of crime." Journal of Research in Crime and Delinquency 30:5–29.

Greenbaum, Stuart
1997 "Kids and guns. From playgrounds to battlegrounds." Juvenile Justice 3:3–10.

Greenberg, David F.
1977 "Delinquency and the age structure of society." Contemporary Crises 1:189–223.

1985 "Age, crime, and social explanation." American Journal of Sociology 91:1–27.

Greenberg, David F., Ronald C. Kessler, and Colin Loftin
1983 "The effect of police employment on crime." Criminology 21:375–394.

Greenfeld, Lawrence A.
1998 Alcohol and Crime. Washington, DC: Bureau of Justice Statistics.

Greenwood, Peter W.
1995 "What works with juvenile offenders: A synthesis of the literature and experience." Federal Probation 58:63–67.

1998 "Investing in prisons or prevention: The state policy makers' dilemma." Crime and Delinquency 44:136–142.

1999 Costs and Benefits of Early Childhood Intervention. Washington, DC: Office of Juvenile Justice and Delinquency Prevention.

Greenwood, Peter W., Karyn E. Model, C. Peter Rydell, and James Chiesa
1996 Diverting Children From a Life of Crime: Measuring Costs and Benefits. Santa Monica, CA: RAND.

Griffiths, M.
1999 "Violent video games and aggression: A review of the literature." Aggression and Violent Behavior 4:203–212.

Grogger, Jeffrey
1997 "Incarceration-related costs of early childbearing." Pp. 231–255 in Rebecca A. Maynard, ed., Kids Having Kids. Washington, DC: Urban Institute Press.

Grossman, Jean Baldwin, and Eileen M. Garry
1997 Mentoring: A Proven Delinquency Prevention Strategy. Washington, DC: Office of Juvenile Justice and Delinquency Prevention.

Guerra, Nancy G.
1997 "Intervening to prevent childhood aggression in the inner city." Pp. 256–312 in Joan McCord, ed., Violence and Childhood in the Inner City. Cambridge, England: Cambridge University Press.

Guerra, Nancy G., Patrick H. Tolan, and W. Rodney Hammond
1994 "Prevention and treatment of adolescent violence." Pp. 383–403 in Leonard D. Eron, Jacquelyn H. Gentry, and Peggy Schlegel, eds., Reason to Hope. Washington, DC: American Psychological Association.

Hagan, John
1989 Structural Criminology. New Brunswick, NJ: Rutgers University Press.

1991 "Destiny and drift: Subcultural preferences, status attainments, and the risks and rewards of youth." American Sociological Review 56:567–581.

1992 "The poverty of a classless criminology." Criminology 30:1–19.

1994 Crime and Disrepute. Thousand Oaks, CA: Pine Forge Press.

Hagan, John, A. R. Gillis, and David Brownfield
1996 Criminological Controversies. Boulder, CO: Westview.

Hagan, John, and Bill McCarthy
1997a Mean Streets. Cambridge, England: Cambridge University Press.

1997b "Anomie, social capital, and street criminology." Pp. 124–141 in Nikos Passas and Robert Agnew, eds., The Future of Anomie Theory. Boston: Northeastern University Press.

Hagan, John, and Ruth D. Peterson
1995 "Criminal inequality in America: Patterns and consequences." Pp. 14–36 in John Hagan and Ruth D. Peterson, eds., Crime and Inequality. Stanford, CA: Stanford University Press.

Hagan, John, John H. Simpson, and A. R. Gillis
1979 "The sexual stratification of social control: A gender-based perspective on crime and delinquency." British Journal of Sociology 30:25–38.

Hagedorn, John
1988 People and Folks: Gangs, Crime and the Underclass in a Rustbelt City. Chicago: Lake View Press.

Hamilton, Robin, and Kay McKinney
1999 Job Training for Juveniles: Project CRAFT. Washington, DC: Office of Juvenile Justice and Delinquency Prevention.

Harris, Anthony R., and James A. W. Shaw
2000 "Looking for patterns: Race, class, and crime." Pp. 128–163 in Joseph F. Sheley, ed., Criminology: A Contemporary Handbook. Belmont, CA: Wadsworth.

Hawkins, Darnell F., John H. Laub, and Janet L. Lauritsen
1998 "Race, ethnicity, and serious juvenile offending." Pp. 30–46 in Rolf Loeber and David P. Farrington, eds., Serious and Violent Juvenile Offenders. Thousand Oaks, CA: Sage.

Hawkins, J. David, Michael W. Arthur, and Richard F. Catalano.
1995 "Preventing substance abuse." Pp. 343–347 in Michael Tonry and David P. Farrington, eds., Crime and Justice: A Review of Research, Volume 19. Chicago: University of Chicago Press.

Hawkins, J. David, Richard F. Catalano, and Devon D. Brewer
1995 "Preventing serious, violent, and chronic juvenile offending: Effective strategies from conception to age 6." Pp. 47–60 in James C. Howell, Barry Krisberg, J. David Hawkins, and John J. Wilson, eds., A Sourcebook: Serious, Violent, and Chronic Juvenile Offenders. Thousand Oaks, CA: Sage.

Hawkins, J. David, David P. Farrington, and Richard F. Catalano
1998 "Reducing violence through the schools." Pp. 188–216 in Delbert S. Elliott, Beatrix A. Hamburg, and Kirk R. Williams, eds., Violence in American Schools. Cambridge, England: Cambridge University Press.

Hawkins, J. David, Todd Herrenkohl, David P. Farrington, Devon Brewer, Richard F. Catalano, and Tracy W. Harachi
1998 "A review of predictors of youth violence." Pp. 106–146 in Rolf Loeber and David P. Farrington, eds., Serious and Violent Juvenile Offenders. Thousand Oaks, CA: Sage.

Hawkins, J. David, and Denise M. Lishner
1987 "Schooling and delinquency." Pp. 179–221 in Elmer H. Johnson, ed., Handbook on Crime and Delinquency Prevention. New York: Greenwood Press.

Heimer, Karen
1995 "Gender, race, and the pathways to delinquency." Pp. 140–173 in John Hagan and Ruth D. Peterson, eds., Crime and Inequality. Stanford, CA: Stanford University Press.
1996 "Gender, interaction, and delinquency: Testing a theory of differential social control." Social Psychology Quarterly 59:36–61.
1997 "Socioeconomic status, subcultural definitions, and violent delinquency." Social Forces 75:799–833.

❖ ❖ ❖ ❖   **Hellman, Daryl A., and Susan Beaton**
1986 "The pattern of violence in urban public schools: The influence of school and community." Journal of Research in Crime and Delinquency 23:102–127.

Henggeler, Scott W.
1989 Delinquency in Adolescence. Newbury Park, CA: Sage.

Hill, Karl G., James C. Howell, J. David Hawkins, and Sara R. Battin-Pearson
1999 "Childhood risk factors for adolescent gang membership: Results from the Seattle social development project." Journal of Research in Crime and Delinquency 36:300–322.

Hindelang, Michael J.
1978 "Race and involvement in common law personal crimes." American Sociological Review 43:93–109.
1981 "Variations in age-race-sex-specific incidence rates of offending." American Sociological Review 46:461–474.

Hindelang, Michael, Michael Gottfredson, and James Garofalo
1978 Victims of Personal Crime. Cambridge, MA: Ballinger.

Hindelang, Michael J., Travis Hirschi, and Joseph G. Weis
1979 "Correlates of delinquency: The illusion of discrepancy between self-report and official measures." American Sociological Review 44:99–101.
1981 Measuring Delinquency. Beverly Hills, CA: Sage.

Hirschi, Travis
1969 Causes of Delinquency. Berkeley: University of California Press.
1977 "Causes and prevention of juvenile delinquency." Sociological Inquiry 47:322–341.
1995 "The family." Pp. 121–140 in James Q. Wilson and Joan Petersilia, eds., Crime. San Francisco: ICS Press.

Hirschi, Travis, and Michael Gottfredson
1983 "Age and the explanation of crime." American Journal of Sociology 89:552–584.

Hirschi, Travis, and Michael J. Hindelang
1977 "Intelligence and delinquency: A revisionist review." American Sociological Review 42:571–587.

Hirschi, Travis, and Hanan C. Selvin
1967 Delinquency Research: An Appraisal of Analytic Methods. New York: Free Press.

Hoffmann, John P., and Felicia Gray Cerbone
1999 "Stressful life events and delinquency escalation in early adolescence." Criminology 37:343–374.

Hoffmann, John P., and Alan S. Miller
1998 "A latent variable analysis of strain theory." Journal of Quantitative Criminology 14:83–110.

Hoffmann, John P., and S. Susan Su
1997 "The conditional effects of stress on delinquency and drug use: A strain theory assessment of sex differences." Journal of Research in Crime and Delinquency 34:46–78.

Hollin, Clive R.
1990a Cognitive-Behavioral Interventions With Young Offenders. New York: Pergamon.
1990b "Social skills training with delinquents: A look at the evidence and some recommendations for practice." British Journal of Social Work 20:483–493.

1992 Criminal Behaviour: A Psychological Approach to Explanation and Prevention. London: Falmer Press.

Hope, Tim
1995 "Community crime prevention." Crime and Justice 19:21–89.

Howell, James C.
1995 "Gangs and youth violence: Recent research." Pp. 261–274 in James C. Howell, Barry Krisberg, J. David Hawkins, and John J. Wilson, eds., A Sourcebook: Serious Violence and Chronic Juvenile Offenders. Thousand Oaks, CA: Sage.

1997a Juvenile Justice and Youth Violence. Thousand Oaks, CA: Sage.

1997b "Youth Gangs." Washington, DC: Office of Juvenile Justice and Delinquency Prevention.

1998a Youth Gangs: An Overview. Washington, DC: Office of Juvenile Justice and Delinquency Prevention.

1998b "Promising programs for youth gang violence prevention and intervention." Pp. 284–312 in Rolf Loeber and David P. Farrington, eds., Serious and Violent Juvenile Offenders. Thousand Oaks, CA: Sage.

1999 "Youth gang homicides: A literature review." Crime and Delinquency 45:208–241.

Howell, James C., and J. David Hawkins
1998 "Prevention of youth violence." Pp. 263–315 in Michael Tonry and Mark H. Moore, eds., Crime and Justice, Volume 24. Chicago: University of Chicago Press.

Howell, James C., Barry Krisberg, J. David Hawkins, and John J. Wilson
1995 A Sourcebook: Serious, Violent, and Chronic Juvenile Offenders. Thousand Oaks, CA: Sage.

Howell, James C., Barry Krisberg, and Michael Jones
1995 "Trends in juvenile crime and youth violence." Pp. 1–35 in James C. Howell, Barry Krisberg, J. David Hawkins, and John J. Wilson, eds., A Sourcebook: Serious, Violent, and Chronic Juvenile Offenders. Thousand Oaks, CA: Sage.

Hsia, Heidi, and Donna Hamparian
1998 Disproportionate Minority Confinement: 1997 Update. Washington, DC: Office of Juvenile Justice and Delinquency Prevention.

Huff, C. Ronald
1996 Gangs in America. Thousand Oaks, CA: Sage.

1998 Comparing the Criminal Behavior of Youth Gangs and At-Risk Youth. Washington, DC: National Institute of Justice.

Huizinga, David
1995 "Developmental sequences in delinquency: Dynamic typologies." Pp. 15–34 in Lisa J. Crockett and Ann C. Crouter, eds., Pathways Through Adolescence. Mahwah, NJ: Lawrence Erlbaum.

1996 The Influence of Delinquent Peers, Gangs, and Co-offending on Violence. Washington, DC: Office of Juvenile Justice and Delinquency Prevention.

Huizinga, David, and Delbert S. Elliott
1986 "Reassessing the reliability and validity of self-report delinquency measures." Journal of Quantitative Criminology 2:293–327.

1987 "Juvenile offenders: Prevalence, offender incidence, and arrest rates by race." Crime and Delinquency 33:206–223.

Huizinga, David, Finn-Aage Esbensen, and Anne Wylie Weiher
1991 "Are there multiple paths to delinquency?" Journal of Criminal Law and Criminology 82:83–118.

❖ ❖ ❖ ❖   **Huizinga, David H., Scott Menard, and Delbert S. Elliott**
1989 "Delinquency and drug use: Temporal and developmental patterns." Justice Quarterly 6:419–455.

Huizinga, David, Anne Wylie Weiher, Scott Menard, Rachele Espiritu, and Finn Esbensen
1998 "Some not so boring findings from the Denver youth survey." Paper presented at the annual meeting of the American Society of Criminology, Washington, DC.

Hundleby, John D.
1987 "Adolescent drug use in a behavioral matrix: A conformation and comparison of the sexes." Addictive Behaviors 12:103–112.

Inciardi, James A., and Karen McElrath
1998 The American Drug Scene. Los Angeles: Roxbury.

Ingersoll, Sarah
1999 Investing in Youth for a Safer Future. Washington, DC: Office of Juvenile Justice and Delinquency Prevention.

Jackson, Pamela Irving
1991 "Crime, youth gangs, and urban transition: The social dislocations of postindustrial economic development." Justice Quarterly 8:379–397.

Jackson, Patrick G.
1990 "Sources of data." Pp. 21–50 in Kimberly L. Kempf, ed., Measurement Issues in Criminology. New York: Springer-Verlag.

Jang, Sung Joon
1999 "Age–varying effects of family, school, and peers on delinquency: A multilevel modeling test of interactional theory." Criminology 37:643–686.

Jang, Sung Joon, and Carolyn A. Smith
1997 "A test of reciprocal causal relationships among parental supervision, affective ties, and delinquency." Journal of Research in Crime and Delinquency 34:307–336.

Jang, Sung Joon, and Terence P. Thornberry
1998 "Self-esteem, delinquent peers, and delinquency: A test of the self-enhancement thesis." American Sociological Review 63:586–598.

Jankowski, Martin Sanchez
1995 "Ethnography, inequality, and crime in the low-income community." Pp. 80–94 in John Hagan and Ruth D. Peterson, eds., Crime and Inequality. Stanford, CA: Stanford University Press.

Jarjoura, G. Roger
1993 "Does dropping out of school enhance delinquent involvement? Results from a large-scale national probability sample." Criminology 31:149–172.
1996 "The conditional effect of social class on the dropout-delinquency relationship." Journal of Research in Crime and Delinquency 33:232–255.

Jarjoura, G. Roger, and Ruth A. Triplett
1997 "Delinquency and class: A test of the proximity principle." Justice Quarterly 14:763–792.

Jenkins, Patricia H.
1997 "School delinquency and the school social bond." Journal of Research in Crime and Delinquency 34:337–367.

Jennings, William S., Robert Kilkenny, and Lawrence Kohlberg
1983 "Moral-development theory and practice for youthful and adult offenders." Pp. 281–355 in William S. Laufer and James M. Day, eds., Personality Theory, Moral Development, and Criminal Behavior. Lexington, MA: Lexington.

Jensen, Gary F.
1972 "Parents, peers, and delinquent action: A test of the differential association perspective." American Journal of Sociology 78:562–575.
1998 "Television and violence: The rest of the story." Paper presented at the annual meeting of the Academy of Criminal Justice Sciences, Albuquerque.

Jensen, Gary F., and David Brownfield
1983 "Parents and drugs: Specifying the consequences of attachment." Criminology 21:543–554.
1986 "Gender, lifestyles, and victimization: Beyond routine activity." Violence and Victims 1:85–99.

Jensen, Gary F., and Raymond Eve
1976 "Sex differences in delinquency." Criminology 13:427–448.

Jensen, Gary F., and Dean G. Rojek
1998 Delinquency and Youth Crime. Prospect Heights, Illinois: Waveland.

Johnson, Richard E.
1979 Juvenile Delinquency and Its Origins. Cambridge, England: Cambridge University Press.
1986 "Family structure and delinquency: General patterns and gender differences." Criminology 24:65–84.

Johnson, Richard E., Anastasios C. Marcos, and Stephen Bahr
1987 "The role of peers in the complex etiology of adolescent drug use." Criminology 25:323–340.

Kappeler, Victor E., Mark Blumberg, and Gary W. Potter
1996 The Mythology of Crime and Criminal Justice. Prospect Heights, IL: Waveland.

Katz, Jack
1988 Seductions of Crime. New York: Basic Books.

Kaufman, Philip, Xianglei Chen, Susan P. Choy, Sally A. Ruddy, Amanda K. Miller, Christopher D. Chapman, Kathryn A. Chandler, Michael R. Rand, and Patty Klaus
1999 Indicators of School Crime and Safety, 1999. Washington, DC: US Department of Education and US Department of Justice.

Kazdin, Alan E.
1994 "Interventions for aggressive and antisocial children." Pp. 341–382 in Leonard D. Eron, Jacquelin H. Gentry, and Peggy Schlegel, eds., Reason to Hope. Washington, DC: American Psychological Association.

Kellermann, Arthur L., Dawna S. Fuqua-Whitley, Frederick P. Rivara, and James Mercy
1998 "Preventing youth violence: What works." Annual Review of Public Health 19:271–292.

Kellermann, Arthur L., and Donald T. Reay
1986 "Protection or peril? An analysis of firearm-related deaths in the home." New England Journal of Medicine 314:1557–1560.

Kellermann, Arthur L., Frederick P. Rivara, Norman B. Rushforth, Joyce G. Banton, Donald T. Reay, Jerry T. Francisco, Ana B. Locci, Janice Prodzinski, Bela B. Hackman, and Grant Somes.
1993 "Gun ownership as a risk factor for homicide in the home." New England Journal of Medicine 329:1084–1091.

Kelley, Barbara Tatem, Rolf Loeber, Kate Keenan, and Mary DeLamatre
1997 "Developmental Pathways in Boys' Disruptive and Delinquent Behavior." Washington, DC: Office of Juvenile Justice and Delinquency Prevention.

❖ ❖ ❖ ❖   **Kelling, George L.**
n.d. What Works—Research and the Police. Washington, DC: National Institute of Justice.
1988 Police and Communities: The Quiet Revolution. Washington, DC: National Institute of Justice.

Kelling, George L., and Catherine M. Coles
1996 Fixing Broken Windows. New York: Martin Kessler Books.

Kelling, George L., Tony Plate, Duane Dieckman, and Charles E. Brown
1974 The Kansas City Preventive Patrol Experiment: A Summary Report. Washington, DC: Police Foundation.

Kempf, Kimberly L.
1990 Measurement Issues in Criminology. New York: Springer-Verlag.
1993 "The empirical status of Hirschi's control theory." Pp. 143–185 in Freda Adler and William S. Laufer, eds., New Directions in Criminological Theory; Advances in Criminological Theory, Volume 4. New Brunswick, NJ: Transaction.

Kennedy, David M.
1997 Juvenile Gun Violence and Gun Markets in Boston. Washington, DC: National Institute of Justice.
1998 "Pulling levers: Getting deterrence right." National Institute of Justice Journal 236:2–8.

Kennedy, Leslie W., and Stephen W. Baron
1993 "Routine activities and a subculture of violence: A study of violence on the street." Journal of Research in Crime and Delinquency 30:88–112.

Kennedy, Leslie W., and David R. Forde
1990 "Routine activities and crime: An analysis of victimization in Canada." Criminology 28:137–152.
1996 "Pathways to aggression: A factorial survey of 'routine conflict'. " Journal of Quantitative Criminology 12:417–438.

Kleck, Gary
1997 Targeting Guns: Firearms and Their Control. New York: Aldine De Gruyter.

Kleck, Gary, and Marc Gertz
1995 "Armed resistance to crime: The prevalence and nature of self-defense with a gun." Journal of Criminal Law and Criminology 86:150–187.

Kleiman, Mark A. R.
1999 "Getting deterrence right: Applying tipping models and behavioral economics to the problems of crime control." Pp. 1–29 in National Institute of Justice (ed.), Perspectives on Crime and Justice: 1998–1999 Lecture Series. Washington, DC: National Institute of Justice.

Klein, Malcolm W.
1971 Street Gangs and Street Workers. Englewood Cliffs, NJ: Prentice Hall.
1995 The American Street Gang. New York: Oxford University Press.
1998 "Street gangs." Pp. 111–132 in Michael Tonry, ed., The Handbook of Crime and Punishment. New York: Oxford.

Klein, Malcolm W., Cheryl L. Maxson, and Jody Miller
1995 The Modern Gang Reader. Los Angeles: Roxbury.

Klepper, Steven, and Daniel Nagin
1989 "The deterrent effect of perceived certainty and severity of punishment revisited." Criminology 27:721–746.

Kohlberg, Lawrence
1976 "Moral stages and moralisation: The cognitive-developmental approach." Pp. 31–53 in T. Lickona, ed., Moral Development and Behavior. New York: Holt, Rinehart and Winston.

Kohn, Paul M., and Jill A. Milrose
1993 "The inventory of high-school students' recent life experiences: A decontaminated measure of adolescents' hassles." Journal of Youth and Adolescence 22:43–55.

Kopka, Deborah L.
1997 School Violence. Santa Barbara, CA: ABC-CLIO.

Kornhauser, Ruth Rosner
1978 Social Sources of Delinquency. Chicago: University of Chicago Press.

Krisberg, Barry, Elliott Currie, David Onek, and Richard G. Wiebush
1995 "Graduated sanctions for serious, violent, and chronic juvenile offenders." Pp. 142–170 in James C. Howell, Barry Krisberg, J. David Hawkins, and John J. Wilson, eds., A Sourcebook: Serious, Violent, and Chronic Juvenile Offenders. Thousand Oaks, CA: Sage.

Krisberg, Barry, and James C. Howell
1998 "The impact of the juvenile justice system and prospects for graduated sanctions in a comprehensive strategy." Pp. 346–366 in Rolf Loeber and David P. Farrington, eds., Serious and Violent Juvenile Offenders. Thousand Oaks, CA: Sage.

Krivo, Lauren J., and Ruth D. Peterson
1996 "Extremely disadvantaged neighborhoods and urban crime." Social Forces 75:619–650.

Krohn, Marvin
2000 "Sources of criminality: Control and deterrence theories." Pp. 373–403 in Joseph F. Sheley, ed., Criminology. Belmont, CA: Wadsworth.

Krohn, Marvin D., William F. Skinner, James L. Massey, and Ronald L. Akers
1985 "Social learning theory and adolescent cigarette smoking: A longitudinal study." Social Problems 32:455–473.

Krohn, Marvin D., Terence P. Thornberry, Lori Collins-Hall, and Alan J. Lizotte
1995 "School dropout, delinquent behavior, and drug use." Pp. 163–183 in Howard B. Kaplan, ed., Drugs, Crime, and Other Deviant Adaptations. New York: Plenum.

Kumpfer, Karol L., and Rose Alvarado
1998 Effective Family Strengthening Interventions. Washington, DC: Office of Juvenile Justice and Delinquency Prevention.

Kumpfer, Karol L., and Connie M. Tait.
2000 Family Skills Training for Parents and Children. Washington, DC: Office of Juvenile Justice and Delinquency Prevention.

Kurlychek, Megan, Patricia Torbet, and Melanie Bozynski
1999 Focus on Accountability: Best Practices for Juvenile Court and Probation. Washington, DC: Office of Juvenile Justice and Delinquency Prevention.

LaGrange, Teresa, and Robert A. Silverman
1999 "Low self-control and opportunity: Testing the general theory of crime as an explanation for gender differences in delinquency." Criminology 37:41–72.

Land, Kenneth C., Patricia L. McCall, and Lawrence E. Cohen
1990 "Structural covariates of homicide rates: Are there any invariances across time and social space?" American Journal of Sociology 95:922–963.

❖ ❖ ❖ ❖   **Landau, Simha F.**
1998 "Crime, subjective social stress and support indicators, and ethnic origin: The Israeli experience." Justice Quarterly 15:243–272.

Larzelere, Robert E., and Gerald R. Patterson
1990 "Parental management: Mediator of the effect of socioeconomic status on early delinquency." Criminology 28:301–324.

Lauritsen, Janet L., and Robert J. Sampson
1998 "Minorities, crime, and criminal justice." Pp. 58–84 in Michael Tonry, ed., The Handbook of Crime and Punishment. New York: Oxford.

Lawrence, Richard
1998 School Crime and Juvenile Justice. New York: Oxford University Press.

Le Blanc, Marc
1993 "Late adolescence deceleration of criminal activity and development of self- and social control." Studies on Crime and Crime Prevention 2:51–68.
1998 "Screening of serious and violent juvenile offenders: Identification, classification, and prediction." Pp. 167–193 in Rolf Loeber and David P. Farrington, eds., Serious and Violent Juvenile Offenders. Thousand Oaks, CA: Sage.

Le Blanc, Marc, and Rolf Loeber
1998 "Developmental criminology updated." Crime and Justice 23:115–198.

Leiber, Michael J., and Jayne M. Stairs
1999 "Race, contexts, and the use of intake diversion." Journal of Research in Crime and Delinquency 36:56–86.

Leonard, Eileen B.
1982 Women, Crime and Society: A Critique of Theoretical Criminology. New York: Longman.

Leonard, Kimberly Kempf, Carl E. Pope, and William H. Feyerherm
1995 Minorities in Juvenile Justice. Thousand Oaks, CA: Sage.

Leonard, Kimberly Kempf, and Henry Sontheimer
1995 "The role of race in juvenile justice in Pennsylvania." Pp. 98–127 in Kimberly Kempf Leonard, Carl E. Pope, and William H. Feyerherm, eds., Minorities in Juvenile Justice. Thousand Oaks, CA: Sage.

Levine, Madeline
1996 Viewing Violence. New York: Doubleday.

Levrant, Sharon, Francis T. Cullen, Betsy Fulton, and John F. Wozniak
1999 "Reconsidering restorative justice: The corruption of benevolence revisted?" Crime and Delinquency, 45:3–27.

Lewit, Eugene M., Donna L. Terman, and Richard E. Behrman
1997 "Children and poverty: Analysis and recommendations." The Future of Children 7:4–24.

Lipsey, Mark W.
1992 "Juvenile delinquency treatment: A meta-analytic inquiry into the variability of effects." Pp. 83–208 in Thomas D. Cook, Harris Cooper, David S. Cordray, Heidi Hartmann, Larry V. Hedges, Richard J. Light, Thomas A. Louis, and Frederick Mosteller, eds., Meta-Analysis for Explanation. New York: Russell Sage.

Lipsey, Mark W., and David B. Wilson
1998 "Effective intervention for serious juvenile offenders." Pp. 313–345 in Rolf Loeber and David P. Farrington, eds., Serious and Violent Juvenile Offenders. Thousand Oaks, CA: Sage.

Lizotte, Alan J., James M. Tesoriero, Terence P. Thornberry, and Marvin Krohn
1994 "Patterns of adolescent firearms ownership and use." Justice Quarterly 11:51–74.

Lockwood, Daniel
1997 "Violence among middle school and high school students: Analysis and implications for prevention." Washington, DC: National Institute of Justice.

Loeber, Rolf, David P. Farrington, Magda Stouthamer-Loeber, Terrie E. Moffitt, and Avshalom Caspi
1998 "The development of male offending: Key findings from the first decade of the Pittsburgh youth study." Studies on Crime and Crime Prevention 7:141–171.

Loeber, Rolf, David P. Farrington, Magda Stouthamer-Loeber, and Welmoet B. Van Kammen
1998 Antisocial Behavior and Mental Health Problems. Mahwah, NJ: Lawrence Erlbaum.

Loeber, Rolf, David P. Farrington, and Daniel A. Waschbusch
1998 "Serious and violent juvenile offenders." Pp. 13–29 in Rolf Loeber and David P. Farrington, eds., Serious and Violent Juvenile Offenders. Thousand Oaks, CA: Sage.

Loeber, Rolf, and Magda Stouthamer-Loeber
1986 "Family factors as correlates and predictors of juvenile conduct problems and delinquency." Pp. 29–149 in Michael Tonry and Norval Morris, eds., Crime and Justice, Volume 7. Chicago: University of Chicago Press.

Loeber, Rolf, Magda Stouthamer-Loeber, Welmoet Van Kammen, and David P. Farrington
1991 "Initiation, escalation and desistance in juvenile offending and their correlates." Journal of Criminal Law and Criminology 82:36–82.

Longshore, Douglas A.
1998 "Self-control and criminal opportunity: A prospective test of the general theory of crime." Social Problems 45:102–113.

Longshore, Douglas, Susan Turner Rand, and Judith A. Stein
1996 "Self-control in a criminal sample: An examination of construct validity." Criminology 34:209–228.

Losel, Friedrich
1995 "The efficacy of correctional treatment: A review and synthesis of meta-evaluations." Pp. 79–111 in James McGuire, ed., What Works: Reducing Reoffending. Chichester, England: Wiley.

Lott, John R.
1998 More Guns, Less Crime. Chicago: University of Chicago Press.

Lotz, Roy, and Leona Lee
1999 "Sociability, school experience, and delinquency." Youth and Society 31:199–223.

Luckenbill, David F.
1977 "Criminal homicide as a situated transaction." Social Problems 25:176–186.

Lundman, Richard J.
1993 Prevention and Control of Juvenile Delinquency. New York: Oxford.

Lykken, David T.
1995 The Antisocial Personalities. Hillsdale, NJ: Lawrence Erlbaum.
1996 "Psychopathy, sociopathy, and crime." Society 34(1):29–38.

❖ ❖ ❖ ❖   **MacCoun, Robert, and Peter Reuter**
1998 "Drug control." Pp. 207–238 in Michael Tonry, ed., The Handbook of Crime and Punishment. New York: Oxford.

MacKenzie, Lynn Ryan
1999 Residential Placement of Adjudicated Youth, 1987–1996. Washington, DC: Office of Juvenile Justice and Delinquency Prevention.

MacLeod, Jay
1987 Ain't No Makin' It. Boulder, CO: Westview Press.

Maguin, Eugene, and Rolf Loeber
1996 "Academic performance and delinquency." Pp. 145–264 in Michael Tonry, ed., Crime and Justice: A Review of Research, Volume 20. Chicago: University of Chicago Press.

Maguire, Kathleen, and Ann L. Pastore
1999 Sourcebook of Criminal Justice Statistics—1998. Washington, DC: Bureau of Justice Statistics.

Majors, Richard, and Janet Mancini Billson
1992 Cool Pose. New York: Lexington Books.

Markowitz, Fred E., and Richard B. Felson
1998 "Socio-demographic differences in attitudes and violence." Criminology, 36:117–138.

Martinson, Robert
1974 "What works? Questions and answers about prison reform." The Public Interest 35:22–54.

Martz, Ron
1999 "Crime stats: Questions linger after Atlanta audit." Atlanta Constitution, January 28, C1, 4.

Marvell, Thomas B., and Carlisle E. Moody
1996 "Specification problems, police levels, and crime rates." Criminology 34:609–646.

Massey, James L., Marvin D. Krohn, and Lisa M. Bonati
1989 "Property crime and the routine activities of individuals." Journal of Research in Crime and Delinquency 26:378–400.

Mastrofski, Stephen D.
2000 "The police in America." Pp. 405–445 in Joseph F. Sheley, ed., Criminology: A Contemporary Handbook. Belmont, CA: Wadsworth.

Matsueda, Ross L.
1988 "The current state of differential association theory." Crime and Delinquency 34:277–306.
1992 "Reflected appraisals, parental labeling, and delinquency: Specifying a symbolic interactionist theory." American Journal of Sociology 97:1577–1611.

Matsueda, Ross L., and Kathleen Anderson
1998 "The dynamics of delinquent peers and delinquent behavior." Criminology 36:269–308.

Matsueda, Ross L., and Karen Heimer
1987 "Race, family structure, and delinquency: A test of differential association and social control theories." American Sociological Review 52:826–840.

Matza, David
1964 Delinquency and Drift. New York: John Wiley and Sons.

Matza, David, and Gresham Sykes
1961 "Juvenile delinquency and subterranean beliefs." American Sociological Review 26:713–719.

Maxson, Cherly L.
1995 "Research in brief: Street gangs and drug sales in two suburban cities." Pp. 228–235 in Malcolm W. Klein, Cherly L. Maxson, and Jody Miller, eds., The Modern Gang Reader. Los Angeles: Roxbury.

Maxson, Cherly L., and Malcolm W. Klein
1990 "Street gang violence: Twice as great, or half as great?" Pp. 71–100 in C. Ronald Huff, ed., Gangs in America. Newbury Park, CA: Sage.

1996 "Defining gang homicide: An updated look at member and motive approaches." Pp. 3–20 in C. Ronald Huff, ed., Gangs in America. Thousand Oaks, CA: Sage.

Maynard, Rebecca A.
1997 Kids Having Kids. Washington, DC: Urban Institute Press.

Maynard, Rebecca A., and Eileen M. Garry
1997 Adolescent Motherhood: Implications for the Juvenile Justice System. Washington, DC: Office of Juvenile Justice and Delinquency Prevention.

Mazerolle, Paul, and Alex Piquero
1997 "Violent responses to strain: An examination of conditioning influences." Violence and Victims 12:323–343.

1998 "Linking exposure to strain with anger: An investigation of deviant adaptations." Journal of Criminal Justice 26:195–211.

McBride, Duane C., and Clyde B. McCoy
1993 "The drugs-crime relationship: An analytical framework." The Prison Journal 73:257–278.

McCabe, Donald L.
1992 "The influence of situational ethics on cheating among college students." Sociological Inquiry 62:365–374.

McCarthy, Bill
1995 "Not just 'for the thrill of it': An instrumentalist elaboration of Katz's explanation of sneaky thrill property crimes." Criminology 33:519–538.

McCord, Joan
1991 "Family relationships, juvenile delinquency, and adult criminality." Criminology 29:397–417.

McDermott, Joan
1993 "Crime in the school and in the community: Offenders, victims, and fearful youths." Crime and Delinquency 29:270–282.

McDonald, Lynn, and Heather E. Frey
1999 Families and Schools Together: Building Relationships. Washington, DC: Office of Juvenile Justice and Delinquency Prevention.

McDowell, David, Alan J. Lizotte, and Brian Wiersema
1991 "General deterrence through civilian gun ownership: An evaluation of the quasi-experimental evidence." Criminology 29:541–559.

McDowell, David, and Brian Wiersema
1994 "The incidence of defensive firearm use by U.S. crime victims, 1987 through 1990." American Journal of Public Health 84:1982–1984.

McEwen, T.
1994 "National assessment program: 1994 survey results." Washington, DC: National Institute of Justice.

McGuire, James
1995 What Works: Reducing Offending. Chichester, England: Wiley.

❖ ❖ ❖ ❖   **Mears, Daniel P., Matthew Ploeger, and Mark Warr**
1998 "Explaining the gender gap in delinquency: Peer influence and moral evaluations of behavior." Journal of Research in Crime and Delinquency 35:251–266.

**Meich, Richard A., Avshalom Caspi, Terrie E. Moffitt, Bradley R. Entner
Wright, and Phil A. Silva**
1999 "Socioeconomic status and mental disorders: A longitudinal study of selection
and causation during young adulthood." American Journal of Sociology
104:1096–1131.

Meier, Robert F., Steven R. Burkett, and Carol A. Hickman
1984 "Sanctions, peers, and deviance: Preliminary models of a social control process." Sociological Quarterly 25:76–82.

Meier, Robert F., and Gilbert Geis
1997 Victimless Crime? Los Angeles: Roxbury.

Merton, Robert K.
1938 "Social structure and anomie." American Sociological Review 3:672–682.
1968 Social Theory and Social Structure. New York: Free Press.

Messerschmidt, James W.
1993 Masculinities and Crime. Lanham, Maryland: Rowman and Littlefield.

Messner, Steven F., and Reid M. Golden
1992 "Racial inequality and racially disaggregated homicide rates: An assessment of
alternative theoretical explanations." Criminology 30:421–447.

Messner, Steven F., Marvin D. Krohn, and Allen E. Liska
1989 Theoretical Integration in the Study of Deviance and Crime: Problems and
Prospects. Albany: State University of New York Press.

Messner, Steven F., and Richard Rosenfeld
1997 Crime and the American Dream. Belmont, CA: Wadsworth.

Miethe, Terance D., and Richard McCorkle
1998 Crime Profiles. Los Angeles: Roxbury.

Miethe, Terance D., and Robert F. Meier
1990 "Opportunity, choice, and criminal victimization: A test of a theoretical model."
Journal of Research in Crime and Delinquency 27:243–266.
1994 Crime and Its Social Context. Albany: State University of New York Press.

Miller, Jerome
1996 Search and Destroy. Cambridge, England: Cambridge University Press.

Miller, Walter
1958 "Lower class culture as a generating milieu of gang delinquency." Journal of Social Issues 14:5–19.
1982 Crime by Youth Gangs and Groups in the United States. Washington, DC: US
Department of Justice.

Minor, William W.
1981 "Techniques of neutralization: A reconceptualization and empirical examination." Journal of Research in Crime and Delinquency 18:295–318.

Moffitt, Terrie E.
1990 "The neuropsychology of juvenile delinquency: A critical review." Pp. 99–169 in
Michael Tonry and Norval Morris, eds., Crime and Justice, Volume 12. Chicago: University of Chicago Press.
1993 " 'Life-course persistent' and 'adolescent-limited' antisocial behavior: A developmental taxonomy." Psychological Review 100:674–701.
1997 "Adolescent-limited and life-course persistent offending: A complementary
pair of developmental theories." Pp. 11–54 in Terence P. Thornberry, ed., Devel-

opmental Theories of Crime and Delinquency: Advances in Criminological Theory, Volume 7. New Brunswick, NJ: Transaction.

Moffitt, Terrie, Avshalom Caspi, Paul Fawcett, Gary L. Brammer, Michael Raleigh, Arthur Yuwiler, and Phil Silva
1997 "Whole blood serotonin and family background relate to male violence." Pp. 231–249 in Adrian Raine, Patricia A. Brennan, David P. Farrington, and Sarnoff A. Mednick, eds., Biosocial Bases of Violence. New York: Plenum.

Moffitt, Terrie E., and Bill Henry
1989 "Neuropsychological assessment of executive functions in self-reported delinquents." Development and Psychopathology 1:105–118.

Moffitt, Terrie E., Donald R. Lynam, and Phil A. Silva
1994 "Neuropsychological tests predicting persistent male delinquency." Criminology 32:277–300.

Moore, Joan
1991 Going Down to the Barrio: Homeboys and Homegirls in Change. Philadelphia: Temple University Press.

Moore, Joan, and John M. Hagedorn
1996 "What happens to girls in the gang?" Pp. 205–218 in C. Ronald Huff, ed., Gangs in America. Thousand Oaks, CA: Sage.

Moore, John P., and Ivan L. Cook
1999 Highlights of the 1998 National Youth Gang Survey. Washington, DC: Office of Juvenile Justice and Delinquency Prevention.

Moore, Kristin Anderson, Donna Ruane Morrison, and Angela Dungee Greene
1997 "Effects on the children born to adolescent mothers." Pp. 145–180 in Rebecca A. Maynard, ed., Kids Having Kids. Washington, DC: Urban Institute Press.

Moore, Mark H., Robert C. Trojanowicz, and George L. Kelling
1988 Crime and Policing. Washington, DC: National Institute of Justice.

Morash, Merry
1983 "An explanation of juvenile delinquency: The integration of moral reasoning theory and sociological knowledge." Pp. 385–409 in William S. Laufer and James M. Day, eds., Personality Theory, Moral Development, and Criminal Behavior. Lexington, MA: Lexington.
1986 "Gender, peer group experiences, and seriousness of delinquency." Journal of Research in Crime and Delinquency 23:43–67.

Morenoff, Jeffrey D., and Robert J. Sampson
1997 "Violent crime and the spatial dynamics of neighborhood transition: Chicago, 1970–1990." Social Forces 76:31–64.

Muller, Janice, and Sharon Mihalic
1999 Blueprints: A Violence Prevention Initiative. Washington, DC: Office of Juvenile Justice and Delinquency Prevention.

Muraskin, Roslyn
1998 "Police work with juveniles." Pp. 151–164 in Albert R. Roberts, ed., Juvenile Justice. Chicago: Nelson-Hall.

Murphy, Kim, and Melissa Healy
1999 "Lawsuits now putting onus of youth crime on parents." Atlanta Constitution, May 2, A15.

Mustaine, Elizabeth Ehrhardt, and Richard Tewksbury
1998a "Predicting risks of larceny theft victimization: A routine activity analysis using refined lifestyle measures." Criminology 36:829–857.

1998b "Specifying the role of alcohol in predatory victimization." Deviant Behavior 19:173–200.

Nagin, Daniel S.
1998a "Criminal deterrence research at the outset of the twenty-first century." Pp. 1–42 in Michael Tonry, ed., Crime and Justice: A Review of Research, Volume 23. Chicago: University of Chicago Press.
1998b "Deterrence and Incapacitation." Pp. 345–368 in Michael Tonry, ed., The Handbook of Crime and Punishment. New York: Oxford.

Nagin, Daniel S., and Raymond Paternoster
1991 "The preventive effects of the perceived risk of arrest: Testing an expanded conception of deterrence." Criminology 29:561–587.
1994 "Personal capital and social control: The deterrence implications of a theory of individual differences in criminal offending." Criminology 32:581–606.

National Institute of Justice
1992 National Institute of Justice Journal, Community Policing, No. 225.
1996 National Institute of Justice Journal, August, No. 231.
1998a National Institute of Justice Journal, October, No. 237.
1998b 1997 Drug Use Forecasting. Washington, DC: National Institute of Justice.

National Television Violence Study
1997 National Television Violence Study, Volume 1. Thousand Oaks, CA: Sage.
1998 National Television Violence Study, Volume 2. Thousand Oaks, CA: Sage.

Nye, Ivan F.
1958 Family Relationships and Delinquent Behavior. New York: Wiley.

O'Brien, Robert M.
2000 "Crime facts: Victim and offender data." Pp. 59–83 in Joseph F. Sheley, ed., Criminology. Belmont, CA: Wadsworth.

Office of Justice Programs
1999 Weed and Seed Best Practices. Washington, DC: Office of Justice Programs.

Office of Juvenile Justice and Delinquency Prevention
1995 Delinquency Prevention Works. Washington, DC: Office of Juvenile Justice and Delinquency Prevention.
1996 Reducing Youth Gun Violence. Washington, DC: Office of Juvenile Justice and Delinquency Prevention.
1998a Guide for Implementing the Balanced and Restorative Justice Model. Washington, DC: Office of Juvenile Justice and Delinquency Prevention.
1998b Juvenile Mentoring Program: 1998 Report to Congress. Washington, DC: Office of Juvenile Justice and Delinquency Prevention.
1999a Report to Congress on Juvenile Violence Research. Washington, DC: Office of Juvenile Justice and Delinquency Prevention.
1999b Title V Incentive Grants for Local Delinquency Prevention Programs: 1998 Report to Congress. Washington, DC: Office of Juvenile Justice and Delinquency Prevention.

Office of National Drug Control Policy
1999 The National Drug Control Strategy, 1999. Washington, DC: Office of National Drug Control Policy.

Olds, David, Peggy Hill, and Elissa Rumsey
1998 Prenatal and Early Childhood Nurse Home Visitation. Washington, DC: Office of Juvenile Justice and Delinquency Prevention.

Olweus, Dan
1986 "Aggression and hormones: Behavioral relationship with testosterone and adrenaline." Pp. 51–72 in Dan Olweus, Jack Block, and Marian Radke-Yarrow,

eds., Development of Antisocial and Prosocial Behavior. Orlando: Academic Press.

1991 "Bully/victim problems among schoolchildren: Basic facts and effects of a school-based intervention program." Pp. 411–448 in Debra J. Pepler and Kenneth H. Rubin, eds., The Development and Treatment of Childhood Aggression. Hillsdale, NJ: Lawrence Erlbaum.

Osgood, D. Wayne, Patrick M. O'Malley, Jerald G. Bachman, and Lloyd D. Johnston
1989 "Time trends and age trends in arrests and self-reported illegal behavior." Criminology 27:389–417.

Osgood, D. Wayne, Janet K. Wilson, Patrick M. O'Malley, Jerald G. Bachman, and Lloyd D. Johnston
1996 "Routine activities and individual deviant behavior." American Sociological Review 61:635–655.

Padilla, Felix
1992 The Gang as an American Enterprise. New Brunswick, NJ: Rutgers University Press.

Paternoster, Raymond
1987 "The deterrent effect of the perceived certainty and severity of punishment: A review of the evidence and issues." Justice Quarterly 4:173–217.

Paternoster, Raymond, and Leeann Iovanni
1989 "The labeling perspective and delinquency: An elaboration of the theory and an assessment of the evidence." Justice Quarterly 6:359–394.

Paternoster, Raymond, and Paul Mazerolle
1994 "General strain theory and delinquency: A replication and extension." Journal of Research in Crime and Delinquency 31:235–263.

Paternoster, Raymond, and Alex Piquero
1995 "Reconceptualizing deterrence: An empirical test of personal and vicarious experiences." Journal of Research in Crime and Delinquency 32:251–286.

Patterson, Gerald R.
1982 Coercive Family Process. Eugene, OR: Castalia.
1986 "Performance models for antisocial boys." American Psychologist 41:432–444.

Patterson, Gerald R., Barbara D. DeBaryshe, and Elizabeth Ramsey
1989 "A developmental perspective on antisocial behavior." American Psychologist 44:329–335.

Patterson, Gerald R., and Thomas J. Dishion
1985 "Contributions of families and peers to delinquency." Criminology 23:63–79.

Patterson, Gerald R., and M. Elizabeth Gullion
1977 Living With Children. Champaign, IL: Research Press Company.

Patterson, Gerald R., John B. Reid, and Thomas J. Dishion
1992 Antisocial Boys. Eugene, OR: Castalia.

Pearson, Frank S., and Neil Alan Weiner
1985 "Toward an integration of criminological theories." Journal of Criminal Law and Criminology 76:116–150.

Peeples, Faith, and Rolf Loeber
1994 "Do individual factors and neighborhood context explain ethnic differences in juvenile delinquency?" Journal of Quantitative Criminology 10:141–157.

Pepler, Debra J., and Ronald G. Slaby
1994 "Theoretical and developmental perspectives on youth and violence." Pp. 27–58 in Leonard D. Eron, Jacquelyn H. Gentry, and Peggy Schlegel, eds., Reason to Hope. Washington, DC: American Psychological Association.

Perkins, Craig A.
1997 Age Patterns of Victims of Serious Violent Crime. Washington, DC: Bureau of Justice Statistics.

Petersilia, Joan
1989 "The influence of research on policing." Pp. 230–247 in Roger G. Dunham and Geoffrey P. Alpert, eds., Critical Issues in Policing. Prospect Heights, IL.: Waveland.
1997 "Probation in the United States." Pp. 149–200 in Michael Tonry, ed., Crime and Justice: A Review of Research, Volume 22. Chicago: University of Chicago Press.

Piliavin, Irving, and Scott Briar
1964 "Police encounters with juveniles." American Journal of Sociology 51:101–119.

Piquero, Alex, and Raymond Paternoster
1998 "An application of Stafford and Warr's reconceptualization of deterrence to drinking and driving." Journal of Research in Crime and Delinquency 35:3–39.

Piquero, Alex, Raymond Paternoster, Paul Mazerolle, Robert Brame, and Charles W. Dean
1999 "Onset age and offense specialization." Journal of Research in Crime and Delinquency 36:275–299.

Piquero, Alex, and Stephen Tibbetts
1996 "Specifying the direct and indirect effects of low self-control and situational factors in an offender's decision making: Toward a more complete model of rational offending." Justice Quarterly 13:481–510.

Platt, Anthony M.
1969 The Child Savers. Chicago: University of Chicago Press.

Ploeger, Matthew
1997 "Youth unemployment and delinquency: Reconsidering a problematic relationship." Criminology 35:659–675.

Plomin, Robert, and Stephen A. Petrill
1997 "Genetics and intelligence: What's new?" Intelligence 24:53–77.

Plotnick, Robert D.
1997 "Child poverty can be reduced." The Future of Children 7:72–87.

Poe-Yamagata, Eileen, and Jeffrey A. Butts
1996 Female Offenders in the Juvenile Justice System. Washington, DC: Office of Juvenile Justice and Delinquency Prevention.

Polakowski, Michael
1994 "Linking self- and social control with deviance: Illuminating the structure underlying a general theory of crime and its relation to deviant activity." Journal of Quantitative Criminology 10:41–78.

Pope, Carl E., and William Feyerherm
1993 Minorities and the Juvenile Justice System. Washington, DC: Office of Juvenile Justice and Delinquency Prevention.

Pulkkinen, Lea
1986 "The role of impulse control in the development of antisocial and prosocial behavior." Pp. 149–175 in Dan Olweus, Jack Block, and Marian Radke-Yarrow, eds., Development of Antisocial and Prosocial Behavior. Orlando, FL.: Academic Press.

Puzzanchera, Charles, Anne L. Stahl, Terrence A. Finnegan, Howard Snyder, Rowen S. Poole, and Nancy Tierney
2000 Juvenile Court Statistics, 1997. Washington, DC: Office of Juvenile Justice and Delinquency Prevention.

Quay, Herbert C.
1983 "Psychological theories." Pp. 330–342 in Sanford H. Kadish, ed., Encyclopedia of Crime and Justice. New York: Free Press.

Raine, Adrian
1993 The Psychopathology of Crime. San Diego, CA.: Academic Press.

Raine, Adrian, Patricia A. Brennan, and David P. Farrington
1997 "Biosocial bases of violence." Pp. 1–20 in Adrian Raine, Patricia A. Brennan, David P. Farrington, and Sarnoff A. Mednick, eds., Biosocial Bases of Violence. New York: Plenum.

Raine, Adrian, Patricia A. Brennan, David P. Farrington, and Sarnoff A. Mednick
1997 Biosocial Bases of Violence. New York: Plenum.

Ramey, Craig T., and Sharon Landesman Ramey
1995 "Successful early interventions for children at high risk for failure in school." Pp. 129–145 in George J. Demko and Michael C. Jackson, eds., Populations at Risk in America. Boulder, CO: Westview.

Rankin, Joseph H.
1983 "The family context of delinquency." Social Problems 30:466–479.

Rankin, Joseph H., and Roger Kern
1994 "Parental attachments and delinquency." Criminology 32:495–515.

Rankin, Joseph H., and L. Edward Wells
1987 "The preventive effects of the family on delinquency." Pp. 257–277 in Elmer H. Johnson, ed., Handbook on Crime and Delinquency Prevention. New York: Greenwood.
1990 "The effect of parental attachments and direct controls on delinquency." Journal of Research in Crime and Delinquency 27:140–165.
1994 "Social control, family structure, and delinquency." Pp. 97–116 in Greg Barak, ed., Varieties of Criminology. Westport, CT: Praeger.

Rebellon, Cesar
1999 "Reconsidering the broken homes/delinquency relationship and specifying its mediating mechanisms." Paper presented at the annual meeting of the American Sociological Association, Chicago.

Reckless, Walter C.
1961 "A new theory of crime and delinquency." Federal Probation 25:42–46.

Reed, Mark D., and Pamela Wilcox Rountree
1997 "Peer pressure and adolescent substance use." Journal of Quantitative Criminology 13:143–180.

Reiman, Jeffrey
1995 The Rich Get Richer and the Poor Get Prison. Boston: Allyn & Bacon.

Reiss, Albert J., Jr.
1951 "Delinquency as the failure of personal and social controls." American Sociological Review 16:196–207.
1988 "Co-offending and criminal careers." Pp. 117–170 in Michael Tonry and Norval Morris, eds., Crime and Justice: A Review of Research, Volume 10. Chicago: University of Chicago Press.

Reiss, Albert J., Jr., and Jeffrey A. Roth
1993 Understanding and Preventing Violence. Washington, DC: National Academy Press.

Rennison, Callie Marie
1999 Criminal Victimization 1998. Washington, DC: Bureau of Justice Statistics.

❖ ❖ ❖ ❖   **Riley, David**
1987 "Time and crime: The link between teenage lifestyle and delinquency." Journal of Quantitative Criminology 3:339–354.

Roberts, Albert R.
1998 Juvenile Justice. Chicago: Nelson-Hall.

Roberts, Julian V., and Loretta J. Stalans
1998 "Crime, criminal justice, and public opinion." Pp. 31–57 in Michael Tonry, ed., The Handbook of Crime and Punishment. New York: Oxford.

Robinson, Laurie
1996 "Linking community-based initiatives and community justice: The office of justice programs." National Institute of Justice Journal 231(August):4–7.

Robinson, Matthew B., and Barbara H. Zaitzow
1999 "Criminologists: Are we what we study? A national self-report study of crime experts." The Criminologist 24(2):1, 4, 17.

Rosen, Lawrence
1985 "Family and delinquency: Structure or function?" Criminology 23:553–573.

Rowe, Alan R., and Charles R. Tittle
1977 "Life cycle changes and criminal propensity." Sociological Quarterly 18:223–236.

Rowe, David C., and David P. Farrington
1997 "The familial transmission of criminal convictions." Criminology 35:177–201.

Rowe, David C., and Bill L. Gulley
1992 "Sibling effects on substance use and delinquency." Criminology 30:217–233.

Rowe, David C., Alexander T. Vazsonyi, and Daniel J. Flannery
1995 "Sex differences in crime: Do means and within-sex variation have similar causes?" Journal of Research in Crime and Delinquency 32:84–100.

Rubin, H. Ted
1998 "The juvenile court landscape." Pp. 205–230 in Albert R. Roberts, ed., Juvenile Justice. Chicago: Nelson-Hall.

Rutter, Michael
1985 "Family and school influences on behavioural development." Journal of Child Psychology and Psychiatry 26:349–368.
1997 "Nature-Nuture Integration." American Psychologist 52:390–398.

Rutter, Michael, and Henri Giller
1983 Juvenile Delinquency. New York: Guilford Press.

Rutter, Michael, Henri Giller, and Ann Hagell
1998 Antisocial Behavior by Young People. Cambridge, England: Cambridge University Press.

Rutter, Michael, Barbara Maughan, Peter Mortimore, Janet Ouston, and Alan Smith
1979 Fifteen Thousand Hours. Cambridge, MA: Harvard University Press.

Salerno, Anthony W.
1991 "The child saver movement: Altruism or a conspiracy?" Juvenile and Family Court Journal 42:37–49.

Samples, Faith, and Larry Aber
1998 "Evaluations of school-based violence prevention programs." Pp. 217–252 in Delbert S. Elliott, Beatrix A. Hamburg, and Kirk R. Williams, eds., Violence in American Schools. Cambridge, England: Cambridge University Press.

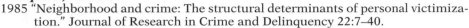

Sampson, Robert J.
1985 "Neighborhood and crime: The structural determinants of personal victimization." Journal of Research in Crime and Delinquency 22:7–40.

1986a "Neighborhood family structure and the risk of personal victimization." Pp. 25–46 in James M. Byrne and Robert J. Sampson, eds., The Social Ecology of Crime. New York: Springer-Verlag.

1986b "Effects of socioeconomic context on official reaction to juvenile delinquency." American Sociological Review 51:876–885.

1987 "Urban black violence: The effect of male joblessness and family disruption." American Journal of Sociology 93:348–382.

1995 "The community." Pp. 193–216 in James Q. Wilson and Joan Petersilia, eds., Crime. San Francisco: ICS Press.

1997 "The embeddedness of child and adolescent development: A community-level perspective on urban violence." Pp. 31–77 in Joan McCord, ed., Violence and Childhood in the Inner City. Cambridge, England: Cambridge University Press.

Sampson, Robert J., and Dawn Jeglum Bartusch
1999 Attitudes Toward Crime, Police, and the Law: Individual and Neighborhood Differences. Washington, DC: National Institute of Justice.

Sampson, Robert J., and W. Byron Groves
1989 "Community structure and crime: Testing social-disorganization theory." American Journal of Sociology 94:774–802.

Sampson, Robert J., and John H. Laub
1993a Crime in the Making. Cambridge, MA: Harvard University Press.

1993b "Structural variations in juvenile court processing: Inequality, the underclass, and social control." Law and Society Review 27:285–311.

Sampson, Robert J., and Janet L. Lauritsen
1993 "Violent victimization and offending: Individual-, situational-, and community-level risk factors." Pp. 1–114 in National Research Council, ed., Understanding and Preventing Violence, Volume 3, Social Influences. Washington, DC: National Research Council.

1997 "Racial and ethnic disparities in crime and criminal justice in the United States." Crime and Justice 21:311–374.

Sampson, Robert J., Stephen W. Raudenbush, and Felton Earls
1997 "Neighborhoods and violent crime: A multilevel study of collective efficacy." Science 277:918–924.

Sampson, Robert J., and William Julius Wilson
1995 "Toward a theory of race, crime and urban inequality." Pp. 37–54 in John Hagan and Ruth Peterson, eds., Crime and Inequality. Stanford, CA: Stanford University Press.

Sampson, Robert J., and John D. Wooldredge
1987 "Linking the micro- and macro-level dimensions of lifestyle-routine activity and opportunity models of predatory victimization." Journal of Quantitative Criminology 3:371–393.

Saum, Christine A.
1998 "Rohypnol: The date-rape drug?" Pp. 254–261 in James A. Inciardi and Karen McElrath, eds., The American Drug Scene. Los Angeles: Roxbury.

Schlossman, Steven
1977 Love and the American Delinquent. Chicago: University of Chicago Press.

Schneider, Anne L.
1990 Deterrence and Juvenile Crime. New York: Springer-Verlag.

❖ ❖ ❖ ❖   **Sealock, Miriam, and Sally S. Simpson**
1998 "Unraveling bias in arrest decisions: The role of juvenile offender type-scripts."
Justice Quarterly 15:427–457.

Sechrest, Lee, and Abram Rosenblatt
1987 "Research methods." Pp. 417–450 in Herbert C. Quay, ed., Handbook of Juvenile Delinquency. New York: Wiley.

Sellers, Christine S.
1999 "Self-control and intimate violence: An examination of the scope and specification of the general theory of crime." Criminology 37:375–404.

Shaw, Clifford R., and Henry D. McKay
1942 Juvenile Delinquency and Urban Areas. Chicago: University of Chicago Press.

Shelden, Randall G., and Lynn T. Osborne
1989 " 'For their own good': Class interests and the child saving movement in Memphis, Tennessee, 1900–1917." Criminology 27:747–767.

Shelden, Randall G., Sharon K. Tracy, and William B. Brown
1997 Youth Gangs in American Society. Belmont, CA: Wadsworth.

Sheley, Joseph F.
1983 "Critical elements of criminal behavior explanations." Sociological Quarterly
24:509–525.

Sheley, Joseph F., and James D. Wright
1995 In the Line of Fire. New York: Aldine De Gruyter.
1998 High School Youths, Weapons, and Violence: A National Survey. Washington,
DC: National Institute of Justice.

Sherman, Lawrence W.
1990 "Police crackdowns." National Institute of Justice Reports No. 219:2–6.
1993 "Defiance, deterrence, and irrelevance: A theory of the criminal sanction." Journal of Research in Crime and Delinquency 30:445–473.
1995 "The police." Pp. 327–348 in James Q. Wilson and Joan Petersilia, eds., Crime.
San Francisco: ICS Press.
1998 "American policing." Pp. 429–456 in Michael Tonry, ed., The Handbook of
Crime and Punishment. New York: Oxford.

Sherman, Lawrence W., Patrick R. Gartin, and Michael E. Buerger
1989 "Hot spots of predatory crime: Routine activities and the criminology of place."
Criminology 27:27–55.

**Sherman, Lawrence W., Denise Gottfredson, Doris MacKenzie, John Eck,
Peter Reuter, and Shawn Bushway**
1998 Preventing Crime: What Works, What Doesn't, What's Promising. Available at
the web site: (*http://www.preventingcrime.org/*)

**Sherman, Lawrence W., Douglas A. Smith, Janell D. Schmidt, and Dennis
P. Rogan**
1992 "Crime, punishment, and stake in conformity: Legal and informal control of domestic violence." American Sociological Review 57:680–690.

Sherman, Lawrence W., and David Weisburd
1995 "General deterrent effects of police patrol in crime 'hot spots': A randomized,
controlled trial." Justice Quarterly 12:625–648.

Shihadeh, Edward S., and Darrell J. Steffensmeier
1994 "Economic inequality, family disruption, and urban black violence: Cities as
units of stratification and social control." Social Forces 73:729–751.

Shoemaker, Donald J.
2000 Theories of Delinquency. New York: Oxford University Press.

Short, James F., Jr. ❖ ❖ ❖ ❖
1997 Poverty, Ethnicity, and Violent Crime. Boulder, CO: Westview.

Short, James F., Jr., and F. Ivan Nye
1958 "Extent of unrecorded juvenile delinquency: Tentative conclusions." Journal of Criminal Law, Criminology, and Police Science 49:296–302.

Short, James F., Jr., and Fred L. Strodtbeck
1965 Group Process and Gang Delinquency. Chicago: University of Chicago Press.

Sickmund, Melissa, Howard N. Snyder, and Eileen Poe-Yamagata
1997 Juvenile Offenders and Victims: 1997 Update on Violence. Washington, DC: National Center for Juvenile Justice.

Siegel, Larry J., and Joseph J. Senna
1997 Juvenile Delinquency. St. Paul, MN.: West.

Simons, Ronald L., Jay Beaman, Rand D. Conger, and Wei Chao
1993 "Stress, support, and antisocial behavior trait as determinants of emotional well-being and parenting practices among single mothers." Journal of Marriage and the Family 55:385–398.

Simons, Ronald L., Martin G. Miller, and Stephen M. Aigner
1980 "Contemporary theories of deviance and female delinquency: An empirical test." Journal of Research in Crime and Delinquency 17:42–53.

Singer, Simon I., Murray Levine, and Susan Jou
1993 "Heavy metal music preference, delinquent friends, social control, and delinquency." Journal of Research in Crime and Delinquency, 30:317–329.

Slaby, Ronald G., and Nancy G. Guerra
1988 "Cognitive mediators of aggression in adolescent offenders: 1. Assessment." Developmental Psychology 24:580–588.

Smith, Bradford
1998 "Children in custody: 20-year trends in juvenile detention, correctional, and shelter facilities." Crime and Delinquency 44:526–543.

Smith, Carolyn, and Terence P. Thornberry
1995 "The relationship between childhood maltreatment and adolescent involvement in delinquency." Criminology 33:451–481.

Smith, Douglas A., and Raymond Paternoster
1987 "The gender gap in theories of deviance: Issues and evidence." Journal of Research in Crime and Delinquency 24:140–172.

Snyder, Howard N.
1999 Juvenile Arrests 1998. Washington, DC: Office of Juvenile Justice and Delinquency Prevention.

Snyder, Howard N., and Melissa Sickmund
1995 Juvenile Offenders and Victims: A National Report. Pittsburg, PA.: National Center for Juvenile Justice.
1999 Juvenile Offenders and Victims: 1999 National Report. Pittsburgh, PA.: National Center for Juvenile Justice.

Snyder, James, and Gerald R. Patterson
1987 "Family interaction and delinquent behavior." Pp. 216–243 in Herberet C. Quay, ed., Handbook of Juvenile Delinquency. New York: Wiley.

Spelman, William, and John E. Eck
1987 Newport News Tests Problem-Oriented Policing. Washington, DC: National Institute of Justice.

Spergel, Irving A.
1995 The Youth Gang Problem. New York: Oxford University Press.

❖ ❖ ❖ ❖   **Stafford, Leon**
1999 "Lawyers: Teen shooter needs psychiatric hospital." Atlanta Constitution, August 10, C1, 6.

Stahl, Anne L.
2000 Offenders in Juvenile Court, 1997. Washington, DC: Office of Juvenile Justice and Delinquency Prevention.

Stark, Rodney, and William Sims Bainbridge
1996 Religion, Deviance, and Social Control. New York: Routledge.

Steffensmeier, Darrell
1993 "National trends in female arrests, 1969–1990: Assessment and recommendations for research." Journal of Quantitative Criminology 9:411–441.

Steffensmeier, Darrell, and Emilie Allan
1995a "Criminal behavior: Gender and age." Pp. 83–113 in Joseph F. Sheley, ed., Criminology. Belmont, CA: Wadsworth.
1995b "Age-inequality and property crime: The effects of age-linked stratification and status attainment processes on patterns of criminality across the life course." Pp. 95–115 in John Hagan and Ruth D. Peterson, eds., Crime and Inequality. Stanford, CA: Stanford University Press.
1996 "Gender and crime: Toward a gendered theory of female offending." Annual Review of Sociology 22:459–487.
2000 "Looking for patterns: Gender, age, and crime." Pp. 85–127 in Joseph F. Sheley, ed., Criminology. Belmont, CA: Wadsworth.

Steffensmeier, Darrell, Emilie Allan, Miles Harer, and Cathy Streifel
1989 "Age and the distribution of crime." American Journal of Sociology 94:803–831.

Steffensmeier, Darrell, Jeffrey Ulmer, and John Kramer
1998 "The interaction of race, gender, and age in criminal sentencing: The punishment cost of being young, black, and male." Criminology 36:763–798.

Steinberg, Laurence
1996 Beyond the Classroom. New York: Simon and Schuster.

Stone, Sandra
1998 "Should the juvenile justice system get tougher on juvenile offenders?" Pp. 199–295 in John R. Fuller and Eric W. Hickey, eds., Controversial Issues in Criminology. Boston: Allyn and Bacon.

Straus, Murray
1994 Beating the Devil Out of Them. New York: Lexington.

Strom, Kevin J.
2000 Profile of State Prisoners Under Age 18, 1985–1997. Washington, DC: Bureau of Justice Statistics.

Strom, Kevin J., and Steven K. Smith
1998 Juvenile Felony Defendants in Criminal Courts. Washington, DC: Bureau of Justice Statistics.

Sullivan, Mercer L.
1989 Getting Paid. Ithaca, NY: Cornell University Press.

Sutherland, Edwin H., Donald R. Cressey, and David F. Luckenbill
1992 Principles of Criminology. Dix Hills, NY: General Hall.

Sutton, John R.
1988 Stubborn Children: Controlling Delinquency in the United States. Berkeley: University of California Press.

Sykes, Gresham M., and David Matza
1957 "Techniques of neutralization: A theory of delinquency." American Sociological Review 22:664–670.

Taylor, E. A.
1986 "Childhood hyperactivity." British Journal of Psychiatry 149:562–573.

Thornberry, Terence P.
1987 "Toward an interactional theory of delinquency." Criminology 25:863–891.

1996 "Empirical support for interactional theory: A review of the literature." Pp. 198–235 in J. David Hawkins, ed., Delinquency and Crime. Cambridge, England: Cambridge University Press.

1997 Developmental Theories of Crime and Delinquency: Advances in Criminological Theory, Volume 7. New Brunswick, NJ: Transaction.

1998 "Membership in youth gangs and involvement in serious and violent offending." Pp. 147–166 in Rolf Loeber and David P. Farrington, eds., Serious and Violent Juvenile Offenders. Thousand Oaks, CA: Sage.

Thornberry, Terence P., and James H. Burch II
1997 Gang Members and Delinquent Behavior. Washington, DC: Office of Juvenile Justice and Delinquency Prevention.

Thornberry, Terence P., and Margaret Farnworth
1982 "Social correlates of criminal involvement: Further evidence on the relationship between social status and criminal behavior." American Sociological Review 47:505–517.

Thornberry, Terence P., David Huizinga, and Rolf Loeber
1995 "The prevention of serious delinquency and violence: Implications from the program of research on the causes and correlates of delinquency." Pp. 213–237 in James C. Howell, Barry Krisberg, J. David Hawkins, and John J. Wilson, eds., A Sourcebook: Serious, Violent, and Chronic Juvenile Offenders. Thousand Oaks, CA: Sage.

Thornberry, Terence P., Marvin D. Krohn, Alan J. Lizotte, and Deborah Chard-Wierschem
1993 "The role of juvenile gangs in facilitating delinquent behavior." Journal of Research in Crime and Delinquency 30:55–87.

Thornberry, Terence P., Marvin D. Krohn, Alan J. Lizotte, Carolyn A. Smith, and Pamela K. Porter
1998 "Taking stock: An overview of findings from the Rochester youth development survey." Paper presented at the annual meeting of the American Society of Criminology, Washington, DC.

Thornberry, Terence P., Alan J. Lizotte, Marvin D. Krohn, Margaret Farnworth, and Sung Joon Jang
1991 "Testing interactional theory: An examination of reciprocal causal relationships among family, school, and delinquency." Journal of Criminal Law and Criminology 82:3–35.

1994 "Delinquent peers, beliefs, and delinquent behavior: A longitudinal test of interactional theory." Criminology 32:47–83.

Thornberry, Terence P., Melanie Moore, and R. L. Christenson
1985 "The effect of dropping out of high school on subsequent criminal behavior." Criminology 23:3–18.

Thornberry, Terence P., Carolyn A. Smith, Craig Rivera, David Huizinga, and Magda Stouthamer-Loeber
1999 Family Disruption and Delinquency. Washington, DC: Office of Juvenile Justice and Delinquency Prevention.

Thornberry, Terence P., Evelyn H. Wei, Magda Stouthamer-Loeber, and Joyce Van Dyke
2000 Teenage Fatherhood and Delinquent Behavior. Washington, DC: Office of Juvenile Justice and Delinquency Prevention.

Thrasher, Federic M.
1927 The Gang. Chicago: University of Chicago Press.

Tibbetts, Stephen G., and Alex Piquero
1999 "The influence of gender, low birth weight, and disadvantaged environment in predicting early onset of offending: A test of Moffitt's interactional hypothesis." Criminology 37:843–878

Tittle, Charles R.
1995 Control Balance: Toward a General Theory of Deviance. Boulder, CO: Westview.

Tittle, Charles R., Marty Jean Burke, and Elton F. Jackson
1986 "Modeling Sutherland's theory of differential association: Toward an empirical classification." Social Forces 65:405–432.

Tittle, Charles R., and Robert F. Meier
1990 "Specifying the sex/delinquency relationship." Criminology 28:271–299.

Tittle, Charles R., Wayne J. Villemez, and Douglas A. Smith
1978 "The myth of social class and criminality: An empirical assessment of the empirical evidence." American Sociological Review 43:643–656.

Tittle, Charles R., and Michael R. Welch
1983 "Religiosity and deviance: Toward a contingency theory of constraining effects." Social Forces 61:653–682.

Tjaden, Patricia, and Nancy Thoennes
1999 "Prevalence and incidence of violence against women: Findings from the National Violence Against Women survey." The Criminologist 24(3):1, 4, 12, 14, 17–19.

Toby, Jackson
1957 "Social disorganization and stake in conformity: Complementary factors in the predatory behavior of hoodlums." Journal of Criminal Law, Criminology, and Police Science 48:12–17.
1995 "The schools." Pp. 141–170 in James Q. Wilson and Joan Petersilia, eds., Crime. San Francisco: ICS Press.

Tolan, Patrick H., and Deborah Gorman-Smith
1998 "Development of serious and violent offending careers." Pp. 68–85 in Rolf Loeber and David P. Farrington, eds., Serious and Violent Juvenile Offenders. Thousand Oaks, CA: Sage.

Tonry, Michael
1995 Malign Neglect. New York: Oxford.

Torbet, Patricia, and Linda Szymanski
1998 State Legislative Responses to Violent Juvenile Crime: 1996–97 Update. Washington, DC: Office of Juvenile Justice and Delinquency Prevention.

Tracy, Paul E., Jr.
1990 "Prevalence, incidence, rates, and other descriptive measures." Pp. 51–77 in Kimberly Kempf, ed., Measurement Issues in Criminology. New York: Springer-Verlag.

Tracy, Paul E., Marvin E. Wolfgang, and Robert M. Figlio
1990 Delinquency Careers in Two Birth Cohorts, New York: Plenum.

Tremblay, Richard E., and Wendy M. Craig
1995 "Developmental Crime Prevention." Crime and Justice 19:151–236.

Trojanowicz, Robert, Victor E. Kappeler, Larry K. Gaines, and Bonnie Bucqueroux
1998 Community Policing: A Contemporary Perspective. Cincinnati, OH.: Anderson.

Turner, C. F., L. Ku, S. M. Rogers, L. D. Lindberg, J. H. Pleck, and F. L. Sonenstein
1998 "Adolescent sexual behavior, drug use and violence: Increased reporting with computer survey technology." Science 280:867–873.

Tygart, C. E.
1991 "Juvenile delinquency and number of children in a family." Youth and Society 22:525–536.

Van Voorhis, Patricia, Francis T. Cullen, Richard A. Mathers, and Connie Chenoweth Garner
1988 "The impact of family structure and quality on delinquency: A comparative assessment of structural and functional factors." Criminology 26:235–261.

VanderVen, Thomas M., Francis T. Cullen, Mark A. Corrozza, and John Paul Wright
1998 "Home alone: The impact of maternal employment on delinquency." Paper presented at the annual meeting of the American Society of Criminology, Washington, DC.

Vaz, Edmund W.
1967 "Juvenile delinquency in the middle class youth culture." Pp. 131–147 in Edmund W. Vaz, ed., Middle-Class Juvenile Delinquency. New York: Harper and Row.

Vigil, James Diego, and Steve C. Yun
1996 "Southern California gangs: Comparative ethnicity and social control." Pp. 139–156 in C. Ronald Huff, ed., Gangs in America. Thousand Oaks, CA: Sage.

Vila, Bryan
1994 "A general paradigm for understanding criminal behavior: Extending evolutionary ecological theory."Criminology 32:311–359.

Visher, Christy A.
2000 "Career offenders and crime control." Pp. 601–619 in Joseph H. Sheley, ed., Criminology. Belmont, CA: Wadsworth.

Vold, George B., Thomas J. Bernard, and Jeffrey B. Snipes
1998 Theoretical Criminology. New York: Oxford University Press.

Wacquant, L. D., and William J. Wilson
1989 "The costs of racial and class exclusion in the inner city." Annals of the American Academy of Political and Social Science 501:8–25.

Walker, Samuel
1998 Sense and Nonsense About Crime and Drugs. Belmont, CA: West/Wadsworth.

Walker, Samuel, Cassia Spohn, and Miriam DeLane
1996 The Color of Justice. Belmont, CA: Wadsworth.

Wang, C. T., and D. Daro
1998 Current Trends in Child Abuse Reporting and Fatalities: The Results of the 1997 Annual Fifty State Survey. Chicago: Prevent Child Abuse America.

Warr, Mark
1993 "Age, peers, and delinquency." Criminology 31:17–40.
1996 "Organization and instigation in delinquent groups." Criminology 34:11–37.
1998 "Life-course transitions and desistance from crime." Criminology 36:183–216.

Warr, Mark, and Mark Stafford
1991 "The influence of delinquent peers: What they think or what they do?" Criminology 29:851–866.

❖ ❖ ❖ ❖   **Wasserman, Gail A., and Laurie S. Miller**
1998 "The prevention of serious and violent juvenile offending." Pp. 197–247 in Rolf Loeber and David P. Farrington, eds., Serious and Violent Juvenile Offenders. Thousand Oaks, CA: Sage.

Weis, Joesph G.
1986 "Issues in the measurement of criminal careers." Pp. 1 51 in Alfred Blumstein, Jacqueline Cohen, Jeffrey A. Roth, and Christy A. Visher, eds., Criminal Careers and Career Criminals, Volume II. Washington, DC: National Academy Press.
1987 "Social class and crime." Pp. 71–90 in Michael Gottfredson and Travis Hirschi, eds., Positive Criminology. Newbury Park, CA: Sage.

Weishew, Nancy L., and Samuel S. Peng
1993 "Variables predicting students' problem behaviors." Journal of Educational Research 87:5–17.

Weissbourd, Richard
1996 The Vulnerable Child. Reading, MA: Addison-Wesley.

Wells, Edward L., and Joseph H. Rankin
1988 "Direct parental controls and delinquency." Criminology 26:263–284.
1991 "Families and delinquency: A meta-analysis of the impact of broken homes." Social Problems 38:71–93.
1995 "Juvenile victimization: Convergent validation of alternative measurements." Journal of Research in Crime and Delinquency 32:287–307.

Welsh, Wayne N., Jack R. Greene, and Patricia H. Jenkins
1999 "School disorder: The influence of individual, institutional, and community factors." Criminology 37:73–116.

Welsh, Wayne N., Patricia H. Jenkins, and Philip W. Harris
1999 "Reducing minority overrepresentation in juvenile justice: Results of community-based delinquency prevention in Harrisburg." Journal of Research in Crime and Delinquency 36:87–110.

White, Garland
1999 "Crime and the decline of manufacturing, 1970–1990." Justice Quarterly 16:81–97.

White, Helene Raskin, and Stephen Hansell
1996 "The moderating effects of gender and hostility on the alcohol-aggression relationship." Journal of Research in Crime and Delinquency 33:450–470.

White, Helene Raskin, and Erich W. Labouvie
1994 "Generality versus specificity of problem behavior: Psychological and functional differences." Journal of Drug Issues 24:55–74.

White, Helene Raskin, Erich W. Labouvie, and Marsha E. Bates
1985 "The relationship between sensation seeking and delinquency: A longitudinal analysis." Journal of Research in Crime and Delinquency 22:197–211.

White, Helene Raskin, Robert J. Pandina, and Randy L. LaGrange
1987 "Longitudinal predictors of serious substance use and delinquency." Criminology 25:715–740.

White, Jennifer L., Terrie E. Moffitt, Avshalom Caspi, Dawn Jeglum Bartusch, Douglas J. Needles, and Magda Stouthamer-Loeber
1994 "Measuring impulsivity and examining its relationship to delinquency." Journal of Abnormal Psychology 103:192–205.

Wiatrowski, Michael D., and Kristine L. Anderson
1987 "The dimensionality of the social bond." Journal of Quantitative Criminology 3:65–81.

Wiatrowski, Michael D., David B. Griswold, and Mary K. Roberts
1981 "Social control theory and delinquency." American Sociological Review 46:525–541.

Wiatrowski, Michael D., Stephen Hansell, Charles R. Massey, and David L. Wilson
1982 "Curriculum tracking and delinquency." American Sociological Review 47:151–160.

Widom, Cathy Spatz
1989 "Does violence beget violence? A critical examination of the literature." Psychological Bulletin 106:3–28.
1997 "Child abuse, neglect, and witnessing violence." Pp. 159–170 in D. M. Stoff, J. Breiling, and J. D. Maser, eds., Handbook of Antisocial Behavior. New York: Wiley.

Widom, Cathy Spatz, and Ashley Ames
1988 "Biology and female crime." Pp. 308–331 in Terrie E. Moffitt and Sarnoff A. Mednick (eds.), Biological Contributions to Crime Causation. Dordrecht: Martinus Nijhoff.

Wiebush, Richard G., Christopher Baird, Barry Krisberg, and David Onek
1995 "Risk assessment and classification for serious, violent, and chronic juvenile offenders." Pp. 171–212 in James C. Howell, Barry Krisberg, J. David Hawkins, and John J. Wilson, eds., A Sourcebook: Serious, Violent, and Chronic Juvenile Offenders. Thousand Oaks, CA: Sage.

Williams, Carolyn L., and Craig Uchiyama
1989 "Assessment of life events during adolescence: The use of self-report inventories." Adolescence 24:95–118.

Williams, Kirk R., and Richard Hawkins
1986 "Perceptual research on general deterrence: A critical review." Law and Society Review 20:545–572.

Williams, Nicolas, Francis T. Cullen, and John Paul Wright
1996 "Labor market participation and youth crime: The neglect of working in delinquency research." Social Pathology 2:195–217.

Wilson, James Q.
1976 Varieties of Police Behavior. New York: Atheneum

Wilson, James Q., and Richard Herrnstein
1985 Crime and Human Nature. New York: Simon and Schuster.

Wilson, James Q., and George L. Kelling
1982 "Broken windows: Police and neighborhood safety." Atlantic Monthly 249 (March):29–38.

Wilson, William Julius
1987 The Truly Disadvantaged. Chicago: University of Chicago Press.
1996 When Work Disappears. Chicago: University of Chicago Press.

Wolfgang, Marvin, and Franco Ferracuti
1982 The Subculture of Violence. Beverly Hills, CA: Sage.

Wolfgang, Marvin E., Robert M. Figlio, and Thorsten Sellin
1972 Delinquency in a Birth Cohort. Chicago: University of Chicago Press.

Wood, Peter B., Betty Pfefferbaum, and Bruce J. Arneklev
1993 "Risk-taking and self-control: Social psychological correlates of delinquency." Journal of Crime and Justice 16:111–130.

❖ ❖ ❖ ❖   **Wordes, Madeline, and Timothy S. Bynum**
1995 "Policing juveniles: Is there bias against youths of color?" Pp. 47–65 in Kimberly Kempf Leonard, Carl E. Pope, and William H. Feyerherm, eds., Minorities in Juvenile Justice. Thousand Oaks, CA: Sage.

Wright, Bradley R. Entner, Avshalom Caspi, Terrie E. Moffitt, Richard A. Meich, and Phil A. Silva
1999a "Reconsidering the relationship between sex and delinquency: Causation but not correlation." Criminology 37:175–194.

Wright, Bradley R. Enter, Avshalom Caspi, Terrie E. Moffitt, and Phil A. Silva
1999b "Low self-control, social bonds, and crime: Social causation, social selection, or both?" Criminology 37:479–514.

Wright, James D., Joseph F. Sheley, and M. Dwayne Smith
1992 "Kids, guns, and killing fields." Society 30:84–89.

Wright, James D., and Teri E. Vail
2000 "The guns-crime connection." Pp. 577–599 in Joseph F. Sheley, ed., Criminology: A Contemporary Handbook. Belmont, CA: Wadsworth.

Wright, John Paul, Francis T. Cullen, and Nicolas Williams
1997 "Working while in school and delinquent involvement: Implications for social policy." Crime and Delinquency 43:203–221.

Wright, Kevin N., and Karen E. Wright
1995 Family Life, Delinquency, and Crime: A Policymaker's Guide. Washington, DC: Office of Juvenile Justice and Delinquency Prevention.

Wright, Richard A.
1994 In Defense of Prisons. Westport, CT: Greenwood.

Wu, Ping, and Denise B. Kandel
1995 "The role of mothers and fathers in intergenerational behavioral transmission: The case of smoking and delinquency." Pp. 49–81 in Howard B. Kaplan, ed., Drugs, Crime, and Other Deviant Adaptations. New York: Plenum.

Yoshikawa, Hirokazu
1994 "Prevention as cumulative protection: Effects of early family support and education on chronic delinquency and its risks." Psychological Bulletin 115:28–54.

Yu, Jiang, and Allen E. Liska
1993 "The certainty of punishment: A reference group effect and its functional form." Criminology 31:447–464.

Zawitz, Marianne W.
1995 "Guns used in crime: Firearms, crime, and criminal justice." Washington, DC: Bureau of Justice Statistics.

Zatz, Marjorie S.
1987 "The changing forms of racial/ethnic biases in sentencing." Journal of Research in Crime and Delinquency 24:69–92.

Zhang, Lening, William F. Wieczorek, and John W. Welte
1997 "The impact of age of onset of substance use on delinquency." Journal of Research in Crime and Delinquency 34:253–268.

Zhang, Quauwu, Rolf Loeber, and Magda Stouthamer-Loeber
1997 "Developmental trends of delinquent attitudes and behaviors: Replications and synthesis across domains, time, and samples." Journal of Quantitative Criminology 13:181–215.

Zigler, Edward, Cara Taussig, and Kathryn Black
1992 "Early childhood intervention: A promising preventative for juvenile delinquency." American Psychologist 47:997–1006.

Zimring, Franklin E.
1998 American Youth Violence. New York: Oxford.

Zimring, Franklin E., and Gordon Hawkins
1997 Crime Is Not the Problem: Lethal Violence in America. New York: Oxford.

1995 Incapacitation: Penal confinement and the restraint of crime. New York: Oxford University Press.

Zingraff, Matthew T., Jeffrey Leiter, Matthew C. Johnsen, and Kristen A. Myers
1994 "The mediating effect of good school performance on the maltreatment-delinquency relationship." Journal of Research in Crime and Delinquency 31:62–91.

Zingraff, Matthew T., Jeffrey Leiter, Kristen A. Meyers, and Matthew C. Johnsen
1993 "Child maltreatment and youthful problem behavior." Criminology 31:173–202.

❖ ❖ ❖ ❖

Subject Index

Author Index